T0214397

Lecture Notes in Computer Science　　11119

Commenced Publication in 1973
Founding and Former Series Editors:
Gerhard Goos, Juris Hartmanis, and Jan van Leeuwen

Editorial Board

David Hutchison
　Lancaster University, Lancaster, UK
Takeo Kanade
　Carnegie Mellon University, Pittsburgh, PA, USA
Josef Kittler
　University of Surrey, Guildford, UK
Jon M. Kleinberg
　Cornell University, Ithaca, NY, USA
Friedemann Mattern
　ETH Zurich, Zurich, Switzerland
John C. Mitchell
　Stanford University, Stanford, CA, USA
Moni Naor
　Weizmann Institute of Science, Rehovot, Israel
C. Pandu Rangan
　Indian Institute of Technology Madras, Chennai, India
Bernhard Steffen
　TU Dortmund University, Dortmund, Germany
Demetri Terzopoulos
　University of California, Los Angeles, CA, USA
Doug Tygar
　University of California, Berkeley, CA, USA
Gerhard Weikum
　Max Planck Institute for Informatics, Saarbrücken, Germany

More information about this series at http://www.springer.com/series/7408

Falk Howar · Jiří Barnat (Eds.)

Formal Methods for Industrial Critical Systems

23rd International Conference, FMICS 2018
Maynooth, Ireland, September 3–4, 2018
Proceedings

 Springer

Editors
Falk Howar
Technical University of Dortmund
Dortmund
Germany

Jiří Barnat
Masaryk University
Brno
Czech Republic

ISSN 0302-9743   ISSN 1611-3349 (electronic)
Lecture Notes in Computer Science
ISBN 978-3-030-00243-5   ISBN 978-3-030-00244-2   (eBook)
https://doi.org/10.1007/978-3-030-00244-2

Library of Congress Control Number: 2018954544

LNCS Sublibrary: SL2 – Programming and Software Engineering

© Springer Nature Switzerland AG 2018
This work is subject to copyright. All rights are reserved by the Publisher, whether the whole or part of the material is concerned, specifically the rights of translation, reprinting, reuse of illustrations, recitation, broadcasting, reproduction on microfilms or in any other physical way, and transmission or information storage and retrieval, electronic adaptation, computer software, or by similar or dissimilar methodology now known or hereafter developed.
The use of general descriptive names, registered names, trademarks, service marks, etc. in this publication does not imply, even in the absence of a specific statement, that such names are exempt from the relevant protective laws and regulations and therefore free for general use.
The publisher, the authors and the editors are safe to assume that the advice and information in this book are believed to be true and accurate at the date of publication. Neither the publisher nor the authors or the editors give a warranty, express or implied, with respect to the material contained herein or for any errors or omissions that may have been made. The publisher remains neutral with regard to jurisdictional claims in published maps and institutional affiliations.

This Springer imprint is published by the registered company Springer Nature Switzerland AG
The registered company address is: Gewerbestrasse 11, 6330 Cham, Switzerland

Preface

This volume contains the papers presented at FMICS 2018, the 23rd International Conference on Formal Methods for Industrial Critical Systems, which was held during September 3–4, 2018, in NUIM, Maynooth, Ireland. The FMICS 2018 conference took place as a collocated event of the 14th International Conference on integrated Formal Methods, iFM 2018.

After 22 successful FMICS workshops held from 1996 to 2017, FMICS has become a conference — such a long-awaited change is probably not a surprise in itself. The aim of the FMICS conference series is to provide a forum for researchers who are interested in the development and application of formal methods in industry. In particular, FMICS brings together scientists and engineers who are active in the area of formal methods and interested in exchanging their experiences in the industrial usage of these methods. The FMICS conference series also strives to promote research and development for the improvement of formal methods and tools for industrial applications. The topics of interest include, but are not limited to:

- Design, specification, code generation, and testing based on formal methods
- Methods, techniques, and tools to support automated analysis, certification, debugging, learning, optimization, and transformation of complex, distributed, real-time systems and embedded systems
- Automated verification (model checking, theorem proving, SAT/SMT constraint solving, abstract interpretation, etc.) of critical systems
- Verification and validation methods that address shortcomings of existing methods with respect to their industrial applicability (e.g., scalability and usability issues)
- Tools for the development of formal design descriptions
- Case studies and experience reports on industrial applications of formal methods, focusing on lessons learned or identification of new research directions
- Impact of the adoption of formal methods on the development process and associated costs
- Application of formal methods in standardization and industrial forums
- Formal methods for mobile and autonomous systems

This year we received 17 submissions. Each of these submissions went through a rigorous review process in which each paper received at least 3 reports. We selected 9 papers for presentation during the workshop and inclusion in these proceedings. The workshop also featured invited talks by Tiziana Margaria (University of Limerick, Lero, and Confirm - Limerick, Ireland) and Susanne Graf (Director of Research at VERIMAG Grenoble, France) and a panel on "Next generation Smart Systems." In addition, 9 invited presentations were given in honour of the 60th birthday of Susanne Graf. The proceedings contain a separate topical part for the accompanying invited contributions.

We would like to thank the ERCIM FMICS working group coordinator Tiziana Margaria for her counselling and support during the organization of FMICS 2018. The iFM 2018 general chair and FMICS local organizer Rosemary Monahan gave us essential help with the local arrangements in Maynooth. We would also like to thank Science Foundation Ireland, Fáilte Ireland, and Maynooth University for the generous sponsoring of the joint events. ERCIM supported the event through the FMICS Working Group, EASST provided the best paper award, and Springer Nature produced the conference proceedings. We would like to thank Bernhard Steffen and Tiziana Margaria for organizing the invited contributions in honor of Susanne Graf's 60th birthday. Finally, we would like to thank the Program Committee members and external reviewers for their useful and detailed reviews and discussions, all authors for their submissions, and all presenters and attendees of the conference.

September 2018   Jiří Barnat
                                                                             Falk Howar

Organization

Program Chairs

Falk Howar	Dortmund University of Technology and Fraunhofer ISST, Germany
Jiří Barnat	Masaryk University, Czech Republic

Program Committee

Alvaro Arenas	IE University, Spain
Michael Dierkes	Rockwell Collins, France
Francesco Flammini	Linnaeus University, Sweden
Wan Fokkink	Vrije Universiteit Amsterdam, The Netherlands
María del Mar Gallardo	University of Malaga, Spain
Marieke Huisman	University of Twente, The Netherlands
Peter Gorm Larsen	Aarhus University, Denmark
Thierry Lecomte	ClearSy Systems Engineering, France
Tiziana Margaria	University of Limerick, Ireland
Radu Mateescu	Inria, France
David Mentré	Mitsubishi Electric R&D Centre Europe, France
Stephan Merz	Inria, France
Manuel Núñez	Universidad Complutense de Madrid, Spain
Peter Ölveczky	University of Oslo, Norway
Charles Pecheur	Université catholique de Louvain, Belgium
Marielle Petit-Doche	Systerel, France
Ralf Pinger	Siemens AG, Germany
Matteo Rossi	Politecnico di Milano, Italy
Marco Roveri	FBK-irst, Italy
Thomas Santen	TU Berlin, Germany
Bernhard Steffen	Dortmund University of Technology, Germany
Jun Sun	University of Technology and Design, Singapore
Maurice ter Beek	ISTI-CNR, Italy
Jaco van de Pol	University of Twente, The Netherlands
Tomáš Vojnar	Brno University of Technology, Czech Republic

Additional Reviewers

Christophe Limbrée
Tomas Kulik
Hugo Daniel Macedo
Tim Willemse

Abstracts of Talks Dedicated to Susanne Graf on the Occasion of Her 60th Birthday

The Quest for Optimality in Stateless Model Checking of Concurrent Programs

Bengt Jonsson

Uppsala University

Abstract. Testing and verification of concurrent programs is hard, as it requires reasoning about all the ways in which operations executed by different processes (or threads) can interfere. Model checking [7, 16] addresses this problem by systematically exploring the state space of a given program and verifying that each reachable state satisfies a given property. A problem in applying model checking to realistic programs is to capture and storing a large number of global states. Two approaches for coping with this problem are abstraction and stateless model checking. *Abstraction techniques* construct a sound overapproximation ofthe state-transition graph, which can then be tractably analyzed. A pioneering work by Graf and Saidi [12] showed how infinite-state systems can be automatically verified in this way. *Stateless model checking* (SMC) [11] explores the state space of the program without explicitly storing global states. The technique requires taking control of the scheduler and subsequently executing the program multiple times, each time imposing a different scheduling of the processes. By considering every process at every execution step, however, the number of possible schedulings grows exponentially wrt. the total length of program execution. Consequently, a number of techniques for reducing this number, without unnecessarily sacrificing coverage, have been developed. The most prominent is Partial order reduction (POR) [8, 10, 15, 17], adapted to SMC as Dynamic POR (DPOR) [9], which exploits the fact that schedulings with the same ordering of dependent operations can be regarded as belonging to the same equivalence class (sometimes called a Mazurkiewicz trace), and that it is sufficient to explore one of them.

In recent years, several techniques have been develop that further increase the efficiency of stateless model checking. One approach has been to develop techniques that are optimal in the sense that they explore exactly one scheduling in each Mazurkiewicz trace [2]. Corresponding minimization techniques for classical (stateful) model checking were pioneered by Graf and Steffen [13]. Other approaches are based on the observation that the notion of Mazurkiewicz trace is unnecessarily refined for the purpose of determining the outcome of a program scheduling. Hence, coarser equivalences have been defined: e.g., based on mapping each read operation to the corresponding write operation that produces its value [6, 14]. For such coarser equivalences, the question of developing optimal exploration algorithms becomes interesting.

In this presentation, we will survey some recent developments and results for making stateless model checking more efficient, also considering different memory models for concurrency [1, 3, 5, 4]. It builds on joint work with Parosh Aziz Abdulla, Stavros Aronis, Mohamed Faouzi Atig, Carl Leonardsson, Magnus Lång, Tuan Phong Ngo, and Konstantinos Sagonas.

References

1. Abdulla, P.A., Aronis, S., Atig, M.F., Jonsson, B., Leonardsson, C., Sagonas, K.: Stateless model checking for TSO and PSO. Acta Inf. **54**(8), 789–818 (2017)
2. Abdulla, P.A., Aronis, S., Jonsson, B., Sagonas, K.: Source sets: a foundation for optimal dynamic partial order reduction. J. ACM **64**(4), 25:1–25:49 (2017)
3. Abdulla, P.A., Atig, M.F., Jonsson, B., Leonardsson, C.: Stateless model checking for POWER. In: Chaudhuri, S., Farzan, A. (eds.) CAV 2016. LNCS, vol. 9780, pp. 134–156. Springer, Cham (2016)
4. Abdulla, P.A., Atig, M.F., Jonsson, B., Ngo, T.P.: Optimal stateless model checking under the release-acquire semantics. In: OOPSLA (2018, to appear)
5. Aronis, S., Jonsson, B., Lång, M., Sagonas, K.: Optimal dynamic partial order reduction with observers. In: Beyer, D., Huisman, M. (eds.) TACAS 2018. LNCS, vol. 10806, pp. 229–248. Springer, Cham (2018)
6. Chalupa, M., Chatterjee, K., Pavlogiannis, A., Sinha, N., Vaidya, K.: Data-centric dynamic partial order reduction. Proc. ACM Program. Lang. **2**(POPL), 31:1–31:30 (2017)
7. Clarke, E.M., Emerson, E., Sistla, A.P.: Automatic verification of finite-state concurrent systems using temporal logics specification: a practical approach. In: Proceedings of 10th ACM Symposium on Principles of Programming Languages, pp. 117–126 (1983)
8. Clarke, E.M., Grumberg, O., Minea, M., Peled, D.A.: State space reduction using partial order techniques. STTT **2**(3), 279–287 (1999)
9. Flanagan, C., Godefroid, P.: Dynamic partial-order reduction for model checking software. In: Principles of Programming Languages, POPL 2005, Long Beach, California, USA, pp. 110–121. ACM (2005)
10. Godefroid, P.: Partial-Order Methods for the Verification of Concurrent Systems: An Approach to the State-Explosion Problem. LNCS, vol. 1032. Springer, Heidelberg (1996). Ph.D. thesis, University of Liège
11. Godefroid, P.: Model checking for programming languages using VeriSoft. In: Principles of Programming Languages, POPL 1997, Paris, France, pp. 174–186. ACM Press (1997)
12. Graf, S., Saidi, H.: Construction of abstract state graphs with PVS. In: Grumberg, O. (eds.) CAV 1997. LNCS, vol. 1254. Springer, Heidelberg (1997)
13. Graf, S., Steffen, B.: Compositional minimization of finite state systems. In: Clarke, E.M., Kurshan, R.P. (eds.) CAV 1990. LNCS, vol. 531, pp. 186–196. Springer, Heidelberg (1991)
14. Huang, J.: Stateless model checking concurrent programs with maximal causality reduction. In: Programming Language Design and Implementation, PLDI 2015, Portland, OR, USA, pp. 165–174. ACM (2015)
15. Peled, D.: All from one, one for all: on model checking using representatives. In: Courcoubetis, C. (eds.) CAV 1993. LNCS, vol. 697, pp. 409–423. Springer, Heidelberg (1993)
16. Queille, J.P., Sifakis, J.: Specification and verification of concurrent systems in CESAR. In: Dezani-Ciancaglini, M., Montanari, U. (eds.) Programming 1982. LNCS, vol. 137, pp. 337–352. Springer, Heidelberg (1982)
17. Valmari, A.: Stubborn sets for reduced state space generation. In: Rozenberg, G. (eds.) ICATPN 1989. LNCS, vol. 483, pp. 491–515 . Springer, Heidelberg (1991)

The Cause-Effect Latency Problem in Real-Time Systems

Wang Yi

Uppsala University, Sweden

Abstract. Real-time systems are often implemented as a set of communicating tasks scheduled and executed with different rates. Functions in such systems are chains of tasks, processing data streams. Ideally each data item (i.e. the "cause") in an input stream corresponds to a data item (i.e. the "effect") in the corresponding output stream. However some input data may be dropped due to the different task execution rates. Data exchange among tasks must be implemented using carefully designed non-blocking protocols to preserve the functional semantics of task chains. In this paper we study such a protocol, the Data Buffering Protocol (DBP) by Paul Caspi et al and the corresponding cause-effect latency problem for DBP. We provide a precise characterization of the problem and a method for estimating the worst-case cause-effect latency of task chains.

Contents

Essays Dedicated to Susanne Graf on the Occasion of Her 60th Birthday

Invited Talks

Generative Model Driven Design for Agile System Design and Evolution: A Tale of Two Worlds

Tiziana Margaria[✉]

Chair of Software Systems, University of Limerick, and Lero, Limerick, Ireland
tiziana.margaria@ul.ie

Abstract. In order to mainstream the production and evolution of IT at the levels of speed, scale, affordability and collaborative effort needed to truly make IT enter the fabric of every economical and societal endeavour, as is the projected future of our society in the next decade, the ease of learning, understanding, and applying new disruptive technologies must drastically improve. We argue that the needs of the people, the economical sectors, and the large-scale trends can only be met if the IT professions embrace and adopt a new way of producing and consuming IT, based on more formal descriptions, more models, more reasoning and analysis before expensive implementations are incurred, coupled with automatic transformations, generations, and analyses that take advantage of the models and formalized knowledge.

We analyse briefly the various dimensions, derive a specification for the new IT and IT platforms, and provide a few examples of how the new thinking can disrupt the status quo but empower a better understanding, a more efficient organization, and a more automatic management of the many cross-dimensional issues that future connected software and systems will depend upon.

1 Introduction

In the increasingly connected and heterogeneous world in which the modern and future industrial critical systems will operate, agility and evolution are of paramount importance. As in Alice in Wonderland, solution providers and technology providers need to run fast in the technology and context evolution race in order to not fall back. The steady evolution of products, infrastructure, as well as design and implementation/manufacturing environments is a continuous source of change. It is additionally topped by disruptions: examples are the inception and then the steady adoption of online-X, self-X and now smart-X approaches across the economy sectors. These disruptions are pervasive and irreversible trends that subvert, one after the other, the well established power and dominance structures in the sectoral, local and global economy. This happens over and over again: in little more than a decade we have seen the inception and then mainstreaming of online communication, marketing, service, and commerce

© Springer Nature Switzerland AG 2018
F. Howar and J. Barnat (Eds.): FMICS 2018, LNCS 11119, pp. 3–18, 2018.
https://doi.org/10.1007/978-3-030-00244-2_1

channels, to the point that Amazon has been for years among the most valuable companies worldwide. The self-X economy has eliminated many service professions though the adoption of online access and individual recognition of the user: travel agencies, ticketing services, booking platforms, and the corresponding service desks of the large providers (like airlines, railways, and event managers like ticket.com or eventbrite), or in the case of science and research, online paper submission systems and online conference management systems. The smart-X economy is the new incipient wave, fuelled by data collection and analysis readily available in a connected and cloud based fashion. The "Smart Anything Everywhere"[1] paradigm builds upon increasingly cheap storage, increasingly cheap and efficient computation power, increasingly powerful and pervasive communication networks, and various advances in traditional algorithms for analysis and optimization, and now also AI/ML style reasoning. Clearly, all these changes separate the current world, as we know it, from a future world where all these connections and enhancements will be accepted, considered normal, and essential part of the established "business practices" for all organisations and companies.

So in such an accelerating, convergent, and individualized socio-technical and economical world, what kind of design and implementation technologies for software and systems will be needed in the future to survive and possibly thrive?

The specification for the fundamental traits of a new generation of technologies comes from the kind of changes demanded by customers and users (at the individual and corporate level). These are either enforced by the economic actors (like the providers of components, systems, the integrators, and the various granularities of cooperation practiced in complex and global supply chains), or mandated by those entities that are responsible for policies and regulations (like the EU in GDPR, the governments, or oversight and standardization bodies, etc.).

So let us have a look at these dimensions of change and forces (Sects. 2–4), in order to derive a characterization of what needs to fundamentally become different if we wish to be ready for the new roaring twenties ahead (2020–2030) in Sect. 5 and propose a new paradigm in Sect. 6.

This space is characterized by a large prevalence of contradictory "needs" and desires, that can only be faced by thinking in a fundamentally different way. Putting a new thinking into practice requires a welcoming adoption of innovations, in spite of the fact that innovations are by definition new unproven paths and means, and as such scary and risky. The lines of resistance to innovation are accordingly high-profile and deeply rooted in the individual fear and organisational inertia. The specific micro- to macrolevel contexts I am prevalently looking at and from which I draw the observations are those of Lero and Confirm, two Irish national research centres that include 8 resp. 10 universities and research institutions, and over 40 companies (SME to multinationals) each. Such centres run 6 years research programs comprising tens of projects, and are embedded in the various layers of decision and management at the single partner level, centre level, national level and EU/international/global level. The global level is due

---

[1] See the EU initiative at https://smartanythingeverywhere.eu.

to strategic partnerships, e.g. with Fraunhofer in Germany, NII in Japan, and CSIRO in Australia and the practice of international collaborations, but also to the fact that several industry partners are Irish branches of multinational corporations.

Examples of the new, future-oriented way of dealing with complex interfaces, new architecture paradigms and security-injecting generative approaches are then provided in Sect. 7.

2   The People

Looking at users as consumers of technology and products, the demand is for significant change already in the close and even immediate future: how can people achieve more complex, more specialized and technically advanced goals and operations by using "simpler" and more supportive tools and infrastructure? In other words, by using tools and systems that "know" more themselves, humans with less and less technical mastery should be quickly enabled to achieve in a more reliable way and at higher quality a wealth of more complex, more precise, more secure and higher quality design, implementation, production, maintenance goals. At the same time, the need for engineers and specialists is growing much faster than their production along the established paths. Along the universities and the universities of applied science, here I see as "producers" of IT specialists also the technical courses in high schools for those countries like e.g. Italy and Germany that have a rich vocational school offering[2].

The requests for producing more specialists and faster are increasingly insistent. These requests come from companies and from professional organizations, both nationally, e.g. from the Irish Computer Society, and internationally, from ACM and IEEE. They also come from the governments and their proxies, like the Irish Higher Education Authority, that design and enforce the policies and programs for the workforce of the future. They ask Universities and research centres to train more people with a large variety of non-traditional backgrounds in these new and wonder-achieving technologies. They dream of an educational system that (a) in a short time span of typically a few weeks to a few months, (b) possibly without direct contact with the teachers nor in-person monitoring (i.e. through online education, or blended forms whereby the on-site presence is extremely compact - one weekend to one week per academic year), and (c) largely virtually, i.e. surely without the need of daily physical presence in dedicated equipped spaces (like classrooms and laboratories), these "fast tracked" individuals become proficient professionals in the new technologies, and future-proof employees of these advanced, leading edge companies.

---

[2] In Italy there is a rich tradition of excellent Istituti Tecnici that form at thousands of qualified experts at the upper secondary school level, leading to chartered professional profiles (e.g. Perito tecnico) under the control of professional Charters (Albo Professionale). The German system has a strong tradition of dual education (duale Berufsausbildung) combining formal education with a training on the job component.

The characteristics and slogans we hear in this context span typically *agile workforce training; training on demand; workforce evolution; off-site approach; flexible, adaptable and smart-sized education; ad-hoc education pills; life-long upskilling; competence building; capability-oriented approaches.*

3   The Economic Domains and Their Convergence

Referring to the Irish and global situation, a number of "needs" are mentioned over and over again:

- the need to integrate across specialization domains, spanning across various disciplines of research and professions;
- the need to become increasingly agnostic about the specific technologies: the programming language, the operating system, the data management/information system, the communication networks, the runtime platforms, and more;
- the need to be future-ready: projects, collaborations, consortia and alliances change. No IT product can afford being locked into technological walled gardens, the need is voiced over and over again to be as technology- and as platform-independent as possible;
- the need to be able to try fast and improve fast: time to market is important, but time to test/time to retest are equally important. What is called "continuous development" or "continuous integration" needs to be supported as the new mainstream paradigm of system design and evolution.

Such demands are brought up consistently across all the economic domains: when we talk about large scale software development and global software development as in Lero or at the EU level, when we address smart advanced manufacturing as in the Irish Confirm or Industry 4.0 in Germany, or smart bio and smart energy (as in the MAREI centre in Ireland), or smart agri (as in an ongoing EU initiative), or new smart materials (as in the Bernal Institute at UL and the ADAPT research centre in Ireland). This uniformity indicates very clearly the convergence of these domains not only in the factual collaboration (e.g. integration to embed smart energy aspects in smart manufacturing and smart agri) but also a higher-level, strategic convergence when anticipating and forecasting what capabilities will be essential to thrive in the next decade.

The characteristics and slogans we hear in this context span *agile development; continuous quality control; evolution-driven design; seamless integration; seamless evolution; continuous development; continuous integration, data-driven development; technology and vendor lock-in.*

4   The Big Picture Context

At a higher abstraction level, the strategists think in terms of paradigms, megatrends, and metaforces that guide the 5 to 10 years cycle length of the market movement and technology adoptions. The moves to *connected, mobile, online, individual, social, green* and now also *smart* fall in this category of strategic, long term and large scale concerns. These cycles are slower, and as such they are both slower to introduce and also slower to pace out. Some consider them to be generation-defining: they lock into the fundamental imprinting and belief system an individual human feels comfortable with. Therefore they are almost impossible to "undo" or to transition to the "next generation values". The *digital natives* vs. *digital immigrants* distinction was an example of this generation-gap defining skill at the turn of the century, and the internet (i.e. the pervasiveness of online, mobile) followed short thereafter. The problem with the big picture is that it suffers disruption too. In a low frequency, long cycle system, a wave of disruption can be even more subversive than in the "normal" tech world. Examples of such fundamental discontinuities have been the oil crisis in the '70s, the internet bubble burst in the '00s, the 9/11-induced shock, freeze and consolidation in a number of markets, like e.g. aviation. Now, we face the potential de-globalization of supply chains following the trade changes due to e.g. Brexit, the current uncertainty concerning trade agreements like the TPP, NAFTA or the Iran deal, and the quick and unexpected resurgence of tariffs.

What we hear in this context sounds like *survival of the fittest is survival of the fastest; agility and quick evolution; flexible contracts; globalization and de-globalization; reframing of supply chains; glocalization.*

5   The Tools and Techniques for the New World

In the new world, the answer in terms of which IT tool and techniques should be researched, produced, and then studied, adopted, and taught today to the traditional and non-traditional students and professionals in order for them to be future-ready needs to capture the essence of these "keywords", which can be summarized in *speed, uncertainty, and change.* Accordingly, the new IT needs to deliver a correspondingly updated, simplified and flexible approach to producing software and systems. It also needs to provide a much simplified and technology-shielding software infrastructure and platform for software and system development itself. This need induces a significant disruption from the past and current culture, where IT production was and is in the hands of (trained or self-taught) specialists who (need to) master coding and (need to) know the details of development systems, programming frameworks, operating systems, communication systems, virtualization systems down to the hardware. In the new world, there is no time and no long-term value anymore in mandating all this knowledge from whoever professionally uses IT and systems and produces IT and systems. So we face deep change, disruptive of how we teach and educate.

As long as we as a community keep practicing and teaching a **code-driven** and **test-driven** approach to (complex) system design, understanding what a system does based on source code will remain a challenge. It is a challenge already now for professionals, as witnessed for meanwhile over 50 years at general software engineering conferences like ICSE and OOPSLA as well at conferences and workshops on software testing, software quality and software maintenance. Works like [5] show that even recovering just the feature level architecture of existing software systems is hard work: it requires both specialized tools and quite some detective work, coupled with technical and domain knowledge, affinity for experimentation and a good pinch of intuition. Few people, even in Software Engineering, satisfy this profile. The mass of people and professionals in need of a system's refactoring, extension, and integration described as "the people" in Sect. 2 isn't equipped to add all these skills to their professional portfolio. The educational system currently for IT is not made either to mainstream deep technology competences. The outcome is that for most IT change projects the need is recognized but there is no follow up. This freeze into past solutions locks entire companies and organisation into outdated systems that impose outdated working patterns. This status quo counters the increasingly flexible workflows and collaborations mandated by both the collaborative economy and the many disruptive opportunities, trends and threats.

The problem is not solved by the run to open source: even if the source code is open, and in theory reusable and modifiable, it still requires comprehension first, then mapping to the concrete situation, and thus all the capabilities mentioned above: it is in practice like starting with legacy. The big boost to adoption of open source has been extremely beneficial for the sharing economy, the commoditization of essential layers of software, the globalisation and mass accessibility of technology and its related knowledge in ways unthinkable even 20 years ago, when entire domains were in the hands of proprietary systems with closed APIs. So, OSS and FOSS [37] work very well, but again they are for specialists.

The Agile movement has sparked a new attitude towards collaborative and fast paced system development, including frequent and consensual meetings with stakeholders that are users and customers, and it is gladly adopted in industry. However, agile thinking addresses the software development process and is agnostic to the means and artefacts. In practice, software is developed again within the "standard best practice": starting from code and with "test first" as a maxime for quality assurance. What this means is twofold:

- Because it is **code**, the artefacts are out of the cultural reach for most of these users and customers, as well as for most of the professional roles essential to the software business that are not directly code-related: sales, marketing, legal, etc. These people have to rely on expert "translation" from the artefacts to the understandable (but possibly incomplete, ambiguous, biased) interpretation of those artefacts and their characteristics into some IT-layman description, that most often is in some natural language prose. We are still trapped here in the **business-IT translation gap**.
- Because quality assurance is prevalently if not exclusively handled via **testing**, it can take place only post-factum: a system is implemented to the code level, and only then it is amenable to validation, verification etc. Given that it is very expensive to write code as well as to debug and test code, this is an inherently and **systematically wasteful** way of managing the production of

software and systems. Also simulation based approaches still require writing simulation code that is quite akin to the production code. Also the verification is still conducted case by case, configuration by configuration, run by run. Once a system is out, any change requires reassessment through regression testing, possibly recertification, skewing even more toward the testing costs the already onerous ratio of cost to develop an increment vs. cost to test that increment.

6 Generative Approaches as the Next Wave

The creation of a software or system is itself *innovation*, and the change or evolution of an existing system is innovation too. Consistently with the widely successful school of *lean* approaches to innovation, one needs to *fail fast* and *eliminate waste*. The key is to recognize as early as possible that something is not as wished, possibly before investing time and resources into producing what will need to be amended, and make changes right away on the artefacts that are available at that stage.

An efficient way to deal with this paradigm addresses a variety of aspects and innovation directions, that we briefly summarize.

– The **cultural aspect** is made accessible by resorting to the description of artefacts within domain models, rather than code: model driven design and development, and model driven and model based testing are already going in this direction.
– The **code aspect** is addressed by separating the (application specific or reusable) "logic" from the implementation of the operations and the system. Service oriented computing leverages component based design together with a high level description of the interfaces and properties of the components as well as the behaviours (described as processes or as APIs) and data they operate upon.
– The **testing aspect** is streamlined by choosing modelling languages that facilitate an early stage "checking" of the model structure, of the architectural and behavioural compatibilities. Architecture Analysis and Description Languages (AADLs) cover the architectural and static aspects, while the use of formal models like the KTS used in jABC [24], DIME [2] and in general graph-based models supported by CINCO [29] allow also a behavioural analysis e.g. by model checking and in some cases a correct-by-construction synthesis of property-conform models, thus delivering the "speed" of early detection and even avoidance of errors that makes then testing on the code much faster.
– The **dissemination aspect** is taken care of by sharing such models (understandable to the domain experts) and possibly also the implementations of the building blocks, this by using for example the existing OSS facilities and structures. Libraries of services have been in use in the telecommunication domain since the '80s [35], they are increasingly in use in bioinformatics, geo-information systems, and are slowly taking a center stage attention also in the

advanced manufacturing community, albeit mostly still in form of reference architectures and shared component models for which standards need to be developed.

– The **speed to change** is accelerated by using generative approaches that transform the models into lower level descriptions, possibly into code, adding one or more model-to-code layers on top of the already long chain of compilers that take UML classes and create skeletons, or Java code and produce bytecode, or C/C++ code and produce executables, and from the executables goes down to the specific instruction set and firmware of the processors, FPGAs and other ASICS. Generation can be partial, as in the UML community, or more extended as e.g. in the Grammatical Evolution approach by [27], that creates in fact programs by successive approximation based on a specific flavour of genetic algorithms that operate along a grammar-driven DSL of the specific domain and operations under consideration. In jABC, CINCO and DIME we use both model-to-model and model-to-code transformations, starting from the Genesys approach of [16,17], up to the generalized approach that Cinco adopts also at the tool metalevel [29].

– The **rich description** of the single components, data, and applications is achieved by means of both domain-independent and domain-specific knowledge about the functionalities, the data and business objects, and the application's requirements and quality profile, as in language-oriented programming [6,39] or language-driven engineering [31].

– The **scalability and speed of education** are supported by teaching domain specialists to deal with these domain specific models, their analysis and composition, and the validation using tools that exploit the domain-specific and contextual knowledge to detect the suitability or not of the current version of the application's models for solving a certain problem in a certain (regulatory, technological, economic) context. We have had successes in the context of school pupils [1,20], postgraduate students with a background in biology and geography [19], and more recently first year students and mature CS students that take a 1 year Higher Diploma [11].

– The **quick evolution** is delivered by means of integrated design environments that support the collaboration of all the professional profiles and stakeholders on the same set of models and descriptions, as in the XMDD and One Thing Approach, applied to models of systems but also of test cases [30].

– The **structuring approaches** based e.g. on hierarchy [32,33], on several notions of features like in [5,14,15,18,25,34], or contracts for abstraction and compositionality as in [13]. These structures allow a nice and incremental factoring of well characterized system components to aide the hierarchical and collaborative organisation of complex or large systems, while supporting the intuition of the domain experts, and the most opportune units of reuse (for development, evolution and testing), and units of localized responsibility, e.g. for maintenance, evolution and support.

Some of this is already in the making even at the level of hardware and platforms, which are essential for the connected and evolving industrial critical systems of tomorrow.

7 Examples of Future-Oriented Rethinking

On the hardware side the foundation of all software executions is the computer architecture, possibly enhanced by various layers of virtualization and resource management. In terms of properties, guarantees, contracts, service level agreements, upper layers of the software and system management stack must rely upon what is known and guaranteed by the underlying layers. So, what is known today about computer architectures and the software layers that enforce essential platform properties? We look at three recent contributions that provide a glimpse of the promising research directions that are amenable to bring formal thinking and generative approaches closer to the mainstream.

7.1 Rich, Formally Specified Interfaces from the Bare Metal Upward

Margaret Martonosi, recent recipient of the IEEE Computer Society Technical Achievement Award "for contributions to power-aware computing and energy-constrained mobile sensor networks", reflected in her recent keynote at IEEE COMPSAC that computer architects are until now required yet to a good extent also restricted to measure in architectures only execution performance, thus sticking to a one-dimensional characterisation of quality that is short of today's architectural demands. Her plea for modern computer systems is towards a far richer and multifaceted characterisation. Such a profile-like characterisation includes next to figures of energy consumption also values for reliability, fairness, portability, scalability, security, and many more. These rich descriptions of the Computer Architecture interfaces should be formulated in an unambiguous language, and she advocates using formal methods for describing and reasoning about interface specification, modeling and metrics [26].

In recent work with Sharad Malik and Aarti Gupta, she used such formal specifications, albeit simple, first to describe the capabilities of an instruction set, an API, and equivalently specifiable behavioural mechanisms for the many other components that do not have an instruction set (called non-ISA components, like most Internet of Things devices), Subsequently they used those descriptions to analyze both the real and the possible behaviours of systems in isolation and in a friendly or hostile context. They used these capabilities and, in a linearized world, the "happens before" behavioural relation that allows to think in terms of system behaviours over sequences of operations, in a trace semantics approach. This led to the development of simple but effective and efficient tools that work as a set of concern-specific lenses to talk about global behaviours at the system level. Tools like Wattch [4], PipeCheck [21] and COATCheck [22] have made the **systematic generation and exploration of architecture-level behavior** both **possible** and **easy**, regarding power optimisation, memory consistency, and memory ordering at the hardware-OS interface, respectively.

Thanks to the rich interface formalisation, it is possible to describe exactly what is intended, what is forbidden, and what happens in a situation-dependent context, and it is consequently possible for the first time to build tools, in this case based on SAT solvers, that systematically explore and classify the behavioural traces.

Eminent achievements have been the automatic and easy reproduction of the Meltdown and Spectre security attacks using the above tools. Not only were such attacks easily "discovered": the discovery came together with an understanding of which design features and mechanisms of interaction led to them, and this understanding of course led to an entire design space of ways to detect and prevent such and similar attacks. Additionally, they were able to generate a large number of other so far unreported attacks that are possible on the same architectures and mechanisms, some of which so relevant that they were reported back to the companies that designed such systems.

Thanks to such behavioural analysis tools, it is made easy for designers of higher level infrastructure software and of applications, to check and recheck that their own designs do not incur in behavioral risks or inconsistencies. Weighted edges on automata-like models can represent latency, power or reliability figures, and provide rich analysis models down to the instruction set layer, which is so far not possible. Upper layers can then rely on the data measured at the lower layers, and enable a systematic design space exploration driven by rich models that embody detailed and multifaceted knowledge at the underlying levels: still a dream for today's system designers, as we will see in Sect. 7.3.

7.2   Ad-Hoc Computing in the World Beyond von Neumann's Architectures

However, considering the future needs, it is even likely that the Von Neumann architectural paradigm will be superseded. As HP Labs Dejian Milojicic foresees [28], architectures for large scale in-memory computing will revolution the operating systems as we know them today and change the entire organization of what is a computer due to he emergence of new nanocomponents. Current research on emerging technologies for memory design, like memristors in HP but also other emergent memory components like Magnetic Random Access Memory (MRAM)[3], studied among others in the TRUDEVICE EU COST Action UL belonged to, are hot candidates to successfully replace actual DRAM-based main memory technology. On the MRAM technology roadmap, the goal is to design and develop ?Service-Oriented? emerging memory devices based on non-volatile MRAM technology, with characteristics and mode of functioning tunable in an ad-hoc fashion by individual application designers, as needed to meet their specific project/work needs. Rapid reconfigurability of the work is here the main benefit, but configurable and controllable (1) reliability, (2) variability, (3) endurance, (4) access time, (5) bandwidth, (6) latency, and (7) power consumption will allow application designers and programmers direct QoS control on memory access services. On the memristor technology roadmap, research leads mainly towards the development of a new kind of passive storage. However, it is known how to produce memristor based devices that implement negation

---

[3] ITRS 2013, http://public.itrs.net/.

and implication and thus generic logic functions. Accordingly, we can envisage scalable architectures where memristor-based memories manage the data, and efficient tiling and interconnections of memristor-based logic organized in crossbar architectures (like for FPGAs) provide easily reconfigurable "control" units that supersede the current Von Neumann architectures. The consequence is a new generation of architectures that provide a memristor-based generic *memory and control* capability that can be configured and used completely on-demand.

Fully exploiting either the Service Oriented MRAM Memory device or the memristor-based architecture requires revolutionizing the current programming model, and the way we organize and handle data, control, and even the set of instructions at the hardware level. In such a post-Neumann architecture, computations consist of

- the data, to be stored e.g. in the memristor storage,
- the "program", to be e.g. "loaded" on the memristor-based control architecture, but whereby
- the Instruction Set of the architecture (i.e., the primitives of the programming language) is not predefined and static like in current architectures, but easily and fully reconfigurable beyond the level of reconfigurability that we know today from FPGAs. In this future, the definition of the instructions in terms of hardware implementation of the primitives will be provided together with the "program", and the instructions will be "mapped" themselves on the control architecture in order to define the set of functionalities available to the specific program.

Taken together, we see here the proposal of a completely ad-hoc and dynamic computation model and system: a Domain Specific Language, and potentially even an Application Specific Language, can be "deployed" case by case, program by program, onto an instruction set-agnostic architecture. By configuring a sea of memristors into instruction-executing logic components, this new paradigm effectively creates a Domain Specific Computer. This computer is then asked to execute a program in that DSL onto given data. When that execution terminates it is ready for a complete reconfiguration to another domain or application. In other words, this future paradigm ditches the inherent dicothomy of the Von Neumann paradigm, and embraces a thorough and generic service-orientation from the hardware up. Once such an architecture is available, implementing language-oriented programming [6,39] and language-driven engineering [31] throughout the entire stack of software layers, down to the hardware, becomes natural and obvious.

Once this is in place, it will be then finally possible to have formally characterized capabilities and interfaces for a new kind of service-oriented general purpose efficient hardware, that is pliable to fast and efficient reconfiguration, and that brings a rich description of both functionality and quality of service in terms of properties and behaviours. The approach just described applies not only to instruction set-based hardware like today's CPUs, but also to API-based components like e.g. Smartcards, which support at different abstraction layers interfaces like the Transmission Protocol Data Units and the Application Protocol Data Units. It applies even to non-ISA components like the FPGAs and most accelerators and IoT devices.

7.3   Security-Injecting Compilers

This is exactly the situation we are currently facing in the project with Blu5 Labs: the SEcube (TM) chip they provide includes three open source components (a CPU, an FPGA and a Smartcard) [38] and is therefore an advanced and open System-on-a-Chip specialised for security applications from the hardware up. However, no formal description of the interfaces of these components is available, as demanded in Sect. 7.1, no formally robust behavioural characterization is available, and as a consequence we cannot bootstrap the formal reasoning from the hardware up as should be the case for an SoC component that is central to a holistic security concept, and responsible for the hardware layers of a security architecture used commercially for top-level security applications.

On the basis of the open source descriptions of the three components and through testing with the SoC programming boards, it is possible to manually write drivers (in machine language and C) that realize several layers of services [8], that are subsequently thoroughly tested in the laboratory. This is still the current state of the art in security architectures: at the hardware interface and at the driver and relative protocols nothing is formal, architectures are designed case by case, software for protocols and low level features is implemented in "coding first" fashion, and architects and designers mostly do not feel the need for introducing formality at all.

In this situation, we built our own model driven, service oriented and generative approach on top of the software layers produced manually by the partners. We produced a DSL library for the multifaceted characterization of security primitives [3], a service library for the primitives at the programming language level, in this case the C language, embedded in the C-IME, our C-applications Integrated Modelling Environment [10,12], and we provided libraries for other domains as in [7,9]. On this basis it is also possible to provide a smart compilation platform, itself realized in a model driven paradigm, that is a model-to-code compiler to normal C or to C with security added through the SEcube platform. This compiler takes security-agnostic models of applications designed in the C-IME environment, and injects during compilation where needed the appropriate security primitives. The result is the same C application, but where all the communication is correctly secured using through the C language libraries and the SEcube security libraries [12].

This generative and model driven approach works in a model driven, service oriented and generative fashion, on security-agnostic application models that are far away from the level of programming, hardware and security competence needed today to create comparably secure software. It successfully frees the application designer from the need of specialized knowledge about security mechanisms and their implementation details. However, in today's world, this ability of modelling, analyzing and proving properties of behaviours is still limited to aim at the provision of executable functionality (of an application). We'd rather like instead to provide a provably bug-free and attack-resilient hardware/software stack. This limitation is due to the informal treatment of hardware interfaces, and to the customary code-based approach to the production and documentation of the low level layers of the SEcube-close software, which are directly implemented in machine language and C and are not accompanied by specifications nor models and are thus in practice not verifiable.

8   The Perspectives Ahead

In spite of the difficulties, we are convinced that this is the way to go in order to mainstream the production and evolution of IT at the levels of speed, scale, affordability and collaborative effort needed to truly make IT enter the fabric of every economical and societal endeavour. It needs to be achieved at a level of competence that can be acquired quickly, in a targeted fashion, and such that the collaboration with the IT specialists is likely to become natural and pervasive. Specialists will still exist and be essential for the implementation and maintenance of the code and of the infrastructure. But the acceptance of formality as a means to clarify interfaces, behaviours and properties and as a precondition to verify and prevent, instead of implementing, testing, and then repairing case by case, is essential to meet the challenges and demands for the future platforms of IT provision and use. In this sense, we need both Archimedean points [36] and future oriented knowledge management for change management [23] in order to make future platforms *easy but powerful for the many*, and *complex yet well structured for the few*.

Acknowledgment. This work was supported, in part, by Science Foundation Ireland grant 13/RC/2094 and co-funded under the European Regional Development Fund through the Southern & Eastern Regional Operational Programme to Lero - the Irish Software Research Centre (www.lero.ie).

References

1. Bakera, M., Jörges, S., Margaria, T.: Test your strategy: graphical construction of strategies for connect-four. In: Proceedings of the 2009 14th IEEE International Conference on Engineering of Complex Computer Systems, pp. 172–181, ICECCS 2009. IEEE Computer Society, Washington, DC (2009). http://dx.doi.org/10.1109/ICECCS.2009.51
2. Boßelmann, S., et al.: DIME: a programming-less modeling environment for web applications. In: Margaria, T., Steffen, B. (eds.) ISoLA 2016. LNCS, vol. 9953, pp. 809–832. Springer, Cham (2016). https://doi.org/10.1007/978-3-319-47169-3_60
3. Boßelmann, S., Neubauer, J., Naujokat, S., Steffen, B.: Model-driven design of secure high assurance systems: an introduction to the open platform from the user perspective. In: Margaria, T., Solo, M.G.A. (eds.) The 2016 International Conference on Security and Management (SAM 2016). Special Track "End-to-end Security and Cybersecurity: from the Hardware to Application", pp. 145–151. CREA Press (2016)

4. Brooks, D., Tiwari, V., Martonosi, M.: Wattch: a framework for architectural-level power analysis and optimizations. In: Proceedings of 27th International Symposium on Computer Architecture, vol. ISSN=1063-6897, pp. 83–94. IEEE (2000)

5. Buckley, J., Rosik, J., Herold, S., Wasala, A., Botterweck, G., Exton, C.: Flints: a tool for architectural-level modeling of features in software systems. In: Proceedings of the 10th European Conference on Software Architecture Workshops, ECSAW 2016, pp. 14:1–14:7. ACM, New York (2016). http://doi.acm.org/10.1145/2993412.3003390

6. Dmitriev, S.: Language oriented programming: the next programming paradigm. JetBrains onBoard Online Mag. **1** (2004). http://www.onboard.jetbrains.com/is1/articles/04/10/lop/

7. Farulla, A., Lamprecht, A.L.: Model checking of security properties: a case study on human-robot interaction processes. In: 12th International Conference on Design Technology of Integrated Systems in Nanoscale Era (DTIS), pp. 1–6. IEEE Computer Society (2017). https://doi.org/10.1109/DTIS.2017.7930158

8. Farulla, G.A., Prinetto, P., Varriale, A.: Holistic security via complex HW/SW platforms. In: 12th International Conference on Design Technology of Integrated Systems in Nanoscale Era (DTIS), pp. 1–6. IEEE Computer Society (2017). https://doi.org/10.1109/DTIS.2017.7930156

9. Farulla, G.A., Indaco, M., Legay, A., Margaria, T.: Model driven design of secure properties for vision-based applications: a case study. In: Margaria, T., Solo, M.G.A. (eds.) The 2016 International Conference on Security and Management (SAM 2016). Special Track "End-to-end Security and Cybersecurity: from the Hardware to Application", pp. 159–167. CREA Press (2016)

10. Gossen, F., Tiziana Margaria, J.N.B.S.: A model-driven and generative approach to holistic security. In: Flammini, F. (ed.) Resilience of Cyber-Physical Systems: From Risk Modeling to Threat Counteraction. Advanced Sciences and Technologies for Security Applications. Springer, Heidelberg (2018). ISBN: 978-3-319-95597-1

11. Gossen, F., Kühn, D., Margaria, T., Lamprecht, A.L.: Computational thinking: learning by doing with the Cinco adventure game tool. In: 42nd IEEE Annual Computer Software and Applications Conference (COMPSAC), CELT Symposium, Tokyo, Japan, 24–27 July 2018. IEEE Computer Society (in press)

12. Gossen, F., Neubauer, J., Steffen, B.: Securing C/C++ applications with a secube^{TM}-based model-driven approach. In: 12th International Conference on Design & Technology of Integrated Systems in Nanoscale Era, DTIS 2017, Palma de Mallorca, Spain, 4–6 April 2017, pp. 1–7. IEEE (2017). https://doi.org/10.1109/DTIS.2017.7930157

13. Graf, S., Quinton, S., Girault, A., Gössler, G.: Building correct cyber-physical systems: why we need a multiview? In: Howar, F., Barnat, J. (eds.) FMICS 2018. LNCS, vol. 11119, pp. 19–31. Springer, Cham (2018)

14. Jonsson, B., Margaria, T., Naeser, G., Nyström, J., Steffen, B.: Incremental requirement specification for evolving systems. In: Calder, M., Magill, E.H. (eds.) Feature Interactions in Telecommunications and Software Systems VI (FIW 2000), pp. 145–162. IOS Press, May 2000

15. Jonsson, B., Margaria, T., Naeser, G., Nyström, J., Steffen, B.: Incremental requirement specification for evolving systems. Nordic J. Comput. **8**, 65–87 (2001). http://dl.acm.org/citation.cfm?id=774194.774199

16. Jörges, S.: Construction and Evolution of Code Generators. A Model-Driven and Service-Oriented Approach. LNCS, vol. 7747. Springer, Heidelberg (2013). https://doi.org/10.1007/978-3-642-36127-2

17. Jörges, S., Margaria, T., Steffen, B.: Genesys: service-oriented construction of property conform code generators. Innov. Syst. Softw. Eng. **4**(4), 361–384 (2008)
18. Karusseit, M., Margaria, T.: Feature-based modelling of a complex, online-reconfigurable decision support service. Electron. Notes Theor. Comput. Sci. **157**(2), 101–118 (2006). http://www.sciencedirect.com/science/article/pii/S1571066106002489
19. Lamprecht, A.-L., Margaria, T. (eds.): Process Design for Natural Scientists. An Agile Model-Driven Approach. CCIS, vol. 500. Springer, Heidelberg (2014). https://doi.org/10.1007/978-3-662-45006-2
20. Lamprecht, A., Margaria, T., McInerney, C.: A summer computing camp using ChainReaction and jABC. In: 40th IEEE Annual Computer Software and Applications Conference, COMPSAC Workshops 2016, Atlanta, GA, USA, 10–14 June 2016, pp. 275–280. IEEE Computer Society (2016). https://doi.org/10.1109/COMPSAC.2016.41
21. Lustig, D., Pellauer, M., Martonosi, M.: PipeCheck: specifying and verifying microarchitectural enforcement of memory consistency models. In: 47th Annual IEEE/ACM International Symposium on Microarchitecture, pp. 635–646. No. ISSN=1072-4451. IEEE (2015)
22. Lustig, D., Sethi, G., Martonosi, M., Bhattacharjee, A.: COATCheck: Verifying memory ordering at the hardware-OS interface. SIGPLAN Not. **51**(4), 233–247 (2016). http://doi.acm.org/10.1145/2954679.2872399
23. Margaria, T.: Knowledge management for inclusive system evolution. In: Steffen, B. (ed.) Transactions on Foundations for Mastering Change I. LNCS, vol. 9960, pp. 7–21. Springer, Cham (2016). https://doi.org/10.1007/978-3-319-46508-1_2
24. Margaria, T., Steffen, B.: Lightweight coarse-grained coordination: a scalable system-level approach. Softw. Tools Technol. Transfer **5**(2–3), 107–123 (2004)
25. Margaria, T., Steffen, B., Reitenspieß, M.: Service-oriented design: the roots. In: Benatallah, B., Casati, F., Traverso, P. (eds.) ICSOC 2005. LNCS, vol. 3826, pp. 450–464. Springer, Heidelberg (2005). https://doi.org/10.1007/11596141_34
26. Martonosi, M.: New metrics and models for a Post-ISA era: managing complexity and scaling performance in heterogeneous parallelism and internet-of-things (keynote talk). In: 42nd IEEE Annual Computer Software and Applications Conference (COMPSAC), CELT Symposium, Tokyo, Japan, 24–27 July 2018. IEEE Computer Society (2018, in press)
27. Medernach, D., Fitzgerald, J., Azad, R.M.A., Ryan, C.: A new wave: a dynamic approach to genetic programming. In: Proceedings of the Genetic and Evolutionary Computation Conference 2016, pp. 757–764. GECCO 2016. ACM, New York (2016). http://doi.acm.org/10.1145/2908812.2908857
28. Milojicic, D.: Generalize or die: operating systems support for memristor-based accelerators (keynote talk). In: 42nd IEEE Annual Computer Software and Applications Conference (COMPSAC), CELT Symposium, Tokyo, Japan, 24–27 July 2018. IEEE Computer Society (2018, in press)
29. Naujokat, S., Lybecait, M., Kopetzki, D., Steffen, B.: CINCO: a simplicity-driven approach to full generation of domain-specific graphical modeling tools. Softw. Tools Technol. Transf. **20**, 327 (2017)
30. Niese, O., Steffen, B., Margaria, T., Hagerer, A., Brune, G., Ide, H.-D.: Library-based design and consistency checking of system-level industrial test cases. In: Hussmann, H. (ed.) FASE 2001. LNCS, vol. 2029, pp. 233–248. Springer, Heidelberg (2001). https://doi.org/10.1007/3-540-45314-8_17

31. Steffen, B., Gossen, F., Naujokat, S., Margaria, T.: Language-driven engineering: from general-purpose to purpose-specific languages. In: Steffen, B., Woeginger, G. (eds.) Computing and Software Science: State of the Art and Perspectives. LNCS, vol. 10000. Springer, Heidelberg (2018)

32. Steffen, B., Margaria, T., Braun, V., Kalt, N.: Hierarchical service definition. Ann. Rev. Commun. ACM **51**, 847–856 (1997)

33. Steffen, B., Margaria, T., Claßen, A.: Heterogeneous analysis and verification for distributed systems. Softw. Concepts Tools **17**(1), 13–25 (1996)

34. Steffen, B., Margaria, T., Claßen, A., Braun, V.: Incremental formalization: A key to industrial success. Softw. Concepts Tools **17**(2), 78–95 (1996)

35. Steffen, B., Margaria, T., Claßen, A., Braun, V., Reitenspieß, M.: An environment for the creation of intelligent network services. In: Intelligent Networks: IN/AIN Technologies, Operations, Services and Applications - A Comprehensive Report, pp. 287–300. IEC: International Engineering Consortium (1996)

36. Steffen, B., Naujokat, S.: Archimedean points: the essence for mastering change. In: Steffen, B. (ed.) Transactions on Foundations for Mastering Change I. LNCS, vol. 9960, pp. 22–46. Springer, Cham (2016). https://doi.org/10.1007/978-3-319-46508-1_3

37. Steinmacher, I., Robles, G., Fitzgerald, B., Wasserman, A.I.: Free and open source software development: the end of the teenage years. J. Internet Serv. Appl. **8**(1), 17:1–17:4 (2017). https://doi.org/10.1186/s13174-017-0069-9

38. Varriale, A., di Natale, G., Prinetto, P., Steffen, B., Margaria, T.: SEcube[TM]: an open security platform: general approach and strategies. In: Margaria, T., Solo, M.G.A. (eds.) The 2016 International Conference on Security and Management (SAM 2016). Special Track "End-to-end Security and Cybersecurity: from the Hardware to Application", pp. 131–137. CREA Press (2016)

39. Ward, M.P.: Language oriented programming. Softw. Concepts Tools **15**(4), 147–161 (1994)

Building Correct Cyber-Physical Systems: Why We Need a Multiview Contract Theory

Susanne Graf[1]([✉]), Sophie Quinton[2], Alain Girault[2], and Gregor Gössler[2]

[1] Univ. Grenoble Alpes, CNRS, Grenoble INP, VERIMAG, Grenoble, France
`susanne.graf@imag.fr`
[2] Univ. Grenoble Alpes, Inria, CNRS, Grenoble INP, LIG, Grenoble, France

Abstract. The design and verification of critical cyber-physical systems is based on a number of models (and corresponding analysis techniques and tools) representing different viewpoints such as function, timing, security and many more. Overall correctness is guaranteed by mostly informal, and therefore basic, arguments about the relationship between these viewpoint-specific models. We believe that a more flexible contract-based approach could lead to easier integration, to relaxed assumptions, and consequently to more cost efficient systems while preserving the current modelling approach and its tools.

1 Introduction

Building correct Cyber-Physical Systems (CPS) is a challenge in critical application domains such as avionics, automotive, etc. It is getting ever more difficult because CPSs are of increasing complexity: indeed, CPS are nowadays composed of a large number of components and subsystems of heterogeneous nature and of different criticality levels. In addition, non-functional aspects, or *viewpoints* – such as timing, memory footprint, energy, dependability, temperature, and more recently also security – are as important as functionality.

There exist many analyses and tools for verifying CPS, but their underlying model is always specific to a *single* viewpoint, and there is currently limited support to relate viewpoints semantically. In practice, the assumptions that a viewpoint-specific analysis makes on the other viewpoints remain mostly implicit, and whenever explicit they are handled mostly manually. In this paper, we argue that the current design process overconstrains the set of possible system designs and that there is a need for methods and tools to formally relate viewpoint-specific models and corresponding analysis results.

More specifically, we claim that *contract-based* design can be relevant to address the challenges raised by the use of multiple viewpoints. The term "design by contract" has been introduced in [30].

This work has been partially supported by the LabEx PERSYVAL-Lab (ANR-11-LABX-0025-01).

© Springer Nature Switzerland AG 2018
F. Howar and J. Barnat (Eds.): FMICS 2018, LNCS 11119, pp. 19–31, 2018.
https://doi.org/10.1007/978-3-030-00244-2_2

The rest of this paper is organized as follows. Section 2 provides a short overview of some viewpoint-specific models and techniques. Section 3 describes existing efforts toward some level of integration of viewpoints. In Sect. 4 we motivate the need for a flexible contract-based approach to formally relate viewpoint-specific models and analysis results. Finally, we present in Sect. 5 initial remarks and possible research directions toward such a framework.

2   Multiple Models for Multiple Viewpoints

In practice, CPS designers make use of several models focusing on specific aspects of a system, called *viewpoints* – typical examples are function, timing, safety, reliability, security, energy, etc. Often, different viewpoints correspond to distinct disciplines, possibly very different levels of granularity, and are supported by their own domain-specific software tools. We now briefly discuss the most relevant ones for CPS.

2.1   Function

The functionality of a system consists of a set of control functions, some of them intended to be executed cyclically with a cycle time that may be specific to each function, and others sporadically, typically for the treatment of alarms. The functionality is itself split between a continuous part (automatic control laws) and a discrete part (finite state machines), hence two viewpoints. Usual requirements for the former part include observability and stability, but also robustness to perturbations, delays, noise, and so on. For the latter part, engineers are concerned with safety and reachability properties. For all of these, a large body of results has been developed.

Function design is nowadays done in a component-based manner, sometimes using directly the C language or using domain specific languages proposed by design environment such as MATLAB Simulink (well suited for ODE based models), Scade [13] (well suited for safety critical systems), or Modelica [33] (well suited for DAE based systems). Most of these design environments include analysis tools to ensure that the control algorithms, provided by the control engineer, are correctly implemented (based on the semantics of the programming language). Analysis tools have also been developed to take into account both the continuous and discrete viewpoints, with tools such as PHAVer [19] or d/dt [4].

2.2   Timing

Timing requirements on CPSs are typically expressed in terms of deadlines on the *Worst-Case Response Time* (WCRT) of the system. The WCRT is the time required to compute and send the outputs of the system to its actuators starting from the values on the inputs obtained from its sensors. Depending on how the system's functionalities are implemented, these deadlines will be expressed in different ways: e.g., end-to-end latency for a task based implementation, or worst-case reaction time for a periodic loop implementation.

The schedulability of a system, that is, the guarantee that no deadline can be missed, is proven in two steps: (i) computing the Worst-Case Execution Time (WCET) of the basic components of the system (e.g., its tasks, its C functions, ...), and (ii) performing the schedulability analysis strictly speaking. The goal of the WCET analysis is to upper bound the time it may take for a program to complete on a given hardware platform, assuming there is no interference from other programs that may concurrently execute. WCET analysis is based on low-level code (obtained by compilation from C) and on an abstraction of the hardware platform of the system under analysis, including memory access policies, caches, pipelines, and so on. Commercial tools like aiT [1, 42] from Absint perform such an analysis.

Schedulability analysis integrates the results of the WCET analysis with an analysis of how different programs (or tasks) may interfere due to the fact that they share computation and communication resources (e.g., on a multi-core processor). Schedulability analysis is based on a model of the software represented as a set of tasks scheduled according to some scheduling policy. Tools performing schedulability analysis include SymTA/S from Symtavision [25] and RT-Druid from Evidence [2].

2.3   Dependability

Dependability is a crucial notion for CPS systems. It is defined as the ability for the system to "deliver a service that can justifiably be trusted" [6]. This generic notion encompasses many concepts, including availability, reliability and safety. Among those, the one on which we focus in this section is *reliability*, which is defined as the probability that the systems works correctly during a given time interval. Being a probability, it varies in the interval $[0, 1]$. For instance, fly-by-wire civil flight control systems must exhibit a reliability greater than $1 - 10^{-9} = 0.999999999$ over 10 h (the "nine nines rule") [37].

When addressing the dependability viewpoint, engineers must provide the *fault model*, which identifies how the components of the CPS being designed can fail: this concerns both the hardware (processors, communication media, memory banks, sensors, actuators, and so on) and the software (tasks, OS, and middleware). For instance, the hardware failures can be transient or permanent. The fault model depends not only on the physical environment of the CPS (the temperature range, vibrations, radiations, and so on), but also on the chosen manufacturing technology (which CMOS size, which packaging), and on the operating mode (which voltage, frequency, and so on).

Then, the user specifies a minimal reliability r that the CPS under design must comply to. Improving the reliability requires some form of *redundancy*, which can be spatial or temporal when dealing with hardware failures [21]. Engineers thus use dedicated analysis tools to derive how much redundancy must be added to the system, and where it must be added, to achieve this bound r. Examples of such tools include fault-trees, reliability block diagrams, and so on.

3 Efforts Toward Integration of Viewpoints

In addition to viewpoint-specific techniques, an increasing number of methods and tools provide some support for handling multiple viewpoints.

3.1 Tool Integration

There exist integration mechanisms between design tools such as MATLAB Simulink, Scade, TargetLink[1], schedulability analysis tools such as SymTA/S or RT-Druid and WCET analysis tools, in particular aiT. This means that the functional model can be annotated with task information allowing for

- the extraction of a scheduling model so as to guarantee that there is always a well defined mapping relating functions and tasks;
- the extraction of low level code for WCET analysis;
- the injection of the computed WCETs into the scheduling model to perform the schedulability analysis.

Such tool support is obviously very useful for guaranteeing the consistency between viewpoint-specific models. Yet, the exchange of information between viewpoints takes place mostly at a syntactical level. For example, the assumption made in the functional model on schedulability is implicit.

3.2 Theoretical Results Relating Automatic Control and Other Viewpoints

Several approaches have been proposed to formally link automatic control objectives with discrete computation and real-time scheduling. Consider for instance the stability objective mentioned in Sect. 2.1. For a given control law, this issue can be addressed purely from the continuous viewpoint (e.g., by defining a suitable Lyapunov function and proving its convergence), but doing so ignores the discrete changes occurring in the system, which may cause the system to switch from one control law to another. Such switches between several control laws make the stability problem very difficult to solve. Taking into account both viewpoints is therefore necessary, and attempts at this have been made in a contract-based manner.

With the goal of reasoning about how discretized signals evolve over time, *change and delay contracts* have been proposed in [32], while [28] introduces a theory of stochastic contracts over Stochastic Signal Temporal Logic.

Co-design of control and real-time scheduling has been studied by many authors, see e.g. [18,20,27]. A set of timing contracts between control and software engineers is proposed in [15]. Stability of embedded control systems under timing contracts, synthesis of timing contracts ensuring stability, and synthesis of scheduling policies ensuring satisfaction of timing contracts are studied in [3].

---

[1] TargetLink is a production code generation tool from dSPACE.

In contrast, [14] proposes a component library for bottom-up construction of hybrid controllers ensuring safety and stability properties.

Of particular interest for multiview contracts is the *symbolic control* [41] approach operating on a finite abstraction of the infinite state space. Control aspects may interfere with other aspects in particular through the system state, the computing power spent to compute the control actions, and through delays and jitter. Consider for instance the delays: they can occur at three places of a controlled closed-loop system: at the inputs (due to sensors dynamics), in the state (due to modeling assumptions), and at the outputs (due to actuators dynamics). These delays have been addressed by the automatic control community and given rise to the "delay systems" research area. Taking into account delay systems within a multiview contract approach and studying the robustness to delays raises several interesting challenges: from the systems and control viewpoint, the control engineer could study the stability, observability, and controllability of their system without considering the delays, and then from the timing viewpoint they could study the robustness of their control law with respect to the delays.

3.3   Other Approaches for the Integration of Multiple Viewpoints

As seen in Sect. 2.1, the continuous and the discrete viewpoints belong both to the functionality of the system. To exemplify the benefits of multiview contracts, it is essential to address also non-functional viewpoints. Consider for instance the timing and the reliability viewpoints. As explained in Sect. 2.3, improving the system's reliability requires some form of redundancy. For instance, a given task (or C function) can be replicated to reach the desired reliability, and potentially, each task can be replicated a different number of times. But this has an obvious negative impact on the timing of the system, because the system's WCRT will increase due to these task replications. So both viewpoints must be addressed jointly, as in [22].

Furthermore, consider now in addition the energy viewpoint. Decreasing the energy consumption of the system is classically achieved thanks to *Dynamic Voltage and Frequency Scaling* (DVFS) by choosing a lower (frequency, voltage) operating point for some tasks of the system. Potentially, each task can use a different (frequency, voltage) operating point. Again, this incurs an obvious negative impact on the timing viewpoint, because lowering the frequency increases the WCET of the tasks. But, perhaps less known is the negative impact on the system's reliability, because lowering the voltage makes the system sensitive to noise and lower energy particles, which are likely to create a critical charge leading to a transient failure [44]. Here again, these intricate dependencies between the viewpoints call for integrated methods and tools, as in [39] for the timing, energy, and temperature viewpoints, or in [5] for the timing, energy, and reliability viewpoints.

A large number of results exist as well on the connection between real-time and fault tolerance [7,12], and more recently on the integration of real-time and security [17,26].

Still, these multiview approaches consider two, at most three viewpoints and are not compatible with the existing workflow discussed previously.

In practice, the overview on all models and corresponding analysis activities is mostly in the hands of a human. As a consequence, the reasoning must be kept simple and thus the constraints imposed on each individual model are very restrictive, as we discuss in more detail in the next section.

4   Problem Statement

We have explained in the previous sections that the verification of cyber-physical systems is mostly performed on viewpoint-specific models. If all these models were completely independent, this would be sufficient [29] but this is of course not the case, as discussed in Sect. 3.3. We see two main issues with the current situation:

1. There is no theoretical framework that can encompass all viewpoints.
2. As a result, the interface between viewpoints must be simple enough to be handled manually, possibly while remaining implicit.

Let us illustrate the above mentioned shortcomings on an example. Functional analysis is based on some ideal (possibly mathematical) semantics of a programming language. In practice, the actual platform on which the code will be running may be compromised by various kinds of failures occurring at runtime, which can be due to insufficient resources (memory, computation time, etc.) or due to physical faults of the hardware platform. In particular, a major verification effort is spent to guarantee the absence of such runtime errors due to timing (thanks to schedulability analysis), as well as to guarantee a very low probability of failures due to the hardware components (thanks to dependability analysis).

Note that in the function model a property requiring *absence of runtime errors* cannot even be expressed. This property is an *assumption* to guarantee the *validity of the idealized mathematical semantics* used to make functional analysis feasible. It must be guaranteed by the platform, and at analysis level by the viewpoints dealing with those errors explicitly.

In the current methodology, this assumption is not explicitly formulated, and this means also that it cannot be relaxed.

Indeed, it has been proven to be unnecessarily restrictive for a large class of CPSs. A system may still satisfy its functional requirements under a *weaker* assumption: for example, a component implementing some continuous control law may still be perfectly safe (i.e., stable in the sense of automatic control) even if a deadline is missed – that is, an increased control delay is observed – from time to time [16,20].

This example underlines the need for a comprehensive tool support backed by a strong formal theory to handle explicitly the dependencies between any two viewpoints. The contract framework we are aiming at must permit to guarantee system properties based on analysis results obtained on viewpoint-specific models. In this context, contracts are attached to viewpoints which may be of very different nature, but all model the same system. Note that existing contract frameworks do not solve our problem.

In the Design-by-Contract approach introduced in [30] for the programming language Eiffel, and in all similar frameworks, proving contract satisfaction boils down to pre/post condition reasoning, which does clearly not fit our needs. Closer to our needs are general frameworks proposed for components composed under some parallel composition operators.

The meta-theory of contracts proposed in [11] extends many existing contract frameworks. It proposes a set of interesting concepts based on work done in the SPEEDS project [34] and a very powerful theory at semantic level. Unfortunately, it assumes a unifying formalism and all concepts are represented as an algebra on sets of runs. We want to reason at a higher level.

Rely/Guarantee[2] reasoning frameworks [31, 36] consider, like we, contracts $(\mathcal{A}, \mathcal{G})$ where $\mathcal{A}$ is an assumption on the environment under which the component is able to guarantee $\mathcal{G}$, and they propose proof rule based reasoning frameworks. In our case, contracts are attached with viewpoints instead of components. In the already mentioned project, we have also developed a general contract framework, with proof rules for avoiding the composition of heterogeneous models by composing verification results instead [23] but it is too abstract to be directly usable.

We aim at building *domain specific reasoning frameworks* adapted to a multi-model and multi-tool based methodology: basic facts should be derived on individual viewpoint models using their specialized tools, the system designer should be able to prove integration correctness using a set of domain specific contracts and proof rules, where the deep semantic level proofs requiring reasoning on the underlying *global system model* are only used to prove the correctness of the framework, or to extend the framework when needed.

5   Discussion

In this section, we emphasize what we believe are key issues that must be taken into account by a multiview contract theory. Our aim is to provide the system engineer who is currently in charge with system integration in a multi-model based approach, with additional tool support for guaranteeing their consistency.

5.1   On Abstraction and Proof Rules

Recall that the proof system that we want to develop is meant to ensure system properties from viewpoint specific analysis results. For now, let us consider some of the problems we may face with preserving properties from viewpoints to the system.

---

[2] more commonly called Assume/Guarantee reasoning, but we adopt here the terminology of [11].

In the simplest case, a viewpoint model M_{vp} is an *abstraction* of the global model M_G, that is, $M_{vp} = \alpha(M_G)$ for a function α preserving a class of properties Φ. In this case, using results on property preserving abstractions (e.g. [29]), for any $\varphi \in \Phi$ we get immediately the proof rule[3]

if (1) M_{vp} satisfies φ then (2) M_G satisfies φ

In practice, the mapping α does quite often not define such a "property preserving abstraction". Only when some property $\mathcal{A}$ holds, α is a Φ-preserving abstraction. We say that M_{vp} is a *conditional abstraction*, and the assumption $\mathcal{A}$ is the condition that guarantees that it is a Φ-preserving abstraction. As an example take the already mentioned condition of *absence of failures and timing errors*, or more generally that no other viewpoint can "break" the function model, which is indeed required to guarantee that the function model M_{Fun} represents a correct abstraction of the system. This gives us immediately the proof rule

if (1) M_G satisfies $\mathcal{A}$ and (2) M_{vp} satisfies φ then (3) M_G satisfies φ

Because of the restriction that verification should be restricted to individual viewpoint models (or small groups of them that can be handled jointly by the same tool), (1) cannot be checked directly, but $\mathcal{A}$ has to be "projected" on individual viewpoints, and therefore (1) can be replaced by verification condition of the form

(1') M_{vp}^1 satisfies $\mathcal{A}_1$, ..., and M_{vp}^k satisfies $\mathcal{A}_k$

On our running example, this means: in all viewpoints one has to identify events that could "break" M_{Fun}, and prove that such events will never occur. This demonstrates that projecting $\mathcal{A}$ on individual viewpoints may be reasonably simple.

We now have given a hint on how to formalize the current proof methodology for strong "cannot break" assumptions. But our aim is to be able to propose more relaxed assumptions. For example, in [24] we have proposed "interface automata" to represent more general "no break" conditions.

But we want to go beyond conditional abstraction. What can we propose, if for example, the condition "absence of deadline misses" is not satisfied, that is, the function model M_{Fun} is *not* an abstraction, at least not for the standard definition[4]? Current practice cannot handle this case in a satisfactory manner. Even if one knows that occasional deadline misses do not harm, it makes it mandatory to achieve schedulability (if needed by adding more resources) because there is no possibility to modify the "contract".

Could one replace this "contract"? Could one come up with a set of proof rules that would allow us to conclude from (1) M_{sched} satisfies *schedulable 9*

---

[3] where it may be necessary to "translate" the viewpoint property to a system property, but this requires technical arguments which beyond the purpose of this paper.

[4] Note that sometimes it may be sufficient to relax the notion of abstraction to obtain a conditional abstraction.

times out of 10, (2) M_{Fun} satisfies *always outputs a correct control action or does nothing* – that is, we replace the guarantee by a weaker one, and (3) possibly some more proofs, that M_{Fun} satisfies *outputs a correct control action 9 times out of 10*? This would then allow us to come up with a set of contracts to be satisfied by the set of viewpoint models.

Finally, could one systematize this approach for more complex "conditions" involving several viewpoints? possibly in a very viewpoint specific manner, using results mentioned in Sect. 3.

5.2 Viewpoint Composition

In order to *prove the correctness* of the reasoning framework to be defined, one obviously needs to reason on the global semantic model $\mathcal{M}_{\mathcal{G}}$, hopefully without ever building it. There are many proposals of unifying semantic frameworks proposed with the aim to provide a uniform representation of systems consisting of heterogeneous viewpoints or composed from parts based on different *models of computation*. We can here discuss only a few of them. One may in particular distinguish work on unified behaviour models whose purpose is the expression of behaviours stemming from heterogeneous viewpoints. We would like to mention in particular stochastic hybrid automata (SHA) [35] or at a lower semantic level Tag machines [10]. Another line of interesting work is on heterogeneous composition, in particular Metropolis [8], Ptolemy [43] or BIP [9]. There is also some work with a similar motivation as ours, where unifying models explicitly address viewpoint integration. We would like to mention [38] which defines a framework for a discrete setting and discusses problems of inter-viewpoint validation, and [40] which discusses a framework for service oriented systems. It proposes to restrict inter-viewpoint verification to verification of their consistency.

To summarize, in order to define a global model representing all relevant viewpoints, we need:

1. a common semantic model, rich enough to represent the behaviour of any viewpoint model
2. define the actual mappings from viewpoint models to the common semantic model
3. a notion of viewpoint composition

Let us discuss some of the needs and difficulties.

1. Behaviour semantics: the needs depend on the considered viewpoints. In those we are aware of, runs can be naturally represented as sequences of events representing *discrete state changes*, where between events, the discrete state remains stable, and the continuous state evolves according some laws. Some viewpoints may constrain the frequency of the occurrence of events by probabilities, occurrence patterns or other distributions. For the viewpoints mentioned in Sect. 2, a formalism such as the already mentioned SHA may be an option.

2. Semantic mapping: A difficulty for defining such a mapping stems from the fact that in different viewpoints, events may have a different granularity. To obtain a set of behaviour models that can be composed, each viewpoint model has to be refined sufficiently to be able to interact with other viewpoints on all relevant events.

Consider a well-known example that illustrates the granularity problem: in a function model according to a synchronous approach, in the simplest case, events are "ticks" representing the cycle period in which states and outputs are updated "instantaneously". This semantic model is useful as it simplifies verification of temporal properties, but using it makes the implicit assumption that the computation can always be completed within the cycle period. And the combined semantic model of both, the function and the corresponding task model, requires to refine "tick events" into event sequences such that all events of the kind *start task* and *end task* of the task model can be identified with some event in the function model.

This combined model may for example be used to easily prove the correctness of the contract saying that "as long as no deadline misses occur, the task model cannot disturb/break the function model".

6   Conclusion

This paper has been motivated by actual difficulties that system designers of large safety-critical cyber-physical systems have to face: how to keep consistent a system design without overconstraining it, in a context where multiple viewpoints are addressed separately using specialized tools. There is presently no framework that would allow a system engineer to manage the interplay between all viewpoints and the overall consistency in a flexible way.

There is a large body of theoretical work addressing interdependency and contracts for specific pairs or small groups of viewpoint; few of them are used in actual design processes. Among the contract frameworks that have been proposed for the purpose of achieving consistent integration, most consist in general theory.

The framework we have in mind would provide viewpoint specific contract patterns guaranteeing inter-viewpoint consistency in a flexible manner. We tried to motivate that this is a meaningful approach on hand of examples.

But most of the work remains to be done. On the application side, we need a more complete picture of existing inter-viewpoint models. The theory that will allow us to do the correctness proofs is also needed, but the theory should be done depending on the needs on the application side.

References

1. aiT. https://www.absint.com/ait/
2. RT-Druid. http://www.evidence.eu.com/products/rt-druid.html
3. Al Khatib, M., Girard, A., Dang, T.: Scheduling of embedded controllers under timing contracts. In: Proceedings of the 20th International Conference on Hybrid Systems: Computation and Control, HSCC 2017. ACM, New York (2017)

4. Asarin, E., Dang, T., Maler, O.: The d/dt tool for verification of hybrid systems. In: Brinksma, E., Larsen, K.G. (eds.) CAV 2002. LNCS, vol. 2404, pp. 365–370. Springer, Heidelberg (2002). https://doi.org/10.1007/3-540-45657-0_30

5. Assayad, I., Girault, A., Kalla, H.: Tradeoff exploration between reliability, power consumption, and execution time for embedded systems. Int. J. Software Tools Technol. Transfer **15**(3), 229–243 (2013)

6. Avizienis, A., Laprie, J.-C., Randell, B., Landwehr, C.: Basic concepts and taxonomy of dependable and secure computing. IEEE Trans. Dependable Secure Comput. **1**(1), 11–33 (2004)

7. Axer, P., Ernst, R.: Stochastic response-time guarantee for non-preemptive, fixed-priority scheduling under errors. In: The 50th Annual Design Automation Conference 2013, DAC 2013, Austin, TX, USA, 29 May–07 June 2013. ACM (2013)

8. Balarin, F., Watanabe, Y., Hsieh, H., Lavagno, L., Passerone, C., Sangiovanni-Vincentelli, A.: Metropolis: an integrated electronic system design environment. Computer **36**(4), 45–52 (2003)

9. Basu, A., et al.: Rigorous component-based system design using the BIP framework. IEEE Software **28**(3), 41–48 (2011)

10. Benveniste, A., Caillaud, B., Carloni, L.P., Caspi, P., Sangiovanni-Vincentelli, A.L.: Composing heterogeneous reactive systems. ACM Trans. Embedded Comput. Syst. **7**(4), 43 (2008)

11. Benveniste, A., et al.: Contracts for system design. Found. Trends Electron. Design Autom. **12**(2–3), 124–400 (2018)

12. Bhat, A., Samii, S., Rajkumar, R.R.: Recovery time considerations in real-time systems employing software fault tolerance. In: Altmeyer, S. (ed.) 30th Euromicro Conference on Real-Time Systems (ECRTS 2018), vol. 106. Leibniz International Proceedings in Informatics (LIPIcs), Dagstuhl, Germany. Schloss Dagstuhl-Leibniz-Zentrum fuer Informatik (2018)

13. Brière, D., Ribot, D., Pilaud, D., Camus, J.-L.: Methods and specifications tools for Airbus on-board systems. In: Avionics Conference and Exhibition, London, UK. ERA Technology (1994)

14. Damm, W., Dierks, H., Oehlerking, J., Pnueli, A.: Towards component based design of hybrid systems: safety and stability. In: Manna, Z., Peled, D.A. (eds.) Time for Verification. LNCS, vol. 6200, pp. 96–143. Springer, Heidelberg (2010). https://doi.org/10.1007/978-3-642-13754-9_6

15. Derler, P., Lee, E., Tripakis, S., Törngren, M.: Cyber-physical system design contracts. In: Proceedings of the ACM/IEEE 4th International Conference on Cyber-Physical Systems, ICCPS 2013. ACM, New York (2013)

16. Ernst, R., Henia, R., Quinton, S.: Beyond the deadline: new interfaces between control and scheduling for the design and analysis of critical embedded systems. Tutorial at ESWeek (2017)

17. Fellmuth, J., Göthel, T., Glesner, S.: Instruction caches in static WCET analysis of artificially diversified software. In: Altmeyer, S. (ed.) 30th Euromicro Conference on Real-Time Systems (ECRTS 2018), vol. 106. Leibniz International Proceedings in Informatics (LIPIcs), Dagstuhl, Germany. Schloss Dagstuhl-Leibniz-Zentrum fuer Informatik (2018)

18. Fontanelli, D., Greco, L., Palopoli, L.: Soft real-time scheduling for embedded control systems. Automatica **49**(8), 2330–2338 (2013)

19. Frehse, G.: PHAVer: algorithmic verification of hybrid systems past HyTech. In: Morari, M., Thiele, L. (eds.) HSCC 2005. LNCS, vol. 3414, pp. 258–273. Springer, Heidelberg (2005). https://doi.org/10.1007/978-3-540-31954-2_17

20. Frehse, G., Hamann, A., Quinton, S., Woehrle, M.: Formal analysis of timing effects on closed-loop properties of control software. In: Proceedings of the IEEE 35th IEEE Real-Time Systems Symposium, RTSS 2014, Rome, Italy, 2–5 December 2014. IEEE Computer Society (2014)

21. Gärtner, F.: Fundamentals of fault-tolerant distributed computing in asynchronous environments. ACM Comput. Surv. **31**(1), 1–26 (1999)

22. Girault, A., Kalla, H.: A novel bicriteria scheduling heuristics providing a guaranteed global system failure rate. IEEE Trans. Dependable Secure Comput. **6**(4), 241–254 (2009)

23. Graf, S., Passerone, R., Quinton, S.: Contract-based reasoning for component systems with rich interactions. In: Sangiovanni-Vincentelli, A.L., Zeng, H., Natale, M.D., Marwedel, P. (eds.) Embedded Systems Development: From Functional Models to Implementations. Springer, New York (2014). https://doi.org/10.1007/978-1-4614-3879-3_8

24. Graf, S., Steffen, B.: Compositional minimization of finite state systems. In: Clarke, E.M., Kurshan, R.P. (eds.) Computer-Aided Verification, Proceedings of a DIMACS Workshop 1990, New Brunswick, New Jersey, USA, 18–21 June 1990, vol. 3. DIMACS Series in Discrete Mathematics and Theoretical Computer Science (1990)

25. Henia, R., Hamann, A., Jersak, M., Racu, R., Richter, K., Ernst, R.: System level performance analysis–the symta/s approach. In: IEE Proceedings - Computers and Digital Techniques, vol. 152 (2005)

26. Krüger, K., Völp, M., Fohler, G.: Vulnerability analysis and mitigation of directed timing inference based attacks on time-triggered systems. In: Altmeyer, S. (ed.) 30th Euromicro Conference on Real-Time Systems (ECRTS 2018), vol. 106. Leibniz International Proceedings in Informatics (LIPIcs), Dagstuhl, Germany. Schloss Dagstuhl-Leibniz-Zentrum fuer Informatik (2018)

27. Kumar, P., Goswami, D., Chakraborty, S., Annaswamy, A., Lampka, K., Thiele, L.: A hybrid approach to cyber-physical systems verification. In: Proceedings of the 49th Annual Design Automation Conference, DAC 2012. ACM (2012)

28. Li, J., Nuzzo, P., Sangiovanni-Vincentelli, A., Xi, Y., Li, D.: Stochastic contracts for cyber-physical system design under probabilistic requirements. In: Proceedings of the 15th ACM-IEEE International Conference on Formal Methods and Models for System Design, MEMOCODE 2017, New York, NY, USA. ACM (2017)

29. Loiseaux, C., Graf, S., Sifakis, J., Bouajjani, A., Bensalem, S.: Property preserving abstractions for the verification of concurrent systems. Formal Methods Syst. Design **6**(1), 11–44 (1995)

30. Meyer, B.: Applying "design by contract". IEEE Computer **25**(10), 40–51 (1992)

31. Misra, J., Chandy, K.M.: Proofs of networks of processes. IEEE Trans. Software Eng. **7**(4), 417–426 (1981)

32. Müller, A., Mitsch, S., Retschitzegger, W., Schwinger, W., Platzer, A.: Change and delay contracts for hybrid system component verification. In: Huisman, M., Rubin, J. (eds.) FASE 2017. LNCS, vol. 10202, pp. 134–151. Springer, Heidelberg (2017). https://doi.org/10.1007/978-3-662-54494-5_8

33. Otter, M., Mattsson, S., Elmqvist, H.: Multidomain modeling with Modelica. In: Handbook of Dynamic System Modeling. Chapmanand Hall/CRC (2007)

34. Passerone, R., et al.: Metamodels in Europe: languages, tools, and applications. IEEE Des. Test Comput. **26**(3) (2009)

35. Castaneda, G.A.P., Aubry, J.-F., Brinzei, N.: Stochastic hybrid automata model for dynamic reliability assessment. Proc. Inst. Mech. Eng. Part O J. Risk Reliab. **225**(1), 28–41 (2011)

36. Pnueli, A.: In transition from global to modular temporal reasoning about programs. In: Apt, K.R. (ed.) Logics and Models of Concurrent Systems. NATO ASI Series (Series F: Computer and Systems Sciences), vol. 13. Springer, Heidelberg (1985). https://doi.org/10.1007/978-3-642-82453-1_5

37. Powell, D.: Failure mode assumption and assumption coverage. In: International Symposium on Fault-Tolerant Computing, FTCS-22, Boston, MA, USA. IEEE. Research report LAAS 91462 (1992)

38. Reineke, J., Tripakis, S.: Basic problems in multi-view modeling. In: Ábrahám, E., Havelund, K. (eds.) TACAS 2014. LNCS, vol. 8413, pp. 217–232. Springer, Heidelberg (2014). https://doi.org/10.1007/978-3-642-54862-8_15

39. Sheikh, H., Ahmad, I.: Sixteen heuristics for joint optimization of performance, energy, and temperature in allocating tasks to multi-cores. ACM Trans. Parallel Comput. **3**(2), 9 (2016)

40. Steffen, B.: Unifying models. In: Reischuk, R., Morvan, M. (eds.) STACS 1997. LNCS, vol. 1200, pp. 1–20. Springer, Heidelberg (1997). https://doi.org/10.1007/BFb0023444

41. Tabuada, P.: Verification and Control of Hybrid Systems - A Symbolic Approach. Springer, New York (2009). https://doi.org/10.1007/978-1-4419-0224-5

42. Theiling, H., Ferdinand, C., Wilhelm, R.: Fast and precise WCET prediction by separated cache and path analyses. Real-Time Syst. **18**(2/3), 157–179 (2000)

43. Zhao, Y., Xiong, Y., Lee, E.A., Liu, X., Zhong, L.C.: The design and application of structured types in ptolemy II. Int. J. Intell. Syst. **25**(2), 118–136 (2010)

44. Zhu, D., Melhem, R., Mossé, D.: The effects of energy management on reliability in real-time embedded systems. In: International Conference on Computer Aided Design, ICCAD 2004, San Jose, CA, USA (2004)

Formal Methods for Industrial Critical Systems

Automated Functional Safety Analysis of Automated Driving Systems

Martin Kölbl$^{(\boxtimes)}$ and Stefan Leue$^{(\boxtimes)}$

University of Konstanz, Konstanz, Germany
{martin.koelbl,stefan.leue}@uni.kn

Abstract. In this paper, we present a method to assess functional safety of architectures for Automated Driving Systems (ADS). The ISO 26262 standard defines requirements and processes in support of achieving functional safety of passenger vehicles, but does not address in particular autonomous driving functions. Autonomous driving will bring with it a number of fundamental changes affecting functional safety. First, there will no longer be a driver capable of controlling the vehicle in case of a failure of the ADS. Second, the hardware and software architectures will become more complex and flexible than those used for conventional vehicles. We present an automated method to assert functional safety of ADS systems in the spirit of ISO 26262 in light of these changes. The approach is model-based and implemented in the QuantUM analysis tool. We illustrate its use in functional safety analysis using a proposed practical ADS architecture and address, in particular, architectural variant analysis.

1 Introduction

The functional safety of software-driven functions in passenger vehicles is currently the subject of the ISO 26262 [8] international standard. It specifies development processes and requirements ensuring functional safety of software defined safety-critical functions, also referred to as items, in automobiles. The ISO 26262 standard focuses primarily on the safety of the software-defined items in the presence of systematic software and random hardware faults.

The advent of assisted and autonomous driving is fundamentally changing the architecture of software-defined critical automotive systems. As a consequence the methodological foundations of asserting functional safety of such systems will have to be redeveloped. The current version of the ISO 26262 standard, as well as the current proposed revision on this standard [9], do not account for the functional safety of autonomous driving functions.

First, the development of autonomous driving systems (ADS) will at some point lead to vehicles in which a human driver will no longer be available to take over control of the vehicle. Following the classification in the SAE J3016 standard [20], this will be the case starting at level 4. Whereas classical functional safety approaches follow a *fail-safe* approach, which in case of a failure relies

© Springer Nature Switzerland AG 2018
F. Howar and J. Barnat (Eds.): FMICS 2018, LNCS 11119, pp. 35–51, 2018.
https://doi.org/10.1007/978-3-030-00244-2_3

on a driver being able to take over control of the vehicle and bring it into a safe state, ADS systems have to be designed to operate in a *fail-operational* manner. This means that in the presence of the failure of some ADS function, the overall vehicle system will remain operational for a certain period of time, with a given probability, in order to navigate the vehicle automatically into a safe location, for instance the shoulder [24]. This is frequently also referred to as "limp-home" mode. For the analysis of functional safety properties this means that the availability of these limp-home mode functions in the presence of a system failure needs to be proven.

Second, the conventional approach to functional safety, as reflected by the current ISO 26262 standard, is highly "item-oriented". This means in particular that one driving function, or item, is implemented by one software component executing exclusively on one hardware unit, referred to as electronic control unit (ECU). Current systems already break with this strict concept and run a low number of functions on a single ECU. However, safety arguments largely rely on execution in isolation, with the exception that some degree of freedom of interference, including that caused by concurrency problems, at the level of the underlying execution platform has to be proven. This will not be the appropriate paradigm for ADS. In those systems, many sub-functions will co-operate and be highly interdependent in order to implement an overall system function, namely to drive safely from location A to location B [18]. Furthermore, for cost, performance, flexibility and dependability reasons, ADS will be implemented on networked computing platforms that encompass a low number of processors, connected by high bandwidth real-time networks, and potentially possessing multiple cores [13]. To increase reliability, redundant software functions can be mapped to different hardware components, both statically and possibly also dynamically. As a consequence, many functions will be mapped to a single or more hardware components, which means that a software-hardware mapping problem needs to be considered in the system and safety design. Again, current ISO 26262-type functional safety analyses do not account for this type of architectures.

Third, ADS will be highly concurrent, due to the parallel processing of sensor data and decision making to support different driving functions, leading to concurrency non-determinism. Another change with ADS is the application of non-linear machine-learning algorithms based on neural networks that are heavily used in environment perception. Non-determinism and non-linearity make it particularly difficult to use classical safety analysis techniques, such as Fault Tree Analysis (FTA) or Failure Mode and Effects Analysis (FMEA) proposed for piloted driving in ISO 26262, in a non-automated, manual fashion.

In this paper we propose a method to analyze functional safety of ADS "in the spirit" of ISO 26262, to the extent that it is applicable, and address some of the challenges pointed out above. The method is model-based and relies on SysML [19] models that describe the nominal and the failure behavior of components, as well as software-hardware mappings. We embed these models into the QuantUM method and tool [15,17] for analyzing causes of safety violations. QuantUM employs automated causality checking [16] in order to compute, depicted as a probabilistic fault tree, ordered sequences of events that are deemed to be causes for safety violations. The benefits of this approach include the following aspects.

- The algorithmic model analysis methods employed in QuantUM (model checking, causality checking) are well suited to deal with concurrency induced non-determinism. Dealing adequately with the non-linearity caused by using neural networks based machine learning is not addressed in this paper.
- The proposed analysis avails itself to an implementation in an automated software tool. Once the models and properties are defined, the analysis performed by QuantUM requires no further interaction with an engineer.
- The SysML models can easily be modified, for instance to analyze architectural alternatives as well as alternative software-hardware mappings during design space exploration. The functional safety analysis can then easily be repeated at little cost by invoking QuantUM on the modified model.
- The developed tools can be qualified according to, for instance, ISO 26262.

We evaluate our approach by applying it to a case study in which we perform a functional safety analysis for a practical ADS architecture [5] for which we analyze two mappings of ADS functions to hardware. The analyzed system failures can be used to assess the impact of single or multiple faults on the overall failure probability, as requested by ISO 26262. The analysis also enables an engineer to select efficient failure handling concepts and to evaluate different possible architectures while meeting safety goals as specified by ISO 26262.

Related Work. The most closely related work on automated model-based safety analysis for autonomous vehicles is [7]. It uses a block definition diagram and a manually created fault tree to compute probabilities for the purpose of safety analysis. In contrast to our work, no causal explanations for failures are automatically derived from the model.

Model-based techniques are applied to evaluate an automotive architecture in several papers. The approach of [6] is not automated, and it does not address the specifics of ADS. UML models, which are similar to SysML models, are also verified in [2,22], but both do not quantify system failures.

The paper [1] also addresses safety engineering for autonomous vehicles. It proposes an approach that differs from that of ISO 26262 by focussing on safety mechanism to detect all malfunctions.

Structure of the Paper. In Sect. 2 we present the foundations of our work which includes the demands of ISO 26262 on vehicles, the change in the architecture with the development of ADS and the QuantUM approach, which we will extend. In Sect. 3 we explain the analysis steps to verify an ADS architecture in the "spirit" of ISO 26262. In Sect. 4 illustrate our approach by applying the steps on two ADS architectures. In Sect. 5 we draw conclusions and suggest future developments.

2   Preliminaries

Functional Safety and Autonomous Driving. The ISO standard 26262 [8] as well as its recently proposed revision [9] define requirements on software development processes for safety-critical functions of an automotive passenger vehicle. This is to ensure that the functional safety of a passenger vehicle is challenged by no more than an acceptable residual risk. The standard is focused on mechanisms that ensure functional safety of critical software-driven functions in the presence of systematic faults and random hardware faults. It assumes that systematic faults can be eliminated by verification and validation techniques, in particular testing. The standard does not tackle random software failures, which happen non-deterministic, for instance, due to concurrency issues or special environment influences. Notice that the ISO 26262 standard does not address techniques to ensure "Safety of the Intended Function" (SOTIF), i.e., the safety of intended functionalities of the vehicle itself. A standard addressing this safety aspect is currently under development [10].

Two characteristics of the ISO 26262 standard are important in the context of this work. First, the standard is "item-oriented", which means that it addresses safety mechanisms for items, such as airbag control, steering, braking, light control, etc., in isolation. This approach is inappropriate for ADS since different vehicle functions will be interdependent by acting as backup functions for others. Further, the driver as the function integrator and coordinator in piloted driving is not available, which means that the software has to take over these integration functions. Second, neither the published version of the ISO 26262 standard nor the its proposed revision address assisted or autonomous driving per se [11]. To the contrary, the ISO 26262 standard allows safety mechanisms to rely on the driver taking over control of the vehicle in order to mitigate the impact of function failures, which in ADS at SAE level 3 is likely not to be practical [23], and at levels 4 and 5 is not even foreseen [20]. Nonetheless, we show how formal analysis techniques can be used to support the safety engineering of ADS in the spirit of ISO 26262. According to ISO 26262, different driving functions, referred to as "items", are assigned an Automotive Safety Integrity Level (ASIL), ranging from the least critical ASIL A to the most critical ASIL D. The determined ASIL implies the design methods that are to be used. As argued above, we will consider the ADS driving function as a unique "item" in the ISO 26262 sense and perform a safety analysis on this set of functions as a whole, including an assignment of an ASIL.

According to ISO 26262, safety goals need to be defined to ensure that the failure probability of software functions in the presence of random hardware faults lies at an acceptable minimum. For each ASIL, a maximum tolerable probability of failing a safety goal due to random hardware faults is specified. A system failure may be a result of a single fault (single-point failure) or a combination of faults (multiple-point failure). From the safety goals, functional safety requirements are derived. In safety analyses one will also have to consider fault rates of the underlying hardware, for instance sensor faults, as well as the hardware-specific fault detection rates. Those will later occur as parameters of our models.

Following ISO 26262, the system architecture design is derived from technical safety requirements. For ASILs A to D, the standard recommends documenting the architecture using a semi-formal notation, such as the SysML, for ASIL A and B, and strongly recommends this for ASIL C and D [9, Part 6]. The system architecture then needs to be verified against the safety requirements [8, Part 4]. The process mandated by ISO 26262 for this verification includes a system design analysis to identify possible effects of faults, the causes of possible failures and a quantification of failures. Applicable methods include Fault Tree Analysis (FTA) and Markov models. The use of formal verification techniques, including model checking [4], is recommended for software architecture verification for ASIL C and D [8, Part 6]. This includes a verification that certain safety goals are met by a given system design [8, Part 8]. We propose that an automated approach based on a formal analysis of the state space described by the system architecture helps to detect and explain safety goal violations at an early stage in the safety engineering process, thereby meeting the requirements of ISO 26262. It also enables automated, tool-supported architectural variant analysis during safety and system engineering, greatly contributing to reducing the related costs.

Model-Based Safety Analysis - The QuantUM Approach. Safety analysis relies on the establishment of cause-effect relationships between states or events in a system. Causality checking [16] is an automated, algorithmic approach to compute cause-effect relationships for events in a model of a system. It is based on model checking and systematic, complete state space exploration. Based on a counterfactual reasoning argument, it computes ordered sequences of events as being causal for the violation of a safety specification, defined as the (un-)reachability of a hazard state. In the context of the QuantUM toolset [15,17], causality checking is used to automatically compute sequences of sequentially ordered events with minimal length which are causal for violations of the reachability property representing the hazard. The SysML model is given by block definition diagrams (bdd) to depict units of the architecture, and state chart diagrams (stm) to specify their behavior. The SysML model contains both the nominal and the failure behavior of the architectural components. In QuantUM, the computed causal events are then depicted as a fault tree [17], with the considered hazard forming the top level event.

The causes for a model failure that QuantUM calculates are represented by a fault tree including the calculated probabilities. In the interpretation of the fault tree notation that QuantUM uses, the nodes in the graph do not all correspond to subsystem faults, but rather to events belonging to the causal process leading up to a hazard. The top level event is connected to an or gate. The or gate is connected to a number of ordered and gates, each one representing a causality class. A causality class is specified by a minimal ordered sequence of events that jointly, and in that order, cause the occurrence of the hazard. Notice that QuantUM can also determine the non-occurrence of single events as the cause of a hazard.

System Architectures for ADS. A functional architecture for autonomous driving is proposed in [5]. The authors extract, from several conceptual as well as practical implemented architectures, a layered architecture. The semantic understanding of the external world is calculated in the *perception layer*. It computes an external world model based on a fusion of the various forms of external sensor information that it receives. The external world model in conjunction with the internal state of the car, which is defined among others by the energy management and failure states of the platform, are used by the *decision and control layer* to make decisions about the execution of a trajectory. The trajectory is then used by the *vehicle platform manipulation* layer to drive the actors, like steering and braking, and keeping the platform overall stable. All three layers have a complex structure of interdependent, cooperating elements, each representing a specific function.

Functional Safety Goals for ADS. A predominant idea in ISO 26262 is that a system needs to reach a safe state in the event of a system failure, in other words, that it is *fail-safe*. When the driving is piloted, this can often be achieved by switching the defective subsystem off and leaving it up to the driver to deal with the situation. In autonomous driving, this option does not exist, as argued above. The objective here needs to be that in the presence of the failure of one function in an ADS, the overall system architecture needs to remain operational for a certain period of time so as to ensure that a safe state can be reached. This capability is often referred to as "fail-operational". The ISO 26262 standard states: "If a safe state cannot be reached by a transition within an acceptable time interval, an emergency operation shall be specified." [8, Part 3]. This means that designing safety mechanisms that ensure a limited backup capability for a defective functionality for a certain period of time is within the practices recommended by ISO 26262. A typical example would be that the braking system takes over functionalities of a failed steering control system by applying differential torque or braking for a limited period of time so as to "limp home" to a safe part of the road, such as the shoulder. The safety goals that we pursue in our analysis will, hence, have to reflect the probabilities of remaining *fail-operational* for a certain period of time.

3 Safety Analysis of an ADS Architecture

Safety Goals for an ADS. Following the earlier made argument we consider the driving function of an ADS to be one item, i.e., one driving function. Using this assumption we perform a safety analysis for this item in the spirit of ISO 26262.

As argued above, we need to consider a fail-operational architecture. When reaching a failure state, the ADS reacts by switching to an emergency mode that handles the failure situation. For a safety analysis of an ADS, we consider possible hazards of an architecture and derive appropriate safety goals to prevent the hazards:

1. When a vehicle is operating as an ADS it has to control the vehicle platform even if it is in an emergency mode. If the control is lost, then the vehicle will

crash. To prevent this hazard we derive the safety goal SG1: *Ensure that the ADS provides driving information to the vehicle platform at any time.*

2. The ADS can have an undetected failure. As a consequence, the emergency mode may not be activated. The detection of a failure ensured by the safety goal SG2: *Ensure that the emergency mode is enabled when a failure of the ADS occurs.*

3. If the system cannot enter or remain in the emergency operation mode for a specified period of time, a safe state may not be reachable. We assume the period of time necessary to reach a safety state to be t_1 seconds and derive the safety goal SG3: *Ensure that the emergency mode of the ADS is available on demand for at least t_1 seconds.*

The ASIL classification of a safety goal is determined according to the severity of a function failure caused by a hazard, the probability of exposure to a situation with a potential failure, and the controllability of the failure situation by the driver. We assume the severity of each hazard of the ADS to be potentially life-threatening (S3 according to [8, Part 3]). Since the ADS system will be active most of the time when the vehicle is in operation, certainly during more than 10% of the operation time, we assume the probability of exposure to be high (E4 according to [8, Part 3]). We also assume the controllability to be very low (C3 according to [8, Part 3]), since in the case of SAE level 3 driving the driver may be surprised by a failure situation, or unable to handle it due to the low occurrence rate of such a situation. These valuations hold for all three safety goals and consequently this implies, according to ISO 26262, an ASIL-D classification for each safety goal.

As argued above, ISO 26262 recommends the use of formal methods, including model checking, for the analysis of ASIL D safety goals.

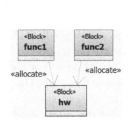

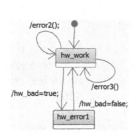

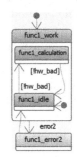

Fig. 1. Mapping 1 (Color figure online)

Fig. 2. Stm `hw` (Color figure online)

Fig. 3. Stm `func1` (Color figure online)

Automated Safety Analysis of an ADS Architecture. We now describe how an extended version of the QuantUM tool can be used to perform an automated safety analysis for a given ADS architecture with respect to safety goals SG1 - SG3.

Step 1: ADS Modeling. The system architecture of a vehicle consists of several software function units executing on a number of hardware units. Each unit is represented by a block in a SysML bdd, see the example in Fig. 1. It depicts two software function units, represented by blocks colored blue, executing on one hardware unit, colored yellow. Assigning a software function to a hardware unit on which the function is executed is referred to as software-hardware mapping. In our bdds, mappings are depicted using dashed arrows with the label <<allocate>>. The behavior of each unit is modeled by a SysML stm. The stms of different units execute concurrently. For the example in Fig. 1 the behavior of the blocks hw and func1 are exemplified in Figs. 2 and 3, respectively.

In the stms, the blue states represent the nominal behavior of the units, and the red states represent its failure behavior. The state machines execute their normal behavior by staying in a "work" state. To reach a failure state, a fault event has to occur. The first type of fault directly leads to a failure of the unit. This can for instance be caused by a loss of power, or by a permanent error such as a broken hardware element. These faults are modeled by a transition to a failure state, such as hw_error1 in Fig. 2. The unit remains in this state until it is repaired, represented by a repair transition to the work state. As a result of entering a failure state, a hardware unit stops executing and any software function, executing on this hardware unit, will cease to operate as well. To model this behavior, the Boolean variable hw_bad is set to true and all transitions of the function unit are disabled by a guard !hw_bad (see Fig. 3). The second type of fault leads to an error inside of the hardware unit, such as a bit flip, even though the unit continues to operate. The hardware unit is not corrupted, but an error is propagated to functions executing on that unit. In the SysML model, error propagation is modeled by message passing. In the example in Fig. 2, two errors are propagated by messages error2 and error3 to the respective software functions. With the receive of such an error the function 1 enters the func1_error2 state and function 2 enters the func2_error3 state upon receiving error3. From these states, the function can return to its normal behavior by a transition representing failure repair.

Step 2: System Failure Modeling. The ADS fails if one of the safety goals SG1-SG3 is violated. The violation of these system goals needs to be mapped to states that the different stms in the system are entering. QuantUM offers the possibility to tag states in the stms of different blocks as error states, and then permits to either use a logical *or* or a logical *and* between all tagged states in order to characterize a violation state of the system. To model the safety goals needed here we extend this rather inflexible scheme. An ADS has the structure of a set of channels. Sensory input data is processed by a function and the output data is forwarded to the next function, forming one channel called the primary channel. The emergency mode adds a second, partly redundant backup channel to the ADS. The ADS fails and violates SG1 if there is a function failure in each of the channels. We attach a Boolean variable bad to each function and permit forming logical expressions on these variables to express the failure of one channel. We combine the failure expressions of each channel with an "and"

and add the result to the property. For example, in order to check two redundant channels the resulting property has the form *it is never the case that step1 or step2 or ... of channel1 is bad and step1 or step2 or ... of channel2 is bad.*

Step 3: Analysis of Emergency Mode Failures. A violation of SG3 implies that the normal ADS behavior has a failure and either the emergency mode functionality is not available on demand, or it is not provided for at least a certain period of time and therefore constitutes a fundamental challenge to the safety of the vehicle. In the following we compute the probability P_{fail} for a violation of SG3. The analysis performed by QuantUM works on a global state graph obtained by interleaving the local behaviors of the concurrent system hardware and software components. A path in this graph, representing an execution of the ADS, constitutes a violation of SG3 if in a state the emergency mode is being activated but not going to be available for at least a period of time t_1. We characterize the set of all emergency activation states S in the global state graph using a Boolean expression e formed as described in Step 2. In accordance with the foundations of probabilistic model checking we will consider reaching a first state $s_i \in S$ as a stochastic event, with the path consisting of a stochastic experiment. The event of reaching a state s_i first, denoted by $reach\_s_i$, precludes the event of reaching another state $s'_i \in S$ first, which means that stochastic events we consider do not overlap. As a consequence we may partition the sample space, which consists of all possible paths in the global state graph, according to the events $reach\_s_i$. In a first probabilistic model checking step performed by QuantUM we compute the probability $P(reach\_s_i)$ to reach each state in S within a period of a driving cycle t_dc. In a second model checking step we compute the probability $P(fail_i|reach\_s_i)$ to reach a failure from state s_i within a time t_1. To enable the first model checking step we change the model in such a way that we conjoin $\neg e$ with all transition guards. This means that when the system enters a state in which e becomes true, this state is turned into an end state with no enabled exit transition. For each end state we calculate its probability. For the second model checking step we compute the probability $P(fail\_s_i|reach\_s_i)$ by starting in any state defined by expression e. The probability P_{fail} is computed by a summation over all products of $P(fail_i|reach\_s_i) \cdot P(reach\_s_i)$, which is justified by the memoryless nature of CTMCs. No causality checking will be performed and no fault trees will be computed by QuantUM during SG3 violation analysis.

Step 4: Probability Rates. Probability rates, in particular for hardware failures, repairs and failure detection, are difficult to determine and usually depend on a specific domain and the concrete hardware used. However, even if precise rates are not available, the comparison of the relative failure probabilities of architectural variants with identical and with different estimated or assumed rates can be of great importance. This can for instance answer the question how architectural variants will affect failure probabilities, or what error detection rates are required to achieve a desired level of failure probability. In QuantUM, the SysML model is labeled with probability rates, for instance for the probability of executing a failure or repair transition. QuantUM uses probabilistic model checking, in particular model checking for Continuous Time Markov Chains (CTMCs) [3], in order to compute the probabilities for the causes leading to a violation of safety properties. A fault event of the hardware may lead to different faults in a system. In this situation we distribute the fault rate over the different fault transitions. The portion of the fault rate that each transition receives relies on domain specific knowledge that the designer needs to provide. For example, in Fig. 2, a bit flip with a probability rate of 10^{-4} can cause an error2 or an error3. Notice that throughout the paper, rates are assumed to be per hour. Assume that it is typical that 40% of the errors are of type error2 and 60% are of type error3. This leads to a fault rate of $0.4 \cdot 10^{-4}$ for error2 and a fault rate of $0.6 \cdot 10^{-4}$ for error3. To split the fault rate in this way is appropriate for CTMCs, cf. [3].

A potential threat to the validity of the failure probabilities computed by QuantUM and the probabilistic model checker Prism [12] that QuantUM uses, is the fact that the original SysML model mixes non-probabilistic and probabilistic transitions. For the non-probabilistic transitions Prism assumes a default rate of 1. Assuming that we consider one time step, based on the negative exponential distribution on which CTMCs are based this translates into a probability of less that 1 of taking this transition with which the accumulated path probability up to this step will be multiplied. However, we do not experience a negative effect on the total failure probability since the SysML model structure that we propose implies that the system will cycle through non-probabilistic normal behavior, for which the path probability is 1, until it performs one probabilistic failure transition to enter a failure state. For example, the state func1_work in Fig. 3 has non-probabilistic transitions between the states func1_calculation and func1_idle with a default rate of 1, remaining is state func1_run until the probabilistic transition error2 is taken.

4   Case Study: A Comparison of Autonomous Driving Architectures

Step 1: ADS Modeling. [5] proposes a functional architecture generalized from real architectures. We use part of this functional model and add several hardware units. The resulting mapping problem leads to a number of architectures. The SysML bdd in Fig. 4 gives an overview of the structure of the first architectural variant that we consider. We model the perception layer by a block Perception and the motion and control layer by a block Trajectory. Since the functions represented by these two blocks are critical for the proper functioning of the ADS we add blocks PerceptionSafe and TrajectorySafe to provide redundant backup functionality. The function represented by the block Trajectory_Selection selects by default the trajectory of block Trajectory, but switches in case of a failure of these blocks to the alternative trajectory computed by block TrajectorySafe. The block MotionControl represents the interface with the vehicle platform manipulation layer by providing it with control parameters, such as steering angle, braking force or differential torque, that the vehicle platform will translate into commands for the actuators of the vehicle. Figure 4 also illustrates the software-hardware mapping that we propose for the first architectural variant. Notice that the primary functionalities for perception and trajectory computation are mapped to the hardware block ADS_primary, while the backup functionality ADS_backup is mapped to a separate hardware unit ADS_backup, thus increasing the probability that the backup functionality will be available even in the case of a failure of the primary hardware represented by block ADS_primary.

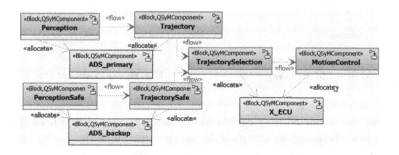

Fig. 4. Architectural variant 1 for ADS

The state machine modeling the behavior or block ADS_primary is given in Fig. 5. The hardware operates correctly in state run. In this state, the occurrence of a detected error inside the hardware, for instance a memory bit flip, is communicated to the Perception block using a perception_error message in case the perception function is currently executing on ADS_primary. In case a trajectory computation function is executing, the hardware error will be communicated using a trajectory_error message to the Trajectory block. If in the run state an undetected hardware error occurs, the impact on the hardware is unknown. We model this by a transition into state undetected along which we set the failure variable bad to true. In this state, no software function can be executed on the hardware.

The behavior of the block Perception is defined by the hierarchical state machine in the stm diagram in Fig. 6. The normal behavior is modeled in the nested state Normal. The function starts its computation in the state idle and cycles through states idle and calculate, which represents the processing of sensor information, as long as the variable ADS_primary.bad is false. When returning to idle it sends the message trajectory_input to the function trajectory in order to indicate that input data for the trajectory function is available. Upon receipt of a message perception_error, the perception function can decide either to handle this message and remain in the Normal state, or it can decide to enter the ErrorData state and set its bad value to true. Upon repair it can return to the idle state and resume execution. Deviating from the classical ISO 26262 viewpoint to only consider hardware failures, we also consider software failures. Such a failure in the block Perception is modeled by a non-deterministic group transition from the Normal state to the CalculationError state in the course of which the bad variable will be set to false. We assume that these errors can

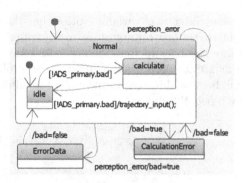

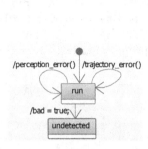

Fig. 5. Stm ADS_primary   **Fig. 6.** Stm Perception

also be repaired, modeled by a return to the Normal state. Space limitations do not allow us to present the complete behavioral model of the ADS. The other blocks representing hardware and software functions have behaviors similar to the ones described above.

Step 2: System Failure Modeling. We characterize a system failure of the ADS violating SG1 or SG2 using different Boolean expressions for each architectural variant and safety goal. The Boolean propositions refer to the bad variables of the blocks in the SysML model. For architectural variant 1, a system failure violating SG1 happens when a software function or a hardware unit fails in both channels, or when at least one of the functions TrajectorySelection or MotionControl or the hardware X_ECU fails. This leads to the Boolean failure expression

$$((ADS\_primary.bad \lor Perception.bad \lor Trajectory.bad)$$
$$\land(ADS\_backup.bad \lor PerceptionSafe.bad \lor TrajectorySafe.bad)) \quad (1)$$
$$\lor(TrajectorySelection.bad) \lor (MotionControl.bad \lor X\_ECU.bad).$$

Architectural variant 2 differs from the first in that the block TrajectorySelection is mapped to the block ADS_backup. As a consequence, architectural variant 2 fails under the same failure condition as variant 1, and additionally by a failure of ADS_backup. This leads to the Boolean failure expression

$$((ADS\_primary.bad \lor Perception.bad \lor Trajectory.bad)$$
$$\land(ADS\_backup.bad \lor PerceptionSafe.bad \lor TrajectorySafe.bad))$$
$$\lor(ADS\_backup.bad \lor TrajectorySelection.bad) \quad (2)$$
$$\lor(MotionControl.bad \lor X\_ECU.bad).$$

The function TrajectorySelection is responsible for selecting the emergency trajectory in case of a failure. The function fails if the function itself or the underlying hardware is in a failure state. This leads to a violation of SG2, expressed by the Boolean failure expression *TrajectorySelection.bad* $\vee$ *X_ECU.bad* for architectural variant 1 and *TrajectorySelection.bad* $\vee$ *ADS_backup.bad* for variant 2.

Step 3: Analysis of Emergency Mode Failures. For the computation of the failure probability of the emergency mode we need to determine the expected operation time of the emergency mode t_1, a Boolean expression representing a failure of the ADS and a Boolean expression characterizing the activation of the emergency mode. We assume t_1 to be 10 s. The failure states of the ADS for the two architectural variants are encoded by the Boolean expressions 1 or 2, respectively. The emergency mode of the ADS is activated in both architectural variants if a software function running on hardware ADS_primary or the hardware ADS_primary itself fails. We encode these states using the Boolean expression (*ADS_primary.bad* $\vee$ *Perception.bad* $\vee$ *Trajectory.bad*).

Step 4: Probability Rates. In order to determine rates in the context of our case study we assume ADS_primary and ADS_backup to be implemented using "standard" hardware without hardware checks in order to meet the high computing power demands of the software functions executing on them. In such hardware components most faults happen because of memory errors [21], and we assume typical fault rates of 10^{-4}. Since there are no special computing power demands that apply to X_ECU and since we have not accounted for any redundancy here we assume safety hardware to be used with a fault rate of 10^{-8}. We further assume a hardware fault detection rate of 99%, i.e., 1% of the errors remain undetected. As described above, the probability of detected hardware faults are distributed evenly over all software functions running on the considered hardware unit. For instance, perception_error and trajectory_error are assumed to each have a probability of 49.5%, i.e., a rate of $0.495 \cdot 10^{-4}$. We assume that a software function affected by a detected hardware error handles the error with a probability of 90%, but will fail with a probability of 10%. For software failures of the perception function we assume a fault rate of 10^{-4}. Functions in a failure state can resume by a repair transition. We assume a repair rate of $4 \cdot 10^{-2}$ for software functions (cf. [7]).

Analysis using QuantUM. We assume a driving cycle duration t_{dc} of 1 h in all of the analyses. The result of the analysis for violating SG1 is a fault tree with the state representing the SG1 violation as top level event, and 19 disjunctive tree branches for architectural variant 1 and 16 disjunctive tree branches for architectural variant 2. We call the disjunctive tree branches *causes*. For both variants, space limitations do not permit us to present the full fault tree here. Architectural variant 1 has the probability of $1.31998187 \cdot 10^{-8}$ and architectural variant 2 the probability of $4.30677042 \cdot 10^{-6}$ to violate SG1. Due to the redundant structure of the architecture in both variants, analyzing SG2 in isolation leads to two single source failures already detected by SG1. One single source failure involves trajectory_selection_error for both variants and the other failure involves X_ECU_undetected for variant 1 and ADAS_backup_undetected

Table 1. Computational effort for SG violation analyses

	Architectural variant 1			Architectural variant 2		
	Memory	Time	States	Memory	Time	States
SG1	143.27 MB	63.79 min	235,765	124.84 MB	57.14 min	207,052
SG2	284.11 MB	4.93 min	321,133	310.35 MB	1.12 min	324,464
SG3	99.25 MB	6.59 min	349,937	160.04 MB	4.96 min	354,943

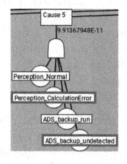

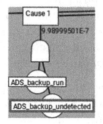

Fig. 7. Cause 5 of architectural variant 1 (Color figur online)

Fig. 8. Cause 1 of architectural variant 2

for variant 2. The probability of a violation of SG3 is $6.399474 \cdot 10^{-9}$ for variant 1 and $6.164128 \cdot 10^{-9}$ for variant 2.

The experiments were performed on a computer with an i7-6700K CPU (4.00 GHz), 60 GB of RAM and a Linux operation system. The computational efforts in memory, time and for the architectural variants are depicted in Table 1. The column *States* gives the number of states explored by QuantUM, in the case of SG3 this only comprises the number of states analyzed by Prism.

The memory effort for SG1 and SG2 is small in comparison to previous models [14]. The small memory effort is due to the fact, that the current implementation of QuantUM, does not compute duplicate state prefix matching as described in [14]. However, for the analyzed models, the current version of QuantUM computes all causes, since each failure state of the stms is only reached by a single trace. All other traces leading to a failure state are extensions of the single trace and so not minimal.

Result Interpretation. The architectural variant 1 has a lower probability of violating SG1. This result can be explained as follows. The fault trees for the two architectural variants differ mainly in the probability of the causes that contain the event ADS_backup_undetected, representing an undetected hardware failure in the hardware unit that is subject to the altered software-hardware mapping. The fault tree of architectural variant 1 contains four causes that contain the event ADS_backup_undetected, of which one cause is depicted in Fig. 7, with a probability of $9.91367948 \cdot 10^{-11}$ and thus not contributing significantly to the total SG1 violation probability. All other causes that contain ADS_backup_undetected have a similarly insignificant probability. Notice that failure events in the fault trees are marked in red.

The fault tree of architectural variant 2 contains one cause with this event, depicted in Fig. 8, with a probability of $0.99899950 \cdot 10^{-6}$, thus contributing significantly to the SG1 violation. While in architectural variant 1 the ADS_back-up_undetected fault needs to coincide with a Perception_CalculationError, in architectural variant 2 the occurrence of ADS_backup_undetected suffices to lead to an SG1 violation. The difference in the probabilities of the two considered causes is due to the fact that the conditional occurrence of two failure events, such as in cause 5 of architectural variant 1, is less probable than the unconditional occurrence of a fault event as in cause 1 of architectural variant 2. Due to the software-hardware mapping in architectural variant 2, the fault event ADS_backup_undetected directly leads to an SG2 violation, and this scenario has a high probability. The difference in the probabilities of SG1 violations can hence be traced back to the difference in the hardware-software mappings used in both architectural variants.

In the following, we discuss the influence of the detection and error handling rates. We first increase the detection rate of ADS_backup for variant 2 from 99% to 99.99%. The higher detection rate decreases the failure probability of cause 2 from $9.98999501 \cdot 10^{-7}$ to $9.98999995 \cdot 10^{-9}$. This change has no significant effect since the probability of reaching error state undetected is decreased by the same amount that the error probability of the functions running on the hardware is increased. The probability of violating SG1 is now mainly due to reaching failure state ErrorData of function TrajectorySelection, which is $3.32799547 \cdot 10^{-6}$. In a second step we increase the error handling rate of function TrajectorySelection from 90% to 99%. This decreases the failure probability for ErrorData in function TrajectorySelection to $3.32805910 \cdot 10^{-8}$. As a consequence the overall failure probability of violating SG1 decreases from $4.30677042 \cdot 10^{-6}$ to $5.60069041 \cdot 10^{-8}$. We notice that detection and error handling rates have an essential influence on the failure probability of the ADS.

A violation of SG3 is less probable than 10^{-9} for both variants. The small probabilities are reasonable since the ADS remains in the emergency mode for only 10 s, which is much shorter than the assumed driving cycle of one hour. Unexpectedly, a violation of SG3 is more probable for variant 1 ($6.399474 \cdot 10^{-9}$) than for variant 2 ($6.164128 \cdot 10^{-9}$). The difference is due to the fact that variant 2 fails more probable without entering the emergency mode.

ISO 26262 requires an analysis of single and multiple point failures, and whether failures are detected or undetected. We extract this information from the causes in the fault trees. A cause representing a single point failure contains a single failure event, other causes are multiple point of failure. For example, Cause 1 of variant 2 is a single point failure since it contains the single failure event ADS_backup_undetected. An undetected failure is represented by a cause that contains at least one undetected failure event. Cause 5 of variant 1 represents such an undetected failure. With this information it is possible to perform further analyses on undetected failure rates and to relate them to single and multiple point faults, as required by ISO 26262.

5 Conclusion

We have presented an automated approach to support the design time functional safety analysis for architectures supporting ADS. The paper addresses the handling of the complexity of future ADS by analyzing a flexible mapping of hardware and software functions. We have applied the proposed approach to two variants of a practical ADS architecture and compared the two variants. We have shown that the proposed approach gives necessary information to perform functional safety analyses in the spirit of ISO 26262. The analysis included fail-operational behavior, software faults and interdependent driving functions which are so far not adequately addressed by ISO 26262. We see great potential in supporting ISO 26262 style functional safety analyses of innovative automotive architectures using the formal algorithmic analyses that QuantUM supports.

Future research will address an improved integration of the analysis into existing tools and methods, for instance by incorporating automated Failure Mode and Effects Analysis (FMEA), more flexible property specification, and an improved scalability of the method, in particular using symbolic analysis techniques.

Acknowledgements. We wish to thank Stephan Heidinger, Matthias Kuntz and Majdi Ghadhab for discussions at the early stages of this work.

References

1. Adler, R., Feth, P., Schneider, D.: Safety engineering for autonomous vehicles. In: DSN Workshops, pp. 200–205. IEEE Computer Society (2016)
2. Bahig, G.M., El-Kadi, A.: Formal verification of automotive design in compliance with ISO 26262 design verification guidelines. IEEE Access **5**, 4505–4516 (2017)
3. Baier, C., Haverkort, B., Hermanns, H., Katoen, J.P.: Model-checking algorithms for continuous-time Markov chains. IEEE Trans. Softw. Eng. **29**(6), 524–541 (2003)
4. Baier, C., Katoen, J.: Principles of Model Checking. MIT Press, Cambridge (2008)
5. Behere, S., Törngren, M.: A functional reference architecture for autonomous driving. Inf. Softw. Technol. **73**, 136–150 (2016)
6. Cuenot, P., Ainhauser, C., Adler, N., Otten, S., Meurville, F.: Applying model based techniques for early safety evaluation of an automotive architecture in compliance with the ISO 26262 standard. In: Proceedings of the 7th European Congress on Embedded Real Time Software and Systems (ERTS^2) (2014)
7. Ghadhab, M., Junges, S., Katoen, J.-P., Kuntz, M., Volk, M.: Model-based safety analysis for vehicle guidance systems. In: Tonetta, S., Schoitsch, E., Bitsch, F. (eds.) SAFECOMP 2017. LNCS, vol. 10488, pp. 3–19. Springer, Cham (2017). https://doi.org/10.1007/978-3-319-66266-4_1
8. ISO: Road vehicles - functional safety. ISO 26262, International Organization for Standardization, Geneva, Switzerland (2011)

9. ISO: Draft international standard, road vehicles - functional safety. Technical report ISO/DIS 26262, International Organization for Standardization, Geneva, Switzerland (2016)
10. ISO: Road vehicles - safety of the intended functionality. Technical report ISO/WD PAS 21448, International Organization for Standardization, Geneva, Switzerland (2017)
11. Koopman P., Wagner, M.: Challenges in autonomous vehicle testing and validation (2016). Preprint https://users.ece.cmu.edu/~koopman/pubs/koopman16_sae_autonomous_validation.pdf
12. Kwiatkowska, M., Norman, G., Parker, D.: PRISM 4.0: verification of probabilistic real-time systems. In: Gopalakrishnan, G., Qadeer, S. (eds.) CAV 2011. LNCS, vol. 6806, pp. 585–591. Springer, Heidelberg (2011). https://doi.org/10.1007/978-3-642-22110-1_47
13. Leitner, A., Ochs, T., Bulwahn, L., Watzenig, D.: Open dependable power computing platform for automated driving. In: Watzenig, D., Horn, M. (eds.) Automated Driving, pp. 353–367. Springer, Cham (2017). https://doi.org/10.1007/978-3-319-31895-0_14
14. Leitner-Fischer, F.: Causality checking of safety-critical software and systems. Ph.D. thesis, University of Konstanz, Germany (2015)
15. Leitner-Fischer, F., Leue, S.: QuantUM: quantitative safety analysis of UML models. In: QAPL. EPTCS, vol. 57, pp. 16–30 (2011)
16. Leitner-Fischer, F., Leue, S.: Causality checking for complex system models. In: Giacobazzi, R., Berdine, J., Mastroeni, I. (eds.) VMCAI 2013. LNCS, vol. 7737, pp. 248–267. Springer, Heidelberg (2013). https://doi.org/10.1007/978-3-642-35873-9_16
17. Leitner-Fischer, F., Leue, S.: Probabilistic fault tree synthesis using causality computation. IJCCBS 4(2), 119–143 (2013)
18. Martin, H., Tschabuschnig, K., Bridal, O., Watzenig, D.: Functional safety of automated driving systems: does ISO 26262 meet the challenges? In: Watzenig, D., Horn, M. (eds.) Automated Driving, pp. 387–416. Springer, Cham (2017). https://doi.org/10.1007/978-3-319-31895-0_16
19. OMG: Systems Modeling Language (SysML), Version 1.5. Technical report, OMG (2017)
20. SAE: J3016_201609: Taxonomy and definitions for terms related to driving automation systems for on-road motor vehicles, September 2016. https://www.sae.org/standards/content/j3016_201609
21. Schroeder, B., Pinheiro, E., Weber, W.: DRAM errors in the wild: a large-scale field study. Commun. ACM 54(2), 100–107 (2011)
22. ter Beek, M.H., Gnesi, S., Koch, N., Mazzanti, F.: Formal verification of an automotive scenario in service-oriented computing. In: ICSE, pp. 613–622. ACM (2008)
23. Watzenig, D., Horn, M.: Introduction to automated driving. In: Watzenig, D., Horn, M. (eds.) Automated Driving, pp. 3–16. Springer, Cham (2017). https://doi.org/10.1007/978-3-319-31895-0_1
24. Weiss, G., Schleiss, P., Drabek, C., Ruiz, A., Radermacher, A.: Safe adaptation for reliable and energy-efficient E/E architectures. In: Watzenig, D., Brandstätter, B. (eds.) Comprehensive Energy Management - Safe Adaptation, Predictive Control and Thermal Management. SAST, pp. 1–18. Springer, Cham (2018). https://doi.org/10.1007/978-3-319-57445-5_1

Safety Interlocking as a Distributed Mutual Exclusion Problem

Alessandro Fantechi[1]([✉]) and Anne E. Haxthausen[2]

[1] DINFO, University of Florence, Firenze, Italy
alessandro.fantechi@unifi.it
[2] DTU Compute, Technical University of Denmark, Lyngby, Denmark
aeha@dtu.dk

Abstract. In several large scale systems (e.g. robotic plants or trans-portation systems) safety is guaranteed by granting to some process or physical object an exclusive access to a particular set of physical areas or objects before starting its own action: some mechanism should in this case *interlock* the action of the former with the availability of the latter. A typical example is the railway interlocking problem, in which a train is granted the authorisation to move only if the tracks in front of the train are free. Although centralised control solutions have been imple-mented since decades, the current quest for autonomy and the possibil-ity of distributing computational elements without wired connection for communication or energy supply has raised the interest in distributed solutions, that have to take into account the physical topology of the controlled areas and guarantee the same level of safety. In this paper the interlocking problem is formalised as a particular class of distributed mutual exclusion problems, addressing simultaneous locking of a pool of distributed objects, focusing on the formalisation and verification of the required safety properties. A family of distributed algorithms solving this problem is envisioned, with variants related to where the data defining the pool's topology reside, and to how such data rules the communication between nodes. The different variants are exemplified with references to different distributed railway interlocking algorithms proposed in the lit-erature. A final discussion is devoted to the steps needed to convert the proposed definitions into a generic plug-and-play safety-certified solution.

1 Introduction

The current quest for autonomy of cyber-physical systems and the possibility of distributing computational elements without wired connection for communica-tion or energy supply has raised the interest in distributed software solutions in which several computational elements cooperate to guarantee global properties. In the case of safety-critical systems, mastering the complexity of distributed solutions so to guarantee that safety is maintained is a hard task.

In this paper we address a particular class of safety-critical cyber-physical systems, showing how a systematic adoption of known distributed algorithms and of formal specifications can help to master the complexity.

© Springer Nature Switzerland AG 2018
F. Howar and J. Barnat (Eds.): FMICS 2018, LNCS 11119, pp. 52–66, 2018.
https://doi.org/10.1007/978-3-030-00244-2_4

In several large scale systems (e.g. robotic plants or transportation systems) safety is guaranteed by granting to some process or physical object an exclusive access to a particular set of physical areas or objects before starting its own action: some mechanism should in this case *interlock* the action of the former with the availability of the latter. A typical example is the railway interlocking problem, in which a train is granted the authorisation to move only if the track segments in front of the train are free.

The problem resembles a classical mutual exclusion problem: there are several active, or moving, physical objects (called from now on *processes*), that compete for the exclusive access for one or more free areas, which are actually shared *resources*.

Centralised solutions for this problem maintain the state of all shared resources, receive access requests and grant the exclusive access to the requesting process only if all the requested resources are free. Each resource can therefore have state = {available, requested by P_i, accessed by P_i}.

Notice that, since we are actually dealing with physical systems, the state of the resource has to reflect the actual state of a physical object: this may require that the *accessed* state is actually split in a state in which the resource is locked (meaning that the request by P_i has been met), and one in which the resource is physically *visited* by the process (see Fig. 1). Furthermore, the *requested* state may include not only a check that the related physical object is free, but also a command to the object to physically prepare it to be available to be visited, and a check that it is actually prepared, and this may take quite a long time. The subsequent states as well require some interaction with the physical object. Since a resource may be engaged in the *requested* state for long, concurrent requests by other processes should be served in the meanwhile. Atomicity of the treatment of a request is therefore guaranteed by denying requests of an already requested resource by other processes.

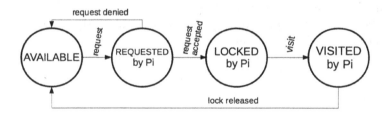

Fig. 1. States of a shared resource (*node*)

To guarantee safety of an interlocking system built according to this principle it is enough to prove that in any case two different processes cannot visit simultaneously the same resource, that is, any resource is exclusively locked by a single process. Putting this in temporal logic (CTL), it is sufficient to verify for each resource, and for each $i \neq j$ the formula $AG \sim (R\_visited\_by\_P_i \wedge R\_visited\_by\_P_j)$. Not a big task for a model checker, if the principles above are expressed in a single finite-state model that takes into account the actual topology of the controlled areas. However, the experience with railway interlocking systems says that when several trains (processes) may require tens of track circuits and points, out of a pool of some hundreds, the combinatorial combination of the possibilities produces a state space explosion problem. This problem asks for suitable abstraction or compositional techniques, and for the power of recently available SAT and SMT-solvers to verify safety of the largest systems of realistic size [9, 28].

In this paper we suggest how a distributed formalisation of the interlocking problem can decompose this verification problem into manageable verification steps: the problem is formalised as a particular class of distributed mutual exclusion problems (Sects. 2, 3, 4), addressing simultaneous locking of a pool of distributed objects, focusing on the formalisation and verification of the required safety properties. A family of distributed algorithms solving this problem is envisioned, with variants related to where the data defining the pool's topology reside, and to how such data rules the communication between nodes (Sect. 5). The different variants are exemplified with reference to different distributed railway interlocking algorithms proposed in the literature (Sect. 6). A final discussion is devoted to the steps needed to convert the proposed definitions in a generic plug-and-play safety-certified solution (Sect. 7).

2   Distributed Mutual Exclusion

In general, the Distributed Mutual Exclusion problem is typically characterised by the following statements:

- Concurrent access of processes to a shared resource or data is executed in mutually exclusive manner.
- Only one process is allowed to execute the *critical section*, that is, to access the shared resources, at any given time.
- In a distributed system there are no shared variables that can be used to implement mutual exclusion and semaphores.
- Message passing is the only means for exchanging information.

Either centralised or distributed Mutual Exclusion algorithms have typically to satisfy the following properties:

1. **Safety:** At any instant, only one process can execute the critical section.
2. **Liveness:** (absence of deadlock and starvation). Two or more processes should not endlessly wait for messages which will never arrive.
3. **Fairness:** Each process gets a fair chance to execute the critical section. Fairness generally means that the critical section execution requests are executed in the order of their arrival in the system.

Several Distributed Mutual Exclusion algorithms have been defined, especially in relation to distributed transactions, among which the most cited ones are Lamport's Algorithm [19], Ricart-Agrawala Algorithm [24], Maekawa's Algorithm [21].

Such algorithms actually guarantee safety, that is Mutual Exclusion, as obviously expected, and guarantee fairness and deadlock freedom at different degrees, with different performance parameters (number of messages, latency, throughput, response time).

3 The Class of Distributed Mutual Exclusion Problems of our Interest

In the case studied in this paper, we are interested in a Distributed Mutual Exclusion algorithm that primarily guarantees safety. Liveness and fairness are actually not a concern, since the focus is on guaranteeing that safety is not violated by multiple requests. If any process gets a request denial, it can just replay the request later: it is somehow assumed that this delay does not cause any major availability problem, because the normal interval between requests is largely greater than the time taken to accept or deny a request. If this assumption does not hold and hence availability becomes a problem, liveness and fairness should be then taken into consideration. This issue may impact on the definition of criteria to choose among different mutual exclusion algorithm variants (see Sect. 5), but we will not discuss it in details, leaving it to future work: the idea is that we concentrate on safety first, and then we will study availability and performability of the envisaged solutions.

We can recast the above problem as simultaneous locking of a pool of distributed nodes, in the following way:

- In this distributed setting, a physical resource is controlled by a dedicated computer, which is a *node* of a network. Hence, we will speak of nodes, rather than resources, from now on.
- A set of distributed nodes is *visited* by some computation *processes* (set of nodes N, set of processes P).
- In order to avoid conflicts between the computations of the processes, a process can request to exclusively lock a pool of nodes for an exclusive visit (pool of nodes $S \subseteq N$). We assume a predetermined set of possible pools $F_S \subseteq 2^N, \emptyset \notin F_S$, without loss of generality, since F_S can also be 2^N; a process request refers to a pool $S \in F_S$.
- In order to lock a pool of nodes, all nodes should be in (or should be brought to) a state in which they are available to be locked.
- If some node of the pool is not available, the lock request is denied.
- Otherwise, if all nodes are available, the lock is granted, and the process can start the visit of the pool.
- The lock on a node is singularly released after the process has declared to have finished visiting that node[1].

---

[1] This feature allows for partial release of the pool of nodes, at the advantage of other processes that want to request those nodes, so increasing availability.

Figure 1 gives an abstract view of the states of a shared resource, that is, of a node; note that there may also be concrete transient states induced by the locking algorithm, such as "requested but not available".

This Distributed Mutual Exclusion problem is actually a simplified case of the general one presented in Sect. 2. Indeed, it can be reduced to a *Distributed Transaction problem (Distributed Atomic Action)*: in this problem, a set of nodes performs a distributed action, and the decision whether the action is committed has to be agreed among all the participants: if they do not agree, the action is aborted and the participants roll back to their previous state, so that either the distributed action has been fully performed, or it has not at all. In our case, the distributed action is the reservation of the requested pool of nodes.

4   2PC Protocol for Distributed Mutual Exclusion

Algorithms to solve the Distributed Transaction problem have been defined since long time; the most popular one is the Two Phase Commit protocol (2PC) [13,20].

4.1   Classical 2PC Protocol

As the name says, the protocol works in two *phases*, according to the following steps for locking a pool of nodes S:

- Commit request phase (or Prepare phase)
  - The coordinator (a specially selected node in S) sends a *query to commit* message to all participants (all other nodes in S) and waits until it has received a reply from all participants.
  - Each participant replies with an *agreement* message or an *abort* message (an abort message may be due to the explicit denial to commit or the expiration of a timeout on the execution of an action or on a communication).
- Commit phase - *Success*
  - If the coordinator received an *agreement* message from all participants during the commit-request phase:
    * The coordinator sends a *commit* message to all the participants.
    * Each participant sends an *acknowledgement* to the coordinator.
- Commit phase - *Failure*
  - If any participant sends an *abort* during the commit-request phase (or the coordinator's timeout expires):
    * The coordinator sends a *rollback* message to all the participants.
    * Each participant rolls back and sends an *acknowledgement* to the coordinator.

This algorithm requires $4M$ messages, with $M + 1$ nodes in S, and assumes that point to point communication is available, although broadcast communication from the coordinator can reduce the overall number of messages. The algorithm is fail-safe w.r.t. communication failures, in the sense that commit cannot be wrongly reached if communication fails somewhere.

4.2   Linear 2PC Protocol for Distributed Mutual Exclusion

In this variant, participants are linearly ordered and each participant communicates with the previous and with the next participant. In the first phase, the coordinator makes the request to the first element of the pool, and each participant propagates the request to the next node in the list. In the second phase, the last participant replies OK if it is ready to commit, and the OK message is propagated backwards to the other participants; on its reception the first node delivers the OK message to the requesting process. If any of the nodes decides to abort, it propagates the abort messages in both directions. This algorithm needs - in the success case - only $2M$ point to point messages, and is hence favoured by a linear topology of the communication network.

4.3   Formalisation of the Linear 2PC Protocol

Already [26] presented a formal verification that 2PC was able to guarantee commit only if all nodes had reached the commit point and no reason for aborting the protocol was raised. This is what suffices for safety certification.

In order to discuss how a compositional formal verification of safety can be conducted, we show in Fig. 2 a simplified formalisation of the nodes of the

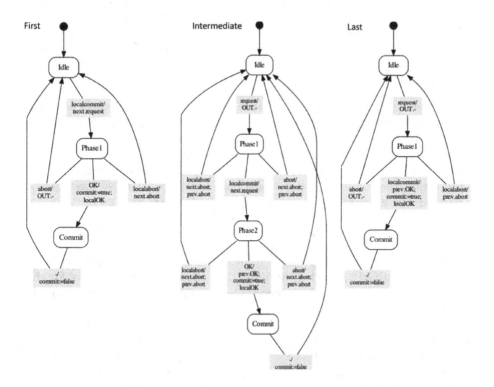

Fig. 2. The Linear 2PC protocol: behaviours of the participating nodes

Linear 2PC protocol, by means of UML Statecharts, representing respectively the *First* node, any *Intermediate* node and the *Last* node of the linear sequence; the Statecharts have been drawn by the UMC tool [5]. The charts show that any Intermediate node goes in state *Phase1* when it receives a *request message* from the previous node, and propagates the message if the node is locally ready to commit. In state *Phase 2*, it waits for the *OK* message from the next node in order to reach the *Commit* state. The node rolls back to the initial state in case of a local abort decision or an abort message from an adjacent node. The *First* and *Last* nodes act similarly upon loosing the communication with the previous or the next node, respectively. The input from the physical environment of the node is abstracted by the incoming *localcommit* and *localabort* actions; the latter abstract communication timeouts as well. Moreover, to keep them simple the shown charts do not model the *release* feature, just exhibiting an unconditional return to the initial state after the *Commit* state. UMC allows any number of *Intermediate* objects to be instantiated, connected in a linear list by means of the *prev* and *next* variables; UMC provides the capability to perform model checking on the modelled network of nodes.

The safety property we are interested to prove can be expressed as: the *First* node reaches the *Commit* state only if all the nodes have locally committed. This can be directly proved on a model consisting of $n + 2$ nodes (*First, Last, n Intermediate* nodes), but when n is already in the order of ten, the state space explosion problem makes the verification time too long to be practical.

We can however decompose this proof noting that it is actually enough to prove that each node can reach its own *Commit* state only if the next one has reached the *Commit* state. This amounts to discharge the following proof obligations:

- locally prove, for each type of node, that reaching the *Commit* states is always preceded by the local commit and by (for the *First* and the *Intermediate* nodes) the reception of the *OK* message from the next node;
- locally prove, for the *Last* and *Intermediate* nodes, that sending the *OK* message to the previous node is always preceded by the local commit;
- prove that the communication means does not forge fake *OK* messages (a received *OK* message has always been sent by the next node).

The first two items above can be easily proved locally for each node. Actually the authors have proved them by model checking for the Statecharts shown in Fig. 2 by means of UMC: the property to be proved has been expressed as a CTL universally quantified "precedes" formula – e.g. the first property above for the *Last* node is: `not E [not (localcommit) U Commit]`. The last item above is actually a security assumption over the communication between nodes.

A similar principle can be used to prove safety of the release features when included in the model, that is, to prove that reserved nodes cannot be released before they have been visited.

While safety is easily assured by employing 2PC, proving liveness and fairness would need to take into account several factors we do not address here, such as synchronous or asynchronous communication, communications faults, ordering of messages, modelling of timeouts, distinguishing successive requests to the same pool, etc.

5 Distributed Mutual Exclusion Variants

The topology of the pool of partners engaged in the 2PC protocol can change at every new invocation of the protocol, since the requesting process may differ, and it might request to lock a different pool of nodes. Different distributed mutual exclusion algorithms can be envisioned, with variants related to the topology of the pool, to where the data defining the pool's topology reside, and how such data rules the communication between nodes. For example, when applied to mutual exclusion of a pool of nodes, the Linear 2PC protocol assumes the knowledge of the linear sequence of nodes of the pool: in particular the formalisation of Linear 2PC provided above assumes that each node can send/receive messages to/from the next and previous elements of the pool. But the list of nodes could also be passed along with the *request* message from the requesting process.

We identify three main variants:

– **Variant (1)** The Classical 2PC algorithm is adopted: the requesting process knows the set S of nodes in the pool and is able to broadcast the request to all the nodes in the pool. The nodes are able to reply to the requesting process.
– **Variant (2A)** The Linear 2PC algorithm is adopted: the pool of nodes S has a linear structure, that is, is composed by a list of nodes. The communication between nodes follows the order of the list. The requesting process knows the list S and sends its request with the list S to the first element of S, each element takes the next and the previous element from the list S and propagates the request, with the list S, according to 2PC: the OK messages are propagated backwards from the last node to the first, by using the knowledge of the previous element for each node. In the case abort messages are generated, they are propagated back and forth in a similar way.
– **Variant (2B)** The Linear 2PC algorithm is adopted, as in Variant 2A: the pool of nodes S has a linear structure, and communication between nodes follows the order of the list. Each node has the knowledge of the previous and next elements for any pool $S \in F_S$ to which it is participating, that is, it knows the adjacent nodes in the pool's topology for each pool to which it belongs. The requesting process sends its request with the requested pool identifier S to the first element of S, and propagates the request, with the S pool id, according to 2PC. Adjacency may be related to physical adjacency or connection between the physical elements controlled by the nodes. Routing mechanisms common to communication networking may be used in each node to determine the next node to which propagate the request, and hence this variant may include limited local rerouting features for availability.

Another source of variability is that actual interlocking algorithms for Cyber-Physical Systems might require two rounds, each employing a 2PC protocol to complete the procedure. In the first round the pool of nodes is locked. In the second round commands are issued to physical objects associated to nodes to move to the desired state, and the acknowledge messages include the check that the physical nodes have actually reached the desired state. Only then the process can start the visit. This behaviour can be needed, e.g., for energy efficiency, because it avoids useless physical movements in case a reservation is aborted.

6 Distributed Interlocking as Distributed Mutual Exclusion

Railway interlocking systems are those systems that are responsible to grant to a train the exclusive access to a *route*: a route is a sequence of track elements that are exclusively assigned for the movement of a train through a station or a network. Actually, railway interlocking systems are the most complex (in term of topological size and structure) instances of the safety interlocking concept defined above.

Granting to a train the exclusive access to a route typically means (i) checking that the route is free from other trains, by means of track circuits or other presence sensors, (ii) commanding points in their correct position, (iii) checking that the points have actually reached the commanded position, and (iv) setting the signals so to give the driver the permission to move. The instantiation of these generic rules on a station topology (made of the track layout and the set of routes) is usually defined in a data structure named *control table*, that is specific for the station where the system resides. The control table drives the subsequent development of a centralised interlocking system. In the usual meaning of railway interlocking, we intend therefore a system that simply receives requests of reservations, and grants reservations or not on the ground of safety rules, until the reservation has been fully used (the track is again free) or has been safely revoked. It is not a burden of the interlocking to look for alternative routes in case the requested one is busy, in order to optimise traffic throughput parameters, nor to guarantee that a train does not enter a not reserved track. These two functions are traditionally in charge of separate systems, namely Automatic Train Supervision (ATS) and Automatic Train Protection (ATP) respectively.

Centralised interlockings are complex and costly to design and especially to be certified against safety guidelines. The complexity is due to the need of verifying every possible conflicting combinations of different routes through the station: adopting model checking to verify the interlocking logic of large stations has indeed proved challenging [11,28].

The distribution of the interlocking logic over a network of computing nodes, according to the spirit of cyber-physical systems, has also the side effect of partitioning the verification effort. According to what was said in Sect. 4, we can think to split the safety certification into simpler and repetitive (hence factorised) proofs that each node verifies the safety requirements, plus a security proof for the employed 2PC protocol. The idea of distributed interlocking has been proposed in several papers [2,8,15], where advantages and possible drawbacks of such a solution are discussed: in practice, preference is still given to centralised solutions, but this may change with the general trend to distribute intelligence.

In a distributed solution, track elements are directly controlled by a set of distributed communicating nodes: each node controls a given layout element.

However, a route is still a global notion: a route has to be established by proper cooperation between the distributed elements. The communication among nodes follows the physical topology of the station/yard and a route is established by the status of the elements that lie along the route.

The following correspondence can be established to consider a distributed railway interlocking as an instance of the general distributed safety interlocking concept:

- Track circuit, point → Node.
- Route → Pool of nodes.
- Trains → Processes.
- A route is requested by a train → A process sends a request for locking a pool - including reserving track circuits and locking points in a specific position.
- A route is reserved for a train → Requested pool is locked - if track elements are free and points are positioned.
- A train occupies a track circuit or a point → Visit of a node.
- A train leaves a track circuit or a point → Release of a node.

A specific characteristic of railway interlocking is that nodes of a route are visited by the movement of the train along the route, hence are visited in a sequential predetermined way. As soon as a track circuit or a point is left by a train, it is available for possibly setting another route: this feature is called *sequential release*, a common feature not needed for safety (a route could also be collectively released when the visit of the last node has ended), but desired to improve availability. Another specific characteristic is that cancellation of an already reserved route may be asked (for example when a train is not able to leave a station due to a mechanical problem). Safe cancellation can be achieved in a similar way to safe reservation.

Some proposed distributed railway interlocking algorithms are discussed in the following and use instances of the Distributed Mutual Exclusion variants shown in Sect. 5:

- Variant (1) [12,15]. The engineering concept was originally developed by INSY GmbH Berlin for their railway control system RELIS 2000 designed for local railway networks. In this solution, the train has an onboard computer with route information. Instead of signals, the computer gives Movement Authorities to the driver. The train broadcasts the request of a route to *distributed switch boxes* that control the track elements. This is actually a special case of Variant 1, since it does not require the locking of the complete route, before the train is allowed to move (*sequential locking*): it is as if the train route is divided into sub-routes, each just containing one track segment, and that the train then sequentially locks these small routes. The protocol implicitly includes sequential release. In [15] the concept has been formalised in the RAISE Specification Language, RSL [27], and the RAISE theorem prover was used for verification. In [12] an extension of RSL, called RSL-SAL [23] was used for the formalisation, and the formal verification was performed using the SAL symbolic model checker.

- Variant (1) US patent 8820685 B2 [22]. A controller onboard the train first identifies a group of resources permitting the vehicle to continue its mission, by querying a local database (which contains the data of the whole railway network) with the mission received from a regulating center. Although details of the communication protocol are not given, the onboard controller broadcasts the locking request to the identified group of resources, and gives the consensus to move only when all the resources are locked in the desired state. Sequential release is considered as well.
- Variant (1) US patent 20120323411 A1 [18]. The concept is not much different from that of patent [22], with the added complexity that the reservation of a route is negotiated first with other trains as well, and the state of the wayside elements is also recorded at a central location as a back-up. Also in this case, details of the protocol are not given, but in reference to our scheme, the distributed protocol concerns the other processes as well, and the central location can be considered as a further node. This patent also includes higher level negotiation mechanisms on board trains to improve availability.
- Variant (2A) [10]. In this proposal, the linear 2PC is adopted. The information about the route to be reserved (that is, the list of nodes) is propagated to the nodes, from the first to the last node of the route: each node knows from this list its adjacent nodes in the route, with which it directly communicates. The concept has been modelled by UML Statecharts, using UMC for formal verification of safety properties.
- Variant (2B) [7]. Again, this proposal adopts linear 2PC. Each node is initialised with a table containing, for each route traversing the node, the adjacent elements with which it has to communicate. Only the route identifier is propagated along the locking request. The concept has been modelled by UML Statecharts, using UMC for formal verification of safety properties.
- Variant (2B) [4]. This paper formalises in SPIN an interlocking system, considered at the level of sections between stations of a metro line: the proposed interlocking model is shown, by model checking, to guarantee that two trains cannot enter the same section. Due to the linear topology of the line, the model is a direct instance of Variant 2B, and does not include the aborting possibility.

A few other attempts at distributing the interlocking logic in separate computations have been developed, starting from the so-called geographic approach [1,3,6], which encodes the interlocking logic in separate objects that each take care of the control of a physical element (point, track circuit, signal, ...) by means of predefined composition rules, mimicking the topology of the specific layout, although the obtained control software is still centralised. In particular, [2] proposes to start from a Statechart geographic model that uses shared variables as a communication means between objects, and to allocate each object on a distributed node. The adoption of standard distributed consistency protocols guarantees that the exchange of information is the same of the full centralised model. However, this approach requires the safety proof of the centralised model, with no attempt to decompose it into simpler proofs. Similarly, in [16,17] an overall Petri Net model of a distributed interlocking system is proposed, by connecting Petri Nets representing the behaviour of each node. Again, the analysis of the model does not employ any decomposition strategy.

Different criteria could be used in practice to choose among the variants; these include for example:

- replicating the network database onboard all trains running in a network can be practically done for a closed network, such as a metro network. Instead, in an open infrastructure, such that envisioned by European interoperability that foresee a train crossing many borders between national network, the size of the database and frequency of its updates would be very high: since these data are critical for safety, trains running with a previous release of the database (maybe due to poor communication) would become dangerous. It seems more reasonable that missions received by a train include a list of identifiers of routes to be followed in each traversed station, to be asked to a local, either distributed or centralised, interlocking system.
- on the other end, keeping route tables on the distributed trackside elements requires robust distributed initialisation, configuration and reconfiguration algorithms to maintain consistency [8].
- resilience to faults of single elements - in view of higher availability, which is one of the advantages of distribution - may require redundancy, replication of data and specific policies that could be favoured by one of the variants.
- another criterion pertains to energy efficiency and reliability of track machinery: if points are soon moved in an attempt to set a route that will fail due to conflicting requests, this may result in a lower reliability and energy waste.

The proposals according to Variant 1 show that moving the network map onboard the train may favour the moving of route decision on board as well: routes are currently predetermined in terms of a pool of elements, and allocated to trains in a centralised way (e.g. by an Automatic Train Supervision (ATS) system). Instead, routes could be dynamically generated in front of the train, allowing for last minute choice according to optimisation strategies computed on board. The push towards a *train-centric vs. infrastructure-centric* decision making is one of the challenges considered in the Multiannual Programme of the Shift2Rail Joint Undertaking Initiative [25].

7   Certification

The certification of safety of a distributed interlocking system, according to what was discussed in Sect. 4, amounts to verify that each component locally complies with the standard communication protocol, plus the verification that the protocol does not forge messages. This makes the basis for a simpler and less expensive certification process. First, the safety distributed protocol should be formally verified once for all – this includes proper security measures against attacks. Assembling off-the-shelf plug-in controller elements, manufactured by different vendors, on top of this safety layer will automatically guarantee overall safety, if they are certified to comply with the standard interlocking protocol.

As we have seen, the verification of the safe behaviour of a node can be cheaply done by automated formal verification. One element that we have ignored so far is that the proofs envisaged in Sect. 4 assume the local knowledge of the previous and next element of the pool. The different variants have different views on how these data are available to the nodes: routing tables may be injected in the node at configuration (or reconfiguration) time, or routing information may arrive together with the locking request. Assuring that the data is always consistent with the physical track layout in each node becomes indeed the major certification effort. The possible application of static analysis techniques, such as those described in [14], is a promising research direction at this regard.

8   Conclusions

In this paper we have shown that *safety interlocking* can be seen as a particular class of *Distributed Mutual Exclusion* problems and consequently distributed algorithms solving this problem can be used for safety interlocking. We presented variants of such distributed algorithms and exemplified them with references to different distributed railway interlocking algorithms proposed in the literature. Finally, we discussed the steps needed to convert the proposed solutions into generic plug-and-play safety-certified solutions. Regarding the possible applications in the railway field, we believe that the achieved gains in the certification effort can significantly decrease costs in the production and deployment of interlocking systems, once a standard communication protocol is emerging: variants presented in this paper aims to be a first step in this direction.

Distributed safety interlocking systems may find application in any domain where safety depends on the guarantee that a set of objects is in a determined state. To our knowledge, however, the only example found in the literature is the one reported (with no details about the adopted algorithms) in [29], aimed to guarantee a safe access to a large physics experiment installation.

We have on purpose focused only on safety, mostly ignoring availability: the proposed protocols do not guarantee liveness and fairness under several conditions, and an accurate analysis of different factors (timing, fault models,. . .) affecting these attributes would be needed. In the case of railway interlocking, low availability can severely impact service performability. Given that safety is granted by principles like those put forward by this paper, distributed solutions can be adopted in practice only if sufficient availability is demonstrated, possibly employing quantitative analysis techniques, as suggested in [8].

References

1. FP7 Project INESS - Deliverable D.1.5 report on translation of requirements from text to UML. Technical report (2009)
2. Banci, M., Fantechi, A., Gnesi, S.: The role of formal methods in developing a distribuited railway interlocking system. In: Proceedings of Formal Methods for Automation and Safety in Railway and Automotive Systems, FORMS/FORMAT, Braunschweig, Germany, pp. 79–91 (2004)
3. Banci, M., Fantechi, A.: Geographical versus functional modelling by statecharts of interlocking systems. Electr. Notes Theor. Comput. Sci. **133**, 3–19 (2005). https://doi.org/10.1016/j.entcs.2004.08.055
4. Basagiannis, S., Katsaros, P., Pombortsis, A.: Interlocking control by distributed signal boxes: design and verification with the SPIN model checker. In: Guo, M., Yang, L.T., Di Martino, B., Zima, H.P., Dongarra, J., Tang, F. (eds.) ISPA 2006. LNCS, vol. 4330, pp. 317–328. Springer, Heidelberg (2006). https://doi.org/10.1007/11946441_32
5. ter Beek, M.H., Fantechi, A., Gnesi, S., Mazzanti, F.: A state/event-based model-checking approach for the analysis of abstract system properties. Sci. Comput. Program. **76**(2), 119–135 (2011). https://doi.org/10.1016/j.scico.2010.07.002
6. van Dijk, F., Fokkink, W., Kolk, G., van de Ven, P., van Vlijmen, B.: EURIS, a specification method for distributed interlockings. In: Ehrenberger, W. (ed.) SAFE-COMP 1998. LNCS, vol. 1516, pp. 296–305. Springer, Heidelberg (1998). https://doi.org/10.1007/3-540-49646-7_23
7. Fantechi, A.: Distributing the challenge of model checking interlocking control tables. In: Margaria, T., Steffen, B. (eds.) ISoLA 2012. LNCS, vol. 7610, pp. 276–289. Springer, Heidelberg (2012). https://doi.org/10.1007/978-3-642-34032-1_26
8. Fantechi, A., Gnesi, S., Haxthausen, A., van de Pol, J., Roveri, M., Treharne, H.: SaRDIn - A safe reconfigurable distributed interlocking. In: Proceedings of 11th World Congress on Railway Research, WCRR. Ferrovie dello Stato Italiane, Milano (2016)
9. Fantechi, A., Haxthausen, A.E., Macedo, H.D.: Compositional verification of interlocking systems for large stations. In: Cimatti, A., Sirjani, M. (eds.) SEFM 2017. LNCS, vol. 10469, pp. 236–252. Springer, Cham (2017). https://doi.org/10.1007/978-3-319-66197-1_15
10. Fantechi, A., Haxthausen, A.E., Nielsen, M.B.R.: Model checking geographically distributed interlocking systems using UMC. In: 25th Euromicro International Conference on Parallel, Distributed and Network-based Processing, PDP, pp. 278–286 (2017). https://doi.org/10.1109/PDP.2017.66
11. Ferrari, A., Magnani, G., Grasso, D., Fantechi, A.: Model checking interlocking control tables. In: Schnieder, E., Tarnai, G. (eds.) FORMS/FORMAT, pp. 107–115. Springer, Heidelberg (2010). https://doi.org/10.1007/978-3-642-14261-1_11
12. Geisler, S., Haxthausen, A.E.: Stepwise development and model checking of a distributed interlocking system - using RAISE. In: Havelund, K., Peleska, J., Roscoe, B., de Vink, E. (eds.) Formal Methods. FM 2018. Lecture Notes in Computer Science, vol. 10951. Springer, Cham (2018). https://doi.org/10.1007/978-3-319-95582-7_16
13. Gray, J.N.: Notes on data base operating systems. In: Bayer, R., Graham, R.M., Seegmüller, G. (eds.) Operating Systems. LNCS, vol. 60, pp. 393–481. Springer, Heidelberg (1978). https://doi.org/10.1007/3-540-08755-9_9, http://dl.acm.org/citation.cfm?id=647433.723863

14. Haxthausen, A.E., Østergaard, P.H.: On the use of static checking in the verification of interlocking systems. In: Margaria, T., Steffen, B. (eds.) ISoLA 2016. LNCS, vol. 9953, pp. 266–278. Springer, Cham (2016). https://doi.org/10.1007/978-3-319-47169-3_19
15. Haxthausen, A.E., Peleska, J.: Formal development and verification of a distributed railway control system. IEEE Trans. Softw. Eng. **26**(8), 687–701 (2000)
16. Hei, X., Takahashi, S., Nakamura, H.: Distributed interlocking system and its safety verification. In: Proceedings of 6th World Congress on Intelligent Control and Automation, Dalian, China, vol. 2, pp. 8612–8615 (2006). https://doi.org/10.1109/WCICA.2006.1713661
17. Hei, X., Ma, W., Gao, J., Xie, G.: A concurrent scheduling model of distributed train control system. In: Proceedings of IEEE International Conference on Service Operations, Logistics, and Informatics, SOLI, pp. 478–483 (2011)
18. Kanner, F.W.A.: Control of automatic guided vehicles without wayside interlocking, Patent US 20120323411 A1 (2012)
19. Lamport, L.: The implementation of reliable distributed multiprocess systems. Comput. Netw. **2**, 95–114 (1978). https://doi.org/10.1016/0376-5075(78)90045-4
20. Lampson, B., Sturgis, H.: Crash recovery in a distributed storage system. Technical report, Comput. Sci. Lab., Xerox Parc, Palo Alto, CA (1976)
21. Maekawa, M.: A $\sqrt{N}$ algorithm for mutual exclusion in decentralized systems. ACM Trans. Comput. Syst. **3**(2), 145–159 (1985). https://doi.org/10.1145/214438.214445
22. Michaut, P.: Method for managing the circulation of vehicles on a railway network and related system, Patent US 8820685 B2 (2014)
23. Perna, J.I., George, C.: Model checking RAISE applicative specifications. In: Proceedings of the Fifth IEEE International Conference on Software Engineering and Formal Methods, SEFM, pp. 257–268. IEEE Computer Society Press (2007)
24. Ricart, G., Agrawala, A.K.: An optimal algorithm for mutual exclusion in computer networks. Commun. ACM **24**(1), 9–17 (1981). https://doi.org/10.1145/358527.358537
25. Shift2Rail Joint Undertaking: Multi-annual action plan, November 2015. http://ec.europa.eu/research/participants/data/ref/h2020/other/wp/jtis/h2020-maap-shift2rail_en.pdf
26. Skeen, D., Stonebraker, M.: A formal model of crash recovery in a distributed systems. IEEE Trans. Softw. Eng. **9**, 219–228 (1983)
27. George, C., Haff, P., Havelund, K., Haxthausen, A.E., Milne, R., Nielsen, C.B., Prehn, S., Wagner, K.R.: The RAISE Language Group. The RAISE Specification Language. The BCS Practitioners Series, Prentice Hall Int. (1992)
28. Vu, L.H., Haxthausen, A.E., Peleska, J.: Formal modeling and verification of interlocking systems featuring sequential release. Sci. Comput. Program. (2016). https://doi.org/10.1016/j.scico.2016.05.010
29. Walz, H.V., Agostini, R.C., Barker, L., Cherkassky, R., Constant, T., Matheson, R.: Distributed supervisory protection interlock system SLC acceleration. Proceedings of the IEEE Particle Accelerator Conference: Accelerator Science and Technology, vol. 3, pp. 1928–1930 (1989). https://doi.org/10.1109/PAC.1989.72972

Checking Consistency of Real-Time Requirements on Distributed Automotive Control Software Early in the Development Process Using UPPAAL

Jan Toennemann[1]([⊠]), Andreas Rausch[1], Falk Howar[2]([⊠]), and Benjamin Cool[1]

[1] Clausthal University of Technology, Clausthal-Zellerfeld, Germany
jan.toennemann@tu-clausthal.de
[2] Dortmund University of Technology and Fraunhofer ISST, Dortmund, Germany
falk.howar@tu-dortmund.de

Abstract. The next generation of automotive control software will run on complex networks of control units, connected by a multitude of different bus systems. With a rising number of safety-critical functions being realized (at least partly) in software, real-time requirements for distributed functions become more important (e.g., time until a system reacts to a perceived driving situation). Defining and refining such requirements consistently during system development is not trivial. Inconsistencies or unrealizability can easily be introduced when decomposing requirements (e.g., time budgets) for functions that run on multiple control units. The automotive industry is actively pursuing methods for finding such problems as early as possible in the system design. In this paper, we present some initial work on the automated verification of requirements on distributed control functions that are deployed to networks of automotive control units. The presented analysis provides insights into the consistency of requirements and relies only on information available at the end of the planning stage in the development process.

1 Introduction

Automotive systems, consisting of a large number of communicating Electronic Control Units (ECUs), are required to handle an ever increasing number of complex tasks and also need to fulfill a multitude of specific requirements related to safety and reliability [15]. Considering a network of real-time systems introduces a whole new layer of complexity, resulting in more complex simulation and analysis. For each new system introduced into the network an additional real-time clock needs to be considered, which might not run synchronous to that of the other systems in the network [20]. Established commercial analysis tools used to test automotive software systems, like TA Simulator [1] or SymTA/S [2], have recently added support for distributed functions. On the one hand, these tools are able to quite accurately simulate the system's behavior and often give very

© Springer Nature Switzerland AG 2018
F. Howar and J. Barnat (Eds.): FMICS 2018, LNCS 11119, pp. 67–82, 2018.
https://doi.org/10.1007/978-3-030-00244-2_5

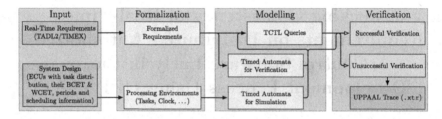

Fig. 1. Workflow for checking consistency of timed requirements with information about system design.

detailed results of tests in the form of exportable statistics and graphs. On the other hand, since the analysis is based on simulation, it requires a lot of information about the final system, e.g., statistical information about bus communcation delays obtained from actual recorded execution.

Moreover, each function or assistance system is mostly tested in isolation by its supplier as the behavior and timing influences of integrating a multitude of functions from various suppliers into a combined system is often very complex [18]. A reliable simulation of the actual behavior and checks on whether the real-time requirements are fulfilled when integrating multiple functions on a network of control units can only be done very late in the development process [8].

Detecting inconsistencies at a stage this late in the development process can require major changes to the system as a whole and introduce a lot of additional work which may delay a project substantially, severely increasing the cost. As defining and refining real-time requirements consistently during system development is not trivial, the automotive industry is actively pursuing methods for finding such problems as early as possible in the system design. Inconsistencies or unrealizability can easily be introduced when decomposing requirements (e.g., time budgets) for functions that run on multiple control units. This calls for methods that enable analysis of real-time requirements even before a final system design is fixed, let alone implemented and ready to be tested.

While analysis in early stages of a project cannot be as precise as late in the process (during the planning phase, a non-negligible number of parameters affecting the final system is still unknown), an approach based on over-approximation of possible behavior can help to discover potential inconsistencies. Inconsistencies can then be addressed by refining requirements or assumptions on system behavior, e.g., when more precise timing information becomes available during the development process.

In this paper, we present such an approach for checking inconsistencies between multiple types of requirements early in the development process, requiring only little information about the final system. Figure 1 shows a high-level overview of the approach. We expect real-time requirements and basic information about the anticipated system design as input. We analyze the following types of requirements:

– Maximum execution time of tasks and reaction time of event chains,
– Data age of task output data,

- Periodicity of tasks,
- Schedulability, and
- Synchronization of tasks.

The analysis is based on the information listed below from the system design:

- A decomposition of functions into sub-functions assigned to control units,
- Data-flow between sub-functions,
- Assumed schedules for electronic control units (ECUs) based on dynamic Earliest Deadline First (EDF) or static priority-based scheduling similar to that of OSEK OS, and
- Assumed best-case and worst-case execution times for sub-functions (including times for bus communication).

Requirements and system design are translated into a network of timed automata, encoding constraints on system behavior and Timed Computation Tree Logic (TCTL) queries representing proof obligations for requirements. The information about the automotive software system is then given as a system definition in UPPAAL [3] utilizing parametrizable templates, encoding scheduling constraints on possible executions and introducing clocks for observing some properties, as well as structures defined in the C-like language provided by UPPAAL. Consistency of requirements can then be evaluated through model checking. We demonstrate the approach on a (fictional) distributed brake-by-wire function.

Related Work. Timing constraints in automotive software systems, especially distributed systems, have been a field of extensive research in recent years and still continues to be. Analyzing and simulating the behavior of a single real-time system is not trivial, but has been reliably accomplished for single core architectures. In recent years many manufacturers of control units have switched to a multi-core approach [10,12,19], where each processor has multiple cores and allows for parallel execution. It has been shown that it is still possible to completely simulate control units with multiple cores and parallel execution in order to ensure that the deployed software will perform reliably under all considered circumstances [5].

Considering a network of real-time systems introduces a whole new layer of complexity, resulting in a more complex simulation and analysis. For each new system introduced into the network an additional real-time clock needs to be considered, which might not run synchronous to that of the other systems in the network [20]. There exist various approaches to develop and test these interconnected systems and generally, the analysis of distributed real-time systems inside certain bounds can also lead to reliable results [7]. But the thorough analysis that is necessary for these results requires a large amount of data about the system, requiring both the system development as well as its implementation and configuration to be already finished when starting the tests.

Moreover, many tasks in automotive software systems do not run periodically in a fixed time grid, but are triggered by events in a non-deterministic matter [16].

Using classic model-checking, these cannot be reliably accounted for, since the worst case assumptions made in the process would be that the event is constantly triggered, resulting in an extremely overloaded system, which is not even close to situations that occur in real-world examinations. There are also propositions to only realize safety-critical functions using periodically triggered tasks [9,17], but as of right now, event-triggered tasks are considered to be an integral part of automotive software systems [16,18]. Several approaches exist to apply statistical analysis to include this type of tasks. The approach presented in [11] uses the experimental statistic model-checking toolkit integrated in the current UPPAAL development snapshots to verify such event properties inside UPPAAL. The model given in [11] is a very detailed representation of the system including a representation of the functional behavior in addition to the timing properties.

An approach similar to the one we present in this paper that does not rely on large amounts of data but rather on over-approximation of possible behavior has been used successfully used for modeling and verification of the Controller Area Network (CAN) bus in [6,14]. For later stages of a development process, when the bus design and message structure are fixed, the behavioral templates developed in these works could be incorporated into our approach in order to generate more realistic model of the underlying bus network.

Outline. The next section presents our motivating example, a distributed brake-by-wire function. Sections 3 and 4 provide technical details on the phenomena that we model in automata templates and the types of properties that can be analyzed using these templates, respectively. Finally, we present results from an initial evaluation of the presented work on the motivating example in Sect. 5 before making some concluding remarks and discussing future work in Sect. 6.

2 Motivating Example

We will demonstrate the key ideas of our approach on the basis of a simplified brake-by-wire architecture (inspired by the example given in [4]) that is broken down into a set of functions running on a distributed system showcasing the various covered types of requirements. While an industrial brake-by-wire system may run on more control units and consist of more or different components than our example, the general architecture of our example is representative of real distributed driving functions, as are analyzed properties and modeled schedulers.

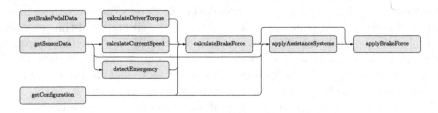

Fig. 2. Functional decomposition of brake-by-wire architecture.

A brake-by-wire system replaces the mechanical connection between the driver and the vehicle by electronic systems [13]. These systems have a number of advantages over mechanical systems (e.g., weight reduction and increased cabin space) and are essential for autonomous driving. Replacing mechanical braking, the software in brake-by-wire systems falls into the highest safety integrity level with strong requirements imposed upon it, since any slightest error could endanger lives.

A high-level point of view of our simplified brake-by-wire architecture is shown in Fig. 2. The distributed brake-by-wire function works by periodically polling the angle of the brake pedal to receive input from the driver, converting the angle to an amount of force that is applied to the brakes, applying additional assistance systems like electronic brake force distribution, and engaging the corresponding actuators in the brakes with the desired force. In addition to this driver-based brake routine, our system includes an emergency brake assistant, periodically analyzing data from various sensors of the car and activating the brake actuators as fast as possible in case of an emergency. We assume several real-time requirements for the functions shown in the figure:

1. The function calculating the force that shall be applied to the brakes must always finish at most 28 ms after it started and the calculations must be done at least every 40 ms.
2. The sensor data used by the assistance systems may at most be 12 ms old and the already pre-processed data from the brake pedal may at most be 16 ms old when the calculations of the brake force start.
3. The driver-triggered brake routine, from the polling of the brake pedal angle to the finished activation of the brake actuators, must finish within 110 ms.
4. The path from the main brake controller calculating the brake force up to the finished activation of the actuators may at most take 80 ms and the input data to the function calculating the brake force must always be from within a time frame of 10 ms.
5. The emergency brake routine, from the polling of the sensor data up to the finished activation of brake actuators, may never surpass a total of 85 ms.

Since we are dealing with automotive software systems, we consider a network of control units using a real-time operating system, where functions are implemented using periodically triggered tasks with deterministic scheduling; we will call such a software system a *processing environment* (PE). We assume that we have a homogeneous hardware architecture, where all tasks have a fixed best-case and worst-case execution time (BCET & WCET, respectively) regardless of the processing environment they are currently deployed on. Having no detailed information about the actual hardware system, we assume each additional processing environment introduced into the system to have a slight clock offset of 1 ms compared to the one added before due to networking and wiring constraints, such that the offset between two processing environments pe_n, pe_m can be calculated as $m - n$ ms, making the processing environment with the lowest index the reference system. If verification is done on processing environments

Table 1. Mapping of functions to tasks for brake-by-wire architecture including estimated time budgets.

Task	Function	BCET	WCET	Description
τ_1	getBrakePedalData	3	4	Receive and store information about the current brake pedal angle
τ_2	getSensorData	6	7	Receive and store information about the sensors (accelero-, gyrometer, camera, ultrasonic sensor, ...)
τ_3	getConfiguration	3	5	Receive and store information about the currently selected user options (engine recuperation, assistance systems, ...)
τ_4	calculateDriverTorque	2	3	Calculate relative torque from brake pedal angle
τ_5	calculateCurrentSpeed	8	10	Use stored sensor data to calculate the current speed
τ_6	detectEmergency	16	22	Use stored sensor data to detect whether an emergency situation is imminent
τ_7	calculateBrakeForce	19	26	Combine current information from the brake pedal, sensors and settings to calculate the force to apply to the brakes
τ_8	applyAssistanceSystems	13	28	Apply enabled assistance systems based on currently stored sensor data and already calculated brake force
τ_9	applyBrakeForce	7	9	Apply the final result of the force calculation to the brakes by activating the brake actuators

modeled after already existing systems, measured data for the delay between the systems should be used to more accurately represent the offset.

Sub-functions are described in Table 1. The noted BCET and WCET are over-approximated and would – in case of a consistent system – be handed to suppliers as timing requirements for the developed functions, since they are then a fundamental base for a consistent system. Possible inconsistencies range from rather simple cases, for example that the time grid assigned to a task fails to make the function run as often as needed for a periodicity requirement to be met, to very complex cases, like for instance when a group of tasks that needs to be run sequentially in a given amount of time (an event chain) does not finish fast enough in edge cases, e.g. when various offsets correlate in a way that is not instantly obvious as the worst-case.

3 Modeling

In this section, we walk through the development process of the templates which we use to simulate the timing behavior of distributed automotive software systems. In order to use UPPAAL as a model-checking tool, we require a model of automotive software systems that can be used as input for the verification. Using UPPAAL global declarations, we have created basic data structures like tasks and implemented several accompanying functions as well as the scheduling. The processing environments are represented using templates, a combination of a modeled timed automaton and accompanying code in the C-like language provided by UPPAAL; an overview of the created documents is shown in Fig. 3. Before setting up the automata and their behavior, we will use the global declarations to implement a task model and scheduling functions, which can then be accessed from the templates.

Fig. 3. Resulting documents of UPPAAL modeling.

Tasks. To be able to refer to tasks, we use the basic structure `Task` composed of a numeric identifier, the `ID` of the task, and the `BCET` and `WCET` as well. Since we require tasks to have scheduling information, the structures `EDF_Task`, comprised of a task, a relative deadline and a period, as well as `OSEK_Task`, consisting of a task, priority and period tuple, were created.

Tasks are not spawned directly but rather as instances, defined as `EDF_Task_Instance` and `OSEK_Task_Instance`, both of which allow us to save their execution time as well as their start time; additionally, the `EDF_Task_Instance` also saves the absolute deadline, which is the absolute deadline of the instance calculated from the start time and the relative deadline of the corresponding `EDF_Task`.

For each task we simulate, we want information about its runtime (its execution time, the time that has passed since the start of the execution) as well as its data age (the time that has passed since the task last finished executing and thus provided new output data). Since we assume tasks to be unique (in the sense that each task ID is only assigned once, globally), we store the runtime and data age clocks using arrays in the global declarations.

We also add broadcast channels to notify of the beginning and end of task execution as well as a Boolean array to save whether a task is currently being executed, as we are unable to compare clock values outside of guards in UPPAAL, including custom functions.

```
int [0 , TASK_QUEUE_MAX]  EDF_schedule (EDF_Task_Queue &tq )  {
  EDF_Task_Instance next_eti = tq [0];
  int [0 , TASK_QUEUE_MAX]  next_eti_pos = 0;
  int [1 , TASK_QUEUE_MAX + 1]  i = 1;
  while (i < TASK_QUEUE_MAX && tq [i]  != NULL_EDF_TI) {
    if (tq [i]. deadline < next_eti . deadline ) {
      next_eti = tq [i];
      next_eti_pos = i ;
    }
    i ++;
  }
  return next_eti_pos ;
}
```

Listing 1. UPPAAL Code for EDF Scheduling.

Scheduling. To create an EDF task instance, we only pass the corresponding task as a reference and the local time of the processing environment as the parameters, since the rest can be calculated from there. The absolute deadline is calculated from the local time of the task-spawning PE and the relative deadline of the EDF task, the start time can be assumed to be the passed local time, and the execution time is zero, since the instance has just been newly generated.

With an initialized system, we are working with EDF task instances in the task queue represented by the data type EDF_Task_Instance. The queue is represented as an array, initialized with the elements NULL_EDF_TI, ordered in a way that we can consider the first encountered NULL_EDF_TI to be the end of the queue. This is a consistency requirement needed by the functions used to enqueue and dequeue the task instances.

Since each task instance in the queue has information about its absolute deadline, the scheduling function shown in Listing 1 simply moves through the queue and returns the instance with the lowest absolute deadline, that is, the instance that needs to be finished next. Should multiple instances have the same deadline, the index of the first one encountered is returned, which is the one with a lower index. The scheduling function does not return the instance, but rather its position in the task queue of the processing environment. This is due to a limitation in UPPAAL, which – while allowing references to be passed to a function – does not allow a function to return a reference. A way to circumvent this would be to pass another reference and set this to the selected instance, but both for consistency and compatibility reasons we chose the approach of just returning the index in the queue. With OSEK instances, scheduling works similar to the presented EDF function, using priority as a parameter instead of a relative deadline.

Processing Environments. We have developed templates that represent processing environments. We create one template for per number of tasks that run on the system and add the tasks dynamically using the parameters. For each task a unique ID, a BCET and a WCET are configured via parameter in the system declarations. All templates share common definitions: two clocks independent from the number of tasks handled (one for the automaton's local time, one for

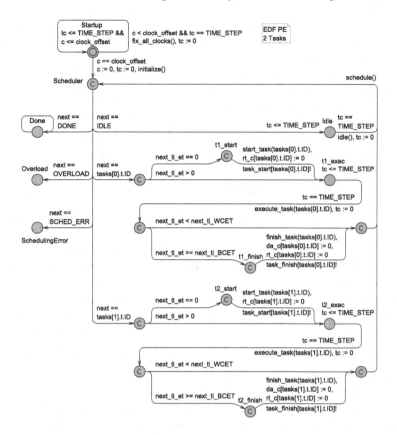

Fig. 4. EDF-scheduled processing environment template with two tasks.

counting to the next time step during any task's execution), a constant for the amount of tasks handled by the template, a variable saving the current local time and an array of the contained task's periods, used as triggers for adding them to the queue. Shorthands are defined to access the next action, determined by the scheduler, for the queue index of the next task instance, the amount of task instances currently in the queue and the execution time of the next task instance, along with the corresponding tasks' WCET and BCET.

Not only definitions, but also some functions are common to all templates. Several functions are used to reset clocks after each tick, e.g. to only allow runtime clocks to progress during actual task execution. While these functions are present in all templates, regardless of the scheduling algorithm used, there are minor differences in the implementations because of different data types. Different functions are run for each task start, finish and execution step.

The generic template for an EDF-scheduled processing environment running two tasks shown in Fig. 4 calls the functions initialize() upon system initialization, schedule() after each time step and idle() when leaving the *Idle* location. For each task, there is a compound of six locations supplied with the numerical task identifiers; in the respective transitions inbetween, the functions

start_task(ID), execute_task(ID) and finish_task(ID) are called
and the broadcast channels for the task ID are used to send the start and finish
signals when appropriate.

The schedule() call first checks the period of the tasks simulated in the
processing environment and adds task instances to the queue in case the the time
grid is met. To this end, variable local_time keeps track of the current time,
as clock valuations cannot be checked against other variables using mathematical
operations, e.g., the time grid triggers, neither can they be passed to other functions, e.g., when calling the function to generate a new EDF task instance. Then,
schedule() calls the template's scheduling function (here EDF) to determine
the next task instance for the processing environment and sets up the shorthands used in the template. It checks if one of the three auxiliary locations
needs to be entered; if the simulations has reached its end, the *Done* location
is entered, if the amount of items in the task queue is larger than allowed by
TASK_QUEUE_OVERLOAD, the *Overload* location is entered and if the deadline
of the currently selected task instance is already in the past, the *SchedulingError*
location is entered.

The auxiliary locations account for limitations of modeling the scheduling in
UPPAAL: clock values and integer variables are limited by int16 bounds of
the underlying C architecture (i.e., by $32,767$). Since a bound on time reduces
the analyzed state space, we allow setting it to even lower values: after having
reached the time set by the TIME_MAX constant, forces all automata to enter
the *Done* location, effectively reaching a verifiable end condition. As long as all
possible scheduling variations occur at least once during the time specified by
TIME_MAX (which has to be assured by the user), this is a sound optimization.

For systems with very large, diverse scheduling periods, the analysis can be
incomplete if not all variations are part of the simulation and verification process.
A possible mitigation might be to introduce an additional integer variable into
the system and increment these at a fixed interval, for example each $30,000$ time
steps, resetting the clock in the process. This would allow to keep track of larger
time spans but, on the other hand, increase the state space.

System Declarations. The system declarations are the last set of declarations in UPPAAL and are used to describe the system, which is the network
of timed automata that shall be simulated and verified. For this system, the
processing environments need to be defined by instantiating the relevant templates. The instantiation of templates works similar to the creation of objects
in object-oriented languages, the parameters are given during creation. After all
templates have been instantiated, the simulatable system must be defined using
the system directive and a comma-separated list of already created templates.
An excerpt of the system definitions covering the tasks of the motivating example is given in Listing 2. These structures cover just the basic task information;
for schedulability, they need to be embedded in either EDF or OSEK tasks and
passed to processing environments in arrays.

```
// Task definitions (ID, BCET, WCET)
const Task T1 = {1, 3, 4};      // getBrakePedalData
const Task T2 = {2, 6, 7};      // getSensorData
...
const OSEK_Task OT3 = { T3, 1, 30 }; // OSEK Task Definitions
const OSEK_Task OT4 = { T4, 2, 30 }; // (Task, Priority, Period)
const OSEK_Task OT6 = { T6, 3, 30 };
const OSEK_Task OT7 = { T7, 1, 30 };
const OSEK_Task OT8 = { T8, 1, 30 };
const EDF_Task ET1 = { T1, 15, 30 }; // EDF Task Definitions
const EDF_Task ET2 = { T2, 20, 30 }; // (Task, rel. Deadline, Period)
const EDF_Task ET5 = { T5, 25, 30 };
const EDF_Task ET9 = { T9, 30, 30 };
const EDF_Task PE1_Tasks[4] = { ET1, ET2, ET5, ET9 }; // Array
const OSEK_Task PE2_Tasks[3] = { OT3, OT4, OT6 };      // Compositions
const OSEK_Task PE3_Tasks[1] = { OT8 };
const OSEK_Task PE4_Tasks[1] = { OT7 };
PE1 = PE_4T_EDF(PE1_Tasks, 0);   // PE Definitions Template
PE2 = PE_3T_OSEK(PE2_Tasks, 1);  // (Task Array, Offset to Reference PE)
PE3 = PE_1T_OSEK(PE3_Tasks, 2);
PE4 = PE_1T_OSEK(PE4_Tasks, 3);
```

Listing 2. System Declaration for some Tasks from the Motivating Example.

4   Verification

In this section, we describe how safety properties can be encoded as TCTL queries using the the small example system from Sect. 3 for illustration. The verification of synchronicity (i.e., multiple tasks finishing within a given period of time) was realized but is not covered here in detail due to space constraints. Due to the way the clocks in timed automata work, each task runtime clock has a valuation of $v(c) \in [0, 1]$ when the corresponding task's simulation state is currently neither executing nor suspended. As a consequence, we are unable to reliably check whether a task has actually just started execution based on the runtime clocks and need to resort to location names and the broadcast channels. The location names used are from the task compounds shown in Fig. 4 (e.g., t1_start) and the indices that need to be used are given using italicized mathematical notation. Requirements are specified using function notation, where each requirement is represented using a function over one or multiple tasks.

4.1   Verification of Properties Using TCTL

We start by covering real-time requirements which we can verify using TCTL queries and the simulated network of timed automata representing processing environments. The requirements covered here are requirements over a single or over two tasks.

Maximum Execution Time of a Task. We will consider the *maximum execution time* (MET) of a task to describe the maximum amount of time that is allowed to pass between the start and finish events of any pair of the task's instances. Due to the existence of runtime clocks, the maximum execution time can easily be verified. As the UPPAAL model is time-bound by the constant

TIME_MAX, we need to prepend a condition to account for this upper bound. Otherwise a system state in which the requirement is not fulfilled can always be found outside of the valid time bounds, as the automata enter the *Done* state and do not continue resetting the clocks.

We have several clocks to choose from that can act as global clocks to compare to this time bound, mainly the clock of the reference system and the runtime or data age clocks of task ID 0; since PE IDs start at 1, those start at the beginning of the simulation and are never reset. Since the reference system may be declared with varying names, we will use rt_c[0] as the global clock for the following verification queries.

Assuming a specific task is represented using a task with the ID n in the UPPAAL model, we use the query

$$\text{A[] (rt\_c[0] <= TIME\_MAX) imply (rt\_c[n] <= MET}(\tau_n))$$

to check for validity of the requirement $\text{MET}(\tau_n)$.

Maximum Data Age. We define the *maximum data age* (MDA) to express the maximum amount of time that may pass between the finish event of one task τ_n and the start event of another task τ_m, essentially the age of the output data provided by τ_n used as input by τ_m. Just like with the execution time, the verification of the data age requirement was made easy in the model-building process by introducing the relevant clocks. Considering two tasks with IDs n, m deployed on the same processing environment with ID i, we can use the formula

$$\text{A[] (PE}i.tj\_start \text{ imply } (da\_c[n] <= \text{MDA}(\tau_n, \tau_m)))$$

to check whether $\text{MDA}(\tau_n, \tau_m)$ is upheld by the given system; where j is the index of task m on the processing environment *pe*, i.e., t1_start or t2_start on a processing environment with two tasks where t1_start belongs to the first task in the passed array and t2_start belongs to the second one.

Periodicity. We assume the *periodicity* (PER) requirement to be describing the maximum amount of time that may pass between two finish events of the same task. The verification of this requirement can be achieved easily as well, due to the fact that the data age clock is reset in the time step *after* the finish state, not before. Using the UPPAAL query

$$\text{A[] (PE}i.tj\_finish \text{ imply } (da\_c[n] <= (\text{PER}(\tau_n))))$$

we can verify whether a task with ID n running on the processing environment with ID i and the task array index j satisfies the requirement $\text{PER}(\tau_n)$.

Schedulability and Queue Overload. While not specifically a requirement, we can check whether a system might encounter an error during the simulation, namely a runtime scheduling error or a queue overload. All auxiliary error states in the templates are states with no outgoing edges. Since these error states are the only states in the whole automaton without outgoing edges, we can check

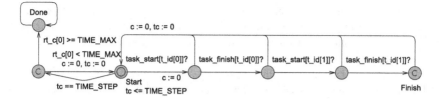

Fig. 5. Template for verification of an event chain of two tasks.

whether it is possible for the automaton to encounter a deadlock. We use the query "A[] not deadlock" to check for deadlock-freeness.

Task Execution. If there is a state in which the runtime clock of a task has a valuation exceeding that of a single time step, we know that the task was executed at least once as there exists at least one system state in which the corresponding runtime clock was not reset; note that this only works if the WCET of the task is indeed larger than the duration of a single tick. To check whether a task instance of a task with ID n is actually ever executed, we can use the query

    E[] (rt_c[0] <= TIME_MAX) and (rt_c[n] > 1)

using a conditional prefix depending on the time limit.

4.2   Verification Using Additional Automata and TCTL

All properties detailed in Sect. 4.1 expressed that either at a certain point in time or at all times the corresponding property must hold. For requirements that need information about a time span rather than a single point in time, or that react based on previous input or actions that cannot be expressed using simple TCTL queries, we will introduce additional automata into the simulated system. These give us the ability to react to multiple events in a single verification run, enabling state-aware verification for our model, which is necessary to verify both the synchronization constraint as well as the maximum reaction time requirement. Note that both of these requirements can range over an arbitrary amount of tasks and span multiple events over a time span.

Maximum Reaction Time of an Event Chain. We consider event chains to be a sequentially ordered set of events and only consider task start and finish events here, such that we can also create parameterizable templates for event chains. The idea is to move through the locations by reacting to the start and the finish events of the contained tasks. To actually catch all valid flows through the event chain, we introduce non-determinism, such that the event chain automaton can switch to the start location from every other location using a non-guarded transition, resetting its internal clock as well as its tick clock. As the automaton is required to transition when receiving on the broadcast channel and because the non-determinism introduces the ability for the automaton to always return to its start location, we need to ensure that there is no single valid event chain flow that violates the requirement. This is accomplished by the verification of the safety property using queries preceded by A[].

As parameters to the template, we can simply pass an array of numeric task IDs representing the tasks in the order they appear in their event chain. For an event chain template of n tasks, we define the parameters as const int[1, TASK_AMOUNT] t_id[n], for n = 2 the template would look like Fig. 5. The code of each event chain automaton template simply contains clock c; clock tc; and does not require any adjustments when changing the amount of tasks. When the automaton is properly defined, we can check for the MRT requirement using the event chain automaton's internal clock. Given an event chain ec_n, we can use a query

```
A[] (ecn.Finish imply ecn.c <= MRT(ecn))
```

to check whether each complete run of the event chain was within the specified bounds. This of course only works when the event chain does reach a finish state, which might not be true in every case. A query to check whether this happens is E<> ecn.Finish.

5   Evaluation

In this section, we briefly demonstrate how the presented approach can be applied using our motivational example. We have formalized the textual requirements from Sect. 2 and are using the system design from Listing 2, specified verification automata and TCTL queries. Table 2 shows an overview of the properties, the queries and their results. As indicated, most requirements are not met in the initial design of the brake-by-wire system. In these cases, using UPPAALs *Diagnostic Trace* option, we can get a snapshot of the automata network in a state where the requirement is violated. This helps us with identifying the root cause of the inconsistencies, assisting in the development of a system consistent with all requirements.

Table 2. TCTL queries and verdicts for the properties from Sect. 2.

Property	UPPAAL query	Verdict
$MET(\tau_7) = 28$	A[] (...) imply (rt_c[7] <= 28)	✔
$PER(\tau_7) = 40$	A[] PE4.t1_finish imply (da_c[7] <= 40)	✔
$MDA(\tau_2, \tau_8) = 12$	A[] PE3.t1_start imply (da_c[2] <= 12)	✘
$MDA(\tau_4, \tau_7) = 16$	A[] PE4.t1_start imply (da_c[4] <= 16)	✔
$MRT(ec_1) = 110$	A[] ec1.Finish imply ec1.c <= 110	✘
$MRT(ec_2) = 85$	A[] ec2.Finish imply ec2.c <= 85	✘
$MRT(ec_3) = 80$	A[] ec3.Finish imply ec3.c <= 80	✘
$SYNC(\tau_3, \tau_4, \tau_5) = 10$	A[] not sync1.Error	✘

We are able to analyze all presented properties of the brake-by-wire example. However, already when analyzing properties on this small example, it become obvious that state space explosion has to be addressed in order to scale to industrial processes and systems with several hundred functions and tens of control units. The **PSPACE**-completeness of model-checking using Timed Automata and TCTL can be partly mitigated by only incorporating the automata required for the verification into the system for each query, but when complex requirements like the reaction time of an event chain need to be checked on very large systems, additional assumptions that reduce the state space will become necessary.

6   Conclusion

We have developed an approach that allows to model-check the consistency of real-time requirements in distributed software systems using UPPAAL early in the development process—and especially long before precise simulations are feasible. With the provided set of UPPAAL templates, multiple timing requirements over such a system can be checked for inconsistencies and used as an indicator whether the basic assumptions require any modification. We have demonstrated the approach on a small brake-by-wire system. In a next step, we plan to evaluate performance and scalability in actual distributed automotive software systems.

References

1. SymTA/S. https://auto.luxoft.com/uth/timing-analysis-tools/
2. TA Simulator. https://www.timing-architects.com/
3. UPPAAL. http://www.uppaal.org/
4. Blom, H., et al.: Timing model - tools, algorithms, languages, methodology, use cases. Technical report (2012)
5. Buttazzo, G.C.: Hard Real-Time Computing Systems. Springer, Boston (2011). https://doi.org/10.1007/978-1-4614-0676-1
6. Cho, B., Kim, T., Choi, J.-Y.: CAN database verification framework using UPPAAL. Int. J. Comput. Theor. Eng. 9(6), 438–442 (2017)
7. Cucinotta, T., et al.: A real-time service-oriented architecture for industrial automation. IEEE Trans. Ind. Inform. 5(3), 267–277 (2009)
8. Frey, P.: A timing model for real-time control-systems and its application on simulation and monitoring of AUTOSAR systems. Ph.D. thesis (2011)
9. Frtunikj, J.: Safety framework and platform for functions of future automotive E/E systems. Automot. Engine Technol. 1, 93–105 (2016)
10. Fuhrman, T., Wang, S., Jersak, M., Richter, K.: On designing software architectures for next-generation multi-core ECUs. SAE Int. J. Passeng. Cars Electron. Electr. Syst. 8, 115–123 (2015)
11. Kim, J.H., Larsen, K.G., Nielsen, B., Mikučionis, M., Olsen, P.: Formal analysis and testing of real-time automotive systems using UPPAAL tools. In: Núñez, M., Güdemann, M. (eds.) FMICS 2015. LNCS, vol. 9128, pp. 47–61. Springer, Cham (2015). https://doi.org/10.1007/978-3-319-19458-5_4

12. Leteinturier, P., Brewerton, S., Scheibert, K.: Multicore benefits & challenges for automotive applications. In: SAE Technical Paper. SAE International, April 2008
13. Line, C., Manzie, C., Good, M.: Control of an electromechanical brake for automotive brake-by-wire systems with an adapted motion control architecture. In: SAE Technical Paper Series. SAE International, May 2004
14. Pan, C., Guo, J., Zhu, L., Shi, J., Zhu, H., Zhou, X.: Modeling and verification of CAN bus with application layer using UPPAAL. Electron. Notes Theor. Comput. Sci. **309**, 31–49 (2014)
15. Pretschner, A., Broy, M., Kruger, I.H., Stauner, T.: Software engineering for automotive systems: a roadmap. In: Future of Software Engineering (FOSE 2007). IEEE, May 2007
16. Rettberg, A., Zanella, M.C., Amann, M., Keckeisen, M., Rammig, F.J. (eds.): IESS 2009. IFIPAICT, vol. 310. Springer, Heidelberg (2009). https://doi.org/10.1007/978-3-642-04284-3
17. Sagstetter, F.: Schedule synthesis for time-triggered automotive architectures. Dissertation, Technische Universität München, München (2016)
18. Scheickl, O.: Timing constraints in distributed development of automotive real-time systems. Dissertation, Technische Universität München, München (2011)
19. Schneider, R., Brewerton, S., Eberhard, D.: Multicore vs safety. In: SAE Technical Paper. SAE International, April 2010
20. Thane, H., Hansson, H.: Testing distributed real-time systems. Microprocess. Microsyst. **24**(9), 463–478 (2001)

Formal Verification of a Programmable Hypersurface

Panagiotis Kouvaros[1], Dimitrios Kouzapas[1], Anna Philippou[1(✉)],
Julius Georgiou[2], Loukas Petrou[2], and Andreas Pitsillides[1]

[1] Department of Computer Science, University of Cyprus, Nicosia, Cyprus
{pkouva01,dkouza01,annap,cspitsil}@cs.ucy.ac.cy
[2] Department of Electrical and Computer Engineering,
University of Cyprus, Nicosia, Cyprus
{julio,lpetro02}@ucy.ac.cy

Abstract. A metasurface is a surface that consists of artificial material, called metamaterial, with configurable electromagnetic properties. This paper presents work in progress on the design and formal verification of a programmable metasurface, the Hypersurface, as part of the requirements of the VISORSURF research program (HORIZON 2020 FET-OPEN). The Hypersurface design is concerned with the development of a network of switch controllers that are responsible for configuring the metamaterial. The design of the Hypersurface, however, has demanding requirements that need to be delivered within a context of limited resources. This paper shares the experience of a rigorous design procedure for the Hypersurface network, that involves iterations between designing a network and its protocols and the formal evaluation of each design. Formal evaluation has provided results that, so far, drive the development team in a more robust design and overall aid in reducing the cost of the Hypersurface manufacturing.

1 Introduction

This paper reports on work-in-progress carried out in the context of the research programme "VISORSURF: A Hardware Platform for Software-driven Functional Metasurfaces" [1], funded by Horizon 2020 FET-OPEN. VISORSURF is an inter-disciplinary programme between computer science (networks/nano-networks and formal methods), computer engineering (circuit design and implementation), and physics (meta-materials). Its main objective is to develop a hardware platform, the *HyperSurface* (HSF), whose electromagnetic behavior can be defined programmatically. The HSF's enabling technology are *metasurfaces*, artificial materials whose electromagnetic properties depend on their internal structure. Controlling the HSF is a network of controller switches which receives external

This work was partially funded by the European Union via the Horizon 2020: Future Emerging Topics call (FETOPEN), grant EU736876, project VISORSURF (http://www.visorsurf.eu).

© Springer Nature Switzerland AG 2018
F. Howar and J. Barnat (Eds.): FMICS 2018, LNCS 11119, pp. 83–97, 2018.
https://doi.org/10.1007/978-3-030-00244-2_6

software commands and alters the metasurface structure yielding a desired electromagnetic behavior, thus allowing a number of high-impact applications. These include electromagnetic invisibility of objects, filtering and steering of light and sound, as well as ultra-efficient antennas for sensors and communication devices.

This paper is concerned with the requirement of the programme for the rigorous design and formal evaluation of the controller-switches network and its protocols. This requirement stems from the project's challenge to provide cutting-edge technology with limitations in both time and cost. Indeed, it is of paramount importance for the produced hardware to adhere to its specification from the very first version of the product, given the high cost of producing the components and the fact that the project's budget is fixed. The specification includes qualitative properties, e.g., the controller network should route all messages correctly to all network nodes, as well as quantitative properties, since nodes need to be reached within specified time bounds in a fault-tolerant manner while preserving power.

Typically, in the networks literature, evaluation of network topologies and protocols is carried out via extensive simulation using discrete-event simulators such as NS-2 or OPNET, or via testbed experiments. While these are important evaluation methods, the results obtained are highly dependent on the physical-layer models supported by the simulators and, in the case of experiments, they are not suitable during the design phase of a protocol. At the same time, as is well known, the simulative approach may discover flaws in a system but it cannot prove their absence. On the other hand, formal analysis techniques allow to formally verify that a system complies to its specifications and check for the absence of flaws. Model checking, in particular, allows to investigate the behavior of a model via an exhaustive search of its state space. Properties of interest may be enunciated in temporal logic and subsequently checked for satisfaction on all possible executions of the system. In case of property violation, counter-examples can be provided to support the designer to diagnose the error. Model checking has been applied for the analysis and design of network protocols in a number of works including [3,10,11].

Unfortunately, a main drawback associated with model checking is the state-space explosion problem and on many occasions analysis cannot be applied on systems of a realistic size. To this effect, the use of statistical model checking (SMC) has been advocated. Statistical model checking [18,20] is a formal-analysis approach that combines ideas of model checking and simulation with the aim of supporting quantitative analysis as well as addressing the state-space explosion problem. It uses Monte Carlo style sampling and hypothesis testing to provide evidence that a system satisfies a given property with high probability. The main idea is to simulate the system for finitely many runs and use hypothesis testing to infer whether the samples provide a statistical evidence for the satisfaction or violation of the specification. Naturally, the greater the number of simulations, the higher the precision achieved. The benefits of employing statistical model checking towards the analysis of network algorithms have been illustrated in various works including [8,12,13].

As required by the project's objectives, our goal has been to develop a set of network protocols (network initialisation, routing and reporting) on a grid network (a Manhattan style topology [16] imposed by the hardware requirements of the project). In this paper we focus on the design of the routing algorithm, which proved to be the main challenge of the work. Routing within grid networks has been a topic of thorough investigation within the network community and it has been of great interest in domains such as networks on chip [2,9]. Various algorithms have been proposed in the literature for mesh topologies where the main challenges posed were towards providing efficiency and tolerance to faults [6,15,17,19]. While these works influenced the development of our routing protocol, the various restrictions imposed by the specific application, such as the limited connectivity as well as the limited resources available to each network node (e.g. limited memory/buffering space, limited computational capabilities) rendered the design of the routing algorithm quite challenging. Indeed, it turns out that apparently innocent characteristics of our model (e.g. the lack of line/-column wrap-arounds) create the risk of deadlocks, even in the absence of faults in the network. To address this problem (discovered via model checking), it was necessary to explore options such as introducing buffers in the nodes or adopting different routing sequences so as to handle the congestion of parts of the network, and to seek methods for assessing these options and provide guarantees that they satisfy the set requirements.

Taking the requirements of VISORSURF into account has led us to employ formal methods from the initial stages of the iterative design of the network protocols via a continuous assessment of design proposals against requirements using model checking. Early on, our experimentation confirmed that the state-space explosion problem is a severe limitation when attempting to analyse a network of a reasonable size. Thus, we turned towards Statistical Model Checking (SMC) and we employed the UPPAAL tool and, more specifically, its SMC extension [5]. In this paper we report on our experience of applying formal methods in the design phase of a routing algorithm on a grid network as imposed by the hardware requirements of the project, and how this led to important design decisions, thus significantly facilitating us towards our goal. Furthermore, we discuss the main challenges we faced in obtaining desired results which point out directions for further research. We believe that our conclusions provide evidence on the impact formal methods may have in the design and implementation of technological applications in the context of small and medium-scale projects.

2 The Hypersurface: Requirements and Design Parameters

In this section we present the main requirements and design parameters of the Hypersurface, as imposed in the context of the VISORSURF programme and as needed in the present discussion. We identify three levels of requirements: (i) architectural/physical constraints as imposed by the physical level of the HSF; (ii) VISORSURF programme requirements as approved by the funding authority; and (iii) resource/manufacturability limitations, in both time and money that make the design phase a non-trivial task.

Architectural/Physical Constraints and Terminology. The *metasurface tile* is a surface consisting of configurable meta-material strips arranged as a grid. A set of four meta-material strips is configured via a controller switch, also called the *intra-tile controller*. All intra-tile controllers of the HSF are interconnected to constitute the *intra-tile network*. Intra-tile controllers will be designed and implemented as a single hardware element and their purpose is to implement basic functionalities, most importantly, support the rudimentary routing of *configuration packets* for configuring the metamaterial.

The intra-tile network receives configuration data from one or more *gateway controllers*. A gateway controller resides on the periphery of the metasurface and it sends configuration packets to controllers throughout the network that, in turn, are programmed by the user. A gateway controller has full computing power. It is envisaged that tiles will be interconnected at the gateway controller level to form larger metasurfaces.

VISORSURF Requirements. As already explained, an intra-tile controller's main task is to set the EM properties of the meta-material strips as directed via configuration packets from the gateway. Note that these packets are directives for appropriately implementing a desired functionality (e.g., to absorb or steer impinging waves) and, for any given function, they consist of one message per network controller. Such a set of configuration packets can be delivered in any order, thus allowing the flexibility to the gateway to decide on the sequence in which the packets will be delivered to the controller nodes. We refer to such sequences as *configuration sequences*.

In addition, intra-tile controllers are expected to report acknowledgements and status to the gateway, thus enabling the monitoring of the state of the controller network in real time and hence "debug" the HyperSurface program. As such, the intra-tile controller network needs to implement routing for both data and acknowledgement packets. The routing should be flexible, scalable, and robust. Furthermore, packets should be delivered in a timely manner (where the timing constraints will be determined in the course of the project). Finally, the intra-tile network needs to provide mechanisms that support a high degree of fault tolerance, where data packets will continue to be delivered to the recipient controllers despite hardware faults.

Resource/Manufacturability Limitations. The programme is required to deliver a functioning HSF prototype within a specific amount of time, money, human, and expertise resources.

The main hardware element to be manufactured is the intra-tile controller. To limit the overall cost, a single uniform type of controller will be designed and manufactured. The selected chip technology for the controller manufacturing allows for a maximum number of 25 pins per intra-tile controller chip. The restriction limits the interconnection capabilities of an intra-tile controller with other components of the metasurface such as its connectivity with its neighbouring controllers as well as with the gateway. A consequence of this restriction is that intra-tile controllers will transmit data in a single bit-by-bit scheme. Moreover, this communication will be implemented asynchronously via an appropriate four-way asynchronous communication hardware protocol. Asynchronous communication uses no clock for synchronisation. Instead, the sender relies on the acknowledgement signal of the receiver to start and end a transmission. The restriction of asynchronous communication was imposed since adding a clock to the chip of the controller would have the following undesirable implications: (i) require more components, such as a crystal that will increase the chip size, and a phase-lock loop responsible for inter-controller synchronisation; (ii) increase power consumption; and (iii) make a total metasurface absorber impossible because of the clock's electromagnetic emissions. Finally, we mention that intra-tile chips will only possess volatile memory since non-volatile memory is expensive and error-prone.

2.1   Hypersurface Manufacturing: Iteration-0

In order to mitigate the implementation risk, manufacturing of the intra-tile chip will take place in iterations. The first manufacturing iteration is expected to implement a basic but working prototype, and the entire design process will be completed for the final deliverable.

The experience presented in this paper will be implemented in the first manufacturing iteration: iteration-0. Despite its basic functionality, iteration-0 identifies the elements that are going to be used by all future iterations: controller hardware and communication protocols, controller pin allocation, network topology, packet format, basic extendable routing protocol, and basic functionalities.

The initial design for iteration-0 can be found in Figs. 1 and 2. The three diagrams in Fig. 1 demonstrate the allocation of the pins and the communication channel endpoints on the intra-tile controller chip. Each channel endpoint requires three pins to implement bit-by-bit asynchronous communication. The limited number of pins (25) limits to a design where only four unidirectional channel endpoints can be allocated (a total of 12 pins) per controller. The physical distribution of the pins is as in diagram (b).

Following the design of the intra-tile controller, the suggestion for a grid topology is a variation of the Manhattan network topology [16] as presented in Fig. 2. Its main characteristic is that the routing direction alternates at each

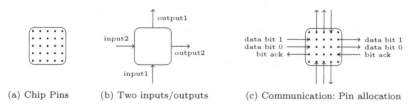

(a) Chip Pins   (b) Two inputs/outputs   (c) Communication: Pin allocation

Fig. 1. Pin allocation.

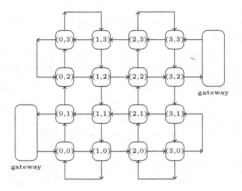

Fig. 2. Manhattan topology with edge wraparound

consecutive row and column. The topology is achieved by rotating the single design intra-tile controller by 90° each time to get the four different orientations (a–d) that are shown in Fig. 3. The interconnection of the four orientations is used to achieve the Manhattan topology; depending on the physical orientation of each intra-tile controller an output endpoint is connected to the corresponding input endpoint of a neighboring intra-tile controller. Each intra-tile controller has knowledge about its type based on its address.

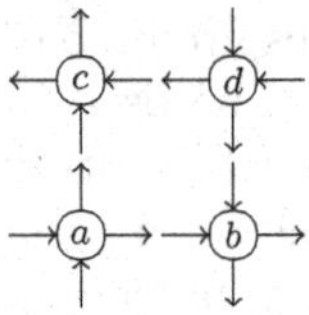

Fig. 3. Controller four different orientations

The proposed topology offers a flexible and robust network, which respects the design constraints: it provides connectivity between the network nodes using only two input and two output edges per node. Unlike the Manhattan networks considered in the literature, the proposed topology provides connections (and consequently bidirectional communication) between neighbouring periphery nodes, which we refer to as *wrap-arounds*, thus employing all communication channels of the nodes and providing connectivity between all nodes. Our design choice of connecting neighboring periphery nodes and not the ends of each row and each column is due to the hardware implementation: crossing the interconnection wires would require to add extra layers on the PCB board that embeds the meta-surface. Furthermore, the edge controllers would require components, e.g. transistors, with more signal drive to send signals over longer wires.

Moving now to the programming of the chip, we point out that there are two modes of operation: the initialisation mode and the normal operation mode. This paper is concerned with evaluating the normal operation mode. The initialisation mode is used to initialise each intra-tile controller with a unique address and with additional initialisation data. This is necessary since, as already discussed, only a single type of controller will be produced and will not possess any non-volatile memory. This has led to the design of a simple initialisation protocol that will assign an address to each controller (its X-Y coordinates), which will be stored at its volatile memory, and, based on which each controller will determine its "type" based on its coordinates.

In the normal operation mode, due to the limited computing power of the intra-tile controller, we are experimenting with variants of the simple XY routing protocol [6], adopted for the Manhattan topology. Below there is the simple XY protocol variant adopted for the iteration-0 design (Table 1). The XY routing protocol assumes a Cartesian coordination system at the intra-tile controllers grid. The implementation assumes a gateway controller connected at the south west corner of the network grid and sending routing packets to intra-tile controller $(0, 0)$. The protocol first routes a packet on the x-axis until it reaches the target x-coordinate and then similarly on the y-axis until it reaches the target. In a Manhattan topology we assume a standard mapping of the four directions "up", "down", "left", "right" on each intra-tile controller depending on its orientation. Upon receiving a configuration packet, an intra-tile controller creates an acknowledgement packet to be routed to a gateway controller.

Table 1. Pseudocode for the XY routing protocol variant

```
 1 XY routing algorithm(packet)
 2      x, y: address a, b: target address
 3
 4 (a, b) = packet
 5   if (x == a) {
 6     if (y == b)
 7        send ack;
 8     else if (y < b)
 9        send packet up
10     else if (y > b)
11        send packet down
12   }
13 else if (x < a - 1)
14     send packet right
15 else if (x == a - 1) {
16      if (x mod 2 = 0 and y < b)
17        send packet up
18      else
19        send packet right
20 }
21 else if (x > a) {
22      if (y == b)
23        send packet left
24      else if (y < b)
25        send packet up
26      else if (y > b)
27        send packet left
28 }
```

The development of the iteration-0 design has undergone several cycles between design and analysis. The parameters considered at each iteration include the number and position of the gateway controllers, the presence of buffer space to store received packets at each intra-tile controller as well as the capability of the controllers for parallel processing/routing of packets. The next section describe the model and the evaluation of each design following the design parameters of the topology.

3   Formal Evaluation

This section describes the encoding of the routing protocol in the input language of the UPPAAL SMC model checker and its subsequent evaluation. UPPAAL SMC is the statistical extension of UPPAAL, a model checker for real-time systems represented by networks of timed automata [5]. The reasons for the selection of the tool to carry out the formal evaluation of the protocols here considered are threefold. First, our design is associated with dense time behaviour and requirements. Second, UPPAAL implements statistical reasoning about properties of timed systems. Given the large state space generated by the models, statistical model checking enables the derivation of results for larger networks than if we had used standard model checking. Second, it supports basic data structures expressed in the syntax of the C programming language, thereby allowing for concise encodings of the system's features, e.g. buffers.

3.1   UPPAAL SMC Models

The modelling here presented admits the following assumptions. First, the network is a 10×10 grid (as discussed in the future work section parameterised model checking techniques are envisaged to enable the effective verification of larger models [4]). Second, in line with the intended operation of the system, the models account only for the routing of configuration sequences and not of arbitrary sequences of packets. Finally, given that nodes are identical (thus have the same speed) and are operating very fast, we assume the presence of a global clock and we assume that at every tick of the clock all nodes that may fire a transition will fire one transition. Following the manufacturing of the first prototype chip, timing measurements (in the form of time bounds for each operation) will be provided and encoded in the model in order to obtain a more precise timing analysis.

Table 2 summarises the system variants that have been considered during the lifetime of the iteration-0 design process. The basic variant is as described above and assumes a single gateway at the south-west corner of the grid. As we show below, the basic system exhibits deadlocks in routing configuration sequences. Consequently, alternative designs had to be evaluated so as to "eliminate" the deadlocks while limiting the time requirements of the routing scheme. In particular, the parallel variant assumes that nodes are equipped with a different processing unit per output. More precisely, this option is implemented in the presence of buffers within the nodes. The buffers are used to store messages received at a node until they are forwarded on the appropriate output, as per their destination node and the XY algorithm. Note, however, that such sending may fail if the recipient node is not ready to receive (e.g. because its buffer is

Table 2. System variants

Variant	Acknowledgements	Parallel processing	Queue size
basic	SW	No	0
parallel	SW	Yes	1 (to model parallelism)
acks-NE	NE	No	0
queue-X	SW	No	X

already full). While in the `basic` mode the sending node will be forced to remain idle and to retry sending the message in the next time unit, in the `parallel` mode, and assuming there exist further messages in its buffer, the node will attempt to send a message on its other output channel, assuming that such a message exists. Note that this mode was implemented in order to explore the design possibility of implementing two independent circuits within a controller chip, one per output channel.

The `acks-NE` variant includes a second gateway taking input from the northeast corner of the network where the acknowledgements are routed as per the XY routing algorithm (see the topology in Fig. 2). Intuitively, this is expected to limit the congestion emerging from routing acknowledgements from north-east coordinates to south-west ones and data packets from south-west coordinates to north-east ones in the `basic` variant. Note that this design choice is also feasible given that multiple tiles, each with its own gateway, are expected to be interconnected in the final metasurface, offering the possibility of connecting multiple tiles to the same gateway. Finally the `queue-X` variant implements a queue of size X for every node in the network.

All system variants are given by the parallel composition of 100 timed automata modelling the nodes, and a timed automaton (automata, respectively) representing the gateway (gateways, respectively). The communication between the nodes is encoded by means of four-dimensional adjacency matrices of pairwise communication channels, where item $[x][y][x'][y']$ denotes the communication channel taking input from node (x, y) and outputting to node (x', y').

Figure 4 depicts the timed automaton modelling the nodes. The automaton is composed of two states (locations) and ten transitions. Initially a node is in state *idle*. On the receipt of a message from either input *in1* or *in2* ($input_1$, $input_2$ in Fig. 1(b)), the node goes to state *Processing*. The state models the processing of the data of the packet before the latter is routed to its destination. Whilst in this state, a node may perform either one of the following actions: (i) if it is not the destination node, then it can route the packet to one of its neighbours according to the XY algorithm; (ii) if it is the destination node, then it will create and route an acknowledgement to one of its neighbours towards a gateway (either in the south-west or the north-east corner depending on the mode of the experiment); (iii) if it is equipped with buffers, then it may receive a second packet which it enqueues in its buffer. In the figure every transition is guarded by a boolean condition determining whether or not the transition

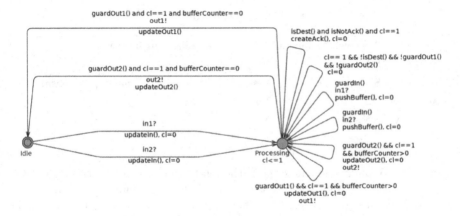

Fig. 4. Timed automaton for intra-tile controller

can be fired. The condition requires from the sender-receiver pair to respect the XY routing scheme and from the receiver to be in a state where the packet can be queued. Further conditions guarding the transitions enable the synchronous evolution of the system. Specifically a node can perform an action only when its local clock is equal to 1; following the action, the node resets its clock; if there is no enabled action the node simply resets its clock whenever this equals 1.

The timed automata modelling the gateways are responsible for generating configuration sequences and for receiving the acknowledgements sent by the nodes. Following the topology of the network, different orderings of the packets in a configuration sequence may induce different settings for deadlocks and time requirements in routing the sequence. We therefore consider the following configuration sequences generated by the gateway:

1. SW → NE(x). The packets are sent row by row from south to north, and the packets in a row are sent from west to east.
2. SW → NE(y). The packets are sent column by column from west to east, and the packets in a column are sent from south to north.
3. NE → SW(x). The packets are sent row by row from north to south, and the packets in a row are sent from east to west.
4. NE → SW(y). The packets are sent column by column from east to west, and the packets in a column are sent from north to south.
5. NE ↔ SW. The packets are sent alternating between the SW → NE(x) and NE → SW(x) orderings at every packet sent.

Indeed, as we show below, the commitment to certain orderings can enable the implementation of simple, deadlock-free designs by building smart gateways.

3.2   Evaluation

We report the experimental results obtained by checking the system variants against specifications pertaining to deadlock-freedom and efficiency in routing configurations sequences:

$$\phi_{ack} \triangleq E[\leq 300; 1000](max : acks)$$
$$\phi_{time} \triangleq E[\leq 300; 1000](max : time)$$

Above, acks is a variable representing the number of acknowledgements that have been received whereas time is a variable expressing the time taken for all acknowledgements to be received. ϕ_{ack} gives the expected maximum value of acks whereas ϕ_{time} determines the expected maximum value of *time*. These are calculated on the first 300 time units, where empirical evaluation showed this to be an upper bound for the completion of the protocol, and for 1000 traces. During the lifespan of the iteration-0 design phase, the specifications were evaluated on progressively more complicated designs so as to derive the simplest one for which ϕ_{ack} is maximised and ϕ_{time} is minimised.

Table 3 summarises the results obtained. The cells with colour demonstrate the cases where not all acknowledgements where received at the gateway, thus the case where a deadlock is present. Note that the times acquired in case of a deadlock include the deadlock traces and are thus irrelevant.

Table 3. Experimental results.

Order	System variant	ϕ_{ack}	ϕ_{time}
SW → NE(x)	basic	40.85 ± 1.23	299.78 ± 0.17
	queue-1	100	216.7 ± 0.35
	parallel	100	211.46 ± 0.34
	acks-NE	99.14 ± 0.27	226.598 ± 0.79
	acks-NE-queue-1	100	201.37 ± 0.22
SW → NE(y)	basic	2.77 ± 0.05	300
	queue-5	100	243.03 ± 0.43
	parallel	98.74 ± 0.68	244.98 ± 0.57
	acks-NE	97.82 ± 0.22	267.38 ± 0.24
	acks-NE-queue-1	100	213.38 ± 0.19
NE → SW(x)	basic	94.27 ± 0.72	258.49 ± 1.43
	queue-5	100	259.54 ± 0.34
	parallel	100	209.19 ± 0.31
	acks-NE	100	218.58 ± 0.12
NE → SW(y)	basic	15.94 ± 0.86	300
	queue-6	100	260.92 ± 0.31
	parallel	98.06 ± 0.84	300
	acks-NE	100	219.53 ± 0.14
NE ↔ SW	basic	71.65 ± 0.94	300
	queue-1	100	216.6 ± 0.37
	parallel	89.04 ± 0.27	300
	acks-NE	100	200.36 ± 0.31

Evidently, the `basic` model exhibits deadlocks under all of the configuration sequence orderings. Figure 5 (left) shows an UPPAAL-generated simulation trace showcasing a deadlock for the SW → NE(x) ordering. In the figure, node $(0, 2)$ is trying to route a data packet to node $(1, 3)$ through node $(0, 3)$, which in turn is trying to route an acknowledgement packet to node $(0, 1)$ through node $(0, 3)$. Consequently node $(0, 2)$ is waiting on node $(0, 3)$ and node $(0, 3)$ is waiting on node $(0, 2)$, thereby creating a deadlock.

The inclusion of queue structures in the nodes may eliminate deadlocks. Interestingly, to achieve this, different sizes of queues are required for different configuration sequence orderings, ranging from size 1 for the SW → NE(x) and NE ↔ SW orderings, to size 6 for the NE → SW(y) ordering. Furthermore, the routing of packets under the former orderings is more efficient. The use of parallel processing can also help to overcome deadlocks, but only in cases SW → NE(x), NE → SW(x), while allowing for more efficient routing in the said cases.

The routing of the acknowledgements to a second gateway attached to the north-east corner of the network can also help alleviate the deadlocks in the NE → SW(x), NE → SW(y) and NE ↔ SW orderings by, intuitively, reducing the congestion near the SW gateway. In the other cases, adding a queue of size 1 is sufficient to prohibit deadlocks from occurring. Given that the size of the queues required is smaller than the corresponding cases with only one gateway, routing in the presence of two gateways appears to be more efficient.

Since the gateways are cheaper than designing and implementing queue systems and/or parallel processing capabilities, the above experimental results suggest the design of a system with two gateways as preferable for the purposes of the project. Moreover, the second gateway design offers additional flexibility and is compatible with the intended design of connecting tiles at the gateway level to form larger metasurfaces.

A point of interest regarding the `acks-NE` design is the nature of the deadlock as illustrated in Table 3. Figure 5 (right) shows a part of an UPPAAL-generated simulation trace that demonstrates the deadlock in a 4×4 size grid. The problem arises when a configuration packet is routed towards controller $(3, 1)$, as shown with red colour. The packet necessarily needs to be routed through controller $(3, 2)$, which is connected to the acknowledgement gateway. Also, in the problematic trace it happens that the configuration packet is interleaved with acknowledgement packets, as shown with green colour, that are routed towards controller $(3, 2)$. The interleaving creates an input/output dependency between controllers $(2, 1)$, $(2, 2)$, $(3, 2)$, and $(3, 1)$. Further experimentation revealed that the presence of deadlocks in the `acks-NE` design is due to similar cyclical dependencies among four interconnected controllers, where acknowledgement packets and configuration packets towards different destinations are interleaved.

Note, however, that deadlocks are removed when adding a queue of size 1. Moreover, further experiments carried out for different grid sizes and various configuration-sequence orderings confirmed the absence of deadlock with such a queue. Intuitively, this can be understood as follows: A queue allows for storing the interleaved packets to the receivers buffer and proceed by processing the next

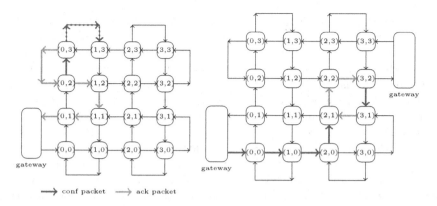

Fig. 5. Left: Trace showcasing a deadlock for the `basic` system under the SW → NE(x) configuration sequence ordering. Right: Trace showcasing a deadlock for the `acks-NE` system under the SW → NE(x) configuration sequence ordering.

packet that will be sent to a different destination. In a set of nodes associated with a circular dependency, there exists at least one node (in Fig. 5 (right) node $(3, 1)$) that cannot receive input on both of its edges. Thus, the buffer of this node will enable to break the circular dependency and allow the flow of packets along the cycle. For instance, in the example of Fig. 5 (right) the configuration packet from controller $(3, 2)$ to controller $(3, 1)$ can be stored in the queue of controller $(3, 1)$, thus breaking the circular dependency.

4   Conclusions and Future Work

The formal analysis here presented provided partial guarantees and useful insights on the behaviour of the protocols and have driven their development. These were used in iterations between designing the Hypersurface and verifying its specifications. The formal evaluation was complemented through extensive simulations via a simulator specifically built in the context of the project to support the protocol evaluation. It is worth mentioning that the formal evaluation was able to pinpoint problems in instances of the model that were not discovered by the simulator (though they were verified by it) and, additionally, the formal approach had the advantage of building models and versions of the algorithm much faster than implementing them within the simulator.

However, a number of obstacles were encountered in the process of analysing the Hypersurface. To begin with, one of the main bottlenecks was that of time. Indeed even in the context of statistical model checking, analysis of values required a non-negligible time: our experiments took up to ten minutes when run on a cluster of 12 dual-core CPUs with 24 GB RAM, and this only for 1000 simulations (which by experimentation we concluded provides an acceptable estimation of the properties in question). Furthermore, also relating to the state-space explosion problem is the fact that we have to limit our analysis for specific configuration sequences, though in principle it would be useful to check algorithm correctness for arbitrary configuration sequences. Finally, the analysis of the results, in the cases where they highlighted problems in the execution of the algorithm, were difficult to interpret. Thus, in order to extract deadlocks in problematic models, it was necessary to devise additional queries which we run by standard model checking. In this respect, it would be useful if the tool could be directed to store specific traces during the analysis.

As future work, there are various directions to explore. In the context of the VISORSURF project, our efforts will continue to improve the design of the algorithms and extend the models with more details (e.g. timing information). At the same time, as the analysis metrics are being developed, further analysis will be carried out to confirm that the network complies to more detailed specifications.

In addition, as we have already pointed out, due to the state-space explosion problem our analysis is restricted by the size of the network and the packet configuration sequences.

To alleviate this shortcoming, sophisticated state-space reduction techniques need to be developed, thereby enabling the effective verification of the Hypersurface. In particular we will develop parameterised model checking techniques that enable conclusions to be drawn *irrespectively* of the size of the network [4]. Specifically we believe the networks will admit *cutoffs* expressing the number of nodes that is sufficient to consider in order to conclude correctness for any number of nodes [7,14].

Finally, the HSF design needs not only to be shown correct but also *robust* against adverse functioning conditions. Thus, we intend to analyse the behaviour of our design under various fault models and extend our routing protocols to fault-tolerant versions, as needed.

References

1. VisorSurf: a hardware platform for software-driven functional metasurfaces. http://www.visorsurf.eu/
2. Benini, L., DeMicheli, G.: Networks on chips: a new SoC paradigm. IEEE Comput. **35**(1), 70–78 (2002)
3. Bhargavan, K., Obradovic, D., Gunter, C.A.: Formal verification of standards for distance vector routing protocols. J. ACM **49**(4), 538–576 (2002)
4. Bloem, R., et al.: Decidability of Parameterized Verification. Morgan and Claypool Publishers, San Rafael (2015)
5. Bulychev, P.E., et al.: UPPAAL-SMC: statistical model checking for priced timed automata. In: Proceedings of QAPL 2012, vol. 85. EPTCS, pp. 1–16 (2012)
6. Chawade, S., Gaikwad, M., Patrikar, R.: Review of XY routing algorithm for network-on-chip architecture. Int. J. Comput. Appl. **43**, 20–23 (2012)
7. Clarke, E., Talupur, M., Touili, T., Veith, H.: Verification by network decomposition. In: Gardner, P., Yoshida, N. (eds.) CONCUR 2004. LNCS, vol. 3170, pp. 276–291. Springer, Heidelberg (2004). https://doi.org/10.1007/978-3-540-28644-8_18

8. Dal Corso, A., Macedonio, D., Merro, M.: Statistical model checking of Ad Hoc routing protocols in lossy grid networks. In: Havelund, K., Holzmann, G., Joshi, R. (eds.) NFM 2015. LNCS, vol. 9058, pp. 112–126. Springer, Cham (2015). https://doi.org/10.1007/978-3-319-17524-9_9

9. Dally, W.J., Towles, B.: Route packets, not wires: on-chip interconnection networks. In: Proceedings of DAC 2001, pp. 684–689. ACM (2001)

10. Dombrowski, C., Junges, S., Katoen, J., Gross, J.: Model-checking assisted protocol design for ultra-reliable low-latency wireless networks. In: Proceedings of SRDS 2016, pp. 307–316. IEEE Computer Society (2016)

11. Fehnker, A., van Glabbeek, R., Höfner, P., McIver, A., Portmann, M., Tan, W.L.: Automated analysis of AODV using UPPAAL. In: Flanagan, C., König, B. (eds.) TACAS 2012. LNCS, vol. 7214, pp. 173–187. Springer, Heidelberg (2012). https://doi.org/10.1007/978-3-642-28756-5_13

12. Höfner, P., Kamali, M.: Quantitative analysis of AODV and its variants on dynamic topologies using statistical model checking. In: Braberman, V., Fribourg, L. (eds.) FORMATS 2013. LNCS, vol. 8053, pp. 121–136. Springer, Heidelberg (2013). https://doi.org/10.1007/978-3-642-40229-6_9

13. Höfner, P., McIver, A.: Statistical model checking of wireless mesh routing protocols. In: Brat, G., Rungta, N., Venet, A. (eds.) NFM 2013. LNCS, vol. 7871, pp. 322–336. Springer, Heidelberg (2013). https://doi.org/10.1007/978-3-642-38088-4_22

14. Kouvaros, P., Lomuscio, A.: Parameterised verification for multi-agent systems. Artif. Intell. 234, 152–189 (2016)

15. Li, M., Zeng, Q., Jone, W.: DyXY: a proximity congestion-aware deadlock-free dynamic routing method for network on chip. In: Proceedings of DAC 2006, pp. 849–852. ACM (2006)

16. Maxemchuk, N.F.: Regular mesh topologies in local and metropolitan area networks. AT&T Tech. J. 64(7), 1659–1685 (1985)

17. Patooghy, A., Miremadi, S.: XYX: a power and performance efficient fault- tolerant routing algorithm for network on chip. In: Proceedings of PDP 2009, pp. 245–251. IEEE Computer Society (2009)

18. Sen, K., Viswanathan, M., Agha, G.A.: VESTA: a statistical model-checker and analyzer for probabilistic systems. In: Proceedings of QEST 2005, pp. 251–252. IEEE Computer Society (2005)

19. Wu, J.: A fault-tolerant and deadlock-free routing protocol in 2D meshes based on odd-even turn model. IEEE Trans. Comput. 52(9), 1154–1169 (2003)

20. Younes, H.S.: Verification and planning for stochastic processes with asynchrounous events. Ph.D. thesis, Carnegie Mellon University (2004)

Modelling and Analysing ERTMS Hybrid Level 3 with the mCRL2 Toolset

Maarten Bartholomeus[1], Bas Luttik[2(✉)], and Tim Willemse[2]

[1] ProRail, Utrecht, The Netherlands
[2] Eindhoven University of Technology, Eindhoven, The Netherlands
{s.p.luttik,t.a.c.willemse}@tue.nl

Abstract. ERTMS Hybrid Level 3 is a recent proposal for a train control system specification that serves to increase the capacity of the railway network by allowing multiple trains with an integrity monitoring system and a GSM-R connection to the trackside on a single section. In this paper we model the principles of ERTMS Hybrid Level 3 in the mCRL2 process algebra and perform an analysis with its associated toolset. Our analysis has resulted in suggestions for improvement of the principles that will be taken into account in the next version of the specification.

1 Introduction

ERTMS (European Rail Traffic Management System) has become the *de facto* international standard for railway traffic management. Its main goals are to improve cross-border interoperability of the European railways, stimulate an open market for equipment, and realise an increase of the capacity of the railway network. ETCS, the train control system part of ERTMS, distinguishes three levels of operation: Level 1, 2, and 3.

Especially Level 3 promises an increase in capacity. Whereas at Levels 1 and 2 train protection relies on train detectors installed at fixed positions along the tracks, at Level 3 both train detection and the issuing of movement authorities to trains is entirely by radio communication between trains and a Trackside System (henceforth abbreviated as TS). Using such a train detection, track sections can be partitioned (virtually) into arbitrarily small sections, and trains can follow each other at close distance.

There are, however, also drawbacks to Level 3. First, to get a reliable position report from a train regarding its location, it must have a train integrity monitoring system (TIMS) to confirm not only the position of its front end, but also the position of its rear end. Not every train on the network is currently equipped with a TIMS, and it will be too costly, if not infeasible, to install a TIMS on every train on short notice. Second, a Level 3 system is intolerant to radio connection problems. As soon as a train loses connection to the TS an unsafe situation occurs from which it is cumbersome to recover.

ERTMS Hybrid Level 3 (HL3) is considered by several European railway inframanagers as an economically viable way to smoothen the transition to

© Springer Nature Switzerland AG 2018
F. Howar and J. Barnat (Eds.): FMICS 2018, LNCS 11119, pp. 98–114, 2018.
https://doi.org/10.1007/978-3-030-00244-2_7

ERTMS Level 3 and increase the capacity on their dense railway networks [8]. ERTMS HL3 assumes a limited installation of conventional trackside train detectors for separating trains without TIMS and for handling degraded situations. The ensuing track sections (referred to as TTDs) are further partitioned into Virtual Sub-Sections (VSSs). Multiple trains equipped with a TIMS and a working radio connection to the TS can be allowed simultaneously on different VSSs of the same TTD, while the system is also still capable of handling trains not equipped with TIMS or without a working radio connection.

TTDs autonomously change between status FREE and OCCUPIED upon detecting trains entering and leaving a track. The status of a VSS, on the other hand, is determined on the basis of position reports emitted by trains, the status of TTDs or other VSSs and various timers. The ERTMS HL3 principles [6] meticulously describe (in plain English) the conditions enabling status updates for VSSs. They do not, however, address, *e.g.*, how to implement the TS and, in particular, the process of updating the status of the VSSs. This is to leave sufficient implementation freedom to suppliers.

By the lack of guiding principles for implementing the TS it is, however, not self-evident that different implementations lead to the same operational behaviour of the TS, nor that interoperability between various TSs is guaranteed under different implementation choices. A further concern is the informal description of how to update the status of VSSs upon external events. While clearly a lot of care went into providing clear and concise descriptions of these updates, each motivated and illustrated through examples, natural language lacks the precision to admit an unambiguous implementation of these.

Ideally, the ERTMS HL3 principles are formulated such that they lead to a correct system independent of the chosen implementation of the TS. To investigate whether this is indeed the case, we have formally modelled those principles and two natural implementations of the TS in mCRL2, a process algebra for formalising specifications of system behaviour. Our models not only allow us to simulate the various operational scenarios documented in [6], but also to analyse exhaustively, using model checking, whether an instantiation of the ERTMS HL3 system with a particular track layout satisfies desirable correctness properties. Moreover, they allow us to formally compare the different implementations of the TS, in order to determine the robustness of the principles against implementation freedom.

There has been extensive research on applying formal methods in the railway domain [7]. For a comparison of the applications directly related to ERTMS [1–3,11,12] we refer to [1, Sect. 10]. Most of these works either focus on the interlocking or on hybrid aspects of ERTMS. In the terminology of [1, Sect. 10], our approach focusses on an extension of a subsystem at the design level. Recent other works modelling and analysing the ERTMS HL3 principles include [5,10].

2 ERTMS HL3 Principles

The ERTMS HL3 principles defined in [6] focus on the different status that a VSS may have and how they are influenced by detected events in the system;

particular attention is paid to how the system should respond to trains losing integrity, disconnecting from and reconnecting with the TS, and recovering from such situations. Moreover, the document [6] discusses several hazards that may affect the safety of the system (trains losing integrity or losing the radio connection with the TS), and how they are mitigated by the principles. The informal description of the system culminates in a state-transition diagram (see Fig. 1) that specifies how the TS should evaluate the status of an individual VSS, based on position reports from trains, reports from train detectors and the expiration of timers. Several scenarios are presented (also in natural language), providing an operational interpretation of the state-transition diagram under various circumstances.

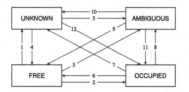

Fig. 1. The VSS state-transition diagram of [6].

As can be seen from Fig. 1, four status are distinguished for a VSS. A VSS has the status FREE if the trackside system is certain that no train is located on it. A VSS has the status OCCUPIED if there is a train located on it according to the most recent position report of this train, and it is certain that there is no other vehicle located in rear of this train on the same VSS. A VSS has the status AMBIGUOUS if there is a train located on it according to the most recent position report of this train, but it is not certain that there is no other vehicle located in rear of this train on the same VSS. A VSS has the status UNKNOWN if according to the most recent position reports from the trains there is no train located on it, but still it is not certain that the VSS is free (*e.g.*, because the TS has reason to suspect that an unconnected train, or part of a train is located on the VSS).

The TS uses the status of the VSSs, on the one hand, to compute so-called *Full-Supervison Movement Authorities*, which it can issue to connected integer trains, and, on the other hand, to present (human) train service controllers with a real-time view on the situation on the railway tracks, allowing them to issue movement authorities to unconnected trains. Full-Supervision Movement Authorities are only issued by the TS for VSSs with the status FREE.

The numbers on transitions in the state-transition diagram in Fig. 1 refer to conditions under which these transitions should take place. These conditions are specified in a 3.5-page table in [6]. Table 1 reproduces, by way of example, a fragment of this table. It shows the first of six parts (#1A–#1F) defining condition #1; these six parts should be read in disjunction. It also shows the first of the two disjuncts (#2A–#2B) defining condition #2. The third column for condition #2A specifies that transition 2 (the transition from FREE to OCCUPIED) has priority over transition 3 (the transition from FREE to AMBIGUOUS)

Table 1. A fragment of the table in [6] specifying the conditions enabling the transitions in Fig. 1.

#	Condition	Priority over	Section ref.
#1A	(TTD is occupied) AND (no FS MA is issued or no train is located on this TTD)		4.2.2
⋮	⋮	⋮	⋮

#2A	(TTD is occupied)
	AND (train is located on the VSS)
	AND (VSS where the estimated front end of the train
	  was last reported, was "occupied" after the
	  processing of this previous position report)
	AND (current state of the VSS where the train was last
	  reported is not "unknown")
		#3	3.3.3
			4.5.1.6

⋮	⋮	⋮	⋮

whenever both the condition for transition #2A and the condition for transition 3 evaluate to true. The last column refers to paragraphs of the document where the rationale for the particular condition is explained.

As is illustrated in Table 1, to be able to evaluate the conditions of the transitions in the state-transition diagram for a particular VSS, the TS needs to be aware of the association between VSSs and TTDs and their relative placement. It needs to keep track of information regarding the status of VSSs and TTDs in the vicinity of the particular VSS under evaluation. Furthermore, it needs to keep track of information about connected trains (their positions, and their movement authorities).

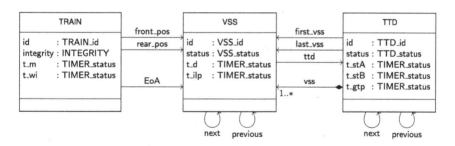

Fig. 2. The data model for the TS.

From the description in [6] we have derived the class diagram shown in Fig. 2. It models the associations between three types of objects about which the TS needs to maintain information: TRAIN, VSS and TTD.

3   mCRL2 model of ERTMS HL3

mCRL2 is a formal language for modelling the behaviour of concurrent systems. It is comprised of an expressive process algebraic language for specifying concurrent processes, a rich language for specifying data types and operations on data, and a requirements language based on a first-order extension of the modal μ-calculus. We explain the relevant mCRL2 language concepts as we go along; for a more detailed account, we refer to [9]. In Sect. 3.1, we describe how we have modelled the static aspects of the ERTMS HL3 principles such as the relevant data types and the conditions governing the VSS state-transition diagram. Section 3.2 describes, at a high level, how we have modelled the behaviour of trains, TTDs and two implementations of the TS.

3.1   Modelling Data and Predicates

The mCRL2 data language is based on algebraic specification. Users can define abstract data types (called *sorts* in mCRL2) by specifying their constructors. As in a functional language, mappings are defined on those data types by means of equations, which are interpreted internally as rewrite rules. Several standard types (*e.g.*, Booleans, natural numbers, integers) together with standard mappings are predefined; mCRL2 also offers the possibility to define lists and sets over a standard or user-defined type. There are two features of the mCRL2 data language that we have extensively used in modelling the ERTMS HL3 principles: *structured types* and *function types*.

Structured types can, on the one hand, be used to specify an enumerated type of constructors; *e.g.*, we defined the sort VSS_status as follows:

```
VSS_status =
  struct free_vss | unknown_vss | ambiguous_vss | occupied_vss;
```

On the other hand, they can also be used to collect information pertaining to a single object; *e.g.*, the sort VSS_info aggregates information regarding a VSS:

```
VSS_info =
  struct vss_info(
    status: VSS_status,
    ttd: TTD_id,
    t_d: TIMER_status,      %% disconnect propagation
    t_ilp: TIMER_status );  %% integrity loss propagation
```

Note that, compared to the class diagram in Fig. 2, the id and the associations next and previous are omitted from the specification of the sort VSS_info. To be able to reuse mCRL2's efficient standard interpretation of the natural numbers and their ordering, it is convenient to, instead, model ids (TRAIN_ids, VSS_ids and TTD_ids) as natural numbers and assume, in particular, that VSSs and TTDs are arranged in accordance with the standard ordering on natural numbers. The TS stores the required information with respect to TRAINs, VSSs and TTDs as functions from the respective ids to the structure type collecting the information per object; *e.g.*, for storing information with respect to the VSSs, we declare a function type VSSs:

```
VSSs = VSS_id -> VSS_info;
```

With the appropriate data types in place, it is, in principle, reasonably straightforward to translate the conditions for the transitions as specified in [6] to mCRL2. The main bottleneck in translating the conditions involves resolving the ambiguity inherently present in a natural language specification. We followed an iterative process of refining and analysing our models, adjusting and validating our interpretation. The excerpt below gives a flavour of our formalisation, illustrating how we formalised condition #2A (*cf.* Table 1):

```
map
  g_f2o_A: VSS_id#TRAIN_id#PTD#VVSs#VSSs#TTDs#TRAINs -> Bool;
var
  v: VSS_id; previous_vs, vs: VSSs; ts: TTDs;
  tr: TRAIN_id; p: PTD; trs: TRAINs;
eqn
  g_f2o_A(v,tr,p,previous_vs,vs,ts,trs) =
      ttd_is_occupied(v,vs,ts)
    && ptd_train_on_vss(v,p)
    && vss_is_occupied(front_pos(trs(tr)),previous_vs)
    && (forall v': VSS_id.( (legal_vss(v') && train_on_vss(tr,v',trs))
          => !(vss_is_unknown(v',vs)))));
```

The mCRL2 code defines a predicate (a Boolean-valued mapping) g_f2o_A that computes a Boolean value on the basis of several parameters. The first parameter v is of type VSS_id and it simply refers to the VSS under consideration. The second and third parameters refer to a train tr through its TRAIN_id and a position report p sent by that train (PTD is a structured type that encapsulates the information that a train sends to the TS). The idea, as will be explained later, is that the evaluation of the conditions is triggered by events and the (implicit) assumption for condition #2A is that it is triggered by the event of a train sending its position report. The fourth and fifth parameters refer, respectively, to the stable information registered by the TS about all VSSs after the *previous* position report, and to the information currently registered about all VSSs by the TS. Note that condition #2A refers to both types of information. By means of the sixth and seventh parameters the information maintained by the TS regarding TTD status and train positions are passed to the predicate.

The definition of the predicate g_f2o_A refers to several auxiliary predicates (*e.g.*, ttd_is_occupied, ptd_train_on_vss, vss_is_occupied, ...), and to a mapping front_pos that retrieves the position of the front-end of train tr in function trs.

3.2   Modelling the Behaviour of Trains, TTDs and the TS

Behaviour is specified in mCRL2 using standard process-algebraic constructions. To denote basic events there is a facility to declare *actions*, which may be parametrised by terms in the data language. The language includes operations for sequential composition, non-deterministic choice, interleaving parallel composition with the facility to enforce communication between actions, and hiding (renaming actions to the special action τ, which can then be treated as unobservable). For the purpose of specifying infinite behaviour, mCRL2 allows the definition of parametrised processes by means of equations, admitting recursive calls. Especially convenient features of the mCRL2 process language are its operation for choice quantification (parametrised non-deterministic choice), conditionals, and multi-actions.

The behaviours of trains, TTDs and the TS are not explicitly described in [6], but the required functionality of these components can be deduced, to a large extent, from explanations in [6]. We have only modelled the behaviour of these components in as far as it is relevant for the analysis of ERTMS HL3 principles.[1]

Trains. Trains may consist of several carriages. To simplify matters, we assume that the length of each individual carriage does not exceed the length of any VSS. A composite train can split into multiple carriages; separated carriages can announce themselves to the TS by means of a start_mission action. We do not yet consider combining trains.

For the purpose of modelling train detection by TTDs, we assume that every carriage has two axles (a front and a rear axle, corresponding with the positions of the front and rear of the carriage). Train movement then consists of an axle moving from one VSS to the next (represented in the mCRL2 model by move actions), in such a way that the front axle of a carriage is never more than one VSS ahead of its rear axle and that similar constraints are obeyed to make sure that carriages of combined trains stay together (cf. the move actions in the specification of the processes Train_move and Train_move_notinteger and its subprocesses). To be able to accurately model train detection by TTDs, a train informs a TTD whenever an axle either enters or leaves the TTD. Furthermore, by means of a multi-action, we achieve that leaving one TTD and entering the next happens simultaneously.

Trains may be connected to the TS or not; to make this explicit in our model, trains can execute connect and disconnect actions, switching between the two states. Connected trains can emit their positions to the TS by means of emit_position actions, and can receive (extensions of their) movement authorities from the TS through extend_EoA actions. As parameter of an emit_position action, a train sends a so-called PTD to the TS, with information about its position and integrity. Trains may be sure about their integrity and confirm it to the TS, or unsure about their integrity and communicate to the TS that their integrity is unknown. We explicitly model integrity loss of a train by including a break action in the specification of train behaviour; we have assumed that after a break action, a train can still continue onto the next VSS (if it has movement authority for it), but then it will stop.

Trackside Train Detection. The TTD processes communicate with trains and with the TS. They maintain an axle counter that is increased when a train notifies the TTD that one of its axles enters the TTD, and it decreases when a train notifies that one of its axles leaves the TTD. When the status of a TTD

---

[1] The mCRL2 code is distributed with the mCRL2 toolset (git commit 2e671cb), which is available from https://www.mcrl2.org.

changes (*i.e.*, the number of detected axles increases from 0 to ≥ 1 or decreases from ≥ 1 to 0), it should notify the TS instantly by an emit_status action. To model this accurately in mCRL2 the communication with the train causing a change of status of the TTD and the notification thereof to the TS are combined in a multi-action.

Trackside System. The TS is the component that determines the status of the VSSs, issues safe Full-Supervision Movement Authorities to connected trains, and provides train controllers with an accurate view on the location of trains on the track.

The ERTMS HL3 principles in [6] prescribe fairly precisely *how*, given a certain state of the system, a new status for each individual VSS should be determined. In our mCRL2 model, it can be determined what should become the new status of a VSS in accordance with the VSS state-transition in Fig. 1 by evaluating the predicates associated with the outgoing transitions. The predicate should take into account the current status of all VSSs, all TTDs, and the locations of all trains, as known to the TS.

The ERTMS HL3 principles are less clear about what triggers the TS to re-evaluate the status of a particular VSS. They do identify the notification from a TTD of a change of status, an incoming position report from a train, and the expiration of a timer as the *events* of the system, suggesting that such events should trigger re-evaluation of the status of VSSs. Furthermore, from the conditions associated with the transitions in Fig. 1 it can be seen that there is a dependency between the status of VSSs; so also a change of status of one VSS may trigger the change of status of another one.

We concluded from the above considerations that, upon the occurrence of an event in the system, it is necessary to re-evaluate the status of *every* VSS, and that the re-evaluation process should continue until a stable state (*i.e.*, a state in which for no VSS a transition is still enabled) is reached. The stabilisation process can be carried out according to various *event-handling strategies*; in the remainder of this paper we restrict our attention to the following strategies:

Immediate update: According to this strategy, upon the occurrence of an event the TS repeatedly chooses non-deterministically a VSS for which a transition is enabled and directly updates the status of this VSS. This process is repeated until for no VSS a transition in its state-transition diagram is enabled. Note that in the course of this process the status of a VSS may be updated multiple times.

Simultaneous update: According to this strategy, upon the occurrence of an event the TS computes, on the basis of the current status of all VSSs and TTDs, and the last known location of every connected train, for which VSSs a status change is enabled. Only after computing the required status changes for all VSS, those status changes are carried out simultaneously. Since the status change of one VSS may trigger the status change of another VSS, this process must still be repeated until for no VSS a status change is enabled.

We note that the simultaneous update strategy is considerably more complex. It requires the update process to proceed in stages. In each stage every VSS should be considered just once, in order to determine whether its status needs to change, given the event that triggered the process and given the current status of all VSSs in the present stage. Computing which updates are still necessary, and whether the update process is completed, requires careful bookkeeping. We therefore expect that the simultaneous update strategy will be harder to implement in practice; we have also observed this while specifying the strategy in mCRL2.

4   Analysis

We have assessed the quality and consistency of our two models (and earlier versions of our models) by attempting to replay the operational scenarios in [6] with mCRL2's simulator and by checking for desirable properties with mCRL2's verification tools. Both simulation and verification reveal issues with the current description of the principles.

4.1   Simulating Operational Scenarios

Several operational scenarios, intended to illustrate the behaviours of the TS are described in [6]. Such scenarios describe both a static track layout and the dynamics, such as trains moving and emitting position and status reports, and VSSs and TTDs changing status. We report on our analysis of two of the more basic scenarios.

Scenario 1. The first scenario, described in [6, p. 29], illustrates nominal behaviour of the TS. It considers a single train running on a track layout consisting of 3 TTDs, see Fig. 3 (top). In the scenario, the train moves from its initial location along TTD10 and TTD20 and reaches VSS31. It reports midway each VSS that it has no integrity information, followed by a report confirming integrity, shortly before leaving the VSS. While doing so, the VSSs on which it resides (and the TTDs containing these VSSs) are expected to change from FREE to OCCUPIED.

As a result of faulty logic in the state-transition diagram of [6], the desired scenario cannot be simulated with our models. When the train enters the TTD20

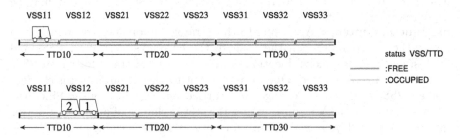

Fig. 3. Configurations defined on [6, p. 29] (top) and [6, p. 31] (bottom).

and the TS has not yet received a position report of a train reporting on TTD20, VSS21-VSS23 all change from FREE to UNKNOWN. This change is triggered by the event emitted by TTD20 which detects the train entering the TTD, enabling condition #1A (see Table 1).

Scenario 2. The second scenario, described on [6, p. 31] describes the expected behaviour of the TS in the presence of a train that splits. The track layout is the same as that of [6, pp. 29], see Fig. 3 (bottom). The scenario starts with composite TRAIN1-2 confirming integrity after which it splits and becomes TRAIN1 and TRAIN2. TRAIN1 confirms integrity and sends a changed train length to the TS after which VSS12 is set to AMBIGUOUS. Next, TRAIN1 starts moving towards VSS31 and reports its position to the TS whereas TRAIN2 remains on VSS12. Each time TRAIN1 enters a new VSS, the status of that VSS becomes AMBIGUOUS, whereas the VSS it left changes from AMBIGUOUS to UNKNOWN. As soon as TRAIN1 leaves TTD20, the TTD informs the TS that it is FREE. This event triggers a change of status for all VSSs on TTD20, which all transition from UNKNOWN to FREE as a result. When TRAIN1 enters VSS31 and reports its presence, this VSS changes from AMBIGUOUS to OCCUPIED.

Again, this scenario cannot be simulated with our models. The status of VSS12 changes to AMBIGUOUS after splitting the composite train. However, the main issue is again that as soon as TRAIN1 enters TTD20, transition #1 is enabled and triggers all VSSs on TTD20 to change from FREE to UNKNOWN instead of the prescribed AMBIGUOUS for VSS21 and FREE for VSS22 and VSS23. Continuing beyond this point for both models furthermore leads to the undesirable situation in which the TS does not stabilise changing status of VSS21, which oscillates between OCCUPIED and AMBIGUOUS. This is a result from an intricate interplay between several conditions.

4.2   Formal Verification

It is not *a priori* clear whether both ways of updating the status of the VSSs discussed in Sect. 3.2 lead to equally desirable implementations. We consider an implementation to be desirable when it meets several high-level correctness criteria that make the TS act reliably and predictably. In general, this means that any implementation needs to satisfy basic sanity properties such as *absence of deadlock*, whether certain actions are present in the state space, *etc.* Verifying such generic requirements has helped us in debugging early versions of our models.

Requirements. Properties that are specific to ERTMS HL3 include *termination of stabilisation*, two forms of *determinism* and *absence of collisions*. Observe that, *e.g.*, determinism is a property that typically requires a branching-time logic and cannot be expressed in, *e.g.*, LTL. We formalise these properties in the first-order modal μ-calculus of mCRL2 and discuss the outcomes of verifying these properties afterwards. We refer to [9] for an in-depth, formal account of this modal logic and here only offer a terse account of the informal reasoning underlying these formulae.

Termination of Stabilisation. Upon receiving events from a train or a TTD, the TS computes new status for the VSSs. Each status change of a VSS may enable a change in another VSS. Once the process reaches a stable state, the TS reports this state via an action stable. There is, however, no *a priori* guarantee that the process stabilises; in fact, simulation of the scenario of [6, pp. 31] has already revealed that the property is violated. We can check this more thoroughly using the following formula; informally it asserts that invariantly (expressed by [true*]), whenever the TS performs a change action, a stable action is inevitable:

$$[\text{true}^*]\,[(\exists v : \text{VSS\_id}, s_1, s_2 : \text{VSS\_status}.\ \text{change}(v, s_1, s_2))]\phi_{\text{stable}}$$

where ϕ_{stable} is the subformula expressing that a stable action cannot be postponed indefinitely by actions taken from a set C of TS-actions involved in the stabilisation computation:

$$\mu X.([\text{C}]X \wedge \langle \text{C} \vee \exists l : \text{List(VSS\_status)}.\text{stable}(l)\rangle\text{true}).$$

Determinacy. The conditions determining the status update of a VSS are intrinsically complex. In particular, it is not obvious whether status updates are deterministic or even desirable: non-determinism may, *e.g.*, be built in to offer freedom when implementing the principles differently by different vendors. On the other hand, non-determinism may be a cause for errors, since it leads to an increase in the number of possible scenarios. *Strong determinacy*, which we define as the absence of non-deterministic status updates, is formalised as $[\text{true}^*]\phi_{\text{strong\_determinacy}}$, where $\phi_{\text{strong\_determinacy}}$ expresses that the state does not have two distinct status updates for a single VSS:

$$\forall v : \text{VSS\_id}, s, s_1, s_2 : \text{VSS\_status}.$$
$$(((\langle\text{change}(v, s, s_1)\rangle\text{true} \wedge \langle\text{change}(v, s, s_2)\rangle\text{true}) \Rightarrow s_1 = s_2)$$

Strong determinism does not guarantee *deterministic stabilisation*, the property that a stable state reached after processing an event is uniquely determined. The reason is that the status of a VSS may be updated based on the status of other VSSs, and the order in which this is done may yield different stabilisations. We deem such a situation highly undesirable as it has a negative impact on the intuition operators have about how the TS operates. Ideally, every event should lead to a stable state that is unique and that is 'known' immediately after the event. Deterministic stabilisation is formalised as:

$$[\text{true}^*]\,[(\exists t : \text{TRAIN\_id}, p : \text{PTD}.\ \text{emit\_position}(t, p))]\phi_{\text{deterministic\_stabilisation}}$$

where $\phi_{\text{deterministic\_stabilisation}}$ is the subformula expressing that there is some stable state l for the VSSs so that whenever the computation stabilises (after a sequence without stable actions), it reaches stable state l:

$$\exists l : \text{List(VSS\_status)}.$$
$$[(\neg\exists l' : \text{List(VSS\_status)}.\ \text{stable}(l'))^*]\forall l'' : \text{List(VSS\_status)}.\ [\text{stable}(l'')](l'' = l)$$

Note that strong determinacy does not imply deterministic stabilisation, nor *vice versa*.

No Collisions. The TS is responsible for sending out a Full-Supervision Movement Authority to a train. It should only extend the movement authority for a train to a VSS if on that VSS no train resides. The property that asserts that this is the case is given by $[\text{true}^*]\phi_{\text{safe}}$ where ϕ_{safe} expresses that no unsafe situation can be reported in a state:

$$\neg(\exists t, t' : \text{TRAIN\_id}, v : \text{VSS\_id}.\langle \text{ExtendEoA}(t, v)\rangle \text{true}$$
$$\wedge \exists l, l' : \text{List}(\text{VSS\_id}).(v = \text{rear}(l') \vee \text{in\_between}(\text{rear}(l'), \text{front}(l), v)) \wedge$$
$$\langle \text{report\_location}(t, l)\rangle \text{true} \wedge \langle \text{report\_location}(t', l')\rangle \text{true})$$

It states that the TS cannot extend a movement authority for a train to a VSS if another train is located in between.

Verification. We verify the requirements listed above on two configurations of varying complexity: the configuration of [6, p. 29], which we also described in Sect. 4.1 and which we here indicate by I, and a configuration inspired by the configuration of [6, p. 31], which we indicate by II. For the latter configuration, we have two TTDs, four VSSs, a composite train and an ordinary train, see Fig. 4. The rear carriage of composite train TRAIN1-2 is located on VSS21 whereas the front is located on VSS22.

Fig. 4. Track layout II, with initial position of TRAIN3 and composite TRAIN1-2.

In addition to considering multiple configurations, we analyse the two different ways in which the TS computes the new stable VSS configurations following an event (*i.e.*, *immediate* versus *simultaneous* update). Table 2 describes the sizes of the state spaces for the respective models and configuration combinations, including the time needed for state space generation. Even though configuration II has fewer VSSs than configuration I, its state space is considerably larger. This is due to the number and composition of trains in configuration II.

The state space for the simultaneous update model of configuration I is smaller than that of the immediate update model. After abstracting from all internal computations of the TS, the state space of the simultaneous update model is weak-trace included in the immediate update model, but not *vice versa*. This means that the immediate update permits more behaviours than the simultaneous update model. For configuration II, both models are equivalent modulo divergence-preserving branching bisimulation. That means that the two modes of updating VSSs are, for all intents and purposes, equivalent for this configuration.

Table 2. Statistics for the state spaces of the various configurations. Time is reported in seconds. For each cell, the first number indicates the result for the *immediate update* mode (Imm) for stabilisation, whereas the second number indicates the *simultaneous update* mode (Simult).

	States		Transitions		Time (s)	
	Imm.	Simult.	Imm.	Simult.	Imm.	Simult.
I	184 139	113 487	591 541	341 427	780	530
II	30 811 310	33 932 280	170 908 128	187 852 936	3 235	2 986

The mCRL2 toolset offers various alternatives for verifying modal formulae. We have mainly used tools that operate directly on the state spaces: ltsconvert is used to minimise the state spaces modulo strong, respectively divergence-preserving branching bisimulation prior to verifying the properties using lts2pbes and pbessolve. The most time consuming part in this workflow is the minimisation of the models, which takes up-to 9 min for the larger models on a 2017 16 Gb Macbook Pro with a 3.5 GHz Intel Core i7. Verifying a formula on the reduced models can be done in seconds. We comment on the results of verifying the requirements formalised above.

On Termination. For both configurations, both the immediate and simultaneous update models of the TS may enter a state in which the process of stabilising the VSS status updates will not terminate. For configuration *I* this happens, *e.g.*, when a train leaves the TTD on which it resided, enters the new TTD and only reports its position when its front is on the second VSS of the new TTD. Since all VSSs on that TTD have status UNKNOWN, the TS cannot decide the status of the VSS on which the front of the train resides and oscillates between AMBIGUOUS and OCCUPIED, see also our explanation for scenario 2. A similar scenario triggers non-termination for configuration *II*.

On Determinacy. Deterministic stabilisation fails for the immediate update model of the TS for configuration *I* but holds for the simultaneous update model for that configuration. The non-determinism results in two stable states in which VSS23 is AMBIGUOUS in one case, but OCCUPIED in the other case. The root cause is a train that moves to VSS23 where it reports to have unknown integrity. The culprit here is a race condition between VSS21-22 changing status from UNKNOWN to AMBIGUOUS, and VSS23 changing status from UNKNOWN to OCCUPIED. If VSS21-22 first change their status, the change of status of VSS23 is stable. If, however, VSS23 first changes status, it can immediately proceed to change its status to AMBIGUOUS. Figure 5 gives an impression of the shape of the counterexample produced by the toolset. Both models for configuration *II* violate the same requirement, non-deterministically reaching a stable configuration with status FREE for VSS21 and another with status UNKNOWN for VSS21.

Strong determinacy holds for configuration *I* for both models of the TS and fails for configuration *II*. In both models for configuration *II*, it is possible to

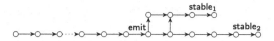

Fig. 5. Shape of the counterexample for deterministic stability of section I. We use the placeholders emit and stable$_1$ and stable$_2$ to indicate the transitions labelled with the parameterised emit_position and stable actions, and suppressed all other actions. We compressed the path towards the emit action (indicated by the dotted edge).

reach a state in which VSS21 can choose to move from OCCUPIED to either FREE or UNKNOWN.

On Collisions. Verifying this property required adding actions report_location to our models. These actions indicate the position of each train at every moment; other than this, they do not affect the model. Both models of the TS for configuration II fail to meet the basic safety requirement that the TS prevents collisions (note that in configuration I only one train is involved, so collisions are impossible). The basic scenario starts by splitting TRAIN1-2 on the TTD20. The rear of that train then becomes a train by itself (*viz.* TRAIN2) but it is invisible to the TS. As a result, TRAIN3, which is on TTD10, gets authorisation to move to VSS21 on which TRAIN2 resides.

5   Lessons Learnt

The goal of [6] is to describe the ERTMS HL3 principles and control logic without unnecessarily restricting vendors in implementing their own solutions. It is, therefore, preferred that the principles do not exclude correct implementations of the ERTMS HL3 idea. It is, however, also desirable that the principles do not admit incorrect implementations. Our analyses of two natural ways of implementing the logic has revealed several issues which are mostly due to the natural language used to phrase the control logic. Moreover, our formalisation suggests that different implementations lead to different functional characteristics of the system. This may be a possible source for a compromised interoperability of implementations by different vendors.

As this case study once more underlines, the act of formalising a specification in itself helps to identify ambiguities and inconsistencies. The richness of the mCRL2 data language, and in particular the possibility to use higher order data types, universal and existential quantifiers, turn out to be essential in concisely and intuitively formalising the required control logic.

Formal analyses, such as simulation and model checking proved to be instrumental in resolving ambiguities and studying the impact of alternative interpretations on the overall system design. Counterexamples and witnesses to system requirements were indispensable tools in this regard, but due to the expressiveness of the logic used in mCRL2, such tools were long missing from mCRL2. The tool pbessolve [13], which implements the theory of [4] for constructing comprehensive counterexamples such as Fig. 5, and which became available to us in the course of our work on this case study, helped to significantly reduce the effort needed to improve our models. *Vice versa*, due to their size and scale, the models and requirements produced in this case study serve as benchmarks for speeding up the algorithmic machinery underlying the counterexample construction, which we found to add a sometimes significant time penalty on top of solving the model checking problem.

From a technical point of view, the *deterministic stabilisation* property and its formalisation in the first-order modal μ-calculus is of interest, not only because it clearly illustrates the strengths and needs for branching time logics, but also because it poses a computational challenge. This challenge consists of efficiently dealing with the outermost existential quantifier ranging over an infinite domain. Using domain knowledge, one can restrict this quantification to range over a finite domain by only considering lists of length n, where n is equal to the number of VSSs in a track layout. While this makes checking deterministic stability decidable for concrete configurations, it may still be intractable in practice, as there are 4^n such lists. However, most of these lists do not represent reachable configurations. In our verification, we utilised this by extracting the reachable configurations from our state spaces, and strengthening the property by quantifying over reachable configurations. A more permanent solution, however, would be to develop different solving strategies such as a (symbolic) solving algorithm that would process the formula essentially inside-out.

We furthermore note that there is an added value to studying the same problem from various angles using different formal methods, and adopting possibly different operational assumptions. For instance, our formalisations of the basics of the ERTMS HL3 principles are conceptually close to how these are formalised in the Electrum language, see [5] and the Event-B language, see [10]. Yet, steered by the strengths of the languages and tools, each method focusses on, and reveals different issues. For instance, the fact that both Electrum and Event-B use a linear time logic means that properties such as deterministic stabilisation (see the previous section) cannot be checked. On the other hand, a language such as Electrum to some extent permits for reasoning about all possible scenarios, allowing to search for scenarios that violate a specific requirement.

6   Conclusion

We formalised and analysed the ERTMS HL3 principles, documented in [6], using the mCRL2 language and toolset. The expressive data language of mCRL2 allowed us to stay close to the concepts used in the informal phrasing of the ERTMS HL3 principles while formalising these. Using simulation and model checking, we revealed a number of hitherto unidentified issues with the current principles. These issues have been communicated to the EEIG ERTMS Users Group and have led to amendments of the document, eliminating several ambiguities in the natural language phrasings. Furthermore, our formal comparison has revealed that the two implementations behave differently, which casts doubt on the robustness of the specification.

Our formalisation and analysis pertains to version 1A of the principles. Recently, version 1B of the principles appeared, and a next version is due in June 2018. It should be reasonably straightforward to adapt our models to the new formulation of the principles and repeat the analysis. It will be interesting to see whether the discovered issues have been resolved in the new versions. In the document describing the principles, also a number of risks are identified and it is explained how these are mitigated. An interesting next step is to, once the currently discovered issues have been resolved, confirm, using model checking, whether these risks have indeed been mitigated.

The recently added facility to generate counterexamples for model checking problems in mCRL2 helped considerably in improving on our models and our understanding of the principles. A strength, and at the same time, a weakness of the mCRL2 toolset is the fact that a verification can be conducted in more than one way. It requires expertise to understand which way is most effective (*e.g.*, fastest) for a particular case. While there is no *one size fits all* work flow, non-expert users can be helped by documenting best-practices and principles. This applies equally to other verification toolsets.

References

1. Berger, U., James, P., Lawrence, A., Roggenbach, M., Seisenberger, M.: Verification of the European rail traffic management system in real-time maude. Sci. Comput. Program. **154**, 61–88 (2018)
2. Canonico, R., Marrone, S., Nardone, R., Vittorini, V.: A framework to evaluate 5G networks for smart and fail-safe communications in ERTMS/ETCS. In: Fantechi, A., Lecomte, T., Romanovsky, A.B. (eds.) RSSRail 2017. LNCS, vol. 10598, pp. 34–50. Springer, Cham (2017). https://doi.org/10.1007/978-3-319-68499-4_3
3. Cimatti, A.: Formal verification and validation of ERTMS industrial railway train spacing system. In: Madhusudan, P., Seshia, S.A. (eds.) CAV 2012. LNCS, vol. 7358, pp. 378–393. Springer, Heidelberg (2012). https://doi.org/10.1007/978-3-642-31424-7_29
4. Cranen, S., Luttik, B., Willemse, T.A.C.: Evidence for fixpoint logic. In: CSL, vol. 41. LIPIcs, pp. 78–93. Schloss Dagstuhl - Leibniz-Zentrum fuer Informatik (2015)
5. Cunha, A., Macedo, N.: Validating the hybrid ERTMS/ETCS level 3 concept with electrum. In: Butler, M., Raschke, A., Hoang, T.S., Reichl, K. (eds.) ABZ 2018. LNCS, vol. 10817, pp. 307–321. Springer, Cham (2018). https://doi.org/10.1007/978-3-319-91271-4_21
6. EEIG ERTMS Users Group. Hybrid ERTMS/ETCS Level 3. Ref: 16E045, Version: 1A, 14 July 2017. http://users.ecs.soton.ac.uk/asf08r/ABZ2018/16E0421A_HL3.pdf
7. Fantechi, A.: Twenty-five years of formal methods and railways: what next? In: Counsell, S., Núñez, M. (eds.) SEFM 2013. LNCS, vol. 8368, pp. 167–183. Springer, Cham (2014). https://doi.org/10.1007/978-3-319-05032-4_13
8. Furness, N., van Houten, H., Arenas, L., Bartholomeus, M.: ERTMS Level 3: the game-changer. IRSE News **232**, 2–9 (2017)
9. Groote, J.F., Mousavi, M.R.: Modeling and Analysis of Communicating Systems. MIT Press (2014)

10. Mammar, A., Frappier, M., Tueno Fotso, S.J., Laleau, R.: An EVENT-B model of the hybrid ERTMS/ETCS level 3 standard. In: Butler, M., Raschke, A., Hoang, T.S., Reichl, K. (eds.) ABZ 2018. LNCS, vol. 10817, pp. 353–366. Springer, Cham (2018). https://doi.org/10.1007/978-3-319-91271-4_24
11. Platzer, A., Quesel, J.-D.: European train control system: a case study in formal verification. In: Breitman, K., Cavalcanti, A. (eds.) ICFEM 2009. LNCS, vol. 5885, pp. 246–265. Springer, Heidelberg (2009). https://doi.org/10.1007/978-3-642-10373-5_13
12. Vu, L.H., Haxthausen, A.E., Peleska, J.: Formal modelling and verification of interlocking systems featuring sequential release. Sci. Comput. Program. **133**, 91–115 (2017)
13. Wesselink, W., Willemse, T.A.C.: Evidence extraction from Parameterised Boolean Equation Systems. In: Benzmüller, C., Otten, J. (eds.) ARQNL, vol. 2095. CEUR Workshop Proceedings, pp. 86–100 (2018). CEUR-WS.org

Progress Checking for Dummies

Antti Valmari[1] and Henri Hansen[2(✉)]

[1] Faculty of Information Technology, University of Jyväskylä,
Jyväskylä, Finland
antti.valmari@jyu.fi
[2] Mathematics, Tampere University of Technology,
P.O. Box 553, 33101 Tampere, Finland
henri.hansen@tut.fi

Abstract. Verification of progress properties is both conceptually and technically significantly more difficult than verification of safety and deadlock properties. In this study we focus on the conceptual side. We make a simple modification to a well-known model to demonstrate that it passes progress verification although the resulting model is intuitively badly incorrect. Then we point out that the error can be caught easily by adding a termination branch to the system. We compare the use of termination branches to the established method of addressing the same need, that is, weak fairness. Then we discuss another problem that may cause failure of catching progress errors even with weak fairness. Finally we point out an alternative notion of progress that needs no explicit fairness assumptions. Our ideas are especially well-suited for newcomers in model checking, and work well with stubborn set methods.

Keywords: Usability of verification methods · Progress · Fairness
Fair testing

1 Introduction

To motivate the present study, let us consider the example system in Fig. 1. It shows Peterson's famous mutual exclusion algorithm [5], and this particular model appears on the home page spinroot.com of the SPIN verification tool.

SPIN reports no errors in this model, as expect, because Peterson's algorithm is correct under the usual assumptions on the execution model. Swapping lines 7 and 8 and running SPIN results in `assertion violated (ncrit==1)`. This is because in the modified system the following scenario is possible: First process 0, followed by process 1, executes `turn = _pid`. Now `turn = 1`. Next process 1 continues to the critical section. It passes line 9 because process 0 has not yet executed `flag[_pid] = 1`, due to swapping lines 7 and 8. Finally process 0 continues to the critical section. It passes line 9 because `turn = 1`. As both processes are now in the critical section, the assertion is violated on line 11. We call the swapping of lines 7 and 8 *modification A* from now on.

© Springer Nature Switzerland AG 2018
F. Howar and J. Barnat (Eds.): FMICS 2018, LNCS 11119, pp. 115–130, 2018.
https://doi.org/10.1007/978-3-030-00244-2_8

```
1    bool turn, flag[2];          // the shared variables, booleans
2    byte ncrit;                  // nr of procs in critical section
3    active [2] proctype user()   // two processes
4    {
5        assert(_pid == 0 || _pid == 1);
6    again:
7        flag[_pid] = 1;
8        turn = _pid;
9        (flag[1 - _pid] == 0 || turn == 1 - _pid);
10       ncrit++;
11       assert(ncrit == 1); // critical section
12       ncrit--;
13       flag[_pid] = 0;
14       goto again
15   }
```

Fig. 1. Peterson's algorithm from the SPIN homepage

Let us now take the original model and remove `|| turn == 1 - _pid` on line 9, and call this *modification B*. For this model, SPIN reports `invalid end state`, because when both processes execute lines 7 and 8, both flags contain the value 1, and neither process can pass the modified line 9. That is, the system is in a deadlock.

We have seeded two different errors to the model, and SPIN has caught them immediately. Finally, let us take the original model and remove `flag[1 - _pid == 0 ||` from line 9. Let us call this *modification C*. This time SPIN reports no errors.

Should we conclude then, that `flag[1 - _pid] == 0 ||` is unnecessary in Peterson's algorithm? In its absence, if a process wants to enter the critical section, it has to wait at line 9 until the other process also seeks entry. Then the former process can enter the critical section. The latter process has to wait until the former process has left the critical section, which is acceptable behaviour. However, the latter process has to wait further still: The latter process is prevented from entering the critical section as long as the former process is not there and does not want to go there; it can only enter *after* the former process has requested entry. Intuitively, this is clearly unacceptable.

The problem is that the (implicit) correctness specification in Fig. 1 is insufficient, and it fails to declare the above scenario as illegal.

Let us now make a small modification to Fig. 1. The modified model is shown in Fig. 2. The cycle consisting of `again:` and `goto again` has been replaced by a do–od-cycle, and a line has been added that makes it possible for each process to exit the cycle. Immediately after exiting the process terminates. Each time when on line 6, the process chooses nondeterministically between terminating and trying to execute the statements in Fig. 1. SPIN reports no errors in this model, and if modification A or B is made to this model, SPIN gives the same error reports as before.

```
1   bool turn, flag[2];         // the shared variables, booleans
2   byte ncrit;                 // nr of procs in critical section
3   active [2] proctype user()  // two processes
4   {
5       assert(_pid == 0 || _pid == 1);
6   do
    :: break
    ::
7       flag[_pid] = 1;
8       turn = _pid;
9       (flag[1 - _pid] == 0 || turn == 1 - _pid);
10      ncrit++;
11      assert(ncrit == 1); // critical section
12      ncrit--;
13      flag[_pid] = 0;
14  od
15  }
```

Fig. 2. Peterson's algorithm with a termination branch

However, now also modification C causes SPIN to report an error. It reports invalid end state. Indeed, if one process terminates and the other goes to line 9, the system is in a deadlock, because the process on line 9 cannot continue.

The theme of the present study is how so-called *progress errors* can sometimes be caught with small tricks that are easier than the standard approach and less vulnerable to accidental misuse that causes failure of catching errors. The addition of the termination branch as was done in Fig. 2 is such a trick. The standard method of obtaining the same effect is via so-called weak fairness assumptions [3], but it is so much more difficult that it was not done in the original model. We do not claim that our tricks cover all progress properties, only that they are an *easy-to-use alternative* that is much better than finding the standard method too difficult to use and therefore not trying to verify progress properties at all. Our tricks thus address usability shortcomings of existing methods with respect to their industrial applicability.

Furthermore, we do not claim that our observations and tricks are fundamentally new. As a matter of fact, the key ideas are two decades old [2,10]. We do claim, however, that their benefits are not sufficiently widely known or have been under-appreciated. Although the addition of the termination branch is easy, gives tangible added value, and is almost free from drawbacks (it makes the size of the state space grow a bit), it seems that it is seldom done. The modelling style in Fig. 1 seems to be the norm, for example among the BEEM benchmarks [4], most models of clients in scheduler or resource allocation systems lack a similar voluntary termination branch.

In Sect. 2 we analyse why the model in Fig. 1 failed and the model in Fig. 2 succeeded in revealing the error. We also compare the addition of the termination branch with the standard solution to the same problem using weak fairness.

In Sect. 3 we discuss a theory that makes it possible to design a model of the user of a service that assumes as much as necessary, but not more, about the behaviour of the user. There is also another kind of problem that may cause an intuitively incorrect model to accidentally pass model checking. It will be solved in Sect. 4. An easy generic approach to progress that is slightly weaker than the standard approach is discussed in Sect. 5.

Full formal treatment of the material in this study would require repeating numerous definitions that can be found in the literature. Because of lack of space, we focus on the intuition and present formally only the concepts which, we believe, are neither obvious nor widely known. Please note that even though the proposed method is suitable "for dummies", this article need not be.

2   Unforced Request

In this section we discuss why and how the addition of the termination branch facilitates the detection of the error caused by modification C. We recall an analogous solution in linear temporal logic [3]. Lastly, we discuss the error detection power and technical difficulty of the methods. When we refer to Fig. 1 or 2, unless otherwise mentioned, we mean both the original figure and modifications A, B and C.

We must first distinguish between a system and its correctness requirements. Lines 2, 10, 11 and 12 of Fig. 1 are not part of Peterson's algorithm, for example, [5] contains nothing corresponding to them. Instead, they express a correctness requirement. They specify that the system should ensure that the two processes are never in the critical section at the same time. This property is usually called *mutual exclusion*. If line 11 is removed, the model loses its ability to catch the error caused by modification A.

There is also an *implicit* correctness requirement arising from the semantics of Promela and the default behaviour of the SPIN tool: in all terminal states, both processes must be at the end of their code, that is, on line 15. (Also line 5 is not part of the algorithm. It expresses a low-level technical correctness requirement related to debugging Promela specifications, and is not important for our discussion.)

In addition to safety properties, systems are usually required to satisfy some progress properties, which in mutual exclusion or resource allocation systems would be called *eventual access*. It says that if a process has requested for access to a resource, then it will eventually get it. In the case of Figs. 1 and 2, a process requests for access by assigning 1 to its flag, that is, by executing line 7. Therefore, eventual access is violated if and only if a process reaches line 8 but then fails to reach line 11. Let P_i denote the line where process i is (at the beginning of the line). In the case of Figs. 1 and 2, eventual access can be specified in linear temporal logic as $\Box(P_0 = 8 \rightarrow \Diamond(P_0 = 11))$ and $\Box(P_1 = 8 \rightarrow \Diamond(P_1 = 11))$.

Figures 1 and 2 specify eventual access, to the extent they specify it, implicitly, via the requirement that the model must not stop while a process is on line 8, 9, or 10 (which follows from the above-mentioned requirement that the model must not stop while a process is on any other line than 15). Indeed, the error caused by modification B is a violation of eventual access, because when both processes are waiting on line 9, process 0 has requested for access but will never get to line 11 (and the same holds also on process 1). In Sect. 1, the error was caught as an unintended terminal state. The users of linear temporal logic would catch it as a violation of eventual access. We will return to this difference towards the end of this section. For the time being, we focus on eventual access.

In the case of Fig. 2, but not Fig. 1, also the error caused by modification C is a violation of eventual access. In the case of Fig. 1 with modification C, eventual access holds formally, and thus it is formally correct not to report any error although intuitively the system is badly wrong. The failure of the model in Fig. 1 to catch the error caused by modification C is *not* due to insufficient specification of correctness requirements, but due to implicit *over-specification* of the users of the algorithm. This is a subtle issue that we will discuss next.

It is obvious that if one process stays in the critical section forever and the other process requests for access, then either safety or progress is violated: If the algorithm lets also the other process enter the critical section, then mutual exclusion is violated, and if it does not, eventual access is violated. This means that to solve the mutual exclusion problem, it is necessary to assume *something* about the behaviour of the clients. In particular, it is necessary to assume that a client will not stay in the critical section forever.

Like most modelling languages and model checking tools, Promela and SPIN implicitly assume that *if something can happen* in the model, *then something will happen*. Most of the time this is a very appropriate assumption. Among other things, if a process of Fig. 1 or 2 is in the critical section, the assumption forces it to leave it at the latest when the other process is waiting on line 9 or 15.

On the other hand, in the case of Fig. 1 with modification C, this implies that each process will always eventually request for access. This is because if we try to execute the model so that one process stays on line 7, eventually the other process reaches line 9, and the only thing that can happen in the model is that the former process executes line 7.

Real-life users of such systems do not necessarily always eventually request for access. This means that Fig. 1 makes an unjustified assumption about the user. It is this assumption that makes Fig. 1 with modification C pass formal verification, although it is intuitively badly incorrect. To avoid this problem, a model where requests are issued should exhibit what we call *unforced request*. Informally, it says that each process must be able to choose not to request for access. We do not call it a property, to emphasize that it is not something that the model checker should check about the system. Instead, it should be enforced by building the model appropriately. It is not a restriction on the behaviour of the processes; it is a requirement that a certain restriction is *not* made.

We conclude that there are two distinct reasons why model checking may fail to reveal an error: *under-specification of the requirements* (such as leaving out line 11) and *over-specification of the model* (such as assuming that each process will always eventually request for access). In Sect. 3 we will discuss over-specification of the model in a solid theoretical framework that makes the notion formally precise. In Sect. 4 we will encounter a third reason. We continue this section by comparing two methods of implementing unforced request.

Figure 2 implements unforced request by adding a termination branch. When a process is on line 6, it is not forced to go to and execute line 7 even when the other process is waiting on line 9, because it can nondeterministically choose to execute the **break** statement instead, thereby going to line 15.

In order to present a theorem later in this section, we make it more formal what we mean by systems, processes, and termination branches. Due to lack of space, we only discuss a minimal set of concepts that will be needed in the sequel. A *system* consists of processes and variables. A *process* is a rooted directed edge-labelled graph whose vertices are called *(local) states*, edges are called *transitions*, and the root is called *initial state*. In addition to the tail and head states, a transition has a *guard* and a *body*. The guard is a Boolean function on the values of the variables. The body assigns values to zero or more variables as a function of the values of the variables.

For instance, in the case of Promela, the set of states is implicit from the code. Line 8 of Fig. 1 expresses a transition whose guard is identically **true** and whose body may change the value of **turn**. Line 9 expresses a transition whose tail state is the head state of the transition on line 8, body makes no assignments, and guard is the condition written on the line.

The addition of a *termination branch* to state s of a process means the addition of one state s' and one transition whose tail state is s, head state is s', guard is the constant function **true**, and body makes no assignments.

In linear temporal logic, instead of adding a termination branch, it is customary to use so-called *weak fairness* assumptions. Intuitively, weak fairness towards transition t means the assumption that if t is enabled for long enough, it will eventually be executed. An execution is thus *weakly unfair* towards t if and only if, from some point on, t is enabled in every state but does not occur. Weakly unfair executions are not treated as valid counterexamples to a property. Typically weak fairness is assumed towards almost all transitions. Not assuming weak fairness towards a transition is thus exceptional and indicates that the transition need not occur even if it is enabled. Weak fairness may also be assumed towards a set of transitions, but we skip that.

The assumption can be thought to reflect that processor time allocation of a real system works well enough that weakly unfair executions do not occur. Strictly speaking, only infinite executions can be weakly unfair, but by a weakly unfair execution in the real world, we mean an execution where t is enabled for "too long" without occurring. Real schedulers are not guaranteed to work that well, of which the Mars Pathfinder priority inversion incident of 1997 [6] is an example (to the extent that such an example can exist). However, to avoid problems like this, schedulers are usually designed to guarantee (some real-world approximation of) weak fairness. This is why it is usually considered reasonable to assume weak fairness in model checking with Promela-like languages. As was discussed in [1], weak fairness may not work as well with process algebras.

To indicate that a process need not execute line 7 if it does not want to, weak fairness is assumed towards every transition except the one that corresponds to line 7. This implies that line 7 need not be executed, even if it is the only thing that can happen in the model.

This method has the advantage that violations of eventual access are caught independently of whether the problem is a deadlock or something else. For instance, assume that line 9 of Fig. 1 is replaced by

```
if
:: flag[1-_pid] == 1 -> flag[_pid] = 0; goto again
:: else -> skip
fi;
```

Let us call this *modification D*. A scenario becomes possible where both processes repeatedly go to this modified line 9, detect that also the other process has made the request, cancel their own request, and go back. This cycle can repeat forever, resulting in neither process ever getting to the critical section. It is weakly fair towards every transition, and thus valid as a counter-example to eventual access. In this case SPIN does not detect the error, but it could be made to detect the error by using standard techniques for linear temporal logic that rely on detecting certain kinds of cycles in the state space.

On the other hand, this approach is more complicated both for the modeller and for the verification tools. Indeed, the authors of spinroot.com were wise enough not to use linear temporal logic in the example, to keep it simple enough to act as a first example to a newcomer who is not familiar with temporal logic. We conclude that it makes sense to have deadlock detection in the toolbox, although its ability to detect errors is restricted. Indeed, SPIN has it. Our contribution here is the remark that it can be made to detect *more* errors by adding termination branches. Although termination branches cannot catch the error caused by modification D, they did catch the error caused by modification C, which is better than nothing and took little extra effort.

We say that an execution is *complete* if and only if it is either infinite or ends in a terminal state. In linear temporal logic, it is customary to extend every complete finite execution to an infinite one by repeating its last state forever, because doing so eliminates a special case and thus simplifies the theory. Deadlocks become infinite executions where, from some point on, nothing useful happens. The notion of weak fairness does not depend on this convention, so we ignore it in the sequel. If the convention is obeyed also in the model checking tool, then no errors are caught as unexpected deadlocks.

We still have to justify that termination branches do not cause false alarms. We first need to introduce yet another concept.

Almost every linear temporal logic property that is relevant for model checking in practice is *stuttering-insensitive*. The formal definition is not important for the present study, so we skip it. Intuitively, a transition is *visible* with respect to a linear temporal logic formula if and only if its occurrence may affect the truth value of an atomic proposition in the formula. Stuttering-insensitivity means that the number of invisible transitions that occur before the first, after the last, or between any two visible transitions is irrelevant. In particular, eventual access is stuttering-insensitive, and the **break** transition in Fig. 2 is invisible with respect to it. By LTL$_X$ we mean the set of the stuttering-insensitive linear temporal logic formulae.

The following theorem implies that violations against an LTL$_X$ formula detected with the termination branch method are errors also when using the weak fairness assumptions, assuming that the formula obeys a mild assumption. The assumption rules out such formulae as $\Box(P_1 \neq 15)$ that directly tests the presence of the termination branch that was added in Fig. 2. Due to lack of space, we formulate and prove the theorem for only a single addition of a termination branch, but the proof can be generalized to multiple additions.

Theorem 1. *Let S be a system, φ an LTL$_X$ formula on it, s a state of a process of S, and $t_1, \ldots, t_n$ be the transitions whose tail state is s, such that weak fairness is not assumed with respect to any of $t_1, \ldots, t_n$. Let S' be obtained from S by adding the termination branch $s -t'\rightarrow s'$. We also assume that t' is invisible with respect to φ. If S' has a deadlocking execution that violates φ and contains t', then S has a weakly fair execution that violates φ.*

Proof. Let ξ' be the execution of S' in the claim. Because the guard of t' tests nothing and the body of t' only changes the local state of the process from s to s', the execution of t' can be removed from within ξ'. The result ξ is an execution of both S and S'. It ends in s. It is weakly fair in S, because weak fairness does not require the execution of any of $t_1, \ldots, t_n$, and no other transition is enabled because ξ' is deadlocking. Because φ is stuttering-insensitive and t' is invisible with respect to it, φ has the same truth value on ξ as on ξ'.   □

Please notice that the theorem holds independently of what weak fairness assumptions are made in S', if any. This is because it follows from the definition of weak fairness that all deadlocking executions are weakly fair.

3   Most General Client

In this section we discuss a theory that makes it possible to avoid over-specification of the kind discussed in the previous section. The theory will lead to the conclusion that the model used in the previous section is, in a rigorous sense, optimal for the verification of eventual access.

If S is a system and φ is an LTL$_X$-formula, then $S \models \varphi$ means that φ holds on S. The following theorem is from [9] and an earlier version appeared in [2]. It establishes a useful link between LTL$_X$ and process algebras. We will introduce the necessary process-algebraic concepts and discuss the link after the theorem.

Theorem 2. *The CFFD-semantics preserves LTL$_X$ in the following sense: If φ is an LTL$_X$-formula whose atomic propositions do not refer to the local states of Q, and if $P_1 \parallel \cdots \parallel P_n \parallel Q \models \varphi$ and $Q' \preceq_{\mathsf{CFFD}} Q$, then $P_1 \parallel \cdots \parallel P_n \parallel Q' \models \varphi$.*

In the theorem, a system is expressed as a parallel composition of *labelled transition systems*, abbreviated *LTS*. Intuitively, an LTS is the representation of the behaviour of a system, subsystem, or individual component of the system as an edge-labelled directed graph. It is the state space of the subsystem, with emphasis on transitions instead of states. Formally, it is a tuple $L = (S, \Sigma, \Delta, \hat{s})$. The set Σ is the set of the visible actions of L, also known as the *alphabet* of L. The symbol τ is used to denote invisible actions, and $\tau \notin \Sigma$. The set of the states of L is S, and $\hat{s} \in S$ is the initial state. The set of the transitions of L is $\Delta \subseteq S \times (\Sigma \cup \{\tau\}) \times S$. The *reachable part* of an LTS $(S, \Sigma, \Delta, \hat{s})$ is the LTS $(S', \Sigma, \Delta', \hat{s})$, where S' and Δ' are the smallest subsets of S and Δ such that $\hat{s} \in S'$ and, if $s \in S'$ and $(s, a, s') \in \Delta$, then $s' \in S'$ and $(s, a, s') \in \Delta'$.

For building a system from its components, many different operators have been defined. We will only need the *parallel composition* operator $\|$. Intuitively, $L_1 \| L_2$ represents the parallel execution of L_1 and L_2, with those actions executed jointly that are in the intersection of their alphabets. Formally, it is the reachable part of $(S, \Sigma, \Delta, \hat{s})$, where $S = S_1 \times S_2$, $\Sigma = \Sigma_1 \cup \Sigma_2$, $\hat{s} = (\hat{s}_1, \hat{s}_2)$, and Δ is defined as follows: $((s_1, s_2), a, (s'_1, s'_2)) \in \Delta$ if and only if either $a \in \Sigma_1 \cap \Sigma_2$, $(s_1, a, s'_1) \in \Delta_1$, and $(s_2, a, s'_2) \in \Delta_2$; $a \notin \Sigma_2$, $(s_1, a, s'_1) \in \Delta_1$, and $s'_2 = s_2 \in S_2$; or $a \notin \Sigma_1$, $(s_2, a, s'_2) \in \Delta_2$, and $s'_1 = s_1 \in S_1$. Because τ is not in any alphabet, invisible actions are not executed jointly. The parallel composition operator is associative and commutative (up to isomorphism on the names of states). So $P_1 \| \cdots \| P_n \| Q$ is now well-defined.

Figure 3 shows the overall structure and one client of a mutual exclusion system as a client–server system. Assume that we want to verify that eventual access holds on Client 0. Then we can let $n = 1$, P_1 be Client 0 and Q be the parallel composition of Server and Client 1 in Theorem 2. Although Q is a single LTS in the theorem, we can use Server $\|$ Client 1 in its place, because Client 0 $\|$ Server $\|$ Client 1 = Client 0 $\|$ (Server $\|$ Client 1) by the associativity of $\|$.

Many process algebras are *compositional*. That is, a subsystem can be replaced by a smaller, semantically equivalent subsystem before model checking. This is a powerful tool for alleviating the state explosion problem. What is more, many process algebras have a *precongruence*. It is defined with respect to a set of operators for building systems from LTSs and subsystems. It is a partial order relation $\preceq$ between LTSs such that if $L_1 \preceq L_2$ and f is a process-algebraic expression that only uses operators from the set, then $f(L_1) \preceq f(L_2)$.

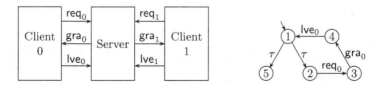

Fig. 3. (Left) A client–server mutual exclusion system (Right) Client 0 as an LTS

By $\preceq_{\mathsf{CFFD}}$ wean mean the preorder in the *Chaos-free Failures Divergences Semantics* [11]. It has some variants depending on the chosen set of operators for building systems. The following is appropriate for the present context.

Let Σ_i denote the alphabet of L_i. A *trace* of L_i is any element of Σ_i^* that can be obtained by picking a finite (not necessarily complete) execution of L_i and dropping all the states and τ-symbols from it. If the same is done to an infinite execution, the resulting sequence of elements of Σ_i is either finite or infinite. If it is finite, it is called a *divergence trace*, and otherwise an *infinite trace*. The sets of divergence and infinite traces of L_i are denoted with $Div(L_i)$ and $Inf(L_i)$.

A *stable failure* of L_i is a pair $(\sigma, A) \in \Sigma_i^* \times 2^{\Sigma_i}$ such that L_i can reach a state s via an execution whose trace is σ, such that no output transition of s is labelled with any element of $A \cup \{\tau\}$. The set of the stable failures is denoted by $Sf(L_i)$. This notion generalizes traces that lead to terminal states. In particular, σ is a trace that leads to a terminal state if and only if $(\sigma, \Sigma_i) \in Sf(L_i)$. In [8] it was proven that to obtain the congruence property with respect to $\parallel$, the semantics must preserve all stable failures.

We define $L_1 \preceq_{\mathsf{CFFD}} L_2$ if and only if $\Sigma_1 = \Sigma_2$, $Sf(L_1) \subseteq Sf(L_2)$, $Div(L_1) \subseteq Div(L_2)$, and $Inf(L_1) \subseteq Inf(L_2)$. We also define $L_1 \approx_{\mathsf{CFFD}} L_2$ if and only if $L_1 \preceq_{\mathsf{CFFD}} L_2$ and $L_2 \preceq_{\mathsf{CFFD}} L_1$.

Intuitively, Theorem 2 says that, when $L \preceq_{\mathsf{CFFD}} L'$, replacing L by L' as a component of a system may introduce new violations of a given LTL$_{\mathsf{X}}$ property. Conversely, if a system with L' is correct with respect to a given formula, replacing it with L is also correct. To put this in another way, if we model a component as L' instead of L, we make *fewer assumptions about its behaviour*.

Consider now Client 0 in Fig. 3. Its interface consists of req_0, gra_0, and lve_0. It is a common assumption in system design that each component of a system may interact via other components only via the interface that was specified in the architecture of the system. Therefore, the alphabet of Client 0 is $\{\mathsf{req}_0, \mathsf{gra}_0, \mathsf{lve}_0\}$.

We require that every trace of Client 0 must be a prefix of $(\mathsf{req}_0\mathsf{gra}_0\mathsf{lve}_0)^\omega$. That is, the client must not try to execute its visible actions in a wrong order. In general in process algebras, the responsibility of this issue may be left on the client or the server, or distributed between them. We could put the responsibility on the server, by extending the client with the construction in automata theory textbooks that extends the transition relation of a deterministic finite automaton from a partial function to a full function. Then the server would have to be designed so that it blocks the added transitions. This difference is not important for the purpose of our present study, and to avoid spending space on it, we put the responsibility on the client.

Our next observation is that Client 0 must have no divergence traces. Letting a client diverge would mean letting it steal all processor time and thus prevent the server and opposite client from making progress. In Sect. 2 we argued that to solve the mutual exclusion problem, it is necessary to assume that a client will not stay in the critical section forever. We are now in a similar situation and make a similar conclusion.

As a consequence, every trace σ of the client must eventually lead to a state such that no output transition of the state is labelled with τ. That is, if σ is a trace of Client 0, then (σ, A) is a stable failure at least when $A = \emptyset$. It follows from the definition of stable failures that if $(\sigma, A) \in Sf(L)$ and $B \subseteq A$, then $(\sigma, B) \in Sf(L)$. Therefore, for each trace σ of Client 0, we have the problem of determining the maximal A's such that (σ, A) is a stable failure of Client 0.

We again appeal to the fact that a client must not stay in the critical section forever. We have chosen that after gra_0, the next visible action of the client may only be lve_0. Together these mean that for the traces that end with gra_0, there is a unique maximal A which is $\{\mathsf{req}_0, \mathsf{gra}_0\}$.

Assume that Client 0 has executed req_0 and the server has committed to give it access. The server is thus ready to execute gra_0 and not gra_1. If Client 0 now refuses to execute gra_0, a correct mutual exclusion system cannot do anything else than deadlock sooner or later. It cannot diverge or choose to execute gra_1, because by the properties of the parallel composition operator, if these options were available now, they would be available also if Client 0 were willing to execute gra_0, compromising the eventual access property towards Client 0. We see that it is not only the critical section where the client must be assumed to not stop. Indeed, we pointed out in Sect. 2 that assuming weak fairness on a transition is the norm and not assuming is exceptional. We conclude that for the traces that end with req_0, there is a unique maximal A which is $\{\mathsf{req}_0, \mathsf{lve}_0\}$.

Similar reasoning does not apply to the empty trace and the traces that end with lve_0. We concluded in Sect. 2 that the client must be given the permission to not execute req_0. So in this case, the maximal A is $\{\mathsf{req}_0, \mathsf{gra}_0, \mathsf{lve}_0\}$.

It follows from the definitions that every finite prefix of an infinite trace is a trace. In the case of Client 0, the only infinite sequence that has this property is $(\mathsf{req}_0 \mathsf{gra}_0 \mathsf{lve}_0)^\omega$. To avoid over-specification, the guiding principle is that if we do not know whether some behaviour must be banned, we must not ban it. If banning it is necessary, then verification will fail, and when analysing the reason for failure, we will find out that banning would have been necessary. Guided by this principle, we do not ban $(\mathsf{req}_0 \mathsf{gra}_0 \mathsf{lve}_0)^\omega$. That Fig. 2 passes verification demonstrates that it need not be banned.

Figure 3(Right) shows a client with precisely the traces, etc., discussed above. It is optimal for the verification of eventual access: if the client may have more behaviour, then mutual exclusion cannot be solved, and if the client has less behaviour, then it has been over-specified, running the risk of intuitively incorrect solutions pass formal verification. From the point of view of this section, the τ-transition from state 1 to state 2 is unnecessary; the req_0-transition could start at state 1. The motivation of the τ-transition will be discussed in Sect. 4.

Figures 1 and 2 do not conform to the architecture in Fig. 3(Left). However, this is not a problem. Consider the system

Client 0 ∥ Server 0 ∥ `flag[0]` ∥ `flag[1]` ∥ `turn` ∥ Server 1 ∥ Client 1

where the clients are like in Fig. 3(Right); the servers are like in Fig. 1 with communication with the clients added; and `flag[0]`, `flag[1]`, and `turn` model the variables in Fig. 1 in a standard fashion used in process algebras to model shared variables. Because of compositionality, this system can be recast as

Client 0 || (Server 0 || flag[0] || flag[1] || turn || Server 1) || Client 1

making it match Fig. 3(Left). It can also be recast as

(Client 0 || Server 0) || flag[0] || flag[1] || turn || (Server 1 || Client 1)

which can be transformed to Fig. 2 by computing (Client 0 || Server 0) and (Server 1 || Client 1), and then translating the system back to Promela.

4   Unprevented Request

In addition to under-specification of the requirements and over-specification of the clients, there is a third way in which an intuitively badly incorrect system may pass verification.

The model in Fig. 4 fails mutual exclusion and SPIN finds the error. Assume that both clients execute line 9, the server executes line 17, and Client 0 continues to the end of line 12. Then the server passes the guard req[0] == 0, and is thus now at -> on line 18. If Client 0 acts fast, it can execute lines 9, 10 and the first statement on line 11 a second time before the server continues. Then the server

```
1    bool req[2], gra[2], turn;
2    byte ncrit;                    // nr of procs in critical section
3    active [2] proctype client()
4    {
5       do
6       :: break;
7       :: // skip
8          // (!gra[_pid]);
9          req[_pid] = 1;
10         (gra[_pid]);
11         ncrit++; assert(ncrit == 1); ncrit--;   // critical section
12         req[_pid] = 0;
13      od
14   }
15   active proctype server()
16   { end: do                       // ok for the server to be blocked here
17      ::  (req[0] == 1 && (req[1] == 0 || turn == 0)) -> gra[0] = 1;
18          (req[0] == 0) -> gra[0] = 0; turn = 1;
19      ::  (req[1] == 1 && (req[0] == 0 || turn == 1)) -> gra[1] = 1;
20          (req[1] == 0) -> gra[1] = 1; turn = 0;
21      od
22   }
```

Fig. 4. A client–server mutual exclusion system with handshake

completes line 18 and executes line 19, letting also Client 1 continue to line 11. Now both clients are in the critical section.

The problem is that Client 0 re-entered the critical section on the basis of the permission that it was given in the previous time, before the server had switched that permission off. This is a well-known problem and is solved by making the client wait until the previous permission has been switched off [3, p. 332]. This can be implemented by removing the comment symbol on line 8. After this modification, SPIN reports no error.

However, if also the comment symbol on line 7 is removed, then SPIN reports an invalid end state. Line 20 contains a bug. It assigns 1 to gra[1], while it should assign 0 to it. As a consequence, after visiting the critical section once, Client 1 can never again pass line 8. This is clearly unacceptable, so it is good that SPIN detects it. (Needless to say, the termination branch on line 6 is necessary for detecting the bug. This further illustrates the benefit of termination branches.)

The problem is that the error was *not detected* while the skip statement on line 7 was commented out. This illustrates another issue that we call *unprevented request*. In the absence of the skip statement, the system does not fail to serve the second, third, and later requests by Client 1, for the vacuous reason that Client 1 does not make such requests. It cannot, because it cannot pass line 8. So the system is formally correct, although it is intuitively unacceptable. Unprevented request means that a client must be able to freely choose whether to issue a request, without being prevented by the rest of the system.

As a matter of fact, if eventual access is expressed as $\square(P_1 = 10 \rightarrow \diamond(P_1 = 11))$, then it holds vacuously also in the presence of the skip statement. Then the model fails unprevented request because of line 8. Therefore, to enforce unprevented request, we must express eventual access as $\square(P_1 = 8 \rightarrow \diamond(P_1 = 11))$. This works in the presence of the skip statement. In its absence it does not work, because then SPIN treats lines 7 and 8 as the same state, making it possible for the client to continue from line 8 by executing line 6, contradicting the idea that it had requested.

The skip statement is thus necessary to enforce unprevented request. The analogue of the skip statement in Fig. 3(Right) is the τ-transition from state 1 to state 2. It is this transition that expresses in the model that the client has decided to seek access, and the next transition simply communicates this request to the rest of the system. The first cannot be blocked by the system even if the latter can be.

After fixing the bug on line 20, the model with line 8 commented out fails and with line 8 present passes verification with SPIN, independently of the presence or absence of the skip statement.

Unfortunately, defining eventual access as $\square(P_1 = 8 \rightarrow \diamond(P_1 = 11))$ introduces a problem. We will discuss it in the next section.

5   AG EF Intended Termination

Consider Fig. 4 after fixing line 20, without the comment symbols on lines 7 and 8, and with eventual access defined as $\square(P_1 = 8 \rightarrow \diamond(P_1 = 11))$. In the absence of fairness assumptions, the system has the execution where Client 1 stays on line 8 or 9 while Client 0 repeatedly visits the critical section. The server repeatedly serves Client 0, because it is not aware of the request by Client 1 before the latter has executed line 9. We see that to verify the formula, it is necessary to assume weak fairness, because otherwise the formula does not hold.

On the other hand, this model did pass verification in the previous section, although weak fairness was not used. This is because eventual access was not checked. Instead, it was checked that the model does not deadlock when the clients have not executed their termination branches.

This illustrates that catching errors as unexpected deadlocks is not sensitive to the nuances of the formalization of eventual access as an LTL_X formula. To the extent that it works, it works without any formalization. It suffices to specify the states where each process is allowed to be when the system terminates. This is often easy, because the default conventions of SPIN and Promela do much of the job. (In Fig. 4 we added **end:** on line 16 for this purpose.) This method specifies progress in general (to the extent it specifies it), instead of specifying one or more particular progress properties. This is an advantage for inexperienced users of LTL_X. On the other hand, as modification D in Sect. 2 demonstrates, not all important progress errors can be caught as unexpected deadlocks.

In [7,13], a theory of *fair testing* was developed that facilitates an intermediate approach between detecting errors as unintended deadlocks and with standard LTL_X-based methods. If it is possible to reach a state from which a desired action d is not reachable, then both LTL_X and fair testing declare that progress was violated. If all paths eventually lead to d, then both declare that progress holds. In the remaining case, there is an infinite path where d does not occur, but repeatedly an alternative path is available that leads to the occurrence of d. Fair testing declares this as progress and LTL_X as non-progress. In terms of the Computation Tree Logic, **AG AF** d expresses progress in the LTL_X sense while **AG EF** d expresses progress in the fair testing sense.

Fair testing does not need explicit formulation of fairness assumptions. It gives a weaker notion of progress than LTL_X, but it is much better than nothing. Checking it from the state space is technically simpler than that of LTL_X. It is exceptionally well suitable to be used together with stubborn set/partial order methods for alleviating the state explosion problem [12].

A generic progress requirement can be stated as *in all futures always, there is a future where eventually all processes are in a legal termination state*. This idea reduces the catching of progress errors to catching terminal strong components of the state space where some process is never in a legal termination state. If all such components happen to be deadlocks, we are back in catching errors as unexpected deadlocks.

6   Conclusions

We argued that a verification model should exhibit unforced request and unprevented request, and this can be obtained by adding termination branches and commitment to request similarly to Fig. 3(Right) and lines 6 and 7 in Fig. 4. Doing so widens the set of progress errors that are caught by catching unexpected deadlocks. This is an advantage, because this method does not need formulating fairness assumptions, and, being technically simple, deadlock detection is available in many tools. Furthermore, the method is compatible with the stubborn set method of alleviating state explosion, as explained in [12].

On the other hand, the method cannot catch all progress errors that can be caught with the standard method based on LTL_X and fairness assumptions. Our method is useful when the standard method is considered too complicated. Furthermore, our observations on the importance of unforced request and unprevented request are worth considering also in the LTL_X context.

We observed that such modelling style is rare. We do not interpret this as a sign of it not being worth using, but as a sign of its benefits not being known, although the idea has been in the literature for decades [10].

Acknowledgements. We thank the anonymous reviewers for their comments.

References

1. Dyseryn, V., van Glabbeek, R.J., Höfner, P.: Analysing mutual exclusion using process algebra with signals. In: Peters, K., Tini, S. (eds.) Proceedings of EXPRESS/-SOS 2017, Berlin, Germany, 4 September 2017. EPTCS, vol. 255, pp. 18–34 (2017)
2. Kaivola, R., Valmari, A.: The weakest compositional semantic equivalence preserving nexttime-less linear temporal logic. In: Cleaveland, W.R. (ed.) CONCUR 1992. LNCS, vol. 630, pp. 207–221. Springer, Heidelberg (1992). https://doi.org/10.1007/BFb0084793
3. Manna, Z., Pnueli, A.: The Temporal Logic of Reactive and Concurrent Systems - Specification. Springer, New York (1992). https://doi.org/10.1007/978-1-4612-0931-7
4. Pelánek, R.: BEEM: benchmarks for explicit model checkers. In: Bošnački, D., Edelkamp, S. (eds.) SPIN 2007. LNCS, vol. 4595, pp. 263–267. Springer, Heidelberg (2007). https://doi.org/10.1007/978-3-540-73370-6_17
5. Peterson, G.L.: Myths about the mutual exclusion problem. Inf. Process. Lett. **12**(3), 115–116 (1981)
6. Reeves, G.E.: What really happened on Mars? (1997). https://www.cs.unc.edu/%7eanderson/teach/comp790/papers/mars_pathfinder_long_version.html. Accessed 7 May 2018
7. Rensink, A., Vogler, W.: Fair testing. Inf. Comput. **205**(2), 125–198 (2007)
8. Valmari, A.: The weakest deadlock-preserving congruence. Inf. Process. Lett. **53**(6), 341–346 (1995)
9. Valmari, A.: A chaos-free failures divergences semantics with applications to verification. In: Davies, J., Roscoe, B., Woodcock, J. (eds.) Millennial Perspectives in Computer Science: Proceedings of the 1999 Oxford-Microsoft Symposium in Honour of Sir Tony Hoare, Cornerstones of Computing, pp. 365–382. Palgrave (2000)
10. Valmari, A., Setälä, M.: Visual verification of safety and liveness. In: Gaudel, M.-C., Woodcock, J. (eds.) FME 1996. LNCS, vol. 1051, pp. 228–247. Springer, Heidelberg (1996). https://doi.org/10.1007/3-540-60973-3_90

11. Valmari, A., Tienari, M.: Compositional failure-based semantics models for basic LOTOS. Formal Asp. Comput. **7**(4), 440–468 (1995)
12. Valmari, A., Vogler, W.: Fair testing and stubborn sets. In: Bošnački, D., Wijs, A. (eds.) SPIN 2016. LNCS, vol. 9641, pp. 225–243. Springer, Cham (2016). https://doi.org/10.1007/978-3-319-32582-8_16
13. Vogler, W. (ed.): Modular Construction and Partial Order Semantics of Petri Nets. LNCS, vol. 625. Springer, Heidelberg (1992). https://doi.org/10.1007/3-540-55767-9

Virtual Integration for Pattern-Based Contracts with the KIND2 Model Checker

Jan Steffen Becker[✉]

OFFIS e.V. Institute for Information Technology,
Escherweg 2, 26121 Oldenburg, Germany
becker@offis.de

Abstract. In component based design of embedded software, virtual integration verifies hierarchical decomposition of components and contracts. In this paper we present a virtual integration analysis that is based on the KIND2 state-of-the-art model checker. Our method focuses on pattern-based requirements with automata-based semantics. We propose the Simplified Universal Pattern that is used in the BTC EmbeddedPlatform as a specification language, but other languages may be used as well. The main contribution is a reduction of virtual integration to a reachability problem on so-called counter automata that form the semantics of the pattern language. The counter automata are translated to the synchronous data flow language LUSTRE, that serves as input for KIND2. KIND2 turns out to be quite powerful in proving the safety properties that result from the reachability problem for the automata. Thus, it yields a positive sound (but not complete) verification technique that gives a sufficient condition for virtual integration.

Keywords: Contract-based design · Formal methods
Virtual integration · Model checking · Requirements engineering
Verification

1 Introduction

In component based design, a system is hierarchically decomposed into components. Component based design is part of recent modeling languages for embedded systems such as Amalthea[1], Autosar[2] and Capella[3], to name only a few. Another popular example are dataflow languages such as Matlab Simulink and Scade.

This work has been partially funded by the German Federal Ministry of Education and Research (BMBF) under research grants 01IS15031H (ASSUME) and 01IS16025A (Aramis II).

[1] https://www.eclipse.org/app4mc/.
[2] https://www.autosar.org/.
[3] https://www.polarsys.org/capella/.

© Springer Nature Switzerland AG 2018
F. Howar and J. Barnat (Eds.): FMICS 2018, LNCS 11119, pp. 131–146, 2018.
https://doi.org/10.1007/978-3-030-00244-2_9

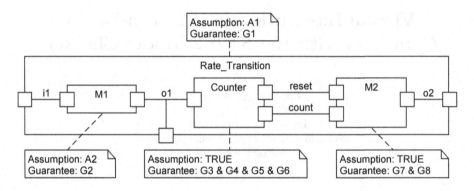

Fig. 1. Running example

Figure 1 shows an imaginary component that is verified in this paper. The component consists of three sub-components M_1, M_2 and *Counter*. The component receives a boolean signal i_1 and outputs two boolean signals o_1 and o_2. The o_1 signal is simply a delayed response of the i_1 signal. As its name suggests, the *Counter* component counts the occurrences of the o_1 signal. If the counter reaches three, the counter is reset and o_2 is set to true.

Many development processes are requirement-driven. State-of-the-art industrial specification tools like BTC EmbeddedPlatform[4] (BTC EP) [2], SESAMM Specifier [14] and STIMULUS [17] assist the engineer in specifying high-quality requirements with unambiguous formal semantics. Pattern languages, such as RSL [20], SPS [12] or TADL [19] are easy to use formalisms to specify functional behavior. In this work we use the Simplified Universal Pattern (SUP) [6]. The SUP is the single pattern that is used for formalization in current versions of the BTC EP. Combining requirements-driven development and component based design leads to *contract based design*. We specify the components using *Assume/Guarantee Contracts* [5]. A contract consists of an *assumption* that describes the allowed behavior of the environment in that the component is going to operate, and the *guarantee* that describes the allowed behavior of the component itself in the environment. Having assumptions and guarantees formalized, it is possible to do formal reasoning among the contracts. The BTC EP assists the engineer in the formalization process, providing traceability from textual to formal requirements and to design and implementation models written in C, Simulink or TargetLink [2]. The focus of BTC EP is verification of the model/code against the formal requirements by formal testing or model checking. Earlier work [1,2,13] already presented a consistency analysis for requirements on one level of the design. However, a *virtual integration analysis* between requirements or contracts on different hierarchical levels has not yet been provided. The question is: Do the contracts on a lower level imply satisfaction of contracts on a higher level? This work presents such an analysis for contracts formalized with the SUP.

---

[4] https://www.btc-es.de/en/products/btc-embeddedplatform/.

We can summarize our approach as follows: We represent the SUP semantics as so-called counter automata that have already been used in [13] for similar patterns. They can precisely encode the original SUP semantics from BTC EP. Because the SUP describes temporal properties of discrete time models with infinite domains, the system specification results in an infinite state transition system. Since verification results shall hold for system runs of arbitrary length, unbounded model checking techniques are needed. KIND2 is a state-of-the-art model checker for verifying safety properties (invariants) of LUSTRE programs. We choose KIND2 as a backend in our approach since it combines different techniques, such as k-induction [21] and IC3 [7], that yield results for the unbounded case as required. The LUSTRE language makes encoding of the counter automata quite easy. KIND2 has been successfully applied in the past for verifying requirements in form of hand-written observers [8] and for virtual integration with contracts written by the user in a LUSTRE dialect [9,11]. In this paper we will (1) show how to encode counter automata in LUSTRE and (2) derive an invariant property for the resulting LUSTRE program that is sufficient to prove virtual integration.

The paper is structured as follows: In Sect. 2 we introduce the SUP and present the details of our running example. In Sects. 3 and 4 counter automata and virtual integration are formally defined. We introduce the LUSTRE language briefly in Sect. 5. We explain the translation process in Sect. 6 including experimental results.

2   Simplified Universal Pattern

The Simplified Universal Pattern (SUP) [6] by BTC is a single pattern with 15 parameters. Most of the parameters have default values. In the Embeddedd Platform a graphical editor is used for formalization that allows the engineer to fill in only needed parameters; parameters with default values are hidden from the user. The SUP defines some trigger/action relationship. Usually, the trigger is some behavior that the system under specification may observe at its ports and the action some behavior it shall perform in response. There are three interpretations for the SUP: progress (the trigger is followed by the action), invariant[5] (trigger and action occur at the same time) and ordering (the action is always preceded by the trigger). In the following, we describe the most common one, progress, from the view point of an observer. An observer is a component that runs in parallel to the system, monitors the ports and rises a failure signal if the specified behavior is violated.

Trigger Phase. The trigger phase is defined by the parameters Trigger Start Event (TSE), Trigger Condition (TC), Trigger End Event (TEE) and Trigger Exit Condition (TEC) as well as two time bounds Trigger Min (TMin) and Trigger Max (TMax). Technically, events are the same as conditions. The term

---

[5] The invariant interpretation is actually a shortcut for the progress interpretation with default values.

event is used to highlight the fact that the condition marks begin or end of a phase. The trigger of the SUP is successfully observed if the TEE occurs within [TMin, TMax] after TSE and TC holds in between. If the TEC occurs, the observation cycle is aborted.

Action Phase. The action phase is defined by the parameters Action Start Event (ASE), Action Condition (AC), Action End Event (AEE), Action Exit Condition (AEC), Action Min (AMin) and Action Max (AMax) analogous to the trigger phase. The AEE must occur within [AMin, AMax] after ASE and AC must hold in between. Otherwise, the observation ends with a failure. If the AEC occurs, the current observation cycle is aborted and a new one starts. If the AEE has been observed successfully the current observation cycle ends successful and a new one starts.

Local Scope. The local scope [LMin, LMax] consisting of two parameters restricts the time span between the TEE and ASE; if the ASE is observed too early or too late, the observation fails.

Furthermore, there is an optional *global scope* parameter that we don't use here and three different *startup phases* and *activation modes* that change the behavior of the SUP. Note that an observer for the SUP is a state machine, so in every observation cycle only the first occurrence of the trigger is noticed. As a default $TSE = TC = TEE$, $ASE = AC = AEE$, $TEC = AEC = false$, $AMin = AMax = TMin = TMax = LMin = Lmax = 0$. In the examples in this paper we assume default values for the SUP and specify only needed values.

2.1   Running Example

As a running example we use the `Rate_Transition` component from Fig. 1 the introduction. In the following we will give a textual explanation of the contracts. The SUP formalization is presented in Table 1. In textual form the assumption for the whole (top-level) component is

(A1) i_1 is *true* once every 35 ms

and the guarantee

(G1) whenever o_1 is *true*, o_2 is *true* within 160 ms.

The component M_1 has some weaker assumption

(A2) i_1 is *true* once every 30 ms to 40 ms.

and the guarantee

(G2) when i_1 is *true* then o_1 is *true* within 10 ms to 20 ms.

The *counter* and M_2 components do not have assumptions. The guarantees for the *counter* component are

Table 1. SUP instances for the running example

ID	Trigger $TSE = TC = TEE$	Local Scope $[Lmin, Lmax]$	Action ASE	AC	AEE	$[Amin, Amax]$
A1	$true$	$[0,0]$	$true$	$\neg i_1$	i_1	$[35\,\text{ms}, 35\,\text{ms}]$
A2	$true$	$[0,0]$	$true$	$\neg i_1$	i_1	$[30\,\text{ms}, 40\,\text{ms}]$
G1	o_1	$[0, 160\,\text{ms}]$	o_2			$[0,0]$
G2	i_1	$[10\,\text{ms}, 20\,\text{ms}]$	o_1			$[0,0]$
G3	$true$	$[0,0]$	$count \geq 0$			$[0,0]$
G4	$o_1 \wedge \neg reset$	$[0,0]$	$count = last(count) + 1$			$[0,0]$
G5	$o_1 \wedge reset$	$[0,0]$	$count = 1$			$[0,0]$
G6	$\neg o_1$	$[0,0]$	$count = last(count)$			$[0,0]$
G7	$count \geq 3$	$[0, 5\,\text{ms}]$	$o_2 \wedge reset$		$count < 3$	$[0, \infty)$
G8	$true$	$[0,0]$	$\neg reset \vee last(count) \geq 3$			$[0,0]$

(G3) *count* is always positive or zero.
(G4) when o_1 is *true* and *reset* is *false*, *count* is inceremented
(G5) when both o_1 and *reset* are *true*, *count* is set to 1
(G6) when o_1 is *false*, *count* is stable

and the guarantee for M_2 is

(G7) when $count \geq 3$ then, after at most 5ms, o_2 and *reset* are *true* until $count < 3$ again.
(G8) *reset* is *true* only if $count \geq 3$ in the last step.

3 Formal Pattern Semantics

We follow the approach in [13] for encoding semantics of pattern instances. A pattern instance $P = \text{P}(\mathbb{Q})$ consists of a pattern P and a parameter substitution $\mathbb{Q}$ that assigns some expression $\mathbb{Q}(q)$ over the system variables to every pattern parameter q. The semantics $[\![P]\!]$ of a pattern instance is a set of traces over the system variables.

3.1 Counter Automata

We use so-called *counter automata* to describe pattern semantics. A counter automaton representing a pattern instance accepts those system executions, called *traces*, that satisfy the pattern semantics.

Definition 1 (Trace). *An evolution ε_X for a variable X is a function $\varepsilon_X : \mathbb{N} \to \mathcal{V}_{type(X)}$ assigning some value X_t from the set of values associated with its type to the variable X at time $t \in \mathbb{N}$.*

A trace *over some set* $\mathbb{X}$ *of variables is a function* $\sigma : X \mapsto \varepsilon_X$ *that maps an evaluation* ε_X *to every variable* $X \in \mathbb{X}$. *The set of all traces over* $\mathbb{X}$ *is denoted by* $\mathcal{T}(\mathbb{X})$.

We denote the value of some variable X at time t in trace σ by $\sigma_X(t)$.

A counter automata is a finite automaton that is equipped with counters. The transitions are labeled with boolean expressions over the input variables and counters, called guard, and with actions on the counters. Starting in the initial state, in every step the guards are evaluated, a transition is taken and the counter values are incremented, reset to an integer value or left unchanged according to the transition's action.

Every pattern P has a corresponding counter automata schema $\mathcal{A}_P$. The automata schema $\mathcal{A}_P$ is used as a template to construct an observer automaton $\mathcal{A}_P(\mathbb{Q})$. We derive $\mathcal{A}_P(\mathbb{Q})$ from $\mathcal{A}_P$ by applying the substitution $\mathbb{Q}$ to the guards in $\mathcal{A}_P$. Technically there is no difference between an observer automaton and an automata schema, except that the observer automaton is defined over the system variables and the automata schema is defined over the pattern parameters.

Definition 2 (Counter automaton). *A counter automaton over a set* $\mathbb{X}$ *of variables is a tuple* $\mathcal{A} = \langle S, \mathbb{X}, \mathbb{W}, I, F, T \rangle$ *with states* S, *integer counter variables* $\mathbb{W}$ *distinct from* $\mathbb{X}$, *initial and failure state* $I, F \in S$ *and a set* T *of transitions. A transition* $\langle s, g, \gamma, s' \rangle \in T$ *consists of source and target states* $s, s' \in S$, *a guard* $g \in Expr_{\mathbb{B}}(\mathbb{X} \cup \mathbb{W})$ *(a boolean expression over* $\mathbb{X} \cup \mathbb{W}$*) and a function* $\gamma : \mathbb{W} \to \mathbb{N} \cup \{INC, STABLE\}$.

A trace σ *over* $\mathbb{X} \cup \mathbb{W} \cup \{s\}$ *(*$s \notin \mathbb{X} \cup \mathbb{W}$ *is a fresh variable with* type$(s) = S$*) is a run for* $\mathcal{A}$ *if* $\sigma_s(0) = I$, $\sigma_c(0) = 0$ *for* $c \in \mathbb{W}$ *and for all* $t \in \mathbb{N}$ *exists* $\langle s, g, \gamma, s' \rangle \in T$ *such that* $\sigma_s(t) = s$, $\sigma_s(t+1) = s'$, $\sigma(t) \models g$ *and* $\sigma_c(t+1) =$

$$\begin{cases} \gamma(c) & \text{if } \gamma(c) \in \mathbb{N} \\ \sigma_c(t) + 1 & \text{if } \gamma(c) = INC \\ \sigma_c(t) & \text{if } \gamma(c) = STABLE \end{cases} \quad \text{for } c \in \mathbb{W}. \text{ A run is accepting if } \sigma_s(t) \neq F \text{ for}$$

all $t \in \mathbb{N}$.

We denote by $\mathcal{T}(\mathcal{A}) = \{\sigma \downarrow \mathbb{X} \mid \sigma \text{ is an accepting run for } \mathcal{A}\}$ *all the accepting runs restricted to the variables in* $\mathbb{X}$.

Here, $\sigma(t) \models g$ denotes satisfaction of g on σ in step t. For the guards we can allow any expression that is valid in LUSTRE. As a direct consequence of using automata for the pattern semantics, the semantics $[\![P(\mathbb{Q})]\!]$ of some pattern instance are the traces accepted by its counter automaton, i.e.

$$[\![P(\mathbb{Q})]\!] = \mathcal{T}(\mathcal{A}_P(\mathbb{Q})).$$

In this paper we allow *complete* and *deterministic* counter automata only. A counter automaton is deterministic if the guards of the outgoing transitions of any state are mutually exclusive, and complete if always at least one outgoing guard is satisfied. Furthermore, failure states are required to be sinks, meaning they have a self-loop as the only outgoing transition.

3.2   Counter Automata for the SUP

The formal semantics [22] that have been kindly provided by BTC Embed-dedSystems to the author, use automata networks that are very close to counter automata. Compared to counter automata, these automata

- synchronize with each other by events,
- may perform arbitrary many steps during one global (i.e. system-level) step, provided that each transition is taken at most once.

Such an automata network can be translated to a single counter automaton by constructing

1. the product of the automata in the network and
2. the transitive closure of the transitions possible during one global step.

Note that computing the transitive closure is a terminating process in our case, since in one global step each transition is taken at most once. Because these steps result in an exponential blow-up of the automaton, we apply standard reduction techniques known from finite automata such as unifying indistinguishable states and removing unreachable ones. From the formal definition of the SUP semantics we derive a single counter automata schema for every combination of interpretation, activation mode and startup phase. Due to the complexity of the SUP that has 15 parameters, the resulting automata are still very big. In practice only a subset of the SUP parameters is used in an instance, e.g. the trigger start and end events equal the trigger condition. This leads to unreachable states and transitions that are never enabled in the observer automaton. Therefore we optimize the automata schema for each pattern instance with respect to the parameters (formally we replace some pattern instance $P(\mathbb{Q})$ by a pattern instance $P'(\mathbb{Q}')$ such that $[\![P'(\mathbb{Q}')]\!] = [\![P(\mathbb{Q})]\!]$ and $|\mathcal{A}_{P'}| \leq |\mathcal{A}_P|$). The local optimization steps include:

1. Substitute parameters that are set to 0, *true*, or *false* in the guards by their value.
2. Unify parameters that have the same value
3. Substitute sub-expressions of the form $X \leq q$ in guards by *true*, if q is a parameter and $\mathbb{Q}(q) = \infty$, i.e. q is set to infinity; the same for other inequalities
4. Remove transitions with unsatisfiable guards; we delegate satisfiability checking to the Z3 SMT solver [18]
5. Remove unreachable states based on the results of step 4

As an example, we show in Fig. 2 the resulting automaton for the SUP instance G1 from Table 1. The engine substituted TC and TEE by TSE, ASE and AC by AEE, and eliminated all time parameters except LMax. Note that the automaton in Fig. 2 is still an automata schema. We do not insert the variables o_1 and o_2 at this point.

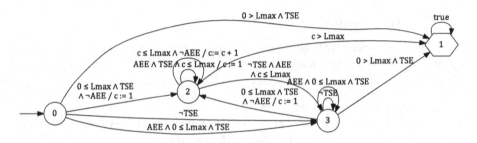

Fig. 2. Counter automaton for guarantee G1; state 0 is the initial and 1 the failure state.

4   Formalizing Virtual Integration

We adopt the theory of *dataflow A/G contracts* from [5] as follows: In this work a contract $\mathcal{C} = (A, G)$ consists of assumptions A and guarantees G which are sets of pattern instances. We specify the semantics in saturated form, i.e. $E_\mathcal{C} = \bigcap_{P \in A} [\![P]\!]$ is the maximal environment and $M_\mathcal{C} = (\mathcal{T}(\mathbb{X}) \setminus E_\mathcal{C}) \cup \bigcap_{P \in G} [\![P]\!]$ is the maximal implementation of $\mathcal{C}$. The semantics $[\![\mathcal{C}]\!] = (\mathcal{E}_\mathcal{C}, \mathcal{M}_\mathcal{C})$ of a contract describes all implementations $\mathcal{M}_\mathcal{C} = \{M \mid M \subseteq M_\mathcal{C}\}$ and allowed environments $\mathcal{E}_\mathcal{C} = \{M \mid M \subseteq E_\mathcal{C}\}$ of $\mathcal{C}$ in form of trace sets.

When composing components, we simply connect signals with the same name as seen in the introduction. In the theory of dataflow A/G contracts we can specify *composition* and *refinement* of contracts.

Definition 3 (Contract operations). *For contracts $\mathcal{C}_1$, $\mathcal{C}_2$, the composition $\mathcal{C}_1 \otimes \mathcal{C}_2$ is a contract such that*

$$M_{\mathcal{C}_1 \otimes \mathcal{C}_2} = M_{\mathcal{C}_1} \cap M_{\mathcal{C}_2} \tag{1}$$

$$E_{\mathcal{C}_1 \otimes \mathcal{C}_2} = \max\{M \mid M \cap M_{\mathcal{C}_2} \subseteq E_{\mathcal{C}_1} \wedge M \cap M_{\mathcal{C}_1} \subseteq E_{\mathcal{C}_2}\} \tag{2}$$

Contract $\mathcal{C}_1$ refines $\mathcal{C}_2$, written $\mathcal{C}_1 \preceq \mathcal{C}_2$, if $M_{\mathcal{C}_1} \subseteq M_{\mathcal{C}_2}$ and $E_{\mathcal{C}_1} \supseteq E_{\mathcal{C}_2}$.

The idea behind Eq. (1) is that an implementation for the composition $\mathcal{C}_1 \otimes \mathcal{C}_2$ has to fulfill the guarantees of both $\mathcal{C}_1$ and $\mathcal{C}_2$. The idea behind Eq. (2) is that we can allow the weakest environment in that both components can operate, whereby part of the assumption of $\mathcal{C}_1$ is already guaranteed by $\mathcal{C}_2$ and vice versa. Refinement $\mathcal{C}_1 \preceq \mathcal{C}_2$ means that $\mathcal{C}_1$ can act as a replacement for $\mathcal{C}_2$, hence the guarantee is stronger and the environment weaker.

For dataflow A/G contracts it is indeed possible to compute the composition of contracts. In this work, however, we prefer to split virtual integration into a set of containment relations that are checked separately. This allows better feedback in case of a failed analysis.

Lemma 1 (Virtual integration). *For contracts $\mathcal{C}_0, \mathcal{C}_1, \dots, \mathcal{C}_n$ refinement $\mathcal{C}_1 \otimes \cdots \otimes \mathcal{C}_n \preceq \mathcal{C}_0$ is equivalent to*

$$\left(\bigcap_{i=1}^{n} M_{\mathcal{C}_i} \subseteq M_{\mathcal{C}_0} \right) \wedge \bigwedge_{i=1}^{n} \left(\left(E_{\mathcal{C}_0} \cap \bigcap_{j=1, j \neq i}^{n} M_{\mathcal{C}_j} \right) \subseteq E_{\mathcal{C}_i} \right). \tag{VIT}$$

Proof. We prove inductively over the number of sub-level contracts that, for assertions $M \subseteq T(\mathbb{X})$,

$$\left(\bigwedge_{i=1}^{n} \left((M \cap \bigcap_{j=1, j \neq i}^{n} M_{\mathcal{C}_j}) \subseteq E_{\mathcal{C}_i} \right) \right) \iff (M \subseteq E_{\mathcal{C}_1 \otimes \cdots \otimes \mathcal{C}_n})$$

in the theory of dataflow A/G contracts. For $n = 1$ this follows directly from Definition 3. Assume we have shown the induction hypothesis for some arbitrary but fixed n. Then we have:

$$\bigwedge_{i=1}^{n+1} \left((M \cap \bigcap_{j=1, j \neq i}^{n+1} M_{\mathcal{C}_j}) \subseteq E_{\mathcal{C}_i} \right)$$

$$\Leftrightarrow \bigwedge_{i=1}^{n} \left(((M \cap M_{\mathcal{C}_{n+1}}) \cap \bigcap_{j=1, j \neq i}^{n} M_{\mathcal{C}_j}) \subseteq E_{\mathcal{C}_i} \right) \wedge \left((M \cap \bigcap_{j=1}^{n} M_{\mathcal{C}_j}) \subseteq E_{\mathcal{C}_{n+1}} \right)$$

$$\overset{\text{ind. hyp.}}{\Leftrightarrow} \left((M \cap M_{\mathcal{C}_{n+1}}) \subseteq E_{\mathcal{C}_1 \otimes \cdots \otimes \mathcal{C}_n} \right) \wedge \left((M \cap M_{\mathcal{C}_1 \otimes \cdots \otimes \mathcal{C}_n}) \subseteq E_{\mathcal{C}_{n+1}} \right)$$

$$\Leftrightarrow M \subseteq \max \left(M \middle| ((M \cap M_{\mathcal{C}_{n+1}}) \subseteq E_{\mathcal{C}_1 \otimes \cdots \otimes \mathcal{C}_n}) \wedge ((M \cap M_{\mathcal{C}_1 \otimes \cdots \otimes \mathcal{C}_n}) \subseteq E_{\mathcal{C}_{n+1}}) \right)$$

$$\Leftrightarrow M \subseteq E_{\mathcal{C}_1 \otimes \cdots \otimes \mathcal{C}_{n+1}}$$

Setting $M = E_{\mathcal{C}_0}$, the VIT condition (VIT) is equivalent to

$$\left(M_{\mathcal{C}_1 \otimes \cdots \otimes \mathcal{C}_n} \subseteq M_{\mathcal{C}_0} \right) \wedge \left(E_{\mathcal{C}_0} \subseteq E_{\mathcal{C}_1 \otimes \cdots \otimes \mathcal{C}_{n+1}} \right).$$

5   Short Introduction to LUSTRE

LUSTRE [16] is a synchronous data flow language. In the following we give a short overview about the key-features of LUSTRE that are relevant for this publication.

Dataflow and Operators. Variables represent streams of data. Analogous to our definition of automata traces, the value of a variable X is an evolution $\varepsilon_X : \mathbb{N} \to \mathcal{V}_{type(X)}$ and $\varepsilon_X : t \mapsto X_t$. LUSTRE supports bool, int and real basic datatypes and user-defined types such as enums. The usual arithmetic, boolean, and comparison operators are defined and have a component-wise semantics, that means

$$\varepsilon_{X \boxplus Y} : t \mapsto \varepsilon_X(t) \boxplus \varepsilon_Y(t)$$

for binary operators $\boxplus \in \{+, -, <, \dots\}$. Furthermore we have the special unary operator *pre* that returns the previous value of expression and binary operator $\to$ that replaces the first component of a stream: $\varepsilon_{X \to Y}(0) = \varepsilon_X(0)$, and $\varepsilon_{pre\ X}(t) = \varepsilon_X(t-1)$, $\varepsilon_{X \to Y}(t) = \varepsilon_Y(t)$ for $t > 0$.

Since LUSTRE does not have imperative aspects, a control flow does not exist. In LUSTRE, statements of the form if P then X else Y have the semantics

$$\varepsilon_{\text{if } P \text{ then } X \text{ else } Y} : t \mapsto \begin{cases} \varepsilon_X(t) & \text{if } \varepsilon_P(t) = true \\ \varepsilon_Y(t) & \text{else} \end{cases}.$$

```
1   type states1 = enum {S1_0, S1_1, S1_2, S1_3};
2   node pattern1(TSE: bool; Lmax: int; AEE: bool) returns (fail: bool);
3     var State: states1; c: int;
4   let
5     (State, c) = (
6         if (not  TSE) then (S1_3, 1)
7         else if ((AEE and (0 <= Lmax)) and TSE) then (S1_3, 1)
8         else if ((not  (0 <= Lmax)) and TSE) then (S1_1, 1)
9         else (S1_2, 1)
10        ) -> (
11        if pre(State) = S1_0 then
12            if (not  TSE) then (S1_3, 1)
13            else if ((AEE and (0 <= Lmax)) and TSE) then (S1_3, 1)
14            else if ((not  (0 <= Lmax)) and TSE) then (S1_1, 1)
15            else (S1_2, 1)
16        else if pre(State) = S1_1 then (S1_1, 1)
17        else if pre(State) = S1_2 then
18            if (not  ((pre c) <= Lmax)) then (S1_1, 1)
19            else if (((not  TSE) and AEE) and ((pre c) <= Lmax))
20                    then (S1_3, 1)
21            else if ((AEE and TSE) and ((pre c) <= Lmax)) then
22                (S1_2, 1)
23            else (S1_2, ((pre c) + 1))
24        else if (not  TSE) then (S1_3, 1)
25            else if ((AEE and (0 <= Lmax)) and TSE) then (S1_3, 1)
26            else if ((not  (0 <= Lmax)) and TSE) then (S1_1, 1)
27            else (S1_2, 1)
28        );
29    fail = false or (State = S1_1);
30  tel;
```

Listing 1.1. LUSTRE node for the SUP used in assertion G1

Nodes. A LUSTRE specification consists of a collection of nodes. From the conceptual perspective, a node encapsulates some behavior as a reusable unit. From the logical perspective, a node definition is a function definition that describes the relation between the inputs and the output types of a node as a set of equations.

6   Translation Schema

After the optimization (see Sect. 3.2) we translate the optimized automata to LUSTRE nodes. The translation of the automaton if Fig. 2 is shown in Listing 1.1. Finally we generate the code for the main node that instantiates all the assertions. An excerpt of the code for our running example is provided in Listing 1.2. For every assertion P a variable $fail_P$ is introduced that becomes *true* upon violation of P. The variable GOAL that is returned by the main node, encodes the virtual integration condition from Lemma 1. We check every part of the conjunction in a separate run of the model checker. If for all parts GOAL can be proven to be an invariant, virtual integration holds.

6.1   From Counter Automata to LUSTRE

Since the translation from counter automata to LUSTRE is quite straight forward, we will not present a formal translation schema here. Instead we explain the

```
 1  node main(count:int; i1:bool; o1:bool; o2:bool; reset:bool)
 2    returns (GOAL:bool);
 3    var failA1, failA2, failG1, (*...*) , failG8: bool;
 4  let
 5    failG1 = pattern1( (* guarantee G1 *)
 6      o1 (* TSE: o1 *) , 32 (* Lmax: 160ms *) ,
 7      o2 (* AEE: o2 *) );
 8    (* ... *)
 9    (* same for failA1, failA2, failG2, ..., failG8 *)
10
11    GOAL = ((failA2 or not failG2) and (not failG3)
12      and (not failG4) and (not failG5) and (not failG6)
13      and (not failG7) and (not failG8)) => (failA1 or not failG1);
14    --%MAIN ;
15    --%PROPERTY GOAL ;
16  tel;
```

Listing 1.2. Main LUSTRE node

translation using the automata schema for guarantee G1, shown in Fig. 2. The code is shown in Listing 1.1.

The node has an input variable for every parameter of the (optimized) pattern, and returns the variable **fail** that is true if the counter automaton is in the failure state. In line 3 a local variable **State** for the state and an integer variable for the counter c are declared. The type of the **State** variable is an enum declared in line 1, that has a literal for every state. Note that the **State** and counter variables look ahead one step: They contain state and counter values in the next instead of the current step. This saves us one unrolling step in the analysis. As a consequence we have to encode the first step (lines 6–9) separately from the other steps (lines 11–27).

The first step is encoded as an if-then-else clause with one branch for each outgoing transition. For example, line 6 encodes the transition from state 0 to state 3 with guard $\neg TSE$. The tuple (S1_3, 1) encodes the next state (S1_3 is the enum literal for state 3) and the new value for c. Here, the translation engine does some optimization: To keep the value range of c as small as possible, we assign the value 1 instead of 0 (as required by Definition 2) to c. We can safely do this, since the value of c is not relevant in state 3. On every path of transitions starting in state 3, c is reset before it is used in a guard.

The encoding of the following steps is a nested if-then-else clause, where the outer if ranges over the current state (the value of **pre State**) and the inner if over the outgoing transitions of each state. For example, in lines 12–15 the outgoing transitions of state 0 are handled and in the last branch, lines 24–27, the outgoing transitions for state 3. Again, we alter the next value of the counter if it is not relevant in the target state, e.g. in line 20 the new value for c is 1 instead of **pre c**.

In the initial version of this paper also upper and lower bounds for the counter variables have been calculated during the translation. Experiments showed that providing this information to KIND2 does not influence the results. It seems that KIND2 finds those bounds itself during invariant generation.

Lemma 2 (Correctness of translation). *For some run σ of a pattern's automata schema $\mathcal{A}_\mathrm{P}$ and data stream ε for the corresponding LUSTRE node* $\mathtt{node_P}$ *with $\varepsilon_q = \sigma_q$ for each parameter q of the pattern is, for all $t \in \mathbb{N}$, $\varepsilon_{\mathtt{fail}}(t) = true$ if $\sigma_s(t+1) = F$.*

Since we have not presented the translation formally, we will not give the proof here. It follows quite straight forward from the translation.

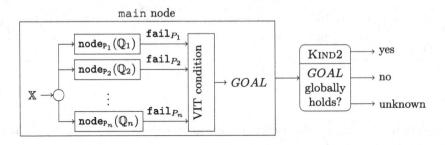

Fig. 3. Calling KIND2

6.2 Checking the VIT Condition

We compose the observers for all pattern instances in a specification, as shown in Fig. 3. An excerpt of the resulting code for the running example is shown in Listing 1.2. For reasons of space we replaced some parts by a comment (*...*). It has an input variable for every system variable (line 1). For every pattern instance $P = \mathrm{P}(\mathbb{Q})$ we introduce some boolean variable $\mathtt{fail}_P = \mathtt{node_P}(\mathbb{Q}(q_1^\mathrm{P}), \ldots, \mathbb{Q}(q_{o_\mathrm{P}}^\mathrm{P}))$ (line 3 in Listing 1.2). For example, in line 5 of Listing 1.2 we instantiate the pattern node $\mathtt{pattern1}$ from Listing 1.1 that we explained in the last section. We choose a step size of 5 ms, so the node parameters are $\mathtt{TSE} = \mathtt{o1}$, $\mathtt{Lmax} = 32$ and $\mathtt{AEE} = \mathtt{o2}$. Analogous code follows for the remaining $\mathtt{fail}$ variables. The step size of 5ms is chosen because it is the largest one that exactly divides all the time constants into integers. As the experimental results in Sect. 6.3 show, a smaller step size would increase the analysis effort.

In order to prove refinement we have to check the set-inclusions $\bigcap_{i=1}^{n} M_{\mathcal{C}_i} \subseteq M_{\mathcal{C}_0}$ and $E_{\mathcal{C}_0} \cap \bigcap_{j \neq i} M_{\mathcal{C}_j} \subseteq E_{\mathcal{C}_i}$ according to Lemma 1. The set expressions reduce to union, intersection and complement of pattern semantics. We translate them to boolean expressions over the $\mathtt{fail}$ variables:

$$Form(\llbracket P \rrbracket) := \neg\mathtt{fail}_P$$
$$Form(F_1 \cup F_2) := Form(F_1) \vee Form(F_2)$$
$$Form(F_1 \cap F_2) := Form(F_1) \wedge Form(F_2)$$
$$Form(\mathcal{T}(\mathbb{X}) \setminus F) := \neg Form(F)$$

where $\mathtt{fail}_P$ is the return value of $\mathtt{node_P}(\mathbb{Q}(q_1^\mathrm{P}), \ldots, \mathbb{Q}(q_{o_\mathrm{P}}^\mathrm{P}))$.

Lemma 3. *For every trace $\varepsilon_{\mathbb{X}} \in \mathcal{T}(\mathbb{X})$ and $F \subseteq \mathcal{T}(\mathbb{X})$ such that $Form(F)$ is defined, exists $t \in \mathbb{N}$ such that*

$$\forall t' \geq t : \varepsilon_{Form(F)}(t') \Leftrightarrow \varepsilon_{\mathbb{X}} \in F.$$

Proof. The basic case $F = \llbracket P \rrbracket$ follows from Lemma 2 together with the fact that we derive $\mathcal{A}_P(\mathbb{Q})$ from $\mathcal{A}_P$ by substitution of the parameters and failure states of $\mathcal{A}_P$ are sinks.

For the case $F = F_1 \cup F_2$ (and $F_1 \cap F_2$ analogously): By induction hypothesis there exist t_i, $i \in \{1, 2\}$ such that $\forall t' \geq t_i : \varepsilon_{Form(F_i)}(t') \Leftrightarrow \varepsilon_{\mathbb{X}} \in F_i$. The lemma holds with $t = \max\{t_1, t_2\}$.

For $\overline{F} = \mathcal{T}(\mathbb{X}) \setminus F$ we have $\varepsilon_{\mathbb{X}} \in \mathcal{T}(\mathbb{X}) \setminus F \Leftrightarrow \neg(\varepsilon_{\mathbb{X}} \in F) \Leftrightarrow \neg\varepsilon_{Form(F)}(t') \Leftrightarrow \varepsilon_{\neg Form(F)}(t')$.

Corollary 1. *If on the parallel composition $fail_P := node_P(\mathbb{Q})$ for all the pattern instances $P = P(\mathbb{Q})$ in contracts $\mathcal{C}_0, \ldots, \mathcal{C}_n$*

- *globally $Form(\bigcap_{i=1}^{n} M_{\mathcal{C}_i}) \Rightarrow Form(M_{\mathcal{C}_0})$ and*
- *globally $Form(E_{\mathcal{C}_0} \cap \bigcap_{j \neq i} M_{\mathcal{C}_j}) \Rightarrow Form(E_{\mathcal{C}_i})$ with i, j ranging from 1 to n*

holds, then refinement $\mathcal{C}_1 \otimes \cdots \otimes \mathcal{C}_n \preceq \mathcal{C}_0$ holds.

Proof. This is a consequence of Lemmas 1 and 3.

Example 1. Listing 1.2, lines 11–13, shows the LUSTRE code for

$$Form((\llbracket \overline{A2} \rrbracket \cup \llbracket G2 \rrbracket) \cap (\llbracket G3 \rrbracket \cap \llbracket G4 \rrbracket \cap \llbracket G5 \rrbracket \cap \llbracket G6 \rrbracket) \cap (\llbracket G7 \rrbracket \cap \llbracket G8 \rrbracket))$$
$$\Rightarrow Form(\llbracket \overline{A1} \rrbracket \cup \llbracket G1 \rrbracket))$$

which checks if the guarantee $G1$ of the top-level contract holds.

Note that Lemma 3 holds only in one direction, so the virtual integration analysis using the corollary is sound, but incomplete.

6.3   Experimental Results

For the running example, checking virtual integration results in two LUSTRE programs to be verified, one that verifies satisfaction of the assumption A2 for the sub-level component M_1, and one that verifies satisfaction of the top-level guarantee G1. Running on a Linux PC with Intel Core i5-3210M CPU @2.50 GHz, KIND2 version 1.1.0 with Z3 4.6.0 as SMT solver backend can prove both in under 1 min.

To give an idea how our method scales, we run some simple experiments with a growing number of requirements and varying time parameters. In the following we denote by $p \xrightarrow{t} q$ an SUP instance with the following parameters: $TSE = TEE = TC = p$, $ASE = AEE = AC = q$, $Lmax = t$ steps, $Tmin = Tmax = Amin = Amax = Lmin = 0$. We prove the refinement

$$(\emptyset, \{P_0 \xrightarrow{\lfloor \frac{m}{n} \rfloor} P_1, P_1 \xrightarrow{\lfloor \frac{m}{n} \rfloor} P_2, \ldots, P_{n-1} \xrightarrow{\lfloor \frac{m}{n} \rfloor} P_n\}) \preceq (\emptyset, \{P_0 \xrightarrow{m} P_n\})$$

(1) with $m = 20$ and $n = 2, 3, 4, \ldots, 10$ and (2) with $n = 2$ and $m = 0, 4, 8, \ldots, 40$. Here $P_0, \ldots, P_n$ are boolean system variables. The tests have been run with the same setup as above. Roughly speaking, KIND2 unrolls the transition system until a k-inductive invariant is found. The empirical results in Fig. 4 suggest that the unrolling depth grows with the maximum time bound (in steps) in the specification.

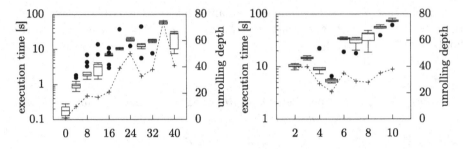

Fig. 4. Detailed results. Left: $n = 2$ and varrying m, right: $m = 20$ and varying n. Box-and-whisker plots show solver run time, the dashed line the unrolling depth.

7   Conclusion and Related Work

In this work we presented an approach for formal verification of virtual integration using the state-of-the art model checker KIND2. KIND2 has been used in the past in different contexts, e.g. the verification of Simulink models [8]. It turns out that KIND2 is also quite powerful in proving virtual integration. In [11] KIND (the predecessor of KIND2) is used in a virtual integration analysis for AADL models, and in [9] the LUSTRE language itself is extended with a notion of contracts in order to facilitate compositional verification of LUSTRE programs. In both cases assertions are written by the end user in a LUSTRE dialect instead of a pattern language that abstracts from the more complex mathematical notation.

We focus on contracts formalized with the SUP in order to integrate with the BTC EmbeddedPlatform, but other pattern languages are possible as well, as long as the semantics can be expressed as counter automata. As shown in [1], most of the SPS patterns can be expressed with the SUP, so it is also possible to define counter automata schemes for them. Automala-like process networks are also verified in [3,4]. Here, the authors present a dedicated algorithm for invariant generation with quite impressing results, that may also be used for proving safety properties. It is not clear, however, if the techniques can be applied to the observer automata used in this work. The counter automata here are synchronous and the interactions, opposed to the presentation in [3,4], purely relies on data. Instead of using a specialized proof system, our approach relies on general purpose methods. In most of our experiments, including the one presented in this paper, KIND2 proves virtual integration by a combination of invariant generation and k-induction.

State of practice virtual integration testing often uses simulation instead of modelchecking. Although simulation-based approaches (e.g. [17]) may scale better, they can only produce counter examples but do not give a formal proof. In other words, simulation, in opposite to our approach, does not give a guarantee that all possible violations of the top level contract are found.

Virtual integration for pattern-based contracts using model checking has already been investigated earlier in [15] based on UPPAAL. However, in [15] only (boolean) events and time constants are allowed as pattern parameters, whereas our approach supports integer band real typed system variables. The OCRA tool [10] also implements a virtual integration analysis that is somewhat closer to our approach. The contract theory behind OCRA is quite similar to the one from [5] that we use in this work. The main difference is that the Othello language that is used for describing contracts in OCRA is more close to LTL extended to numerical data types. OCRA uses the nuXmv model checker as backend and seems not to use k-induction. There is no direct translation between the SUP and Othello and a quantitative comparison of our approach to OCRA is future work.

References

1. Becker, J.S.: Analyzing consistency of formal requirements. In: Automated Verification of Critical Systems (AVOCS 2018) (2018)
2. Becker, J.S., et al.: Interoperable toolchain for requirements-driven model-based development. In: ERTS 2018 (2018)
3. Bensalem, S., Bozga, M., Nguyen, T.H., Sifakis, J.: Compositional verification for component-based systems and application. IET Software 4(3), 181–193 (2010)
4. Bensalem, S., Bozga, M., Sifakis, J., Nguyen, T.-H.: Compositional verification for component-based systems and application. In: Cha, S.S., Choi, J.-Y., Kim, M., Lee, I., Viswanathan, M. (eds.) ATVA 2008. LNCS, vol. 5311, pp. 64–79. Springer, Heidelberg (2008). https://doi.org/10.1007/978-3-540-88387-6_7
5. Benveniste, A.: Contracts for system design. Found. Trends Electron. Design Autom. 12(2–3), 124–400 (2018)
6. Bienmüller, T., Teige, T., Eggers, A., Stasch, M.: Modeling requirements for quantitative consistency analysis and automatic test case generation. In: FM&MDD 2016. Computing Science Technical report Series, vol. CS-TR-1503. Newcastle University (2016)
7. Bradley, A.R.: SAT-based model checking without unrolling. In: Jhala, R., Schmidt, D. (eds.) VMCAI 2011. LNCS, vol. 6538, pp. 70–87. Springer, Heidelberg (2011). https://doi.org/10.1007/978-3-642-18275-4_7
8. Brat, G., Bushnell, D., Davies, M., Giannakopoulou, D., Howar, F., Kahsai, T.: Verifying the safety of a flight-critical system. In: Bjørner, N., de Boer, F. (eds.) FM 2015. LNCS, vol. 9109, pp. 308–324. Springer, Cham (2015). https://doi.org/10.1007/978-3-319-19249-9_20
9. Champion, A., Gurfinkel, A., Kahsai, T., Tinelli, C.: CoCoSpec: a mode-aware contract language for reactive systems. In: De Nicola, R., Kühn, E. (eds.) SEFM 2016. LNCS, vol. 9763, pp. 347–366. Springer, Cham (2016). https://doi.org/10.1007/978-3-319-41591-8_24

10. Cimatti, A., Dorigatti, M., Tonetta, S.: OCRA: a tool for checking the refinement of temporal contracts. In: Proceedings of the 28th IEEE/ACM International Conference on Automated Software Engineering, pp. 702–705. IEEE Press (2013)

11. Cofer, D., Gacek, A., Miller, S., Whalen, M.W., LaValley, B., Sha, L.: Compositional verification of architectural models. In: Goodloe, A.E., Person, S. (eds.) NFM 2012. LNCS, vol. 7226, pp. 126–140. Springer, Heidelberg (2012). https://doi.org/10.1007/978-3-642-28891-3_13

12. Dwyer, M.B., Avrunin, G.S., Corbett, J.C.: Patterns in property specifications for finite-state verification. In: Proceedings of the 21st International Conference on Software Engineering, pp. 411–420. ACM (1999)

13. Ellen, C., Sieverding, S., Hungar, H.: Detecting consistencies and inconsistencies of pattern-based functional requirements. In: Lang, F., Flammini, F. (eds.) FMICS 2014. LNCS, vol. 8718, pp. 155–169. Springer, Cham (2014). https://doi.org/10.1007/978-3-319-10702-8_11

14. Filipovikj, P., Jagerfield, T., Nyberg, M., Rodriguez-Navas, G., Seceleanu, C.: Integrating pattern-based formal requirements specification in an industrial toolchain. In: 2016 IEEE 40th Annual Computer Software and Applications Conference (COMPSAC), vol. 2, pp. 167–173. IEEE (2016)

15. Gezgin, T., Oertel, M., Weber, R.: Multi-aspect virtual integration approach for real-time and safety properties. In: International Workshop on Design and Implementation of Formal Tools and Systems (DIFTS 2014). IEEE, October 2014

16. Jahier, E., Raymond, P., Halbwachs, N.: The Lustre V6 Reference Manual. IMAG, December 2016

17. Jeannet, B., Gaucher, F.: Debugging embedded systems requirements with stimulus: an automotive case-study. In: 8th European Congress on Embedded Real Time Software and Systems (ERTS 2016) (2016)

18. de Moura, L., Bjørner, N.: Z3: an efficient SMT solver. In: Ramakrishnan, C.R., Rehof, J. (eds.) TACAS 2008. LNCS, vol. 4963, pp. 337–340. Springer, Heidelberg (2008). https://doi.org/10.1007/978-3-540-78800-3_24

19. Project TIMMO: TIMMO Partners: TADL: Timing augmented description language version 2. Deliverable d6, The TIMMO Consortium, October 2009

20. Reinkemeier, P., Stierand, I., Rehkop, P., Henkler, S.: A pattern-based requirement specification language: mapping automotive specific timing requirements. In: Software Engineering (Workshops), vol. 184, pp. 99–108 (2011)

21. Sheeran, M., Singh, S., Stålmarck, G.: Checking safety properties using induction and a SAT-Solver. In: Hunt, W.A., Johnson, S.D. (eds.) FMCAD 2000. LNCS, vol. 1954, pp. 127–144. Springer, Heidelberg (2000). https://doi.org/10.1007/3-540-40922-X_8

22. Teige, T.: Simplified Universal Pattern Syntax and Semantics. BTC Embedded Systems, June 2017. Confidential

Active Mining of Document Type Definitions

Markus Frohme[✉] and Bernhard Steffen[✉]

Chair of Programming Systems, Computer Science,
TU Dortmund University, Dortmund, Germany
{markus.frohme,steffen}@cs.tu-dortmund.de

Abstract. In this paper, we present the application of our active learning algorithm for Systems of Procedural Automata (SPAs) for inferring Document Type Definitions (DTDs) via testing of corresponding document validators. The point of this specification mining approach is to reveal unknown (lost or hidden) syntactic document constraints that are automatically imposed by document validators in order to support document writers or to validate whether a certain validator implementation does indeed satisfy its specification. This is particularly interesting in the context of today's General Data Protection Regulation (GDPR) as their violation might lead to substantial penalties. The practicality of this approach is supported by the fact that for inferred complex DTDs, context-free model checking may be used to automatically validate whether business-critical rules are enforced by a validator and therefore automatically prohibited by a corresponding documentation process once and for all.

Keywords: Active automata learning
System of procedural automata · Context-free languages
Document type definitions

1 Introduction

Data integrity is an important aspect of today's software systems. Often, this aspect is only considered from a technical point of view: data integrity should be established in order to guarantee the correct execution of a program. With the ever-growing impact of digitalization on the everyday life, "data" emerges more and more as a political and social issue as well. A prominent example for this effect can be seen in the current enacting of the General Data Protection Regulation (GDPR) [6]. Amongst other, this regulation requires companies that work with user-centric data, to be able to precisely specify, which data is stored, for how long it is stored and for what purpose it is stored. Failing to do so and not confirming to these regulations will result in legal notices causing huge monetary and often prestigious damage, thus making this is a highly critical issue for the industry.

© Springer Nature Switzerland AG 2018
F. Howar and J. Barnat (Eds.): FMICS 2018, LNCS 11119, pp. 147–161, 2018.
https://doi.org/10.1007/978-3-030-00244-2_10

A powerful means to address this problem is to enforce constraints at the data-storage or data-transmission level, to ensure the documentation required by GDPR. A popular format for this regard is the eXtensible Markup Language (XML), because it is easily parsable by machines but still readable for humans. XML as a meta-language, however, only enforces generic constraints (opening tags, closing tags, etc.) and does not allow to specify domain-specific constraints (e.g. "data-usage must be documented"). This either needs to be checked by some custom validation logic or by using one of the many format specifications available (e.g. XML Schema Definitions (XSDs), Document Type Definitions (DTDs) or RELAX NG). In both cases, having an automated approach for inferring constraint specifications (in our case DTDs) proves useful:

- if no actual format specification is used, it allows to extract a DTD specification and consequently allows to check if the (custom) validation logic works correctly.
- if an existing validation framework is used, it allows to check (limited to the capabilities of DTDs) if the expected constraints are correctly implemented in the chosen framework. Especially with the more complex specifications languages (XSD), one faces the difficulty to intuitively express the desired needs.

In this paper, we present the application of our active learning algorithm for inferring Systems of Procedural Automata (SPAs). We show how our algorithm and tool of [7] can be applied in practice in order to infer Document Type Definitions (DTDs) via testing of corresponding document validators. For this presentation, we take a look at a fictitious e-commerce shop, that is storing transaction data (e.g. online orders) along with contact information of their customers. To adhere to GDPR, our shop wants to ensure, that for every contact information, the purpose and duration (if applicable) of its storage is documented alongside the data. To further introduce the running example for this showcase and give a conceptual overview of the learning setup, let us introduce the three fundamental layers of abstraction we pursuit throughout this paper. These are shown in Figs. 1, 2 and 3:

The first layer (cf. Fig. 1) shows the target DTD of our running example as well as an exemplary XML document conforming to the DTD. The DTD describes the structure of records, that store information about transaction information and contact information. Each transaction (tInf, e.g. an order in the shop) needs to reference some sort of external resource (reference) in order to describe the contents of a transaction. For every transaction, it is furthermore possible to store additional contact information (cInf, e.g. delivery address) about persons involved in the transaction. However, for every contact information, it is necessary to document the purpose of their storage (purpose): Transactional information (trans) are only relevant to the specific transaction and will be deleted after the transaction is successfully completed (delDate). Customer-relationship-management data (crm, e.g. account information) are usually stored indefinitely, unless the user explicitly asks for their deletion (disclaimer).

```
<!ELEMENT records (record+)>

<!ELEMENT record (date,
                     ((tInf, reference+) |
                      (cInf, purpose))+
                  )>

<!ELEMENT tInf (#PCDATA)>
<!ELEMENT cInf (#PCDATA)>
<!ELEMENT reference (#PCDATA)>
<!ELEMENT date (#PCDATA)>

<!ELEMENT purpose ((trans, delDate) |
                   (crm, disclaimer) |
                   (adv, agreement)
                  )>

<!ELEMENT trans EMPTY>
<!ELEMENT crm EMPTY>
<!ELEMENT adv EMPTY>
<!ELEMENT delDate (#PCDATA)>
<!ELEMENT disclaimer (#PCDATA)>
<!ELEMENT agreement (#PCDATA)>

<!ATTLIST record id CDATA #IMPLIED>
<!ATTLIST cInf type CDATA #REQUIRED>
```

```
<records>
    <record id="123">
        <date>2018-05-10</date>
        <tInf>Order No. 3434-CBGAE-45</tInf>
        <reference>catalog:CBGAE-4566X</reference>
        <reference>db:0234.23423-2</reference>
        <cInf type="address">Otto-Hahn-Str. 14</cInf>
        <purpose>
            <trans/>
            <delDate>2018-05-17</delDate>
        </purpose>
        <cInf type="e-mail">user@example.org</cInf>
        <purpose>
            <crm/>
            <disclaimer>Until canceled</disclaimer>
        </purpose>
    </record>
</records>
```

Fig. 1. Document Type Definition (DTD) and a valid example document for our running example.

```
RECORDS -> RECORD+
RECORD  -> (id)? date ((tInf, reference+) | (CINF, PURPOSE))+
PURPOSE -> (trans delDate) |
           (crm disclaimer) |
           (adv agreement)
CINF    -> type pcdata*
```

Fig. 2. An context-free grammar (in EBNF form) representing an exemplary procedural view on the DTD of our running example.

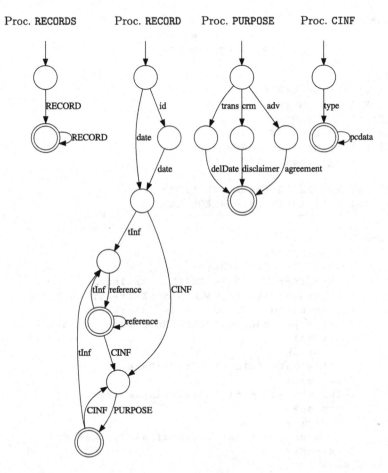

Fig. 3. An SPA representation of the context-free grammar of our running DTD example.

Using contact information for advertisement purposes (adv), needs an explicit agreement from the involved contact (agreement).

The goal of our active mining approach is to extract these characteristics by testing a corresponding document validator (whose internal checking logic is not known beforehand) to verify that indeed no document that violates the required documentation is accepted by the system. Our learning algorithm [7] infers systems of procedural automata, which are based on context-free grammars (CFGs). Therefore, let us present how we see XML documents and DTDs as a system of procedures.

The second layer (cf. Fig. 2) shows a context-free grammar that resembles a procedural view of the DTD of Fig. 1. Our procedural interpretation is as follows: Each non-terminal corresponds to a procedure that can perform certain actions which are defined in its corresponding production rules. A procedure may either perform atomic actions (represented by terminal symbols) or call other procedures (represented by other non-terminal symbols).

In the case of DTDs, we interpret tags as procedures that can perform actions corresponding to the allowed content of the tag. On the one hand, these may be atomic actions, such as specifying attributes or having arbitrary fixed content. On the other hand, these could be calls to other procedures, which in our case correspond to nested tags.

When setting up the learning process, one usually has to define an input alphabet of the system under learning (SUL) which allows to control the granularity of the inferred model. In our example, we are interested in the inner structure of tags such as <record> or <purpose>, so we model them as procedures (non-terminal symbols). For other components, such as the <crm> tag or the id attribute, we are just interested if they have to be specified inside a tag or not, so we model them as terminal symbols. It is worth noting, that we normally speak about *abstract* words on this level of abstraction. However, with a concrete input alphabet definition, we can always transform an abstract word into a *concrete* word (XML document) and transform between the XML/DTD representation and the CFG representation. For a complete alphabet definition of the running example and an exemplary transformation, see Sect. 2.

The third layer (cf. Fig. 3) shows the SPA representation of the context-free grammar of Fig. 2. An SPA is the formal model, that is returned by our learning algorithm. For each non-terminal of the grammar, there exists an independent DFA that accepts the language of right-hand sides of the production rules of the corresponding non-terminal. It is easy to see, how one can construct a CFG from an SPA and vice versa.

For inferring a context-free system by means of an SPA, our learning algorithm requires the entry points and exit points of a procedure to be observable. In the general case, this requires some sort of additional instrumentation of the system under learning. For XML documents (or tag languages in general) this necessary information is naturally integrated into its lexical structure: For each procedure (tag) the entry point (opening tag) and exit point (closing tag) is already given. As a result, no additional work or instrumentation is required, which makes DTD inference a very well suited scenario for our algorithm.

For the inference process, we especially focus on the syntactical structure of XML documents and their description via DTDs and (to a further extent) context-free grammars. The practicality of this approach is supported by the fact that for our inferred complex DTDs, context-free model checking [5] may be used to automatically validate whether business-critical rules are enforced by a validator and therefore automatically prohibited by a corresponding documentation process once and for all.

Outline. We continue in Sect. 2 with introducing the results of related fields of research and preliminary terminology/concepts. Section 3 presents and summarizes the main concepts of our active learning algorithm of [7]: Systems of Procedural Automata and the key concepts that allow for learning these systems. Section 4 showcases the learning setup and the first steps of our algorithm for the e-commerce example presented above. Section 5 concludes the paper and gives an outlook on further concepts we plan to investigate in the future.

2   Preliminaries and Related Work

Specification Mining (as a sub category of the broader field of Data Mining) describes the process of analyzing system traces in order to determine patterns and establishing a specification of some sort to describe the system's behavior. There has been research particularly addressing the inference of DTDs from XML documents [13]. However, many data-mining approaches work in a *passive* fashion, meaning only a fixed set of traces is used for inferring models. As a result, the quality of the inferred specifications highly depends on the quality of the training set. To overcome this issue, our approach follows concepts of the field of *active automata learning* (AAL).

Many AAL algorithms integrate into the minimal adequate teacher (MAT) framework proposed by Angluin [4]. Key to this framework is the existence of a *teacher* that is able to answer *membership queries*, i.e. questions, whether a word is a member of the target language, and *equivalence queries*, i.e. questions, whether a tentative hypothesis exactly recognizes the target language. The process of inferring a (regular) language is then given by discovering the equivalence classes of the Myhill-Nerode congruence [14] for the target language. We expect the reader to be familiar with the general process and formalities of active automata learning. For a thorough introduction (to the regular case) see e.g. [15] or [10, Chap. 8].

In the context of DTD mining, words of the target language are simply XML documents and the membership question can be answered by checking if a particular XML document is accepted by a validator. Equivalence queries then check for XML documents that are accepted by the hypothesis but not by the system under learning (or vice versa). However, regular languages are not powerful enough to capture the key characteristics of XML documents, which inherently support (potentially infinite) recursive nesting of tags. DTDs exhibit a very similar structure to context-free grammars (which has been exploited in the past [12]), making context-free languages a promising abstraction level for XML documents and DTDs. Angluin herself already reasoned about the inference of context-free languages [4], but her extensions required for answering e.g. membership queries have – at least to the knowledge of the authors – prevented any practical application.

A particularly fruitful contribution was made by Alur et al. who proposed the idea of *visibly pushdown languages* [2,3], a subset of context-free languages. The main concept of these languages is that the stack operations of the corresponding *visibly pushdown automaton* (VPA) are bound to the observation of certain symbols. The characterizations given by Alur et al. have been used by Kumar et al. [11] and Isberner [9, Chap. 6] to formulate learning algorithms for visibly pushdown languages, requiring only *classic* membership queries.

The idea of having special input symbols with special semantics is similar to our required instrumentation of making entry points and exit points of procedures observable. Indeed, one can interpret XML documents as a special kind of visibly pushdown language. However, our algorithm not only shows better performance compared to the general-purpose VPL approach [7], but also infers models/specifications that directly correspond to the originating context-free grammar. As discussed in the previous section, the knowledge about the inferred context-free grammar in combination with the specific input alphabet definition allows to directly extract the key properties of the originating DTD.

In the following, we partition the input alphabet to allow for a better distinction of atomic and procedural (entry and exit) actions. For the learning process, we define $\hat{\Sigma} = (\Sigma_c, \Sigma_i, \Sigma_r)$ as the input alphabet, where Σ_c denotes the *call* alphabet, Σ_i denotes the *internal* alphabet and Σ_r denotes the *return* alphabet. For the running example of Fig. 2 the partition is as follows:

- $\Sigma_c = \{\text{RECORDS}, \text{RECORD}, \text{PURPOSE}, \text{CINF}\}$
- $\Sigma_i = \{\text{id}, \text{type}, \text{date}, \text{reference}, \text{tinf}, \text{trans}, \text{crm}, \text{adv}, \text{delDate},$
  $\text{disclaimer}, \text{agreement}, \text{pcdata}\}$
- $\Sigma_r = \{R\}$

Note, that on the abstract language level, we only need a single return symbol. Transforming an abstract word with explicit entry and exit points into a valid XML document can be ensured by using a (context-aware) symbol mapper. For example, the abstract word RECORDS RECORD date tInf reference R R (where we choose arbitrary content for the terminal symbols date, etc.) can be transformed into the following XML document:

```
<records>
    <record>
        <date>...</date>
        <tInf>...</tInf>
        <reference>...</reference>
    </record>
</records>
```

Listing 1.1. An XML document transformed from the abstract word RECORDS RECORD date tInf reference R R.

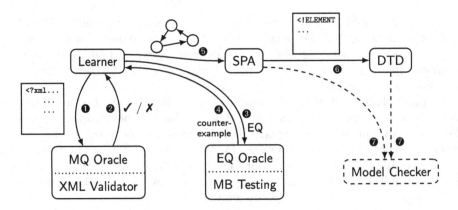

Fig. 4. Our active learning loop for the inference of DTDs.

With this transformation step, we can now show in Fig. 4 the overall configuration of our learning setup for inferring (black-box) DTDs.

The transformed queries of our learning algorithm resemble XML documents, thus the membership queries can be answered by the document validator we want to test (❶). Its response (acceptance, rejection) is directly interpreted as the answer to the query (❷). Refinement steps (❸, ❹) by means of equivalence queries can be realized via (context-free) model-based testing. However, this topic is beyond the scope of this paper – for our example in Sect. 4 we used a set of manually constructed checks. Ultimately, the learning algorithm returns a hypothesis in form of an SPA (❺), which can directly be used to construct a DTD specification for the documents accepted by the tested document validator (❻). Either models may be used for further context-free model checking [5] (❼).

3   Learning Systems of Procedural Automata

In the following subsections we report from [7], the key concepts of our approach: the orchestration of regular systems to obtain a procedural system and how to learn the individual regular systems and the overall procedural system. *Procedural automata* are the core components of our notion of SPAs and are defined as follows:

Definition 1 (Procedural Automaton). *Let* $\hat{\Sigma} = (\Sigma_c, \Sigma_i, \{R\})$ *be an input alphabet and* $c_j \in \Sigma_c$ *denote the j-th procedure (for an arbitrary but fixed order, with* $j \in \{1, ..., |\Sigma_c|\}$*). A procedural automaton for procedure* c_j *over* $\hat{\Sigma}$ *is a deterministic finite automaton* $P^j = (Q^j, q_0^j, \delta^j, Q_F^j)$*, where*

- Q^j *denotes the finite, non-empty set of states,*
- $q_0^j \in Q^j$ *denotes the initial state,*
- $\delta^j : Q^j \times (\Sigma_c \cup \Sigma_i) \to Q^j$ *denotes the transition function, and*
- $Q_F^j \subseteq Q^j$ *denotes the set of accepting states.*

Procedural automata resemble regular DFAs over the joined alphabet of call symbols and internal symbols. Intuitively, they represent the production rules of a non-terminal and the accepted language of a procedural automaton coincides with the language of right-hand sides of the production rules.

A *system* of procedural automata is then given by the set $\{P^1, ..., P^{|\Sigma_c|}\}$. An example for such a system of procedural automata is given by the four DFAs in Fig. 3. SPAs are fully characterized by their internal procedures and therefore, the process of learning SPAs essentially consists of inferring each of the individual procedures. We capitalize on this circumstance by delegating the inference of the procedures to existing learning algorithms for regular systems. Thus, the main task for the learning algorithm of an SPA is managing the learning algorithms of the procedures and serving as a mediator for communication with the (global) learning environment.

3.1   Global and Local Queries

Key to our approach is a translation layer that bridges between the view of the entire system and the local view concerning the individual procedural automata: *Local queries* of procedural automata are expanded to *global queries* of the SUL, and *global counterexample traces* are projected onto *local counterexample traces* of the concerned procedural automata. Key to being able to perform these translations is the maintenance of so-called *access-*, *terminating-* and *return*-sequences. Intuitively, these sequences store information about how a procedural automaton can be accessed, how a successfully terminating run of a procedure looks like and how global termination can be achieved after executing a procedure (accessed by the matching access sequence). Notation-wise we refer to the access-, terminating- and return sequence of a procedure p as $as[p]$, $ts[p]$, $rs[p]$ respectively. The following two subsections explain the two objectives of the translation layer, where we begin with the simpler query expansion:

Membership Query Expansion. Membership query expansion proceeds by symbol-wise processing of the proposed (local) query, which leaves each internal symbol unchanged and replaces each call symbol with the concatenated sequence of the call symbol, the corresponding terminating sequence and the return symbol. Afterwards, the access-sequence of the procedure in question is prepended to the translated query and the corresponding return-sequence is appended as illustrated in Fig. 5. By providing the regular learners with specialized membership oracles that perform this translation steps automatically, no further configuration is necessary as everything is abstracted in the oracle. Technically this is dealt with by a mapper that expands abstract (local) membership queries to concrete (global) ones (similar to [1]). The responses for local queries are simply taken over from the responses of the global queries.

Counterexample Projection. Global counterexamples need to be translated into local counterexamples in order to allow the regular learner to refine the

Local query:

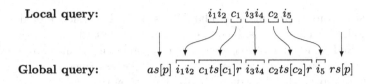

Global query:

Fig. 5. The expansion of a local query of a procedural automaton p to a global query of the SUL.

corresponding local hypothesis. Counterexample analysis allows to pin-point a single input symbol, for which the hypothesis and the SUL transition into two distinct states. This allows us to identify the procedure that needs refinement and to translate the isolated trace into a local context. This is again done by symbol-wise processing, which leaves internal symbols unchanged and whenever a call (return) symbol is encountered, it removes all following symbols until the matching return (call) symbol is encountered. See Fig. 6 for illustration. For refining the concerned hypothesis automaton, we can simply delegate the refinement step to the corresponding learner using the translated counterexample.

Global counterexample:

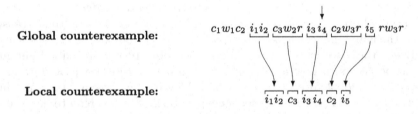

Local counterexample:

Fig. 6. The projection of a global counterexample with critical input i_4 to a local counterexample for the concerned procedural automaton of c_2.

3.2   The Learner

With the concept of query translation, we presented a method that allows to transfer information between local procedures and the global procedural system. Key aspect of this communication is the utilization of access-, terminating and return sequences. Positive counterexamples (i.e. counterexamples that are rejected by the tentative hypothesis but are accepted by the system under learning) play a special role throughout the learning process, because they are witnesses for a successful run of the SUL. In particular, since we are observing well-matched words (i.e. words, in which every call symbol has exactly one matching return symbol), for every procedural call (call symbol) in a positive counterexample, we can automatically extract:

- a corresponding access sequence (everything up until the call symbol),
- a terminating sequence for the procedure (everything in between the call symbol and the matching return symbol), and

– a return sequence for the procedure (everything after the matching return symbol).

Initially, our learning algorithm has no information about any of the required sequences. As a consequence, it is also not possible to construct an initial hypothesis (e.g. a tentative DTD). Instead, an initial (dummy) hypothesis is constructed, that simply rejects all input words. This ensures that the first counterexample our (global) learning algorithm will receive, will always be a positive one[1] , which gives us access to the required sequences and ensures progress.

Upon receiving a (positive) counterexample, we analyze the counterexample to extract the required sequences as described above. Generally, we cannot expect a single counterexample to contain all procedural call symbols at once and therefore giving us access to the information required for activating all local learners and reasoning about procedural invocations. We tackle this issue by introducing the concept of partiality. We keep track of *active* procedures (i.e. procedures for which we have the required sequences) in a special alphabet Σ_{act}. For every procedure in Σ_{act} we can activate the corresponding learning process of the individual procedural automaton and every active (sub-)learner can use $\Sigma_{act} \cup \Sigma_i$ as its input alphabet. By rejecting words that would traverse undefined transitions, counterexamples that introduce previously unobserved call symbols will always be positive, allowing us to activate the local learner for the corresponding procedure. After repeated refinement steps until no further counterexamples are found (cf. Fig. 4), our algorithm terminates with an SPA hypothesis corresponding to the context-free grammar of the target system.

3.3   Correctness and Complexity

Throughout this section we fix the following notation. A canonical SPA is given by the tuple $S = (P^1, ..., P^l)$, such that each P^j is a canonical automaton for the corresponding procedure $c_j \in \Sigma_c$. The size of an SPA is the sum of the individual sizes of the procedures, i.e. the number of their states, so that $|S| = \sum_{j=1}^{l} |P^j| = \sum_{i=j}^{l} n_j = n$.

Similar to the original work by Angluin [4], we assume that so-called *equivalence queries* are available to indicate discrepancies between inferred hypothesis models and the considered SUL (MAT framework). Our following correctness and complexity considerations are based on the assumption that the individual procedural automata are learned using one of the well-known algorithms for regular inference, which incrementally construct hypotheses requiring at most n_j equivalence queries and $kn_j^2 + n_j \log_2 m$ membership queries (for procedure $c_j \in \Sigma_c$) where m denotes the length of the longest counterexample and k the input alphabet size. Under these assumptions it is easy to prove:

Theorem 1 (Correctness and termination [7]). *Having access to a MAT teacher for an instrumented context-free language L (e.g. a DTD), our learning*

---

[1] We assume that a DTD describes at least a root tag.

algorithm determines a canonical SPA $S = (P^1, ..., P^l)$ for L requiring at most n equivalence queries and $\mathcal{O}((\sum_{j=1}^{l}(|\Sigma_i|+|\Sigma_c|)n_j^2)+n\log_2 m)$ membership queries.

4   Example Run of the Algorithm

In order to demonstrate the inner workings of the algorithm and to give a more visual presentation of the learning process, let us present the first steps of the algorithm for our running example of Figs. 2 and 3. As presented in Sect. 3.2, the initial hypothesis of the algorithm is a dummy hypothesis, which rejects all words – thus we will start this example with handling the first positive counterexample.

Let us assume, the first counterexample that is passed to the refinement step is $ce_1 = $ RECORDS RECORD date tInf reference R R, which – when translated – corresponds to the XML document in Listing 1.1. One easily verifies that this document is conforming to the target DTD and thus poses a true counterexample. From this counterexample we can extract for the procedure RECORDS:

- $as[\text{RECORDS}] = \varepsilon$
- $ts[\text{RECORDS}] = $ RECORD date tInf reference R
- $rs[\text{RECORDS}] = \varepsilon$

and for procedure RECORD:

- $as[\text{RECORD}] = $ RECORDS
- $ts[\text{RECORD}] = $ date tInf reference
- $rs[\text{RECORD}] = $ R.

This information can now be used to start the local learning processes for the procedural automata of procedures RECORDS and RECORD, because their local queries can now be embedded into a global context using the access sequences and return sequences. Furthermore, the set of active procedures Σ_{act} is updated to {RECORDS, RECORD}, because we can now simulate their procedural invocation using the corresponding terminating sequence. The resulting intermediate hypothesis for the SPA is shown in Fig. 7.

As one can see, there exist two procedural automata (one for each activated procedure) and both accept their respective (abstracted) terminating sequence that was extracted from the counterexample. However, one can also see their hypothetical properties: The RECORD procedure currently accepts words that may have multiple occurrences of the date symbol. These errors are subject to further refinements triggered by negative counterexamples, i.e. words which are accepted by the SPA, but whose translated XML document is not valid according to the (unknown) DTD.

But to focus on the aspect of discovering new procedures and extending existing knowledge, let us assume we receive the following positive counterexample for our next refinement step: $ce_2 = $ RECORDS RECORD date CINF type R PURPOSE trans delDate R R R. Since the SPA rejects any words that contain unobserved procedures, this is indeed a valid counterexample again. Similar to

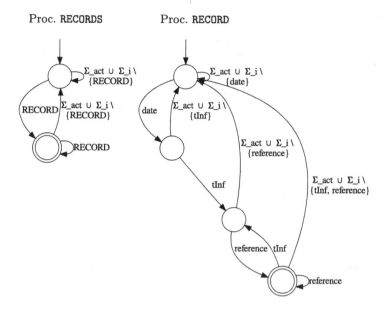

Fig. 7. SPA hypothesis after the first counterexample ce_1.

the first refinement step, we analyze the counterexample for unknown procedures and thereby detect the procedures PURPOSE and CINF and continue to extract the required sequences and adding both procedures to Σ_{act}.

On the one hand, we can now start the (local) learning algorithms for the newly discovered procedures. On the other hand, the existing learners of RECORDS and RECORD can now pose membership queries containing invocations of the new procedures. This is realized by a dynamic extension of the (local) input alphabet of the learner and constitutes one of the core ideas of our algorithm. The resulting hypothesis of the SPA after this second refinement step is shown in Fig. 8.

As one can see, all local learners are activated due to knowledge about the access sequences of the corresponding procedures. Similar to the first counterexample, the initial hypotheses for the PURPOSE and CINF procedure only accept the respective run extracted from the counterexample. However, for the hypothesis of RECORD one can see, that the extension of the input alphabet lead to new hypothesis states, that now describe the (tentative) behavior of the RECORD procedure regarding invocations of PURPOSE and CINF.

From this point on, further equivalence checks may yield positive counterexamples (e.g. the PURPOSE procedure does not accept the valid word crm disclaimer) or negative counterexamples (e.g. the CINF procedure contains accepting runs with multiple occurrences of the type attribute). Subsequent refinement steps eventually lead to the hypothesis of the SPA shown in Fig. 3. From this hypothesis, one can easily construct the corresponding context-free grammar shown in Fig. 2, by performing a DFA-to-regular expression transformation. In combination with the chosen alphabet definition that was used for

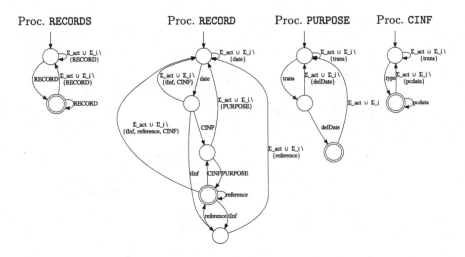

Fig. 8. SPA hypothesis after the second counterexample ce_2.

the active learning process (e.g. mapping `crm` to `<crm/>`) one can ultimately construct the originally unknown DTD of Fig. 1.

5 Conclusion and Future Work

In this paper, we have shown how our active learning algorithm for Systems of Procedural Automata (SPAs) can be employed to infer Document Type Definitions (DTDs) via testing of corresponding document validators. The point of this specification mining approach is to reveal unknown (lost or hidden) syntactic document constraints that are automatically imposed by document validators. Revealed DTDs are particularly interesting in the context of today's GDPR as their violation might lead to substantial penalties. Verifying data integrity (with special regard to documentation) either by a DTD itself or by being able to verify business-critical rules for inferred complex DTDs by context-free model checking [5] suffices to validate whether these rules are enforced by a validator and therefore automatically prohibited by a corresponding documentation process once and for all.

Currently, we are investigating how far this approach might reach. In particular, we are interested to explore which form of integrity checks are covered by our approach and which may be covered by conceptual extensions, e.g. along the lines of the learning of register automata [8].

References

1. Aarts, F., Jonsson, B., Uijen, J., Vaandrager, F.W.: Generating models of infinite-state communication protocols using regular inference with abstraction. Formal Methods Syst. Des. **46**(1), 1–41 (2015)
2. Alur, R., Kumar, V., Madhusudan, P., Viswanathan, M.: Congruences for visibly pushdown languages. In: Caires, L., Italiano, G.F., Monteiro, L., Palamidessi, C., Yung, M. (eds.) ICALP 2005. LNCS, vol. 3580, pp. 1102–1114. Springer, Heidelberg (2005). https://doi.org/10.1007/11523468_89
3. Alur, R., Madhusudan, P.: Visibly pushdown languages. In: Proceedings of the 36th Annual ACM Symposium on Theory of Computing, pp. 202–211. ACM (2004)
4. Angluin, D.: Learning Regular Sets from Queries and Counterexamples. Inf. Comput. **75**(2), 87–106 (1987)
5. Burkart, O., Steffen, B.: Model checking for context-free processes. In: Cleaveland, W.R. (ed.) CONCUR 1992. LNCS, vol. 630, pp. 123–137. Springer, Heidelberg (1992). https://doi.org/10.1007/BFb0084787
6. Regulation (EU) 2016/679 of the European Parliament and of the Council of 27 April 2016 on the protection of natural persons with regard to the processing of personal data and on the free movement of such data, and repealing Directive 95/46/EC (General Data Protection Regulation). Official Journal of the European Union, L119, pp. 1–88 (2016)
7. Frohme, M., Steffen, B.: Compositional Learning of Mutually Recursive Procedural Systems (2018, under submission)
8. Howar, F., Steffen, B., Jonsson, B., Cassel, S.: Inferring canonical register automata. In: Kuncak, V., Rybalchenko, A. (eds.) VMCAI 2012. LNCS, vol. 7148, pp. 251–266. Springer, Heidelberg (2012). https://doi.org/10.1007/978-3-642-27940-9_17
9. Isberner, M.: Foundations of active automata learning: an algorithmic perspective. Ph.D. thesis, Technical University Dortmund, Germany (2015)
10. Kearns, M.J., Vazirani, U.V.: An Introduction to Computational Learning Theory. MIT Press, Cambridge (1994)
11. Kumar, V., Madhusudan, P., Viswanathan, M.: Minimization, learning, and conformance testing of boolean programs. In: Baier, C., Hermanns, H. (eds.) CONCUR 2006. LNCS, vol. 4137, pp. 203–217. Springer, Heidelberg (2006). https://doi.org/10.1007/11817949_14
12. Minamide, Y., Tozawa, A.: XML validation for context-free grammars. In: Kobayashi, N. (ed.) APLAS 2006. LNCS, vol. 4279, pp. 357–373. Springer, Heidelberg (2006). https://doi.org/10.1007/11924661_22
13. Moh, C.-H., Lim, E.-P., Ng, W.-K.: DTD-Miner: a tool for mining DTD from XML documents. In: Proceedings Second International Workshop on Advanced Issues of E-Commerce and Web-Based Information Systems, WECWIS 2000, pp. 144–151 (2000)
14. Nerode, A.: Linear automaton transformations. Proc. Am. Math. Soc. **9**(4), 541–544 (1958)
15. Steffen, B., Howar, F., Merten, M.: Introduction to active automata learning from a practical perspective. In: Bernardo, M., Issarny, V. (eds.) SFM 2011. LNCS, vol. 6659, pp. 256–296. Springer, Heidelberg (2011). https://doi.org/10.1007/978-3-642-21455-4_8

Adaptive Learning for Learn-Based Regression Testing

David Huistra[(✉)], Jeroen Meijer, and Jaco van de Pol

Formal Methods and Tools, University of Twente, Enschede, The Netherlands
{d.j.huistra,j.j.g.meijer,j.c.vandepol}@utwente.nl

Abstract. Regression testing is an important activity to prevent the introduction of regressions into software updates. Learn-based testing can be used to automatically check new versions of a system for regressions on a system level. This is done by learning a model of the system and model checking this model for system property violations.

Learning the model of a large system can take an unpractical amount of time however. In this work we investigate if the concept of adaptive learning can improve the learning speed of a model in a regression testing scenario.

We have performed several experiments with this technique on two systems: ToDoMVC and SSH. We find that there can be a large benefit to using adaptive learning. In addition we find three main factors that influence the benefit of adaptive learning. There are however also some shortcomings to adaptive learning that should be investigated further.

1 Introduction

Successful software systems are often continuously updated throughout their life cycle [1]. Updates to the system often extend or alter the functionality. These changes occasionally unintentionally alter the behavior of existing functionality. This is what we call a regression.

In order to detect regressions, it is important to test from them [2]. Regressions can occur at many different levels of functionality, such as unit or system level.

In practice, regression testing is mostly performed on unit level. Here each code unit is tested independently. Unit testing techniques enjoy a lot of popularity, as it has proven to be an efficient way to identify regressions and it can be automated to test each version of a system [3].

In this work we focus on a testing technique for system level testing called Learn-Based Testing (LBT) [4]. The LBT testing technique is based on model checking and capable of identifying different type of regressions than unit testing. In addition it can also be automated to test each software version for system level regressions.

D. Huistra, J. Meijer—Supported by STW SUMBAT grant: 13859.

J. van de Pol—Supported by the 3TU.BSR project.

© Springer Nature Switzerland AG 2018
F. Howar and J. Barnat (Eds.): FMICS 2018, LNCS 11119, pp. 162–177, 2018.
https://doi.org/10.1007/978-3-030-00244-2_11

Importance of automated testing. To understand why automated testing is important for regression testing, it is important to understand the nature of regression testing. In regression testing there are often only a small number of regressions to be found compared to the amount of functionality that is being tested. Therefore, regression testing often requires a big effort to find only a few regressions. In practice, this means that for many testing techniques, the effort required to apply them is not considered worth the possible reward.

This is however were automated testing stands out. Another aspect of regression testing is that it tends to happen periodically. A lot of versions of the system will all need to be tested for the same regressions. Unit testing can be setup to take advantage of this fact and automatically test all versions in the same manner. The initial setup of writing all unit tests will still require quite a bit of effort, but after this it can be used to test each version with minimal manual effort.

Our hypothesis is that LBT has the same advantages as unit testing, but enables regression testing at the system level. The purpose of this paper is to investigate the use of LBT in the context of regression testing.

How LBT works. The core concept of LBT is to learn a behavioural model of the system. Such a model describes how the system reacts to sequences of inputs. Using such a model the system can then be tested for regressions.

Identifying regressions is done by determining if (the model of) a system adheres to a set of predefined system properties. This can be performed automatically by giving a set of properties and a model to a model checker such as LTSmin [5].

Interaction bottleneck. Learning the behavioural model of a system can be performed automatically. A learning algorithm will interact with the system by performing sequences of actions and observing the outputs. Given a set of input-output combinations a model hypothesis can be constructed.

However, depending on the size of a system (i.e. the amount of interaction required) and how fast interaction with the system is, learning a model can take a significant amount of time. For larger systems the learning time can make the approach unpractical.

To combat this issue, there is an active area of research on the topic of reducing the amount of interaction required with the system. There have been a number of techniques proposed that can be used to reduce the amount of interaction required, such as better learning algorithms or caching mechanisms.

Adaptive learning. When learning a model in the context of regression testing however, there is a specific technique that we believe can aid in reducing the time required to learn a model. We call this technique adaptive learning [6].

When performing regression testing on a system, in all but the first testing of the system, there is a previous regression test of the same system. In the previous regression testing of the system, the model of a previous version of the system was already learned. In most cases, the previous system is very similar to the updated system in terms of behavior. Therefore, the models of these systems will likely also be very similar.

With adaptive learning we want to reuse information about the system learned during the previous test to speed up the new test. Conceptually this is done by 'adapting' the existing model to the updated system.

Our contribution. There is however little known about the effectiveness of this technique. Therefore we wanted to study how much benefit can be gained from using adaptive learning when learning the model of a system in a regression testing context.

In this work we setup an experiment to determine the benefit of adaptive learning when learning a system in a regression testing context. We also discuss several factors we found that influence the benefit of adaptive learning.

We find that in the right situations there can be a large benefit to using adaptive learning. There are however also still some shortcomings that should be investigated further.

Outline. In Sect. 2 we first give more background information about the adaptive learning technique and learning the model of a system in general. In Sect. 3 we then discuss the experiments we performed with adaptive learning and show the outcome. We discuss the main factors that influence the benefit of adaptive learning that we identified in Sect. 4. In the discussion Sect. 5 we discuss the shortcomings of adaptive learning and the experiments and propose what should be done to improve upon this work. Finally in Sect. 6 we conclude this work by summarizing our findings.

2   Background

In this section we explain the technique of adaptive learning. Before that we introduce the reader with the concept of automatically learning a behavioral model of a system called active automata learning.

2.1   Active Automata Learning

In active automata learning, a learning algorithm is given a set of actions it can perform and asked to produce a model that describes the behaviour of a system [7]. It does this by interacting with the system through the set of actions it has been given and observing the outputs. Based on this interaction it will try to determine what states there are in the system and what the result is of applying each action in each state. With this information it will then construct a model hypothesis.

The difficulty lies in determining if all states have been identified. The learner could try all infinite sequences of actions, but this does not scale very well. Therefore the learning algorithm is designed to interact with the system until it has found a consistent set of observations and then produce a minimal model hypothesis.

To determine if the learner has identified all possible states, the model hypothesis is then given to a so called teacher. The teacher will determine if the hypothesis is correct or not. If the hypothesis is not correct, it will return its findings to the learner so the learner can improve the model.

There are different ways to implement the learner and the teacher. These different implementations influence the benefit that can be gained from using adaptive learning.

Learning Algorithms. In general the learning algorithms work by constructing an observation table while interacting with the system. The rows of an observation table are (possible) access sequences to the different states of the system that have been discovered. The columns are separating sequences that are used to distinguish states from each other.

The learner will add access and/or separating sequences to the table when it finds inconsistent observations. When the observations in the table are considered consistent, the learner will construct a model hypothesis. If the learner receives a counterexample back from the teacher it will add this observation to the table and extend the observation table to make it consistent for all observations.

When and how separating sequences are added to the observation table depends on the specific learner implementation. We look at two implementations: L* and R&S.

- The idea of L* [8] is that it will try to learn as much from a counterexample as possible. It will therefore add all prefixes of the counterexample to the observation. By doing this it may find more new states and avoid work of the teacher, but it will require more interaction with the system to fill the observation table.
- R&S [9] will only add a minimal version of the counterexample to the observation table. This keeps the observation table small but reduces the chance of finding additional states from one counter-example.

In addition to observation table based learners, there are also discrimination-tree based learners. These learners are however not yet compatible with adaptive learning, as is discussed in the next section.

Teacher Algorithms. The teacher algorithm is given a model hypothesis and asked to determine if this hypothesis is correct. It does this by attempting to find a counterexample, a sequence of actions that produces a different result in the system compared to in the model. It will try a large set of sequences to see if they are a counterexample. If it cannot find a counterexample, it will determine that the hypothesis is correct.

What sequences and how many sequences the teacher will try depends on the specific implementation. We distinguish between two: the WMethod and RandomWord method.

– The WMethod [10] is an FSM testing method which requires that an upper bound on the number of states is known and systematically tries to find a difference between a hypothesis and a system.
– The RandomWord algorithm will generate a random set of sequences that it will try out on the system. The amount and length of the sequences is given by the user. If the output of the system deviates from the system for one of these sequences, a counterexample is found. Otherwise the model is finalized.

2.2   Adaptive Learning

A learning algorithm will iteratively try to discover all states of a system by extending the access and separating sequences. Once it is able to distinguish between all states using those sequences, it can fill the observation table and construct a model hypothesis.

A large amount of the learning effort goes into discovering all the states of a system. But in a regression testing scenario, an updated version of a system will generally still have most of the states of the previous version. Adaptive learning attempts to reuse knowledge about the states of a system from a previously learned model. This should reduce the amount of effort that goes into the discovery of the states.

After a system is changed, we do now know how the states have changed. So how can we give a learner information about the possible states of a system, even though these states might not exist anymore? In related work there have been two techniques proposed to steer the learning using an older model.

The first is the approach called Adaptive Model Checking by Groce et al. [6]. Their approach is based on calculating the access and separating sequences from an existing model. This information is then added to the observation table before the learner starts interacting with the system. After this the learner will proceed as normal by filling the observation table and constructing a model hypothesis.

The second approach is part of the Active Continuous Quality Control approach by Windmüller et al. [11]. The key idea of this approach is to extract the set of separating sequences from the old observation table and add these to the table of the new learner, and then proceed as normal.

They have found that this approach works well for the R&S learning algorithm suggested by Rivest and Schapire [9]. In this learning algorithm each counterexample is used to extend the set of separating sequences with exactly one element. Therefore, this approach in essence reuses all counterexamples found during the learning of the previous model.

Windmüller et al. also describe why the separating sequences discovered while learning the previous model can be reused to learn the new model. The separating sequences are used by a learner to distinguish between states. A learner will initially start with a minimal set of separating sequences and add sequences to this set if it discovers it can otherwise not distinguish between two states. If a new learner reuses these separating sequences, it will directly be capable of distinguishing between states. Even if the system has been changed and a sequence no longer helps to distinguish two states, the new observations will show this and a correct model will be constructed.

In our experiments we used the second approach, as we believed it to be a good fit for regression testing. It is easy to store the observation table of each learner and initialize the new learner with this information.

2.3 The Role of Separating Sequences

In order to understand how much adaptive learning can help to reduce the interaction needed to learn a model, it is important to better understand the role of separating sequences when learning a model. In this section we give more insight into separating sequences.

The role of separating sequences is to steer the observations the learner makes when learning a model. Initially a learning algorithm does not know what observations to make. It is only given a set of actions it can perform.

Learning algorithms such as R&S will therefore try to develop a minimal viable hypothesis. They will perform a minimal amount of interaction such as performing each action once. If the observations are consistent with each other, it will immediately produce a model hypothesis, otherwise it will keep adding observations until they are consistent. If it cannot distinguish possible states from one another with the observed outputs, the learner will merge these states.

The learner will then ask the teacher for a counterexample. When the learner receives a counterexample, the learner can learn what sequence of actions distinguishes two states from one another. It will add this sequence to the set of separating sequences and perform this sequence in all possible discovered states to determine if it can distinguish two states from one another.

With each separating sequence, the learner learns what observations it should make in order to identify more unique states. And the more states it discovers, the more accurate the model becomes.

Therefore, the set of separating sequences tells the learning algorithm what sequences it should try in the possible states it has discovered to determine if the states can be distinguished from one another.

2.4 Example

In this section we attempt to illustrate the background information through an example of learning a model. In this example we learn a simple system with just two inputs: a and b. The system is shown in Fig. 1. Performing action a and receiving output z is denoted as a/z.

We use the R&S learner and RandomWord teacher in this example.

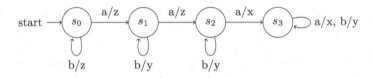

Fig. 1. Model of the system learned in the example

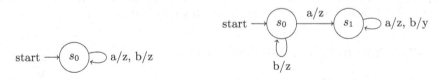

Fig. 2. Model hypothesis 1   **Fig. 3.** Model hypothesis 2

Iteration 0. Input: The user has to specify a system and alphabet of the system that should be learned.

Step 1: The first step of the learner is to process the input alphabet. In our example a and b. Based on this the learner initializes *access sequences* $\leftarrow [a,b]$ and *separating sequences* $\leftarrow []$.

Step 2: Then the learner starts filling the observation table with each combination of a access sequence and a separating sequence element. In the first iteration it makes only two observations: a/z & b/z.

Step 3: Given these observations the learner constructs the model hypothesis shown in Fig. 2. Based on these observations alone, it can only identify one unique state.

Iteration 1. Input: The model hypothesis of iteration 0 is processed by a teacher that attempts to find a counterexample. In our example the teacher finds the following counterexample sequence: $a/z, b/y$.

Step 1: The learner starts with processing the given counterexample. From this counterexample it determines that it should make more observations. It adds action b to the set of separating sequences, as performing b separates two possible states from one another.

Step 2: The learner will than fills the observation table with all combinations of access sequence and separating sequence elements. It identifies that the sequence of action a transitions the system into a unique state. It than adds the sequences a,a and a,b as possible access sequences of new states.

Step 3: The filled observation table produces the hypothesis shown in Fig. 3.

Iteration 2. Input: The teacher will find another counterexample in the model hypothesis. This time $a/z, a/z, a/x$.

Step 1: The learner will process this counterexample and identify that the sequence a, a can be used to identify inconsistent behavior. Therefore a, a will be added to the set of separating sequences.

Steps 2 and 3: We skip the details, but the observation table is extended, new states are identified and new access sequences are added. The resulting hypothesis matches the model shown in Fig. 1.

Output: This time the teacher does not find a counterexample. Therefore the learner will return the model hypothesis as the final hypothesis to the user.

Adaptive Learning. Now we learn the same system once again, but this time we use adaptive learning.

Input: This time the input is the alphabet of the system and a set of separating sequences from the previous learner: *alphabet* ← *[a, b]* and *old separating sequences* ← *[b, (a, a)]*.

Step 1: Once again the learner will use the alphabet to initialize the access sequence. But this time the learner will set the separating sequences to the old separating sequences.

Step 2: When the learner starts filling the observation table, it needs to makes a lot more observations. Using these observations however it can iteratively identify new unique states and add the corresponding access sequences while filling the observation table. While filling the observation table it identifies all possible states in the same iteration.

Step 3: The constructed model hypothesis in the first iteration is equivalent to the system shown in Fig. 1.

3   Experiments

As stated previously, the main practical bottleneck for using learn-based testing is the learning time of a model. Our goal is to determine how much adaptive learning can help to reduce the amount of interaction required to learn a model. In other words, when learning the model of a system, is it more efficient to adapt a (similar) model or to learn a model from scratch?

There is no definitive answer to this question. It depends on the situation. For example, how similar the model to adapt is to the system that is being learnt.

We are however specifically interested to determine the benefit of adaptive learning in the context of regression testing. Here we assume that iterative versions of a system will all need to be learnt to be checked for regressions. This means that for each version of the system that needs to be learnt, the model of a relatively similar previous version was already learnt and that model can be adapted. The result is that models to adapt from are often very similar to the model that is being learnt, which is an optimal scenario for adaptive learning.

To determine the benefit of adaptive learning in a regression testing context in practice, we set up two experiments to compare the performance of adaptive learning to regular learning. In the experiment we learn multiple versions of a system through both adaptive and regular learning and compare the interaction required to learn those versions.

In this section we discuss the setup, procedure and results of this experiment.

3.1   The Setup

In this section we discuss how the experiment was setup to produce a good estimation of the benefit of adaptive learning in a general regression setting context.

Chosen systems. The specific systems that are learnt have a large impact on the interaction required to learn its model. Therefore experiments were performed on two different systems. We chose systems already learnt in related work to build upon those efforts and show the benefit of adaptive learning. In addition, the learnt models of these systems are publicly available. This allowed us to perform the experiments on a simulated version of the real system. We created a simulator that simulates a system's behavior based on a given model. This simulator made it much faster to perform experiments compared to working with a real system.

The chosen systems are as follows:

- **ToDoMVC:** ToDoMVC[1] is a project that contains a large number of implementations of a standardized set of functionalities but implemented using different frameworks/libraries. The main goal is to compare these frameworks/libraries with one another. Bainczyk and Schieweck [12] have learnt the model of a large number of the implementations and shown that they do not all produce the same functionality.
- **SSH:** Models of SSH implementations were previously learnt by Fiterău-Broştean et al. [13] in order to verify these systems using a list of system properties. These system properties were also available and provides a nice template that can be used for model checking different versions after their model is learnt, and gives a good indication as to what type of changes between versions should be detected. We focused our experiments on the DropBear[2] implementation.

Learning parameters. To account for and determine the influence of learning parameters on the benefit of adaptive learning, the experiments were performed with different combination of learning parameters. L* and R&S were used as the learning algorithms, as these are the two main observation table based learners and our adaptive learning approach is developed for those. For the teacher algorithms WMethod and RandomWord were used. See the background section

---

[1] http://todomvc.com/.

[2] https://matt.ucc.asn.au/dropbear/dropbear.html.

for more information. While there are many variations of these learners and teachers, we found that these four were a good representation of the different behaviour we saw during experimentation.

Multiple versions. The difference between two versions of a system can vary. A new version can be a code-refactoring were only the underlying code is changed but the functionality remains the same, or a new version can change a large part of the functionality. When the difference between two versions varies, the benefit of adaptive learning also varies.

In order to take this into account, as well as to determine how much the difference between two versions influences the benefit of adaptive learning, the experiment is based on learning multiple versions of a system with varying degrees of difference to one another. The details are discussed in the next sections.

Measurements. The experiments focus only on the interaction required to learn a model in different situations. The models are not actually checked for regressions, as this is not relevant for measuring the benefit of adaptive learning.

The interaction required to learn a model is measured by the number of queries that have to be processed by the system. We measure both the learning and equivalence queries.

We do not count the queries used to test the final hypothesis for counterexamples. This is a fixed number for each learning experiment and is not relevant when comparing the two approaches. In addition, this number depends on user settings and a hypothesis can already be checked for regressions while the hypothesis is still searched for counterexamples.

3.2   Learning ToDoMVC

In the ToDoMVC experiment we wanted to determine the benefit of adaptive learning in the optimal situation. In the optimal situation, adaptive learning is used to learn a model that is unchanged from the previously learnt model. In this experiment we therefore learn the same system twice, once with regular learning and once with adaptive learning.

We also look at the influence of the different learner and teacher algorithms. We look at the benefit of adaptive learning for all combinations of the L*

Table 1. Queries needed to learn ToDoMVC with different learning parameters

Parameters	Regular learning		Adaptive learning	
	Learner	Teacher	Learner	Teacher
L* + WMethod	2,534	1,944	1,634	0
L* + RandomWord	19,215	3	1,743	0
R& S + WMethod	549	2,037	544	0
R& S + RandomWord	337	2	326	0

and R&S learner and the WMethod and RandomWord teacher algorithms. The results of the experiment can be found in Table 1. We discuss these results in Sect. 3.4

3.3 Learning SSH

For the SSH experiment we manually created several versions of the SSH program with varying degrees of differences between those versions. The experiment is based on learning these different versions of the program by adapting a model of the base system and comparing this to learning from start.

We performed the experiments with the L* and R&S learning algorithms and the WMethod equivalence oracle. The RandomWord oracle was not able to find the required counterexamples within 10 million attempts.

In the following we discuss the versions of the program we created and how we performed the experiment on that version.

Base System. The base system is the system learnt by Fiterău-Broştean et al. [13]. This system is used to learn the initial model without adaptive learning.

Version 1: The first version of SSH that was created is functionally equivalent to the base system. This is for example the case when non-functional changes have been introduced, such as code refactoring or styling adjustments. Even with such changes a system should be tested for regressions, to make sure that the functionality did not change. This is an optimal situation for adaptive learning, as the model will not need to be adapted at all. The model only needs to be verified as correct.

Version 2: The second version of SSH is a system that introduces a regression into the system. We created a version that contains a property violation according to the LTL formulae specified by BroStein et al.

Version 3: The third version of SSH is a system that introduces a special type of new functionality to the system. Here an action needs to be performed twice in order to proceed with a key-reset, which should require an additional separating sequence to identify the new state.

The results of this experiment can be seen in Table 2.

3.4 Discussion

In the ToDoMVC experiment we see that there is a benefit to using adaptive learning with all combinations of learning parameters. However, the benefit reduces when the required teacher queries using traditional learning is reduced. We can summarize the findings as following:

1. When using RandomWord, the effort required to find all separating sequences for ToDoMVC is very small. Therefore little effort can be saved by using adaptive learning.

2. RandomWord produces very long counterexamples. This results in L* creating a large observation table. L* benefits from the shorter counterexamples produced by WMethod, while R&S is better capable of processing large counterexamples.

Table 2. Queries needed to learn SSH with different learning parameters

System	Parameters	Regular learning		Adaptive learning	
		Learner	Teacher	Learner	Teacher
Version 1	L*	15,311	605,534	9,071	0
	R&S	5,310	618,868	5,291	0
Version 2	L*	15,623	503,978	9,071	0
	R&S	5,309	566,240	5,291	0
Version 3	L*	15,911	604,617	10,749	42,356
	R&S	6,081	1,290,732	6,061	42,356

When learning the first version of SSH with regular learning, we saw that L* and R&S performed similar. Both require around 620.000 queries to learn the base system, although R&S required significantly less learning queries. In both cases adapting a model requires significantly less queries than learning a model from scratch.

L* however requires almost twice as much learning queries as R&S. We believe this comes from the fact that the L* learner produces more distinguishing suffixes and thus larger observation tables. Simply filling the observation table of an L* learner requires significantly more queries.

For the learning of version 2 we see the same results as for learning version 1. This indicates that even though a bug has been introduced in version 2, this version of the system can be learnt with the same distinguishing suffixes as the base system. Therefore the learner only needs to fill the observation table to learn the model of this version.

When learning version 3 we see that the learner needs to find additional separating sequences. The effort required to identify the additional sequences is however significantly smaller than finding all of them.

4   A Theory of Reuse

As discussed in Sect. 2, a learning algorithm needs a set of separating sequences to determine what observations it should make to identify and distinguish the states of a system. By reusing an existing set of separating sequences discovered while learning a similar model, adaptive learning aims to reduce the interaction needed to discover the set of separating sequences.

The goal of this research effort is to determine how much interaction can be avoided by using adaptive learning. To this end we performed an experiment to compare adaptive learning to regular learning. We however also identified three main factors that determine the benefit of adaptive learning. In this section we discuss those factors.

4.1 Discovery

The main factor that determines the benefit of adaptive learning is the amount of interaction required to discover a set of separating sequences in the model. The difficulty of discovering a set of separating sequences depends mainly on the behaviour of a system that is being learned and partially on the method used to discover separating sequences.

We can see this when looking at the differences between the experiments on ToDoMVC and SSH. SSH requires a lot more interaction to discover the set of separating sequence, while ToDoMVC showed the difference the teacher algorithm can have on the effort required to discover a set of separating sequences.

The effort that goes into the discovery of a set of separating sequences is a combination of the following two aspects:

1. The number of suffixes that need to be discovered
2. The effort to discover a suffix

The number of suffixes required. A separating suffix is used to distinguish two states from one another. The number of separating sequences required is therefore at most the number of pairs of states that need to be distinguished between, but often pairs can reuse the same suffix. The number of separating sequences is therefore related to the specific behaviour in a system.

Discovering a suffix. The discovery of suffixes is performed by a teacher algorithm. Given a hypothesis, the teacher will attempt to find two states that should be distinguished from each other. It does this by finding a sequence of actions that shows these states have a different behavior/output, i.e. a counterexample.

The teacher algorithm tries to find such a sequences by simply trying (random) sequences of actions on the system. The number of sequences that can be tried and the percentage of sequences that result in a counterexample however depend on the system.

The number of possible sequences of a certain length is simply the number of actions to the power of the length of the sequence. Therefore the number of possible actions significantly increases the average effort required to find a counterexample. The required length of counterexamples and the percentage of sequences that produce a counterexample depend on the behaviour of the system.

For example, a system that resets to the initial state when a wrong action is performed requires a precise set of sequence of actions to reach certain states, thus the percentage of sequences that are a counterexample is reduced. In the experiments we saw for example that SSH resets back to the initial state when a wrong actions is performed, therefore it required very specific sequences of actions to reach certain states. This is also the reason why RandomWord did not perform well for SSH.

4.2   Reuse

Depending on the change between two versions of a system, the number of distinguishing suffixes that can be reused and the number of new suffixes that need to be discovered varies on how much the behaviour of the system changed.

Generally, the more the states of a system have been altered, the number of suffixes that can be reused is reduced.

However, we believe that generally the difference in behaviour between two versions of a system is minor. Therefore in most situations there should be a high number of distinguishing suffixes that can be reused.

When creating versions of SSH we noticed that many small changes did not require the discovery of additional separating sequences and we had to purposefully make changes that would trigger this need.

4.3   Quality

The third factor that influences the benefit of adaptive learning is the quality of the set of separating sequences. The separating sequences guide the learner in what observations it should make. With a bad quality of separating sequences however, the learner can make a large number of observations that does not assist in identifying new states.

Generally a learner will attempt to find a sufficient set of separating sequences, but in most cases it will not find a minimal set of separating sequences.

An example of this is the L* learner. This learner will add a large number of sequences to the set op separating sequences. Not all of these sequences are required. Therefore, this learner will generally make more observations than required.

This can be seen in the ToDoMVC experiment. With adaptive learning, the L* learner required almost twice as much queries compared to the R&S learner. The reason for this is the large set of separating sequences that L* creates.

5   Discussion and Future Work

Our experiments confirm that adaptive learning improves the LBT approach for regression testing: the number of queries needed to learn the adapted system is significantly lower than the number of queries needed to learn a system from scratch.

We also explained the factors that influence this gain. The reusability of the learnt distinguishing suffixes depends on the complexity of the base system, the difference with the updated system, and the quality of the set of suffixes.

These observations lead to two potential improvements that can be studied in future work:

– **Discrimination Tree based learners:** The approach for adaptive learning used in our work is based on observation tree-based learners such as L* and R&S. More recent learners are based on a discrimination tree and have shown to be more efficient in the learning queries they require to create a hypothesis. Therefore, we believe that an adaptive learning approach should be developed for discrimination tree-based learners.

– **Calculate the optimal set of separating sequences:** The quality of the set of separating sequences identified while learning a model can vary. Instead of using a set that is discovered during the learning of a model we can also calculate a set of separating sequences on a given model. An approach to do this was proposed by Smetsers et al. [14]. This operation can be performed in between learning two models. It should provide a better-quality set and also remove sequences if they are no longer required.

6   Conclusion

In the experiments we have seen that adaptive learning can reduce the interaction required to learn the model compared to regular learning. This is especially the case when changes between models are small, such as a regression testing context.

The benefits of adaptive learning can vary a great deal however. We have identified three main factors that influence the benefit of adaptive learning. The first two of these are the specific behavior of the system that is being learned and the amount of change between two versions of a system. These two factors can be used to determine if adaptive learning should be applied when learn-based regression testing a specific system. If the system needs a lot of difficult to find separating sequences and the changes between versions are small, then adaptive learning can provide a large benefit.

The third factor is the quality of the separating sequences and how they are used. We have seen that the learning parameters have a large impact on this. They determine what separating sequences are identified and how they are used to make observations. We have also discussed two ways in which the quality of the separating sequences can be improved.

References

1. Zelkowitz, M.V.: Perspectives in software engineering. ACM Comput. Surv. **10**(2), 197–216 (1978)
2. Wong, W.E., Horgan, J.R., et al.: A study of effective regression testing in practice. In: ISSRE, Albuquerque, NM, USA, 2–5 November, pp. 264–274 (1997)
3. Olan, M.: Unit testing: test early, test often. J. Comput. Sci. Coll. **19**(2), 319–328 (2003)
4. Meinke, K.: Automated black-box testing of functional correctness using function approximation. In: ISSTA, Boston, MA, USA, 11–14 July, pp. 143–153 (2004)
5. Kant, G., Laarman, A., Meijer, J., van de Pol, J., Blom, S., van Dijk, T.: LTSmin: high-performance language-independent model checking. In: Baier, C., Tinelli, C. (eds.) TACAS 2015. LNCS, vol. 9035, pp. 692–707. Springer, Heidelberg (2015). https://doi.org/10.1007/978-3-662-46681-0_61
6. Groce, A., Peled, D.A., Yannakakis, M.: Adaptive model checking. Logic J. IGPL **14**(5), 729–744 (2006)

7. Steffen, B., Howar, F., Merten, M.: Introduction to active automata learning from a practical perspective. In: Bernardo, M., Issarny, V. (eds.) SFM 2011. LNCS, vol. 6659, pp. 256–296. Springer, Heidelberg (2011). https://doi.org/10.1007/978-3-642-21455-4_8

8. Angluin, D.: Learning regular sets from queries and counterexamples. Inf. Comput. **75**(2), 87–106 (1987)

9. Rivest, R.L., Schapire, R.E.: Inference of finite automata using homing sequences. In: Hanson, S.J., Remmele, W., Rivest, R.L. (eds.) Machine Learning: From Theory to Applications. LNCS, vol. 661, pp. 51–73. Springer, Heidelberg (1993). https://doi.org/10.1007/3-540-56483-7_22

10. Chow, T.S.: Testing software design modeled by finite-state machines. IEEE Trans. Softw. Eng. **4**(3), 178–187 (1978)

11. Windmüller, S., Neubauer, J., et al.: Active continuous quality control. In: CBSE, Vancouver, BC, Canada, 17–21 June 2013, pp. 111–120 (2013)

12. Bainczyk, A., Schieweck, A., Steffen, B., Howar, F.: Model-based testing without models: the TodoMVC case study. In: Katoen, J.-P., Langerak, R., Rensink, A. (eds.) ModelEd, TestEd, TrustEd. LNCS, vol. 10500, pp. 125–144. Springer, Cham (2017). https://doi.org/10.1007/978-3-319-68270-9_7

13. Fiterau-Brostean, P., et al.: Model learning and model checking of SSH implementations. In: SPIN, Santa Barbara, CA, USA, 10–14 July 2017, pp. 142–151 (2017)

14. Smetsers, R., Moerman, J., Jansen, D.N.: Minimal separating sequences for all pairs of states. In: Dediu, A.-H., Janoušek, J., Martín-Vide, C., Truthe, B. (eds.) LATA 2016. LNCS, vol. 9618, pp. 181–193. Springer, Cham (2016). https://doi.org/10.1007/978-3-319-30000-9_14

Essays Dedicated to Susanne Graf on the Occasion of Her 60th Birthday

Predicate Abstraction and Such...

Bernhard Steffen[1]($\boxtimes$) and Tiziana Margaria[2]

[1] Chair for Programming Systems,
TU Dortmund University, Dortmund, Germany
`steffen@cs.tu-dortmund.de`
[2] Chair of Software Systems,
University of Limerick, and Lero, Limerick, Ireland
`tiziana.margaria@ul.ie`

Abstract. Predicate abstraction is only a facet of Susanne Graf's work, but an important and characteristic one. Aiming for the essence without being disrupted by 'syntactic sugar' appears like a red thread in her career, and it explains also her current vision for a contract-based composition of viewpoints. This paper sketches her accompanying associated keynote, as well as the nine papers of scientific relatives who came to FMICS for celebrating her 60th birthday.

Keywords: Verification · Tools · State explosion problem
Scalability · Compositionality · Interface specifications
Predicate abstraction · CEGAR · Viewpoints · Cyber-physical systems
Contracts · Refinement · Real time · Security
Communication protocols

1 Introduction

CAV 1989, Grenoble, unforgettable! Who has been there will remember great discussions, nice weather, fantastic food, and Susanne Graf in the middle of all of this, taking care.[1] These were the early days of the tools and techniques that influenced the field for computer-aided verification as it is known today. Spin [21] was in its very beginning, as were, e.g., CESAR/XESAR [34,37] Auto/Autograph [38,39] and the Concurrency Workbench [7].

Susanne Graf's impressive work is in the center of this development, and it is not possible to list all her contributions in this introduction. We therefore focus on a particularly interesting aspect of Susanne's research and its impact, her semantics-first perspective: the aim to characterize the essence of the problem independently of the given (syntactic) representation. This line of work started already in 1984 with her characterizing semantic relations between CCS expression in temporal logics [15] and later [16] following the characterization idea

---

[1] For those who did not know that Susanne easily climbs more than 1000 meters of height with her skies before breakfast, her energy was a miracle.

© Springer Nature Switzerland AG 2018
F. Howar and J. Barnat (Eds.): FMICS 2018, LNCS 11119, pp. 181–188, 2018.
https://doi.org/10.1007/978-3-030-00244-2_12

inspired by [20], which was then generalized to a more general notion of characteristic formulas for fully characterizing certain behavioural relations with a single formula [40].

State explosion was a major issue at CAV 1989 as also visible from Susanne's contribution [11]. Already back then were solutions treating millions of states, an impressive number, but still far from truly capturing industrial relevant examples. Compositional approaches [6][2] and reduction techniques leading to partial order reduction [46] were proposed to achieve better scalability by avoiding full state graph generation.

Susanne contributed also here, introducing the idea of exploiting interface specifications for state space reduction [17,18]. In a sense, this work can be seen as a predecessor for a number of (her) follow-up publications concerning component-based systems and contracts [3,12,19,36]. The general idea here is to constrain how a system can (i.e., is intended to) be used by the environment and thereby reduce the state space required for analysis.

Another dimension of techniques for increasing scalability is abstraction [2,27], whose perhaps most radical form from the semantic perspective is the *predicate abstraction* [14]: Forget about the representational structure of the target system at all and characterize states just by their properties/predicates. In a sense, this reminds of Nerode's characterization of minimal deterministic acceptors [32], but in an approximative fashion, as, e.g., also used for active automata learning [1] or later, more specifically, for a corresponding alphabet abstraction refinement [22,23]. The most visible impact of predicate abstraction, however, can be observed with the counter-example guided abstraction refinement (CEGAR) approach, characterized by incrementally refining abstract models at need [5]: Whenever verification results in terms of counter-example traces on the model cannot be matched on the system, these traces are exploited to refine the abstraction underlying the model by adding 'distinguishing' predicates in a way that eliminates this 'spurious' counter example.

Susanne's keynote *"Building Correct Cyber-Physical Systems: Why we need a Multiview Contract Theory"* reflects on decades of experience with the verification of, in particular, cyber-physical systems [13]: in order to scale to realistic sizes, abstract models focusing on dedicated viewpoints (e.g., function, timing, security) are essential, as is the consistent integration of such viewpoint models to a comprehensive overall model, which is currently treated in a mostly informal way. Susanne advocates to establish a more flexible contract-based approach aiming at a generalized notion of unifying models [41], while easing integration, relaxing assumptions, and preserving current modeling approaches and their tools.

Consistency across large scale systems is also at the core of the other FMICS keynote presented by Margaria on *Generative Model Driven Design for Agile System Design and Evolution* [29]. It has been an ongoing challenge, e.g., concerning the adequate treatment of heterogeneity in Industrial Critical Systems

---

[2] Particularly, entertaining was the related discussion between Ed Clarke and Willem Paul de Roever of what compositionality really means.

[43] and the use of features and their properties as a unit of analysis and configuration [25].

The remainder of this paper sketches the contributions to the FMICS event for the celebration of Susanne's 60th birthday. All contributions aim at increasing the reliability of systems development, but from different angles.

2   Invited Contributions

The nine invited contributions fall into three categories that essentially concern the state explosion problem (scalability), the problem of dealing with the gap between models/programs and running systems, and with time.

2.1   Complex Systems: Components, Procedures, and Concurrency

The first four contributions concern generic approaches towards scalability of distributed system verification.

The paper [9] by Garavel, Lang and Mounier, *Compositional Verification in Action*, addresses compositional verification as a means to overcome the state explosion problem. Specific emphasis is put on the impact of an interface specification-based approach developed by Susanne [18], which can be regarded as an early contribution towards a contract-based treatment of distributed systems.

The second contribution [28], *A Note on Refinement in Hierarchical Transition Systems* by Gerald Lüttgen, sketches how modal transition systems may be applied to formally capture hierarchical refinement. Gerald's approach aims at a formal, operational semantics-based underpinning of the incremental refinement practices of engineers who are used to, e.g., place state machines inside states or add outer transitions to states during design, hoping that no unwanted side effects arise.

The third paper [45], *Modal Meta Model Checking* by Bernhard Steffen and Alnis Murtovi, generalizes context-free model checking [4], a technique for verifying infinite state systems, to a technique for verifying properties for classes of (domain-specific) languages. This technique aims at consistently dealing with view point-specific languages, in particular, by establishing properties that may drastically reduce the effort for the verification of individual systems.

Also the fourth contribution [24], *The Quest for Optimality in Stateless Model Checking of Concurrent Programs* by Bengt Jonsson, aims at taming the state explosion problem. It surveys some recent developments and results for making stateless model checking more efficient, e.g. by considering different memory models for concurrency. The main point here is to avoid the (often prohibitive) construction of the global state graph without imposing too high a degree of redundant computation.

2.2 Formal Methods for IoT Systems

The two contributions of this section aim at extending the reach of verification technology beyond the traditional boundaries.

The paper *Wholly!: A Build System For The Modern Software Stack* by Gelle, Saidi and Gehani [10], presents a system designed for the reproducible and verifiable builds of optimized and bloatware-free software that runs uniformly on traditional desktops, the cloud, and IoT devices. Wholly aims at closing the gap between (verified) models/programs and fully deployed systems by explicitly considering the built process as part of the development.

The paper *A Modeling Language for Security Threats of IoT Systems* by Legay et al. [26] proposes a security-based modeling language for IoT systems with two important features: (i) vulnerabilities are explicitly represented and (ii) interactions are allowed or denied based on the information stored on the IoT devices. This contribution can be regarded as a way to establish a specific viewpoint for dealing with attacks explicitly and ways to prohibit them.

2.3 Analysis of Timed Systems

Time imposes very important and traditional viewpoints. The three contributions of this section deal with different timing issues and their treatment.

The contribution *The Cause-Effect Latency Problem in Real-time Systems* by Yi [48] discusses the Data Buffering Protocol and the corresponding cause-effect latency problem, which arises, e.g., when data items are lost. The problem of preserving the functional semantics of task chains via non-blocking protocols for data exchange among tasks establishes a viewpoint which must be consistently integrated into the corresponding overall modelling.

The paper *Revisiting Bounded Reachability Analysis of Timed Automata-Based on MILP* by Ober [33] studies the reduction of bounded reachability analysis of timed automata to a Mixed Integer Linear Programming (MILP) problem. This switch from the traditional way of dealing with bounded reachability as a satisfiability problem to MILP is a good example for a switch of viewpoint with a corresponding switch of mindset (cf. [42]) whose application profile has to be validated in practice.

The paper *Evaluation and Comparison of Real-Time Systems Analysis Methods and Tools* by Sophie Quinton [35] discusses several experimental and theoretical methods to evaluate and compare real-time systems analysis methods and tools concerning their adequacy for industrial use. In particular, it considers obstacles for industrial uptake and community efforts to overcome them, e.g., based viewpoint-specific contract patterns for establishing inter-viewpoint consistency.

3 Conclusions and Perspectives

Writing this introduction to the topical part for Susanne Graf's 60th birthday celebration and looking back all the way to the first instance of CAV in 89 was an interesting experience. A lot has been achieved in the last three decades as also apparent from the papers of this topical part, but some hurdles seem to be persistent. There are still no truly compositional methods for dealing with concurrent systems, and much of today's progress is due to Moore's law and intelligent heuristics. We had to learn that (problem) (de)composition requires care which can rarely be automated. Susanne's vision for viewpoint compositions therefore foresees contracts as a way of manual support. It seems that this is the way to go: Ease the required manual support, make it reusable, and automate its use. In a sense, this pattern also underlies Wholly [10] as well as the idea of domain-specific languages: factor complexity out and conquer! This approach invites to a new art of development along the lines of language-oriented programming [8,47] or language-driven engineering [42], supported by automated composition, e.g. in the line of [30,44]. In fact, there is a trend to move from the concrete level to the meta-level, which is also apparent in Susanne's vision: rather than establishing ways to show that certain properties are preserved in a specific context, she aims at conditions that enforce the concept of property preservation. We envision that this will lead to new generations of integrated development environments which are themselves generated from meta model specifications (cf. [31]) that may well comprise contracts.

References

1. Angluin, D.: Learning regular sets from queries and counterexamples. Inf. Comput. **75**(2), 87–106 (1987)
2. Bensalem, S., Graf, S., Lakhnech, Y.: Abstraction as the key for invariant verification. In: Dershowitz, N. (ed.) Verification: Theory and Practice. LNCS, vol. 2772, pp. 67–99. Springer, Heidelberg (2003). https://doi.org/10.1007/978-3-540-39910-0_4
3. Bozga, M., Graf, S., Mounier, L.: IF-2.0: a validation environment for component-based real-time systems. In: Brinksma, E., Larsen, K.G. (eds.) CAV 2002. LNCS, vol. 2404, pp. 343–348. Springer, Heidelberg (2002). https://doi.org/10.1007/3-540-45657-0_26
4. Burkart, O., Steffen, B.: Model checking for context-free processes. In: Cleaveland, W.R. (ed.) CONCUR 1992. LNCS, vol. 630, pp. 123–137. Springer, Heidelberg (1992). https://doi.org/10.1007/BFb0084787
5. Clarke, E.M., Grumberg, O., Jha, S., Lu, Y., Veith, H.: Counterexample-guided abstraction refinement for symbolic model checking. J. ACM **50**(5), 752–794 (2003)
6. Clarke, E.M., Long, D.E., McMillan, K.L.: Compositional model checking. In: Proceedings of Fourth Annual Symposium on Logic in Computer Science (LICS), pp. 353–362 (1989)
7. Cleaveland, R., Parrow, J., Steffen, B.: The concurrency workbench: a semantics-based tool for the verification of concurrent systems. ACM Trans. Program. Lang. Syst. **15**(1), 36–72 (1993). http://doi.acm.org/10.1145/151646.151648
8. Dmitriev, S.: Language oriented programming: the next programming paradigm. JetBrains onBoard Online Mag. **1** (2004). http://www.onboard.jetbrains.com/is1/articles/04/10/lop/

9. Garavel, H., Lang, F., Mounier, L.: Compositional verification in action. In: Howar, F., Barnat, J. (eds.) FMICS 2018. LNCS, vol. 11119, pp. 189–210. Springer, Cham (2018)

10. Gelle, L., Saidi, H., Gehani, A.: Wholly!: a build system for the modern software stack. In: Howar, F., Barnat, J. (eds.) FMICS 2018. LNCS, vol. 11119, pp. 242–257. Springer, Cham (2018)

11. Graf, S., Richier, J.-L., Rodríguez, C., Voiron, J.: What are the limits of model checking methods for the verification of real life protocols? In: Sifakis, J. (ed.) CAV 1989. LNCS, vol. 407, pp. 275–285. Springer, Heidelberg (1990). https://doi.org/10.1007/3-540-52148-8_23

12. Graf, S., Passerone, R., Quinton, S.: Contract-based reasoning for component systems with rich interactions. In: Sangiovanni-Vincentelli, A., Zeng, H., Di Natale, M., Marwedel, P. (eds.) Embedded Systems Development. Embedded Systems, vol. 20, pp. 139–154. Springer, New York (2014). https://doi.org/10.1007/978-1-4614-3879-3_8

13. Graf, S., Quinton, S., Girault, A., Gössler, G.: Building correct cyber-physical systems: why we need a multiview contract theory? In: Howar, F., Barnat, J. (eds.) FMICS 2018. LNCS, vol. 11119, pp. 19–31. Springer, Cham (2018)

14. Graf, S., Saidi, H.: Construction of abstract state graphs with PVS. In: Grumberg, O. (ed.) CAV 1997. LNCS, vol. 1254, pp. 72–83. Springer, Heidelberg (1997). https://doi.org/10.1007/3-540-63166-6_10

15. Graf, S., Sifakis, J.: A modal characterization of observational congruence on finite terms of CCS. In: Paredaens, J. (ed.) ICALP 1984. LNCS, vol. 172, pp. 222–234. Springer, Heidelberg (1984). https://doi.org/10.1007/3-540-13345-3_20

16. Graf, S., Sifakis, J.: A logic for the description of non-deterministic programs and their properties. Inf. Control **68**(1–3), 254–270 (1986)

17. Graf, S., Steffen, B.: Compositional minimization of finite state systems. In: Proceedings of 2nd International Conference on Computer-Aided Verification (CAV 1990) (1990)

18. Graf, S., Steffen, B., Lüttgen, G.: Compositional minimisation of finite state systems using interface specifications. Formal Aspects Comput. **8**(5), 607–616 (1996)

19. Gössler, G., Graf, S., Majster-Cederbaum, M., Martens, M., Sifakis, J.: An approach to modelling and verification of component based systems. In: van Leeuwen, J., Italiano, G.F., van der Hoek, W., Meinel, C., Sack, H., Plášil, F. (eds.) SOFSEM 2007. LNCS, vol. 4362, pp. 295–308. Springer, Heidelberg (2007). https://doi.org/10.1007/978-3-540-69507-3_24

20. Hennessy, M., Milner, R.: On observing nondeterminism and concurrency. In: de Bakker, J., van Leeuwen, J. (eds.) ICALP 1980. LNCS, vol. 85, pp. 299–309. Springer, Heidelberg (1980). https://doi.org/10.1007/3-540-10003-2_79

21. Holzmann, G.J.: The model checker SPIN. IEEE Trans. Softw. Eng. **23**(5), 279–295 (1997)

22. Howar, F., Steffen, B., Merten, M.: Automata learning with automated alphabet abstraction refinement. In: Jhala, R., Schmidt, D. (eds.) VMCAI 2011. LNCS, vol. 6538, pp. 263–277. Springer, Heidelberg (2011). https://doi.org/10.1007/978-3-642-18275-4_19

23. Isberner, M., Howar, F., Steffen, B.: Inferring automata with state-local alphabet abstractions. In: Brat, G., Rungta, N., Venet, A. (eds.) NFM 2013. LNCS, vol. 7871, pp. 124–138. Springer, Heidelberg (2013). https://doi.org/10.1007/978-3-642-38088-4_9

24. Jonsson, B.: The quest for optimality in stateless model checking of concurrent programs. In: Howar, F., Barnat, J. (eds.) FMICS 2018. LNCS, vol. 11119, pp. XI–XII. Springer, Cham (2018)

25. Karusseit, M., Margaria, T.: Feature-based modelling of a complex, online-reconfigurable decision support service. Electron. Notes Theor. Comput. Sci. **157**(2), 101–118 (2006). http://www.sciencedirect.com/science/article/pii/ S1571066106002489

26. Legay, A.: A modeling language for security threats of IoT systems. In: Howar, F., Barnat, J. (eds.) FMICS 2018. LNCS, vol. 11119, pp. 258–268. Springer, Cham (2018)

27. Loiseaux, C., Graf, S., Sifakis, J., Bouajjani, A., Bensalem, S.: Property preserving abstractions for the verification of concurrent systems. Formal Methods Syst. Des. **6**(1), 11–44 (1995)

28. Lüttgen, G.: A note on refinement in hierarchical transition systems. In: Howar, F., Barnat, J. (eds.) FMICS 2018. LNCS, vol. 11119, pp. 211–222. Springer, Cham (2018)

29. Margaria, T.: Generative model driven design for agile system design and evolution: a tale of two worlds. In: Howar, F., Barnat, J. (eds.) FMICS 2018. LNCS, vol. 11119, pp. 3–18. Springer, Cham (2018)

30. Margaria, T., Steffen, B.: Backtracking-free design planning by automatic synthesis in metaframe. In: Astesiano, E. (ed.) FASE 1998. LNCS, vol. 1382, pp. 188–204. Springer, Heidelberg (1998). https://doi.org/10.1007/BFb0053591

31. Naujokat, S., Lybecait, M., Kopetzki, D., Steffen, B.: CINCO: a simplicity-driven approach to full generation of domain-specific graphical modeling tools. Softw. Tools Technol. Transf. **20**, 327–354 (2017)

32. Nerode, A.: Linear automaton transformations. Proc. Am. Math. Soc. **9**(4), 541–544 (1958)

33. Ober, I.: Revisiting bounded reachability analysis of timed automata based on MILP. In: Howar, F., Barnat, J. (eds.) FMICS 2018. LNCS, vol. 11119, pp. 269–283. Springer, Cham (2018)

34. Queille, J.P., Sifakis, J.: Specification and verification of concurrent systems in CESAR. In: Dezani-Ciancaglini, M., Montanari, U. (eds.) Programming 1982. LNCS, vol. 137, pp. 337–351. Springer, Heidelberg (1982). https://doi.org/10.1007/ 3-540-11494-7_22

35. Quinton, S.: Evaluation and comparison of real-time systems analysis methods and tools. In: Howar, F., Barnat, J. (eds.) FMICS 2018. LNCS, vol. 11119, pp. 284–290. Springer, Cham (2018)

36. Quinton, S., Graf, S.: Contract-based verification of hierarchical systems of components. In: Proceedings of the 6th IEEE International Conference on Software Engineering and Formal Methods (SEFM 2008), pp. 377–381. IEEE (2008)

37. Richier, J.L., Rodriguez, C., Sifakis, J., Voiron, J.: Verification in XESAR of the sliding window protocol. In: Protocol Specification, Testing and Verification VII, Proceedings of the IFIP WG6.1 Seventh International Conference on Protocol Specification, Testing and Verification, Zurich, Switzerland, 5–8 May 1987 (1987)

38. Roy, V., de Simone, R.: Auto/Autograph. In: Computer-Aided Verification, Proceedings of a DIMACS Workshop 1990, New Brunswick, New Jersey, USA, 18–21 June 1990. DIMACS Series in Discrete Mathematics and Theoretical Computer Science, vol. 3, pp. 477–492. DIMACS/AMS (1990)

39. Roy, V., de Simone, R.: Auto/Autograph. Formal Methods Syst. Des. **1**(2/3), 239–249 (1992)

40. Steffen, B.: Characteristic formulae. In: Ausiello, G., Dezani-Ciancaglini, M., Della Rocca, S.R. (eds.) ICALP 1989. LNCS, vol. 372, pp. 723–732. Springer, Heidelberg (1989). https://doi.org/10.1007/BFb0035794
41. Steffen, B.: Unifying models. In: Reischuk, R., Morvan, M. (eds.) STACS 1997. LNCS, vol. 1200, pp. 1–20. Springer, Heidelberg (1997). https://doi.org/10.1007/BFb0023444
42. Steffen, B., Gossen, F., Naujokat, S., Margaria, T.: Language-driven engineering: from general-purpose to purpose-specific languages. In: Steffen, B., Woeginger, G. (eds.) Computing and Software Science: State of the Art and Perspectives, LNCS, vol. 10000. Springer (2018)
43. Steffen, B., Margaria, T., Claßen, A.: Heterogeneous analysis and verification for distributed systems. Softw. Concepts Tools **17**(1), 13–25 (1996)
44. Steffen, B., Margaria, T., Freitag, B.: Module Configuration by Minimal Model Construction. Technical report, Fakultät für Mathematik und Informatik, Universität Passau (1993)
45. Steffen, B., Murtovi, A.: M3C: modal meta model checking. In: Howar, F., Barnat, J. (eds.) FMICS 2018. LNCS, vol. 11119, pp. 223–241. Springer, Cham (2018)
46. Valmari, A.: A stubborn attack on state explosion. In: Computer-Aided Verification, Proceedings of a DIMACS Workshop 1990, New Brunswick, New Jersey, USA, 18–21 June 1990. DIMACS Series in Discrete Mathematics and Theoretical Computer Science, vol. 3, pp. 25–42. DIMACS/AMS (1990)
47. Ward, M.P.: Language oriented programming. Softw. Concepts Tools **15**(4), 147–161 (1994)
48. Yi, W.: The cause-effect latency problem in real-time systems. In: Howar, F., Barnat, J. (eds.) FMICS 2018. LNCS, vol. 11119, p. XIII. Springer, Cham (2018)

Compositional Verification in Action

Hubert Garavel[1]([✉]), Frédéric Lang[1], and Laurent Mounier[2]

[1] Univ. Grenoble Alpes, Inria, CNRS, Grenoble INP, LIG,
38000 Grenoble, France
{hubert.garavel,frederic.lang}@inria.fr
[2] Univ. Grenoble Alpes, CNRS, Grenoble INP, Verimag,
F-38000 Grenoble, France
laurent.mounier@univ-grenoble-alpes.fr

Abstract. Concurrent systems are intrinsically complex and their verification is hampered by the well-known "state-space explosion" issue. Compositional verification is a powerful approach, based on the divide-and-conquer paradigm, to address this issue. Despite impressive results, this approach is not used widely enough in practice, probably because it exists under multiple variants that make knowledge of the field hard to attain. In this article, we highlight the seminal results of Graf & Steffen and propose a survey of compositional verification techniques that exploit (or not) these results.

1   Introduction

The present article was written in honour of Susanne Graf and Bernhard Steffen at the occasion of their 60th birthdays.

Concurrent systems are commonly found in software programs, hardware circuits, and telecommunication networks, where many processes have to execute simultaneously, synchronise to properly access shared resources, and communicate together to achieve common tasks. Concurrent systems are notoriously hard to design correctly, as they are prone to subtle errors, such as deadlocks, livelocks, or synchronisation issues. To avoid or detect such errors, formal methods, supported by computer-aided verification tools, are established techniques for the design of concurrent systems [22].

Unfortunately, verification algorithms for concurrent systems are often hampered by the "state-space explosion" issue, which arises when the complexity of verification (which can be exponential in the number of concurrent processes) exceeds the capabilities of the computer on which verification is performed. This makes it difficult, if not unfeasible, to analyse large systems with many processes, such as most industrial case studies. Various verification approaches have been proposed to fight state-space explosion, but there is no silver bullet, as each approach works under specific assumptions, for particular classes of problems.

The present article focuses on one of these approaches, *compositional verification*, which relies on "divide-and-conquer" strategies that decompose a global system into local concurrent processes and seek to exploit locality properties of

© Springer Nature Switzerland AG 2018
F. Howar and J. Barnat (Eds.): FMICS 2018, LNCS 11119, pp. 189–210, 2018.
https://doi.org/10.1007/978-3-030-00244-2_13

these processes. There are many different branches of formal methods and, consequently, very diverse forms of compositional verification. The present article is centred around a series of papers published between 1990 and 1996 by Susanne Graf and Bernhard Steffen [36–40], the three latter ones being co-authored with Gerald Lüttgen. More precisely, the scope of the present article is defined as follows:

- We consider the established framework of *asynchronous concurrency*, in which concurrent processes execute without assumption about their respective speeds. These processes can synchronise and communicate using Hoare's rendezvous[1] [44]. Communicating automata [1] and process calculi [7] naturally fit in this setting. Other communication schemes, such as shared memories or message queues, can be expressed, as particular cases, in terms of rendezvous.
- We do not consider compositional verification techniques designed for theorem proving or static analysis, but only those designed for *enumerative verification* (or *reachability analysis*) methods, which rely on state-space exploration and include both *model checking* (in which the properties to be verified are expressed in some temporal logic) and *equivalence checking* (in which the properties to be verified are expressed using bisimulations or behavioural preorders).
- We do not consider *state-based* models, such as Kripke structures (in which relevant information is attached to the states, usually in the form of *state variables*, so that the properties to be verified are expressed using predicates or invariants relating these variables); instead, we consider *action-based* models, such as labelled transition systems (in which relevant information is attached to the transitions, usually in the form of *transition labels*, so that the properties are expressed as sequences, trees, or graphs of actions).
- We consider both *explicit-state* methods (in which reachable states and transitions are analysed individually) and *symbolic* methods (in which sets of reachable states are analysed collectively). Actually, many papers discussed in this survey use explicit-state methods, but symbolic methods are also applicable. There is a common belief that symbolic methods systematically outperform explicit-state ones, which hardly exceed 10^{12} states on current machines; this is a misconception and the situation is more contrasted. In particular, explicit-state methods handle dynamic data structures (e.g., lists, trees, etc.) more easily, and, even in the case of pure control structures (e.g., Petri nets), recent results [49] show that explicit-state methods, combined with appropriate reductions, compete well with symbolic methods.

The compositional verification approaches we consider here are traditionally referred to as *compositional minimisation* or *compositional reachability analysis*; they are *action-based* and rely on *equivalence-checking* concepts, especially

---

[1] Some authors consider rendezvous as synchronous and message queues as asynchronous.

behavioural equivalence and preorder relations between labelled transition systems. In the sequel, *compositional verification* is often used as a synonym for *compositional minimisation*, although the latter is clearly more specific.

There exist indeed alternative approaches, referred to as *compositional reasoning*, *assume-guarantee*, or *rely-guarantee*, which are often *state-based* and rely on *model-checking* concepts, including assertions, logic formulas and satisfaction relations. See, e.g., [33,67] for detailed presentations of these approaches.

The present article is organised as follows. Section 2 introduces compositional minimisation in its simplest forms. Section 3 recalls the main concepts, namely *interfaces* and *semi-composition*, put forward in the seminal papers of Graf, Steffen & Lüttgen. Section 4 discusses enhanced compositional approaches that use interfaces without semi-composition. Section 5 presents the most advanced approach, in which interfaces and semi-composition are both used. Practical applications of compositional verification to realistic case studies are reported whenever possible. Finally, Sect. 6 gives a few concluding remarks.

2   Compositional Minimisation Without Interfaces

2.1   Principles

To perform compositional minimisation in an action-based setting, one needs six ingredients carefully designed to fit well together:

1. A *low-level model* M, which is a state-transition formalism[2] in which the behaviour of the system S under verification can be encoded. This model is usually very simple, with a low abstraction level, so that the properties to be verified for S can be easily checked on M. As a counterpart, the encoding of S in M can get large and verbose. Two famous examples of such models are: *labelled transition systems* [64], which are the underlying semantic model of most process calculi and play a central role in major functional verification tools, and *interactive Markov chains* [42], which are performance evaluation models that combine ordinary transitions and stochastic ones, the firing time of the latter being governed by exponential distributions.
2. A *parallel composition operator* $\|$ that takes n models $M_1, ..., M_n$ and returns a new model $M' = M_1\|...\|M_n$. The notation $\|$ is a crude simplification, as parallel composition operators usually carry extra information to determine which synchronisations have to be done (see, e.g., [29]). The resulting model M' is often referred to as a *composition*, while $M_1, ..., M_n$ are referred to as *components*[3]. More often than not, the complexity of M' (measured in number of states and transitions) is the product (rather than the sum) of the complexities of $M_1, ..., M_n$: the state-space explosion problem precisely lies in such complexity growth.

---

[2] For conciseness, we use the same term "model" and the same letter M to refer both to the "meta-model" (i.e., the low-level formalism) and the "models" (i.e., all particular instances expressed in this formalism).

[3] Also called *subsystems*, *agents*, or *processes* in the literature.

3. An *equivalence relation* $\approx$ defined over models. This relation (which differs from graph isomorphism noted $=$) should be a congruence with respect to parallel composition, i.e., if $M_i \approx M_i'$ for all $i \in \{1, ..., n\}$, then $M_1||...||M_n \approx M_1'||...||M_n'$. Two examples of such equivalences are: strong bisimulation [61], which is a congruence for the parallel composition operators of most process calculi (see [88] for a discussion) and branching bisimulation [34]. Equivalence relations may incorporate *abstractions*: for instance, branching bisimulation can remove some τ-transitions ($\tau.M \approx M$), and Markov-chain lumpability can merge some stochastic transitions ($\lambda.M + \mu.M \approx (\lambda + \mu).M$).

4. A *minimisation function* min : $M \to M$ that maps each model to a distinguished element of its equivalence class in the quotient set $M/\approx$; this distinguished element is usually chosen to minimise some complexity criterion. For bisimulation relations, for example, one chooses a labelled transition system that has the least number of states. Minimising a model applies to this model the abstractions inherent to relation $\approx$. Because of the congruence property, one has $M_1||...||M_n \approx \min(M_1)||...||\min(M_n)$ and $\min(M_1||...||M_n) = \min(\min(M_1)||...||\min(M_n))$.

5. A *high-level language* L in which the system S can be specified. Theoretical papers on compositional verification often use M in place of L, but this is not realistic, as complex systems are never described using low-level models only. The language L should be equipped with a concept of components and a parallel composition, also noted $||$, for assembling these components. A composition $C_1||...||C_n$ is said to be *flat* if all components C_i are sequential, or *hierarchical* if some components C_i are themselves compositions.

6. A *translation function* $[\![\cdot]\!] : L \to M$ that maps each system S written in L to a corresponding low-level model $[\![S]\!]$. This function should be able to translate components taken individually, and should be a morphism for parallel composition, meaning that, given n components C_1, ..., C_n, $[\![C_1||...||C_n]\!] \approx [\![C_1]\!]||...||[\![C_n]\!]$. The translation of an entire system may very well fail due to state explosion[4], but the translation of individual components is expected to succeed, at least for a majority of them.

Given a system $S = C_1||...||C_n$ such that $[\![S]\!]$ is excessively large, compositional minimisation, in its simplest form, avoids to compute $[\![S]\!]$ directly and computes $\min[\![C_1]\!]||...||\min[\![C_n]\!]$ instead. This idea was advocated in many papers, both in the functional verification setting [17, 55, 69, 76, 77, 80, 81, 84, 88] and in the performance evaluation setting [23, 42].

2.2   Strategies

In practice, compositional minimisation is more complex than the simple form exposed above. For systems with many components, there are multiple ways (called *strategies*) to perform compositional minimisation, and all strategies do

---

[4] In theoretical papers that use M in place of L, there is a notational confusion between C_i and $[\![C_i]\!]$, which is particularly annoying when the latter cannot be computed.

not necessarily have the same efficiency, i.e., provide the same amount of state-space reduction. The efficiency of a strategy is inversely proportional to the size (e.g., number of states) of the largest intermediate model that is generated; a good strategy strives to keep this size as small as possible, in order to avoid state-space explosion during the compositional verification process. There are several causes leading to the existence of multiple strategies.

First, if the system has a hierarchical structure, e.g., $(C_1||C_2)||(C_3||C_4)$, minimisation can be applied either to the leaf components only, i.e., $(\text{min}\ [\![C_1]\!]\ ||\ \text{min}\ [\![C_2]\!])||(\text{min}\ [\![C_3]\!]\ ||\ \text{min}\ [\![C_4]\!])$, or to every intermediate level in the hierarchy, i.e., $\text{min}(\text{min}(\text{min}\ [\![C_1]\!]\ ||\ \text{min}\ [\![C_2]\!])||\ \text{min}(\text{min}\ [\![C_3]\!]\ ||\ \text{min}\ [\![C_4]\!]))$, or any intermediate combination between these two extremes. Such strategies are called *static* as they are uniformly applied to all components.

Second, compositional minimisation is sometimes counterproductive. Replacing, in a parallel composition $M_1||...||M_n$, some model M_i by its quotient $\text{min}(M_i)$ never increases the complexity, but computing $(\text{min}\ [\![C_1]\!]||...||\text{min}\ [\![C_n]\!])$ rather than $[\![C_1||...||C_n]\!]$ may fail if the complexity of some $[\![C_i]\!]$ is larger than that of $[\![C_1||...||C_n]\!]$. This may very well occur when components are so tightly synchronised that the behaviour of a component C_i is strongly constrained by the other components; ignoring such components may lead to a huge, or even unbounded, state space for C_i. Shared memories, network links, and hardware buses are typical examples of components C_i whose models $[\![C_i]\!]$ cannot be generated in isolation because they allow a potentially infinite number of read/write or send/receive operations, whereas the components that use these memories, links, or buses actually employ a much smaller set of operations. Thus, when performing compositional minimisation on a system $S = C_1||...||C_n$, it is not necessarily optimal to minimise all components one by one; it might be more efficient to consider them two by two, three by three, etc., leading to a number of combinations that is an exponential of n.

Finding an optimal strategy is difficult, and computationally out of reach if the number of components is large. So, one can only rely on heuristics. Rather than using the aforementioned static strategies, which are probably suboptimal, it is more suitable to use *dynamic* strategies that decide, at each verification step, which subset of components is the best candidate for being generated and minimised.

Such a heuristic (called *smart reduction*) is proposed in [16], based on metrics that consider both the amount of synchronisations between components (trying to compose the most tightly synchronised components first, to avoid state-space explosion arising from the interleaving of loosely coupled components) and the proportion of transitions that can be hidden after composition (the more hidden transitions, the greater the gains during subsequent minimisation steps if a weak equivalence, e.g., branching bisimulation, is used).

2.3   Applications

Implementing compositional minimisation is a difficult challenge, because many software tools are required to implement M, $||$, $\approx$, min, L, and $[\![\cdot]\!]$. Moreover, if any of these tools is poorly implemented, the entire tool chain may become inefficient and useless for non-trivial applications.

A handful of tool prototypes have been developed in the 90s, but the best implementation of compositional minimisation available today is unquestionably the CADP toolbox [26], the development of which started in the late 80s and has been steadily pursued until now. Compositional verification, at large, is a particular strength of CADP [25]. Concerning compositional minimisation, CADP provides the following software tools and libraries:

- M is implemented by BCG[5] (*Binary-Coded Graphs*), a compact format, with its associated software tools and libraries, that enable large transition systems (with billions of states and transitions) to be stored as computer files.
- $\|$ is implemented by EXP.OPEN[6], a tool that, among other features, computes the parallel composition of transition systems executing concurrently and synchronised using the parallel operators of various process calculi.
- $\approx$ and min are respectively implemented by BCG_CMP[7] and BCG_MIN[8], two state-of-the-art tools (see [9] for an assessment) that compare and minimise transition systems modulo various equivalence and preorder relations.
- L is implemented in multiple ways, as the CADP toolbox supports several high-level languages for describing value-passing concurrent systems. For many years, LOTOS (ISO/IEC international standard 8807) [46] has been the language of choice but, since 2010, it has been progressively replaced by LNT [27], a modern specification language combining features from process calculi, imperative languages, and functional languages.
- $[\![\cdot]\!]$ is implemented by the two LOTOS compilers CÆSAR[9] and CÆSAR.ADT[10], and by the LNT2LOTOS[11] translator, the combination of which delivers state-of-the-art user-friendliness and performance (see [58,59] for an assessment).

Moreover, a unique feature of CADP is its scripting language SVL[12] [24], which can be seen as a process calculus extended with operations on labelled transition systems, e.g., comparison, minimisation, hiding and renaming of transition labels, detection of deadlocks and livelocks, etc. Designed with the goal of making compositional verification easily accessible to non-experts [52], SVL and its associated compiler[13] implement the aforementioned static and dynamic strategies, including smart reduction.

Compositional minimisation, as implemented in CADP, has been successfully used in many case studies. A dozen of small- or medium-size examples are

---

[5] http://cadp.inria.fr/man/bcg.html.
[6] http://cadp.inria.fr/man/exp.open.html.
[7] http://cadp.inria.fr/man/bcg_cmp.html.
[8] http://cadp.inria.fr/man/bcg_min.html.
[9] http://cadp.inria.fr/man/caesar.html.
[10] http://cadp.inria.fr/man/caesar.adt.html.
[11] http://cadp.inria.fr/man/lnt2lotos.html.
[12] http://cadp.inria.fr/man/svl-lang.html.
[13] http://cadp.inria.fr/man/svl.html.

available online, as part of the CADP demos[14]. In four of these examples (demos No. 05, 18, 25, and 35, which have between 5 and 20 components), compositional minimisation easily succeeds (generating intermediate models with 2.10^6 states at most) where direct generation fails. In seven other examples (demos No. 01, 02, 08, 17, 27, 28, and 36, which have between 4 and 11 components), the largest intermediate model generated by compositional minimisation is between 1.7 and 24 times smaller than the model obtained using direct generation.

Here is a chronological list (since 1991) of case studies in which compositional minimisation, as implemented in CADP, has been used to achieve functional verification. For conciseness, we use the symbol ⋆ to indicate those case studies in which the author's laboratories (INRIA Grenoble, LIG, and/or Verimag) have been involved:

- rel/REL reliable atomic multicast protocol[15] [3,18], Hewlett-Packard (UK)⋆.
- Transit Node message router[16] [62]⋆.
- CoopScan framework for cooperative applications development[17] [48]⋆.
- Transmission Control Protocol (TCP)[18] [74], Berlin (DE).
- Distributed leader election for unidirectional ring networks[19] [28]⋆.
- Bus arbitration of the Powerscale architecture[20] [11], Bull, Les Clayes (FR)⋆.
- Eurocontrol's Departure Clearance Protocol[21] [47], Brussels (BE).
- OM/RR protocol for traffic control[22] [85,86], Eindhoven (NL).
- INRES protocol[23] [54], Nokia Research Center (FI).
- Bull's CFS distributed file system for AIX[24] [65]⋆.
- Philips' HAVi leader election protocol[25] [68], Amsterdam (NL).
- Single pulser and bus arbitration hardware designs[26] [41], Stirling (UK).
- Sync-stop & Chandi-Lamport checkpoint algorithms[27] [35], Bucharest (RO)⋆.
- Chilean electronic invoices system[28] [2,6], Sophia Antipolis (FR).
- FRACTAL software components[29] [4,5], Sophia Antipolis (FR), London (UK).
- FAUST asynchronous network-on-chip[30] [72,73], CEA/Leti, Grenoble (FR)⋆.

---

[14] http://cadp.inria.fr/demos.
[15] http://cadp.inria.fr/case-studies/91-c-relrel.html.
[16] http://cadp.inria.fr/case-studies/94-a-transitnode.html.
[17] http://cadp.inria.fr/case-studies/95-c-groupware.html.
[18] http://cadp.inria.fr/case-studies/96-d-tcp.html.
[19] http://cadp.inria.fr/case-studies/96-f-leaderelection.html.
[20] http://cadp.inria.fr/case-studies/96-h-powerscale.html.
[21] http://cadp.inria.fr/case-studies/97-c-dcl.html.
[22] http://cadp.inria.fr/case-studies/98-d-omrr.html.
[23] http://cadp.inria.fr/case-studies/98-g-inres.html.
[24] http://cadp.inria.fr/case-studies/98-i-cfs.html.
[25] http://cadp.inria.fr/case-studies/99-a-havi.html.
[26] http://cadp.inria.fr/case-studies/99-b-dill.html.
[27] http://cadp.inria.fr/case-studies/01-d-checkpointing.html.
[28] http://cadp.inria.fr/case-studies/04-a-electronic-invoices.html.
[29] http://cadp.inria.fr/case-studies/05-c-components.html.
[30] http://cadp.inria.fr/case-studies/07-a-faust.html.

- Diagrams for choreographies[31] [71], Málaga (ES) and Santa Barbara (US).
- Trivial File Transfer Protocol (TFTP)[32] [30], Airbus, Toulouse (FR)*.
- CRESS diagrams for Web and grid services[33] [78], Stirling (UK).
- Logical regulatory modules[34] [60], Oeiras (PT), Evry-Paris-Marseille (FR)*.
- Fault-tolerant routing algorithm for a network-on-chip[35] [89], Utah (US)*.
- Graphical user interfaces[36] [63], Atos, Grenoble (FR)*.

Compositional minimisation has also been used for performance evaluation:

- Performance analysis of a Plain Old Telephone System[37] [43], Erlangen (DE).
- SCSI-2 bus arbitration protocol[38] [23], Twente (NL)*.
- European Train Control System[39] [8], Saarbrücken (DE), Freiburg (DE).

3   The Seminal Papers of Graf, Steffen, and Lüttgen

In spite of these achievements, compositional minimisation still faces practical limitations when some components (such as the aforementioned shared memories, network links, and hardware buses) cannot be analysed separately from their neighbour components. This problem was addressed, as early as 1990, by Graf & Steffen in a series of five scientific papers:

- [36]: the original paper, published at the first CAV workshop in 1990, which contains all the fundamental contributions;
- [37]: a technical report from RWTH Aachen, published in 1991, which gives the proofs for the theorems of [36];
- [38]: a technical report from Universität Passau, with Gerald Lüttgen as third author, published in 1995, which extends the theoretical developments of the former papers and includes a running example that illustrates the key steps of the approach;
- [39]: a 10-page extended abstract published in the paper version of the *Journal on Formal Aspects of Computing*; due to constraints on the number of pages, this paper does not contain more material than the initial paper [36];
- [40]: a 28-page journal article, which is based on [38] and can be considered as the most complete version; this article is available online from the electronic repository of the *Journal on Formal Aspects of Computing*[40].

---

[31] http://cadp.inria.fr/case-studies/09-a-collab-diag.html.
[32] http://cadp.inria.fr/case-studies/09-h-tftp.html.
[33] http://cadp.inria.fr/case-studies/09-p-web-and-grid.html.
[34] http://cadp.inria.fr/case-studies/13-c-regulatory-modules.html.
[35] http://cadp.inria.fr/case-studies/13-f-utahnoc.html.
[36] http://cadp.inria.fr/case-studies/14-d-hmi.html.
[37] http://cadp.inria.fr/case-studies/98-b-markov-pots.html.
[38] http://cadp.inria.fr/case-studies/02-f-scsi-2.html.
[39] http://cadp.inria.fr/case-studies/06-e-etcs.html.
[40] Online manuscript at http://www-verimag.imag.fr/~graf/PAPERS/GLS96.pdf.

These papers are a breakthrough in compositional verification, as they target the difficult case where some component C_i of a system $S = C_1||...||C_n$ cannot be minimised in isolation from its *environment*, i.e., from the other components $C_1||...||C_{i-1}||C_{i+1}||...||C_n$. Precisely, this is the case where the behaviour of C_i is potentially huge, so that state-space explosion occurs when computing $[\![C_i]\!]$, but only a fraction of this behaviour is actually permitted by the environment of C_i. To address such situations, Graf & Steffen propose the following approach, which we reformulate here in a didactic manner:

- The constraints[41] exerted on C_i by its neighbour components must be expressed as an *interface*[42] noted I, which is intended to be a set of traces containing all the sequences of actions allowed by the environment. Concretely, the interface is represented as a labelled transition system, and the traces are the words of the language recognised by this automaton. In practice, I is usually specified in the same high-level language L as the components $C_1, ..., C_n$ and later translated to the low-level formalism M. It is assumed that I is small enough that state-space explosion never occurs when computing $[\![I]\!]$.
- Graf & Steffen assume that the interface I is provided by the user, based on his/her own intuition of how the environment behaves. Thus, the interface is not necessarily *exact* because of human errors or approximations:
  - If the interface is too *restrictive*, i.e., if it contains less traces than allowed by the environment, this is a severe problem, as the model computed for C_i will be truncated, so that subsequent verification steps will be done under false assumptions. In such case, the interface is said to be *incorrect*.
  - If the interface is too *permissive*, i.e., if it contains more traces than allowed by the environment, there is no correction problem, but there might be a performance problem, as the model computed for C_i will be larger than actually needed. The most permissive interface is the "chaos" automaton that accepts all actions of C_i in any order, which is equivalent to having no interface for C_i.
  So, a correct interface should be a superset of the traces allowed by the environment. Said differently, a correct interface should express some of, but not necessarily all, the constraints exerted by the neighbour components.
- Graf & Steffen define a *semi-composition*[43] operator $\Pi_I(C_i) = \pi_1([\![C_i||I]\!])$, where $||$ denotes the parallel composition operator of CSP [45] that forces C_i and I to synchronise on their common actions, while letting C_i (resp. I) interleave on its actions that are absent from I (resp. C_i), and where π_1 is a function that projects the product labelled transition system $[\![C_i||I]\!]$ onto the states of $[\![C_i]\!]$, meaning that each product state (x, y) is mapped to x and

---

[41] Also called *context constraints* or *environment constraints* in the literature.

[42] Also called *behavioural interface*, *interface specifications*, or *process interface*.

[43] This operator was actually named *reduction* in [36], but we prefer the term *semi-composition* later introduced by Krimm & Mounier [51], because the former term often denotes a minimisation operation that is incompletely done, yielding a smaller yet not necessarily minimal result: partial-order reduction, symmetry reduction, tau-confluence reduction, etc.

each product transition $(x, y) \xrightarrow{a} (x', y')$ is either mapped to $x \xrightarrow{a} x'$ if a is an action of C_i, or ignored otherwise.

- The semi-composition operator enjoys nice properties: (i) $\Pi_I(C_i)$ is behaviourally included in $[\![C_i]\!]$, in the sense that both models have the same initial state and that any transition $x \xrightarrow{a} x'$ of $\Pi_I(C_i)$ is also a transition of $[\![C_i]\!]$; (ii) the number of states in $\Pi_I(C_i)$ is thus less or equal to the number of states in $[\![C_i]\!]$ (the more restrictive the interface, the smaller this number); (iii) if I is the chaos automaton allowing all the actions of C_i, then $\Pi_I(C_i) = [\![C_i]\!]$; (iv) interfaces can be safely minimised using language equivalence or any stronger equivalence.

- But the most important property is the following one: if interface I is correct, then $[\![C_1||...||C_n]\!] = [\![C_1]\!]||...||[\![C_{i-1}]\!]||\Pi_I(C_i)||[\![C_{i+1}]\!]||...||[\![C_n]\!]$, meaning that $[\![C_i]\!]$ can be safely replaced with $\Pi_I(C_i)$, which is presumably less complex[44], or even with $\min(\Pi_I(C_i))$, because $[\![C_1||...||C_n]\!] \approx [\![C_1]\!]||...||[\![C_{i-1}]\!]||\min(\Pi_I(C_i))||[\![C_{i+1}]\!]||...||[\![C_n]\!]$ since $\approx$ is a congruence.

- Graf & Steffen also address the case of incorrect interfaces by extending $\Pi_I(C_i)$ with *undefinedness predicates* that indicate, for each state, which actions of C_i have been cut off by I. Later, when recombining $\Pi_I(C_i)$ with its environment, the parallel composition operator discharges those predicates corresponding to transitions of C_i that the environment is never ready to synchronise with, and would indeed never fire. If some predicates remain undischarged when the parallel composition is done, then I is incorrect; the user should analyse these predicates to understand why/where I is too restrictive, and restart compositional verification with a modified interface[45].

Figure 1 illustrates the semi-composition of a component C_i with an interface I, both having 0 as their initial state. All transitions of C_i labelled by actions a_0, a_2, b_0, b_2, c_0, and c_2 are cut off, because they never synchronise in the parallel composition with I. The action sets attached to the states 0, 2, and 5 of $\Pi_I(C_i)$ represent the undefinedness predicates; for instance, the set attached to state 0 indicates that transitions labelled by a_0 and a_2 have been cut off in this state.

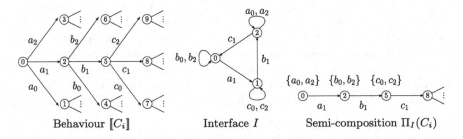

Behaviour $[\![C_i]\!]$ Interface I Semi-composition $\Pi_I(C_i)$

Fig. 1. Reduction achieved using semi-composition with an interface

---

[44] In some cases [36, Sect. 6], interfaces reduce complexity from exponential to linear.
[45] Such an iterative approach based upon incremental refinement was very much the CEGAR idea published ten years later [15].

4 Compositional Minimisation with Interfaces but Without Semi-composition

We now examine two approaches that, given a set of asynchronous components $S = C_1||...||C_n$ synchronised by rendezvous, reuse the idea of interfaces to avoid state-space explosion when generating certain components. These approaches do not borrow the semi-composition operator concept, and thus technically differ from the work of Graf & Steffen.

The first approach was proposed by Cheung & Kramer [12–14] and implemented in the TRACTA tool [32]:

- In this approach, a component C_i having an interface I is replaced by $[\![C_i||I]\!]$ instead of being replaced by the semi-composition $\Pi_I(C_i) = \pi_1([\![C_i||I]\!])$.
- To ensure that $[\![C_1]\!]||...||[\![C_{i-1}]\!]||[\![C_i||I]\!]||[\![C_{i+1}]\!]||...||[\![C_n]\!]$ is strongly bisimilar to $[\![C_1||...||C_n]\!]$, the interface I must not only be correct in the sense of Graf & Steffen, but also deterministic and free of internal actions[46].
- The initial paper [12] assumes that interfaces are correct without checking for correctness. In [13,14], the approach is refined as follows to deal with incorrect interfaces. An *output-completion* operation is applied to transform the user-given interface I into an extended interface I': this is done by adding an *undefined* state π and by creating, for each state y of I and each action a not enabled in y, an additional transition $y \xrightarrow{a} \pi$. When computing $S' = [\![C_1]\!]||...||[\![C_{i-1}]\!]||[\![C_i||I']\!]||[\![C_{i+1}]\!]||...||[\![C_n]\!]$, each transition $(x,y) \xrightarrow{a} (x',\pi)$ of $[\![C_i||I']\!]$ should normally disappear (i.e., be blocked) unless it can synchronise with another action a present in the environment of C_i, i.e., $[\![C_1]\!]||...||[\![C_{i-1}]\!]||[\![C_{i+1}]\!]||...||[\![C_n]\!]$, thus signalling that I is too restrictive. Hence, interface I is correct iff S' contains no reachable state whose i^{th} element has the form (x',π).

The second approach was proposed by Valmari [82] and implemented in the ARA tool [83]. This approach is similar to the one of Cheung & Kramer, with two differences: interfaces are allowed to be nondeterministic, and the user must explicitly introduce the undefined state[47] π in the interface, i.e., provide an interface I' rather than I.

At first sight, these two approaches may look simpler and more elegant than the one of Graf & Steffen, because they do not require a semi-composition operator, but they are actually inferior (although they were published later than [36]), for at least three reasons:

1. Semi-composition is a reduction, meaning that $\Pi_I(C_i)$ is smaller than $[\![C_i]\!]$, but parallel composition is not. Indeed, $[\![C_i||I]\!]$ can be (much) larger than $[\![C_i]\!]$. Figure 2 shows a simple example in which $[\![C_i||I]\!]$ has three times more states than $[\![C_i]\!]$. Thus, using interfaces without semi-composition can be counter-productive, keeping in mind that $[\![C_i]\!]$ is expected to be huge.

---

[46] Internal actions are usually noted τ in most process calculi.
[47] This state is called *cut state* in [82].

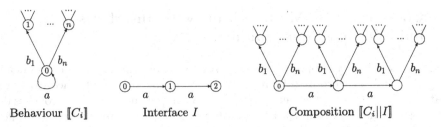

Behaviour $[\![C_i]\!]$ Interface I Composition $[\![C_i\|I]\!]$

Fig. 2. Example where $[\![C_i\|I]\!]$ is larger than $[\![C_i]\!]$

2. The approach of Cheung & Kramer requires nondeterministic interfaces to be determinised [12, Sect. 5.1]. In the worst case, this may cause an exponential blowup in the number of states of the interface (e.g., a small interface with 40 states may get larger than one trillion states), thus compromising the compositional verification approach.

3. The approach of Valmari requires the introduction of the state π and its associated transitions into (possibly nondeterministic) interfaces. No algorithm is provided for such an operation, which might be trivial only for deterministic interfaces — unless determinisation (at the risk of exponential blowup) is first applied to nondeterministic interfaces. Figure 3 shows indeed that the aforementioned output-completion operation works for a deterministic interface I_1, but not for a nondeterministic interface I_2 language-equivalent to I_1: the output-complete interfaces I_1' and I_2' are not language-equivalent (e.g., I_2' accepts a trace $a.b$ ending in π, whereas I_1' does not).

For the sake of completeness, one can mention a third approach [87] that, strictly speaking, does not use interfaces, but simulates their effect by introducing additional synchronisation actions *sleep* and *wake*. From a practical perspective, this approach is not suitable, as it requires to modify the code of components to insert these actions, and also changes the well-established semantic rules for the parallel composition operator, so as to perform look-ahead of *sleep* actions.

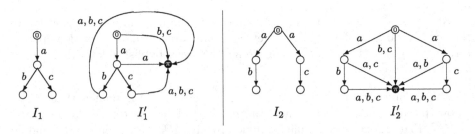

I_1 I_1' I_2 I_2'

Fig. 3. Example where language equivalence is not preserved by output completion

5   Compositional Minimisation with Interfaces and Semi-composition

5.1   Principles

The first (and, to the best of our knowledge, the only) complete implementation of the ideas of Graf & Steffen has been done by Krimm & Mounier [50,51], who adapted the approach to the case of LOTOS [46]. Such adaptation faces various changes in the base assumptions:

– Graf & Steffen (but also Cheung & Kramer and Valmari) consider the parallel composition operator $\|$ of CSP [45], which forces synchronisation on all common actions. On the contrary, the parallel composition operator $|[g_1, ..., g_n]|$ forces synchronisation only on actions whose gate[48] belongs to the (possibly empty) list $g_1, ..., g_n$, whereas all other actions do not synchronise (i.e., interleave).
– The LOTOS operator enables components to have common, yet non-synchronised actions, e.g., between two components C_1 and C_2 executing in full interleaving (i.e., $C_1 |[]| C_2$) and proposing the same actions.
– The LOTOS operator also enables nondeterministic synchronisations, e.g., between three components C_1, C_2, and C_3 connected using $(C_1 |[]| C_2) |[g]| C_3$: any action having gate g proposed by C_3 may synchronise either with C_1 or C_2. This is a most useful pattern to describe pools of clients and servers.
– The parallel operator of CSP is associative whereas, in LOTOS, $(C_1 |[g]| C_2) |[g']| C_3$ may be different from $C_1 |[g]| (C_2 |[g']| C_3)$ when $g \neq g'$.
– The LOTOS operator for action hiding, which was not considered by Graf & Steffen, needs to be taken into account.

In a nutshell, the solution proposed by Krimm & Mounier works as follows:

– Interfaces are labelled transition systems, which can be nondeterministic and contain internal actions (same as in the approach of Graf & Steffen).
– The semi-composition operator $\Pi_I(C_i)$ is generalised to a new operator with four arguments: (i) a component C_i; (ii) an interface I; (iii) a list of gates $g_1, ..., g_n$ on which C_i and I must synchronise; (iv) a Boolean stating whether I is surely correct or possibly incorrect, the former case avoiding correctness checks. The useful properties of $\Pi_I(C_i)$ also hold for this new operator.
– The undefinedness predicates of [36], which are a state-based concept incompatible with labelled transition systems, are encoded by means of *fail-transitions*. In the labelled transition system computed by the semi-composition operator for a possibly incorrect interface I, state s has a self-loop transition $s \xrightarrow{\text{fail}(a)} s$ iff the interface has cut off action a in that state. The parallel composition operator of LOTOS is also slightly modified to handle these fail-transitions.

---

[48] A LOTOS action can be seen as a value tuple, the first element of which is the gate.

The prototype tools developed by Krimm & Mounier have been rewritten and integrated in CADP, which has become the reference framework for compositional minimisation techniques [25]. The DES2AUT tool has been subsumed by SVL[49]. The PROJECTOR tool[50] implements the semi-composition operator; it is built upon the OPEN/CÆSAR application programming interface [21], which enables $\Pi_I(C_i)$ to be computed on the fly, without computing $[\![C_i]\!]$ first (this could cause state-space explosion), and also enables C_i to be expressed in any specification language connected to OPEN/CÆSAR, including LOTOS, LNT, EXP, etc.

5.2 Interface Synthesis

Assume a system $S = C_1 || ... || C_n$, some components of which are too large to be generated separately from their neighbour components and thus require interfaces. Is it possible to generate automatically and correctly these interfaces, rather than asking the user to provide them, at the risk of human mistakes? This question has been studied in two papers.

The first paper [51] considers a process-algebraic setting in which components are combined inside expressions by means of the LOTOS operators for action hiding and parallel composition. An algorithm is given [51, Sect. 3, operator Ψ] to automatically compute an interface for a given component, seen as a subexpression contained in a larger expression describing the entire system or a part of it. This algorithm works recursively by structural induction on the syntax of LOTOS expressions and calculates the set of actions on which the component and its environment have to synchronise.

The second paper [53] considers a more expressive setting, communicating-automata networks, the components of which are combined using synchronisation vectors [1] that can encode action hiding, action renaming, and the parallel composition operators of most process calculi (including CCS, CSP, μCRL, LNT, LOTOS, etc.) as particular cases. An algorithm is given, which explores the synchronisation graph to compute a correct interface for a given component. This algorithm, which has been implemented in SVL[51], improves over the one of [51] in several respects:

– It is applicable to other process calculi than LOTOS.
– It can compute an interface for a component, the environment of which can be arbitrarily chosen to be any subset of components, without requiring these components to be adjacent or closely connected in a process-algebraic expression (this is useful in presence of parallel composition operators that are not associative because they synchronise on different action sets).
– It handles the possible existence of common, yet non-synchronised actions between the component and its environment.

---

[49] http://cadp.inria.fr/man/svl-lang.html (see "abstraction").

[50] http://cadp.inria.fr/man/projector.html.

[51] http://cadp.inria.fr/man/svl-lang.html (see "refined abstraction").

- It handles the possible existence of common, nondeterministically synchronised actions between the component and its environment (i.e., the environment can synchronise on a given action either with the component or with another component, and vice versa). Such actions are ignored in [51], leading to over-permissive interfaces.
- It can generate, in the case of LOTOS, less permissive interfaces than [51], possibly leading to better reductions [53, Examples 2–3 and Fig. 1].

5.3 Applications

Four examples of compositional verification with interfaces and semi-composition are available online, as part of the CADP demos (see footnote 14). For these examples (demos No. 20, 33, 37, and 38, which have between 3 and 60 components), both direct generation and compositional minimisation without interfaces fail, but compositional minimisation with interfaces and semi-composition succeeds, the largest intermediate model generated having less than $700,000$ states.

Compositional verification with interfaces and semi-composition, as implemented in CADP, has also been used with success in various (mostly industrial) case-studies:

- rel/REL reliable atomic multicast protocol[52] [51] Hewlett-Packard (UK)*.
- Distributed leader election for unidirectional ring networks[53] [51]*.
- ATC (Air Traffic Control) system[54] [70], Glasgow (UK).
- PolyKid CC-NUMA multiprocessor architecture[55] [31], Bull, Pregnana (IT)*.
- ScalAgent's deployment protocol for software components[56] [79]*.
- Mutual exclusion protocols for CC-NUMA architectures[57] [56,57]*.
- Asynchronous circuit for the DES (Data Encryption Standard)[58] [75]*.
- Asynchronous Memory Protection Unit[59] [10], Tiempo, Grenoble (FR)*.

6   Conclusion

Although compositional verification is now thirty years old, and despite its true potential in overcoming state-space explosion (as demonstrated in many convincing case studies), it is not yet a widespread verification technique, and its use for practical problems remains rather an exception than the rule.

A major breakthrough was made in 1990 with a series of papers by Graf, Steffen & Lüttgen [36–40]. Unfortunately, the merits of these papers are not

---

[52] http://cadp.inria.fr/case-studies/91-c-relrel.html
[53] http://cadp.inria.fr/case-studies/96-f-leaderelection.html
[54] http://cadp.inria.fr/case-studies/99-e-atc.html.
[55] http://cadp.inria.fr/case-studies/00-c-polykid.html.
[56] http://cadp.inria.fr/case-studies/03-e-parfums.html.
[57] http://cadp.inria.fr/case-studies/10-f-mutex.html.
[58] http://cadp.inria.fr/case-studies/15-f-des.html.
[59] http://cadp.inria.fr/case-studies/18-1-mpu.html.

sufficiently understood. Either these papers are not mentioned in surveys [19, 20, 66] or they are merely cited without any further comment on the significance of their contributions [33]. These are injustices the present article tries to remedy.

The approach of [36] relies upon two key concepts: *interfaces* and *semi-composition*. Using these concepts is not mandatory, as it is possible to perform compositional minimisation without interfaces (Sect. 2) or with interfaces but without semi-composition (Sect. 4). We have shown, however, that the best results are obtained when both concepts are taken advantage of (Sect. 5).

The approach of [36] has been generalised to the case of LOTOS and its descendent languages, and fully implemented in the CADP verification toolbox [25] and successfully applied to numerous case studies, the most recent of which [10] shows impressive results, as an asynchronous hardware block containing not less than 660 concurrent processes was fully verified in a few hours by an industry engineer without prior training in formal methods. This is a clear indication that compositional minimisation techniques have reached a maturity level sufficient to enable their use in industry.

Concerning future research, we envision enhanced approaches for interface synthesis so as to generate interfaces automatically in complex cases that, today, must be dealt with manually, as well as applications of the ideas of Graf & Steffen to quantitative verification, including probabilistic, timed, and hybrid systems.

Acknowledgements. The present work has been partly funded by BPI France and FEDER (*Fonds Européen de Développement Economique Régional*) Rhône-Alpes Auvergne under national project SecurIoT-2 supported by the four competitiveness clusters Minalogic, SCS, Systematic Paris-Région, and Derbi.

References

1. Arnold, A.: Synchronized behaviours of processes and rational relations. Acta Inf. **17**, 21–29 (1982)
2. Attali, I., Barros, T., Madelaine, E.: Parameterized specification and verification of the Chilean electronic invoices system. In: Proceedings of the 24th International Conference of the Chilean Computer Science Society (SCCC 2004), Arica, Chili, pp. 14–25. Society for Computer Simulation International, IEEE, November 2004
3. Bainbridge, S., Mounier, L.: Specification and verification of a reliable multicast protocol. Technical report HPL-91-163, Hewlett-Packard Laboratories, Bristol, UK, October 1991
4. Barros, T., Henrio, L., Madelaine, E.: Behavioural models for hierarchical components. In: Godefroid, P. (ed.) SPIN 2005. LNCS, vol. 3639, pp. 154–168. Springer, Heidelberg (2005). https://doi.org/10.1007/11537328_14
5. Barros, T., Henrio, L., Madelaine, E.: Verification of distributed hierarchical components. In: Proceedings of the International Workshop on Formal Aspects of Component Software (FACS 2005), Macao. Electronic Notes in Theoretical Computer Science, October 2005
6. Barros, T., Madelaine, E.: Formalization and proofs of the Chilean electronic invoices system. INRIA Research Report 5527, INRIA, June 2004
7. Bergstra, J.A., Ponse, A., Smolka, S.A. (eds.): Handbook of Process Algebra. Elsevier, Amsterdam (2001)

8. Böde, E., et al.: Compositional performability evaluation for Statemate. In: Proceedings of the 3rd International Conference on the Quantitative Evaluation of Systems (QUEST 2006), Riverside, California, USA, pp. 167–178. IEEE Computer Society Press, September 2006

9. Boulgakov, A., Gibson-Robinson, T., Roscoe, A.W.: Computing maximal weak and other bisimulations. Form. Asp. Comput. **28**(3), 381–407 (2016)

10. Bouzafour, A., Renaudin, M., Garavel, H., Mateescu, R., Serwe, W.: Model-checking synthesizable SystemVerilog descriptions of asynchronous circuits. In: Krstic, M., Jones, I.W. (eds.) Proceedings of the 24th IEEE International Symposium on Asynchronous Circuits and Systems (ASYNC 2018), Vienna, Austria. IEEE, May 2018

11. Chehaibar, G., Garavel, H., Mounier, L., Tawbi, N., Zulian, F.: Specification and verification of the PowerScale bus arbitration protocol: an industrial experiment with LOTOS. In: Gotzhein, R., Bredereke, J. (eds.) Proceedings of the IFIP Joint International Conference on Formal Description Techniques for Distributed Systems and Communication Protocols, and Protocol Specification, Testing, and Verification (FORTE/PSTV 1996), Kaiserslautern, Germany, pp. 435–450. Chapman & Hall, October 1996. Full version available as INRIA Research Report RR-2958

12. Cheung, S.C., Kramer, J.: Enhancing compositional reachability analysis with context constraints. In: Proceedings of the 1st ACM SIGSOFT International Symposium on the Foundations of Software Engineering, Los Angeles, CA, USA, pp. 115–125. ACM Press, December 1993

13. Cheung, S.C., Kramer, J.: Compositional reachability analysis of finite-state distributed systems with user-specified constraints. In: Proceedings of the 3rd ACM SIGSOFT International Symposium on the Foundations of Software Engineering, Washington, DC, USA, pp. 140–150. ACM Press, October 1995

14. Cheung, S.C., Kramer, J.: Context constraints for compositional reachability. ACM Trans. Softw. Eng. Methodol. (TOSEM) **5**(4), 334–377 (1996)

15. Clarke, E., Grumberg, O., Jha, S., Lu, Y., Veith, H.: Counterexample-guided abstraction refinement. In: Emerson, E.A., Sistla, A.P. (eds.) CAV 2000. LNCS, vol. 1855, pp. 154–169. Springer, Heidelberg (2000). https://doi.org/10.1007/10722167_15

16. Crouzen, P., Lang, F.: Smart reduction. In: Giannakopoulou, D., Orejas, F. (eds.) FASE 2011. LNCS, vol. 6603, pp. 111–126. Springer, Heidelberg (2011). https://doi.org/10.1007/978-3-642-19811-3_9

17. Fernandez, J.C.: ALDEBARAN: un système de vérification par réduction de processus communicants. Thèse de Doctorat, Université Joseph Fourier (Grenoble), May 1988

18. Fernandez, J.C., Garavel, H., Mounier, L., Rasse, A., Rodríguez, C., Sifakis, J.: A toolbox for the verification of LOTOS programs. In: Clarke, L.A. (ed.) Proceedings of the 14th International Conference on Software Engineering (ICSE '14), Melbourne, Australia, pp. 246–259. ACM, May 1992

19. Fogel, J.: A survey of verification techniques for solving the state explosion problem. In: Proceedings of the IFAC Conference on Control Systems Design (CSD 2000), Bratislava, Slovak Republic, IFAC Proceedings Volumes, vol. 33(13), pp. 361–366, June 2000

20. Furia, C.: A compositional world: a survey of recent works on compositionality in formal methods. Technical report 2005.22, Dipartimento di Elettronica e Informazione, Politecnico di Milano, Italy, March 2005

21. Garavel, H.: OPEN/CÆSAR: an open software architecture for verification, simulation, and testing. In: Steffen, B. (ed.) TACAS 1998. LNCS, vol. 1384, pp. 68–84. Springer, Heidelberg (1998). https://doi.org/10.1007/BFb0054165. Full version available as INRIA Research Report RR-3352

22. Garavel, H., Graf, S.: Formal methods for safe and secure computers systems. BSI Study 875, Bundesamt für Sicherheit in der Informationstechnik, Bonn, Germany, December 2013

23. Garavel, H., Hermanns, H.: On combining functional verification and performance evaluation using CADP. In: Eriksson, L.-H., Lindsay, P.A. (eds.) FME 2002. LNCS, vol. 2391, pp. 410–429. Springer, Heidelberg (2002). https://doi.org/10.1007/3-540-45614-7_23. Full version available as INRIA Research Report 4492

24. Garavel, H., Lang, F.: SVL: a scripting language for compositional verification. In: Kim, M., Chin, B., Kang, S., Lee, D. (eds.) Proceedings of the 21st IFIP WG 6.1 International Conference on Formal Techniques for Networked and Distributed Systems (FORTE 2001), Cheju Island, Korea, pp. 377–392. Kluwer Academic Publishers, August 2001. Full version available as INRIA Research Report RR-4223

25. Garavel, H., Lang, F., Mateescu, R.: Compositional verification of asynchronous concurrent systems using CADP. Acta Inform. **52**(4), 337–392 (2015)

26. Garavel, H., Lang, F., Mateescu, R., Serwe, W.: CADP 2011: a toolbox for the construction and analysis of distributed processes. Springer Int. J. Softw. Tools Technol. Transf. (STTT) **15**(2), 89–107 (2013)

27. Garavel, H., Lang, F., Serwe, W.: From LOTOS to LNT. In: Katoen, J.-P., Langerak, R., Rensink, A. (eds.) ModelEd, TestEd, TrustEd. LNCS, vol. 10500, pp. 3–26. Springer, Cham (2017). https://doi.org/10.1007/978-3-319-68270-9_1

28. Garavel, H., Mounier, L.: Specification and verification of various distributed leader election algorithms for unidirectional ring networks. Sci. Comput. Program. **29**(1–2), 171–197 (1997). Special issue on Industrially Relevant Applications of Formal Analysis Techniques. Full version available as INRIA Research Report RR-2986

29. Garavel, H., Sighireanu, M.: A graphical parallel composition operator for process algebras. In: Wu, J., Gao, Q., Chanson, S.T. (eds.) Proceedings of the IFIP Joint International Conference on Formal Description Techniques for Distributed Systems and Communication Protocols, and Protocol Specification, Testing, and Verification (FORTE/PSTV 1999), Beijing, China, pp. 185–202. Kluwer Academic Publishers, October 1999

30. Garavel, H., Thivolle, D.: Verification of GALS systems by combining synchronous languages and process calculi. In: Păsăreanu, C.S. (ed.) SPIN 2009. LNCS, vol. 5578, pp. 241–260. Springer, Heidelberg (2009). https://doi.org/10.1007/978-3-642-02652-2_20

31. Garavel, H., Viho, C., Zendri, M.: System design of a CC-NUMA multiprocessor architecture using formal specification, model-checking, co-simulation, and test generation. Springer Int. J. Softw. Tools Technol. Transf. (STTT) **3**(3), 314–331 (2001). Also available as INRIA Research Report RR-4041

32. Giannakopoulou, D.: Model checking for concurrent software architectures. Ph.D. thesis, Imperial College of Science, Technology and Medicine, University of London, Department of Computer Science, January 1999

33. Giannakopoulou, D., Namjoshi, K.S., Păsăreanu, C.S.: Compositional reasoning. In: Clarke, E., Henzinger, T., Veith, H., Bloem, R. (eds.) Handbook of Model Checking, pp. 345–383. Springer, Cham (2018). https://doi.org/10.1007/978-3-319-10575-8_12

34. van Glabbeek, R.J., Weijland, W.P.: Branching time and abstraction in bisimulation semantics. J. ACM **43**(3), 555–600 (1996)

35. Godza, G., Cristea, V., Mateescu, R.: Formal specification of checkpointing algorithms. In: Proceedings of 13th International Conference on Control Systems and Computer Science (CSCS 2013), Bucharest, Romania, pp. 311–317. Polytechnic University of Bucharest, May 2001

36. Graf, S., Steffen, B.: Compositional minimization of finite state systems. In: Clarke, E.M., Kurshan, R.P. (eds.) CAV 1990. LNCS, vol. 531, pp. 186–196. Springer, Heidelberg (1991). https://doi.org/10.1007/BFb0023732

37. Graf, S., Steffen, B.: Compositional minimization of finite state systems. Aachener Informatik-Berichte AIB 1991-23, RWTH Aachen University, Department of Computer Science, Germany (1991)

38. Graf, S., Steffen, B., Lüttgen, G.: Compositional minimization of finite state systems using interface specifications. Research Report MIP-9505, Universität Passau, Fakultät für Mathematik und Informatik, Germany (1995)

39. Graf, S., Steffen, B., Lüttgen, G.: Compositional minimization of finite state systems using interface specifications. Form. Asp. Comput. **8**(5), 607–616 (1996). 10-page article published in the paper version of the journal

40. Graf, S., Steffen, B., Lüttgen, G.: Compositional minimization of finite state systems using interface specifications. Form. Asp. Comput. **8E**, 286–313 (1996). 28-page article published in the electronic repository of the journal. http://static-content.springer.com/esm/art%3A10.1007%2FBF01211911/MediaObjects/165_2005_BF01211911_MOESM1_ESM.pdf

41. He, J., Turner, K.J.: Specification and verification of synchronous hardware using LOTOS. In: Wu, J., Chanson, S.T., Gao, Q. (eds.) Proceedings of the IFIP Joint International Conference on Formal Description Techniques for Distributed Systems and Communication Protocols and Protocol Specification, Testing, and Verification (FORTE/PSTV 1999), Beijing, China, pp. 295–312. Kluwer Academic Publishers, October 1999

42. Hermanns, H.: Interactive Markov Chains. LNCS, vol. 2428. Springer, Heidelberg (2002). https://doi.org/10.1007/3-540-45804-2

43. Hermanns, H., Katoen, J.P.: Automated compositional Markov chain generation for a plain-old telephone system. Sci. Comput. Program. **36**, 97–127 (2000)

44. Hoare, C.A.R.: Communicating sequential processes. Commun. ACM **21**(8), 666–677 (1978)

45. Hoare, C.A.R.: Communicating Sequential Processes. Prentice-Hall, Englewood Cliffs (1985)

46. ISO/IEC: LOTOS - A Formal Description Technique Based on the Temporal Ordering of Observational Behaviour. International Standard 8807, International Organization for Standardization - Information Processing Systems - Open Systems Interconnection, Geneva, September 1989

47. de Jacquier, A., Massart, T., Hernalsteen, C.: Vérification et correction d'un protocole de contrôle aérien. Technical report 363, Université Libre de Bruxelles, May 1997

48. Kerbrat, A., Ben Atallah, S.: Formal specification of a framework for groupware development. In: Bochmann, G., Dssouli, R., Rafiq, O. (eds.) FORTE 1995. IFIPAICT, pp. 303–310. Springer, Boston (1996). https://doi.org/10.1007/978-0-387-34945-9_22

49. Kordon, F., et al.: MCC'2017 - The Seventh Model Checking Contest. Transactions on Petri Nets and Other Models of Concurrency (2018, to appear)

50. Krimm, J.-P.: Une approche compositionnelle pour la vérification de programmes LOTOS. Master's thesis, Université Joseph Fourier (Grenoble), June 1996

51. Krimm, J.-P., Mounier, L.: Compositional state space generation from LOTOS programs. In: Brinksma, E. (ed.) TACAS 1997. LNCS, vol. 1217, pp. 239–258. Springer, Heidelberg (1997). https://doi.org/10.1007/BFb0035392. Extended version with proofs available as Research Report VERIMAG RR97-01

52. Lang, F.: Compositional verification using SVL scripts. In: Katoen, J.-P., Stevens, P. (eds.) TACAS 2002. LNCS, vol. 2280, pp. 465–469. Springer, Heidelberg (2002). https://doi.org/10.1007/3-540-46002-0_33

53. Lang, F.: Refined interfaces for compositional verification. In: Najm, E., Pradat-Peyre, J.-F., Viguié Donzeau-Gouge, V. (eds.) FORTE 2006. LNCS, vol. 4229, pp. 159–174. Springer, Heidelberg (2006). https://doi.org/10.1007/11888116_13. Full version available as INRIA Research Report RR-5996

54. Luukkainen, M., Ahtiainen, A.: Compositional verification of large SDL systems. In: Proceedings of the 1st Workshop of the SDL Forum Society on SDL and MSC (SAM 1998), Berlin, Germany, June 1998

55. Malhotra, J., Smolka, S.A., Giacalone, A., Shapiro, R.: A tool for hierarchical design and simulation of concurrent systems. In: Proceedings of the BCS-FACS Workshop on Specification and Verification of Concurrent Systems, Stirling, Scotland, UK, pp. 140–152. British Computer Society, July 1988

56. Mateescu, R., Serwe, W.: A study of shared-memory mutual exclusion protocols using CADP. In: Kowalewski, S., Roveri, M. (eds.) FMICS 2010. LNCS, vol. 6371, pp. 180–197. Springer, Heidelberg (2010). https://doi.org/10.1007/978-3-642-15898-8_12

57. Mateescu, R., Serwe, W.: Model checking and performance evaluation with CADP illustrated on shared-memory mutual exclusion protocols. Sci. Comput. Program. **78**(7), 843–861 (2013)

58. Mazzanti, F., Ferrari, A.: Ten diverse formal models for a CBTC automatic train supervision system. In: Gallagher, J.P., van Glabbeek, R., Serwe, W. (eds.) Proceedings of the 3rd Workshop on Models for Formal Analysis of Real Systems and the 6th International Workshop on Verification and Program Transformation (MARS/VPT 2018), Thessaloniki, Greece. Electronic Proceedings in Theoretical Computer Science, vol. 268, pp. 104–149, April 2018

59. Mazzanti, F., Ferrari, A., Spagnolo, G.O.: Towards formal methods diversity in railways: an experience report with seven frameworks. Springer Int. J. Softw. Tools Technol. Transf. (STTT) **20**(3), 263–288 (2018)

60. Mendes, N., Lang, F., Cornec, Y.S.L., Mateescu, R., Batt, G., Chaouiya, C.: Composition and abstraction of logical regulatory modules: application to multicellular systems. Bioinformatics **29**(6), 749–757 (2013)

61. Milner, R. : A Calculus of Communicating Systems. LNCS, vol. 92. Springer, Heidelberg (1980). https://doi.org/10.1007/3-540-10235-3

62. Mounier, L.: A LOTOS specification of a transit-node. Rapport SPECTRE 94-8, VERIMAG, Grenoble, March 1994

63. Oliveira, R., Dupuy-Chessa, S., Calvary, G., Dadolle, D.: Using formal models to cross check an implementation. In: Luyten, K., Palanque, P. (eds.) Proceedings of the 8th ACM SIGCHI Symposium on Engineering Interactive Computing Systems (EICS 2016), Brussels, Belgium, pp. 126–137. ACM, June 2016

64. Park, D.: Concurrency and automata on infinite sequences. In: Deussen, P. (ed.) GI-TCS 1981. LNCS, vol. 104, pp. 167–183. Springer, Heidelberg (1981). https://doi.org/10.1007/BFb0017309

65. Pecheur, C.: Advanced modelling and verification techniques applied to a cluster file system. In: Hall, R.J., Tyugu, E. (eds.) Proceedings of the 14th IEEE International Conference on Automated Software Engineering (ASE 1999), Cocoa Beach, Florida, USA. IEEE Computer Society, October 1999. Extended version available as INRIA Research Report RR-3416

66. Peng, H., Tahar, S.: A survey on compositional verification. Technical report, Department of Electrical and Computer Engineering, Concordia University, Montreal, Canada, November 1998

67. Roever, W., et al.: Concurrency Verification - Introduction to Compositional and Noncompositional Methods. Cambridge Tracts in Theoretical Computer Science, vol. 54. Cambridge University Press, Cambridge (2001)

68. Romijn, J.: Analysing industrial protocols with formal methods. Ph.D. thesis, University of Twente, The Netherlands, September 1999

69. Sabnani, K.K., Lapone, A.M., Uyar, M.U.: An algorithmic procedure for checking safety properties of protocols. IEEE Trans. Commun. **37**(9), 940–948 (1989)

70. Sage, M., Johnson, C.: A declarative prototyping environment for the development of multi-user safety-critical systems. In: Proceedings of the 17th International System Safety Conference (ISSC 1999) Orlando, Florida, USA. System Safety Society, August 1999

71. Salaün, G., Bultan, T.: Realizability of choreographies using process algebra encodings. In: Leuschel, M., Wehrheim, H. (eds.) IFM 2009. LNCS, vol. 5423, pp. 167–182. Springer, Heidelberg (2009). https://doi.org/10.1007/978-3-642-00255-7_12

72. Salaün, G., Serwe, W.: Translating hardware process algebras into standard process algebras: illustration with CHP and LOTOS. In: Romijn, J., Smith, G., van de Pol, J. (eds.) IFM 2005. LNCS, vol. 3771, pp. 287–306. Springer, Heidelberg (2005). https://doi.org/10.1007/11589976_17. Full version available as INRIA Research Report RR-5666

73. Salaün, G., Serwe, W., Thonnart, Y., Vivet, P.: Formal verification of CHP specifications with CADP - illustration on an asynchronous network-on-chip. In: Beerel, P., Roncken, M., Greenstreet, M., Singh, M. (eds.) Proceedings of the 13th IEEE International Symposium on Asynchronous Circuits and Systems (ASYNC 2007), Berkeley, California, USA, pp. 73–82. IEEE Computer Society Press, March 2007

74. Schieferdecker, I.: Abruptly-terminated connections in TCP - a verification example. In: Brezočnik, Z., Kapus, T. (eds.) Proceedings of the COST 247 International Workshop on Applied Formal Methods in System Design, Maribor, Slovenia, pp. 136–145. University of Maribor, Slovenia, June 1996

75. Serwe, W.: Formal specification and verification of fully asynchronous implementations of the data encryption standard. In: van Glabbeek, R., Groote, J.F., Höfner, P. (eds.) Proceedings of the International Workshop on Models for Formal Analysis of Real Systems (MARS 2015), Suva, Fiji. Electronic Proceedings in Theoretical Computer Science, vol. 196 (2015)

76. Tai, K.C., Koppol, V.: An incremental approach to reachability analysis of distributed programs. In: Proceedings of the 7th International Workshop on Software Specification and Design, Los Angeles, CA, USA, pp. 141–150. IEEE Press, Piscataway, December 1993

77. Tai, K.C., Koppol, V.: Hierarchy-based incremental reachability analysis of communication protocols. In: Proceedings of the IEEE International Conference on Network Protocols, San Francisco, CA, USA, pp. 318–325. IEEE Press, Piscataway, October 1993

78. Tan, L.: Case studies using CRESS to develop web and grid services. Technical report, Department of Computing Science and Mathematics, University of Stirling, Scotland, UK, December 2009

79. Tronel, F., Lang, F., Garavel, H.: Compositional verification using CADP of the ScalAgent deployment protocol for software components. In: Najm, E., Nestmann, U., Stevens, P. (eds.) FMOODS 2003. LNCS, vol. 2884, pp. 244–260. Springer, Heidelberg (2003). https://doi.org/10.1007/978-3-540-39958-2_17. Full version available as INRIA Research Report RR-5012

80. Valmari, A.: Compositional state space generation. In: Rozenberg, G. (ed.) ICATPN 1991. LNCS, vol. 674, pp. 427–457. Springer, Heidelberg (1993). https://doi.org/10.1007/3-540-56689-9_54

81. Valmari, A.: Compositionality in state space verification methods. In: Billington, J., Reisig, W. (eds.) ICATPN 1996. LNCS, vol. 1091, pp. 29–56. Springer, Heidelberg (1996). https://doi.org/10.1007/3-540-61363-3_3

82. Valmari, A.: Composition and abstraction. In: Cassez, F., Jard, C., Rozoy, B., Ryan, M.D. (eds.) MOVEP 2000. LNCS, vol. 2067, pp. 58–98. Springer, Heidelberg (2001). https://doi.org/10.1007/3-540-45510-8_3

83. Valmari, A., Kemppainen, J., Clegg, M., Levanto, M.: Putting advanced reachability analysis techniques together: The "ARA" tool. In: Woodcock, J.C.P., Larsen, P.G. (eds.) FME 1993. LNCS, vol. 670, pp. 597–616. Springer, Heidelberg (1993). https://doi.org/10.1007/BFb0024669

84. Valmari, A., Kokkarinen, I.: Unbounded verification results by finite-state compositional techniques: 10^{any} states and beyond. In: Proceedings of the 1st International Conference on Application of Concurrency to System Design (ACSD 1998), Fukushima, Japan, pp. 75–85. IEEE Computer Society, March 1998

85. Willemse, T.: The specification and validation of the OM/RR-protocol. Master's thesis, Department of Mathematics and Computing Science, Eindhoven University of Technology, Eindhoven, The Netherlands, June 1998

86. Willemse, T., Tretmans, J., Klomp, A.: A case study in formal methods: specification and validation of the OM/RR protocol. In: Gnesi, S., Schieferdecker, I., Rennoch, A. (eds.) Proceedings of the 5th International Workshop on Formal Methods for Industrial Critical Systems (FMICS 2000), Berlin, Germany, pp. 331–344. GMD Report 91, Berlin, April 2000

87. Yeh, W.J.: Controlling state explosion in reachability analysis. Ph.D. thesis, Software Engineering Research Center (SERC) Laboratory, Purdue University, December 1993. Technical report SERC-TR-147-P

88. Yeh, W.J., Young, M.: Compositional reachability analysis using process algebra. In: Proceedings of the ACM SIGSOFT Symposium on Testing, Analysis, and Verification (SIGSOFT 1991), Victoria, British Columbia, Canada, pp. 49–59. ACM Press, October 1991

89. Zhang, Z., Serwe, W., Wu, J., Zheng, T.Y.H., Myers, C.: An improved fault-tolerant routing algorithm for a network-on-chip derived with formal analysis. Sci. Comput. Program. **118**, 24–39 (2016)

A Note on Refinement in Hierarchical Transition Systems

Gerald Lüttgen[⊠]

Software Technologies Research Group,
University of Bamberg, Bamberg, Germany
gerald.luettgen@swt-bamberg.de

Abstract. Software engineers frequently employ notations and tools based on transition systems, such as UML state machines and State-charts, for specifying and reasoning about reactive behaviour. While these notations are typically supported by an operational semantics, they lack a formal underpinning of the incremental refinement practices of engineers who, e.g., place state machines inside states or add outer transitions to states during design. This note sketches how modal transition systems may be applied to formally capture such refinements along state hierarchies, using a hierarchical extension of labelled transition systems that permits engineers to explicitly allow or disallow state refinement and transition extension at each state. A small example testifies to the utility of this framework for hierarchically refining reactive systems.

1 Introduction

Context and motivation. Hierarchical state machines play an important role when specifying and designing embedded systems. They are employed by software and systems engineers, e.g., in the form of *UML state machines* or *Statecharts* [6,16]. These visual notations are supported by modern tools for the model-driven engineering of embedded and reactive systems, and are typically equipped with operational semantics [7,14,17,19]. However, these semantics focus only on formalizing reactive execution, and not on the refinement practices employed by engineers who often start with an empty canvas, i.e., a single state. This is then refined incrementally by placing state machines inside states – which leads to a sequential, *vertical refinement* – and next to each other – which captures a concurrent, *horizontal refinement*.

Refinement has been studied intensively in the field of concurrency theory, where systems are built of concurrently interacting components. There, refinement means restricting nondeterminism [10], but not adding behaviour as is required for vertical refinement. Care is taken for refinement preorders to be pre-congruences, so as to enable *compositional reasoning*. Two examples of concurrency settings based on labelled transition systems are the interface theory *Interface Automata* [1] and the component framework *BIP* [2]. Interface theories model the assumptions and guarantees that a component expects from and

© Springer Nature Switzerland AG 2018
F. Howar and J. Barnat (Eds.): FMICS 2018, LNCS 11119, pp. 211–222, 2018.
https://doi.org/10.1007/978-3-030-00244-2_14

assures to its environment. A notion of compatibility defines when several components are compatible to each other, and a compositional alternating simulation preorder ensures that compatibility is preserved under refinement. Hence, interface theories support horizontal but not vertical composition and refinement.

The BIP (Behaviour-Interaction-Priority) framework for composing heterogeneous components is more flexible than Interface Automata, as it permits the specification of different kinds of component interaction, ranging from fully synchronous to fully asynchronous, and of priorities between interactions. BIP has been extended to hierarchical components in [11], thereby offering vertical composition, and has been equipped with contract-based reasoning along component hierarchies. However, the concern here is guaranteeing safety and progress properties [13], such as freedom of component interference [11], rather than supporting vertical refinement. In general, it may be fair to say that concurrency theory has focussed on horizontal refinement and often neglected vertical refinement.

Content and contributions. In this note, we sketch how vertical refinement of hierarchical state machines can be supported by the popular concurrency framework of *Modal Transition Systems* (MTS) [18]. MTS allows one to attach must- and may-modalities to transitions in order to model required and permitted behaviour, resp., and is equipped with the *modal refinement* preorder that supports the refinement of permitted to required behaviour. The utility of the MTS framework is quite versatile, as can be seen in the contribution by Steffen and Murtovi to this Festschrift volume [25].

To apply MTS for addressing vertical refinement, we first introduce in Sect. 2.1 a hierarchical version of event-labelled transition systems, called *Hierarchical Transition Systems* (HTS). A state of an HTS has an inner and an outer context, where the former allows one to place an HTS inside a *simple* state, which then becomes *compound*, and where the latter permits one to extend the outer state by adding transitions leaving that state [15,24]. Here, a compound state describes the usual sequential behaviour as defined in Statecharts [16], i.e., when the outer state is active, the inner state machine executes from its initial state until it is aborted by a transition emanating from the outer state. To indicate whether a state is refinable and open for extension wrt. a particular event, it is annotated with a *refinability flag* and *extensibility flags* [24], resp., so that an engineer can gradually disallow refinement and extension during vertical refinement and, thereby, successively close the state.

We then give, in Sect. 2.2, each HTS a semantics as an MTS and lift modal refinement to HTS. Intuitively, a transition in an HTS corresponds to a must-transition in the MTS; a refinable state has a may-transition to itself, for each event; a state has an outgoing may-transition to a special state tt, for each event for which it is extensible; and state tt has a may-loop for each event and no outgoing must-transition. We argue in Sect. 3.1 that this encoding is sufficient to correctly capture vertical refinement as employed by engineers, by considering popular refinement operations and proving that these do indeed modally refine the MTS underlying the manipulated HTS. A small example in Sect. 3.2 illustrates our semantic framework for hierarchically refining reactive systems, while the implications of our approach are discussed in Sect. 4.

Dedication. The author dedicates this paper to Susanne Graf, on the occasion of her 60th birthday. My first ever publication on the compositional minimization of finite state systems [12] has been a collaboration with Susanne (and Bernhard Steffen). I have closely followed Susanne's numerous scientific contributions ever since, and share with her many interests in concurrency theory and automated verification, especially on the utility of contracts and the importance of compositional reasoning. I wish her continued scientific success for years to come, and that she remains the outstandingly sympathetic person she is.

2   Hierarchical Transition Systems

A *hierarchical transition system* is a labelled transition system over a set of events, where states can themselves be hierarchical transition systems. Plain states are referred to as *simple*, while states with an embedded transition system are called *compound*. As in UML state machines and Statecharts [6,16], entering a compound state means entering the initial state of the inner transition system, and exiting some active state implies exiting also any active inner state. Hence, state hierarchy allows for a compact representation when several transitions with the same label and target state emanate from multiple states. Hierarchy has also been introduced to automata, and *hierarchical automata* have been employed as a model for Statecharts in the context of model checking [20].

Regarding *vertical refinement*, a state can be seen as having an inner and an outer context. The state's inner context refers to the transition system embedded in the state, which is empty in the case of a simple state, while the state's outer context relates to transitions leaving the state. Because we wish to semantically model vertical refinement as behaviour containment, we interpret a state as permitting arbitrary behaviour. To restrict behaviour, we introduce a *refinability flag* for each state and an *extensibility flag* for each state and event. If the refinability flag of a state is switched to *false*, the state's interior may no longer be changed. Similarly, if the extensibility flag for a state and event is switched to *false*, then no outgoing transition labelled with the event may be added to the state. The addition of these flags thus allows one to switch off permitted but optional behaviour, while retaining required behaviour.

2.1   Syntax of HTS

Let E be a set of *events* and N be set of state names, or *states* for short. In practice, E and N are often finite. Moreover, we assume that every $n \in N$ is associated with a hierarchical transition system:

Definition 1 (HTS). *The set HTS of* Hierarchical Transition Systems *over E and N is inductively defined as follows:*

- $n = (ext, ref)$ *is an HTS for any $n \in N$, extensibility flags $ext(e) \in \mathbb{B} =_{df}$ {true, false} for each $e \in E$, and refinability flag $ref \in \mathbb{B}$.*

– Let HTS $n_1, \ldots, n_k$ for some $k > 0$ and $n \in N$ be such that n does not occur in any n_i, for $1 \leq i \leq k$. Then, $n = (\{n_1, \ldots, n_k\}, \longmapsto, n_0, \text{ext}, \text{ref})$ is an HTS, where (a) n is the name of the hierarchical transition system, (b) $\longmapsto \subseteq \{n_1, \ldots, n_k\} \times E \times \{n_1, \ldots, n_k\}$ is the transition relation, (c) $n_0 \in \{n_1, \ldots, n_k\}$ is the initial state, and (d) ext and ref are the extensibility flags and the refinability flag as above. We require that such an HTS satisfies the following conditions, where $\text{ref}(m)$ and $\text{ext}(m, e)$ stand for the refinability flag of some $m \in N$ and the extensibility flag of m wrt. e, resp.:

(e) $\text{ref}(n)$ if $\text{ref}(n_i)$ for some $1 \leq i \leq k$;
(f) $\text{ref}(n)$ if $\text{ext}(n_i, e)$ for some $1 \leq i \leq k$ and some $e \in E$;
(g) $\text{ext}(n, e)$ if $\text{ext}(n_i, e)$ for some $1 \leq i \leq k$.

In the following, we identify an HTS with its name n, and refer to n of the first (second) kind above as simple state (compound state). We also expect that the outermost state n of an HTS satisfies $\text{ext}(n, e)$ for all $e \in E$.

Intuitively, Condition (e) of a compound HTS demands that all ancestor states of a refinable state are refinable or, equivalently, all descendant states of a non-refinable state or also non-refinable. Conditions (f) and (g) require that all ancestor states of an extensible state are refinable and extensible, resp.

2.2   Semantics of HTS

Hierarchical transition systems are given a semantics in terms of *modal transition systems* (MTS) [18], and the standard notion of *modal refinement* on such systems is lifted to HTS. An MTS is a transition system in which each transition is labelled with an event and assigned a must- or may-modality, where a must-transition (may-transition) specifies required (permitted) behaviour. Moreover, each required behaviour must also be permitted, which is known as *syntactic consistency*. Consequently, a state s that does not have an outgoing e-may-transition, specifies that event e is forbidden in s.

Definition 2 (MTS). *A Modal Transition System (MTS) over event set E is a tuple $(S, \longrightarrow, \dashrightarrow, s_0)$, where S is the set of states, $s_0 \in S$ is the initial state, and $\longrightarrow \subseteq \dashrightarrow \subseteq S \times E \times S$ are the must- and may-transition relations, resp.*

In the following, we often abbreviate an MTS by its initial state. MTSs can be related by an alternating simulation relation, called *modal refinement* [18]:

Definition 3 (MTS refinement). *Given two MTS $(S_1, \longrightarrow_1, \dashrightarrow_1, s_{01})$ and $(S_2, \longrightarrow_2, \dashrightarrow_2, s_{02})$, a relation $\mathcal{R} \subseteq S_1 \times S_2$ is a modal refinement relation if the following conditions hold, for all $(s_1, s_2) \in \mathcal{R}$ and $e \in E$:*

1. $s_2 \xrightarrow{e}_2 s_2'$ implies $\exists s_1'. s_1 \xrightarrow{e}_1 s_1'$ and $(s_1', s_2') \in \mathcal{R}$,
2. $s_1 \overset{e}{\dashrightarrow}_1 s_1'$ implies $\exists s_2'. s_2 \overset{e}{\dashrightarrow}_2 s_2'$ and $(s_1', s_2') \in \mathcal{R}$.

We write $s_1 \sqsubseteq_{MTS} s_2$ if $(s_1, s_2) \in \mathcal{R}$ for some modal refinement relation $\mathcal{R}$, and $S_1 \sqsubseteq_{MTS} S_2$ if $s_{01} \sqsubseteq_{MTS} s_{02}$.

Modal refinement is a preorder, i.e., it is reflexive and transitive. Intuitively, one MTS refines another MTS if the required behaviour of the latter can be simulated by the former, and the permitted behaviour of the former is simulated by the latter. Thus, refining an MTS allows changing permitted behaviour into required behaviour, while adding non-permitted behaviour is prohibited.

Definition 4 (HTS semantics). *The semantics of an HTS n is the modal transition system $MTS(n)$, which is inductively defined along the structure of n as follows, where tt denotes a special state not in N:*

If $n = (ext, ref)$, then $MTS(n) =_{df} (\{n, tt\}, \emptyset, \dashrightarrow, n)$, where $\dashrightarrow$ is least such that, for all $e \in E$, (a) $n \overset{e}{\dashrightarrow} n$ if ref, (b) $n \overset{e}{\dashrightarrow} tt$ if ext(e), and (c) $tt \overset{e}{\dashrightarrow} tt$.

If $n = (\{n_1, \ldots, n_k\}, \longmapsto, n_0, ext, ref)$ and $MTS(n_i) = (S_i, \longrightarrow_i, \dashrightarrow_i, s_{0i})$ for $1 \leq i \leq k$, then $MTS(n) =_{df} (S, \longrightarrow, \dashrightarrow, n_0)$, where $S =_{df} \{tt\} \cup \bigcup \{n.s \mid s \in S_i \setminus \{tt\}, 1 \leq i \leq k\}$ and $\longrightarrow, \dashrightarrow$ are the least relations satisfying, for all $e \in E$:

(a) $n.s \overset{e}{\dashrightarrow} n.s$ if ref and $s \in S \setminus \{tt\}$

(b) $n.s \overset{e}{\dashrightarrow} tt$ if ext(e) and $s \in S \setminus \{tt\}$

(c) $tt \overset{e}{\dashrightarrow} tt$

(d) $n.s_i \overset{e}{\longrightarrow} n.s_j$ if $n_i \overset{e}{\longmapsto} n_j$, $s_i \in S_i \setminus \{tt\}$ and $s_j = init(n_j)$

(e) $n.s_i \overset{e}{\dashrightarrow} n.s_j$ if $n_i \overset{e}{\longmapsto} n_j$, $s_i \in S_i \setminus \{tt\}$ and $s_j = init(n_j)$

(f) $n.s \overset{e}{\longrightarrow} n.s'$ if $s \overset{e}{\longrightarrow}_i s'$ and $s, s' \in S_i \setminus \{tt\}$

(g) $n.s \overset{e}{\dashrightarrow} n.s'$ if $s \overset{e}{\dashrightarrow}_i s'$ and $s, s' \in S_i \setminus \{tt\}$

(h) $n.s \overset{e}{\dashrightarrow} tt$ if $s \overset{e}{\dashrightarrow}_i tt$ and $s \in S_i \setminus \{tt\}$

Here, $init(m) =_{df} m.init(m_0)$ if $m = (\{m_1, \ldots, m_k\}, \longmapsto, m_0, ext, ref)$ is compound, and $init(m) =_{df} m$ if m is simple.

Intuitively, the MTS semantics of some HTS n flattens the state hierarchy of n, so that states in $MTS(n)$ are sequences of successively nested states in n. A transition $n_i \overset{e}{\longmapsto} n_j$ of a compound HTS n is translated to a must-transition with underlying may-transition (Conds. (d)–(e)). According to the semantics of state hierarchy in Statecharts dialects [6,16], this implies that each flattened state of the form $n.n_{i.\_}$ in $MTS(n)$ has an outgoing e-must-transition to the initial state to which n_j points, which is inductively defined via function $init()$ along the hierarchy of n_j. In addition, $MTS(n)$ inherits all must- and may-transitions in the semantics of its children n_i, where states get prefix "$n.$" because n_i is a child of n (Conds. (f)–(h)). Refinability of some basic HTS n is naturally defined via an e-may-loop on n for all events e (Condition (a)), while e-extensibility of n for some e is realized by an e-may-transition to a special, universal state tt (Condition (b)). This state captures arbitrary behaviour and is thus also modelled in MTS by an e-may-loop for all events e (Condition (c)). For compound HTS, the semantic interpretation of refinability and extensibility is analogous.

Regarding extensibility, Schmidt introduced in [24] the notion of n *is open for e*, in the context of refinement patterns for the top-down refinement of hierarchical state machines. This notion specifies that e-transitions leaving n can no longer be added to and removed from n. Although he used transition systems with simulation instead of MTS and modal refinement for defining the semantics of hierarchical state machines, our notion of an e-extensible state n closely relates to his *open* notion.

Definition 5 (HTS refinement). *An HTS m refines an HTS n, in signs $m \sqsubseteq_{HTS} n$, if $MTS(m) \sqsubseteq_{MTS} MTS(n)$.*

HTS refinement is compositional for substitution within a compound HTS n, i.e., n is refined when replacing one of its children n_i with a refined HTS m:

Definition 6 (Substitution). *For states $n, m, m' \in N$ with m' not occurring in n, the name substitution $n[m'/m]$ is defined by $n[m'/m] =_{df} m'$ if $n = m$, and $n[m'/m] =_{df} n$, otherwise.*

For a compound HTS $n = (\{n_1, \ldots, n_k\}, \longmapsto, n_0, ext, ref)$, some HTS m and $1 \leq i \leq k$ such that m does not occur in n_i, the compound HTS $n\{m/n_i\}$ is given by $(\{n_1, \ldots, n_{i-1}, m, n_{i+1}, \ldots, n_k\}, \longmapsto', n_0[m/n_i], ext, ref)$, where $n'[m/n_i] \overset{e}{\longmapsto}' n''[m/n_i]$ if $n' \overset{e}{\longmapsto} n''$, for all $n', n'' \in \{n_1, \ldots, n_k\}$.

Theorem 7 *[Compositionality]. Let n, m be HTS as in Definition 6 and such that $m \sqsubseteq_{HTS} n_i$ for some $1 \leq i \leq k$. Then, $n\{m/n_i\} \sqsubseteq_{HTS} n$.*

Observe that compositionality as treated here is somewhat restricted in that substitutions are only considered at the outermost hierarchy level of a compound HTS, and not also at arbitrary inner levels. Such latter substitutions of some deeper descendant n^* of n must be conducted first for n^*, and the outer context must be reconstructed step-by-step along the ancestors of n^* until n is reached, by repeatedly applying Theorem 7. We believe that a general compositionality result can in principal be obtained, but this requires a more complex semantic construction.

3   Vertical Refinement

This section (i) formally describes several vertical *refinement operations* that are popular with software engineers, (ii) shows how these operations can be casted in our HTS setting, and (iii) proves that each operation indeed refines an HTS according to $\sqsubseteq_{HTS}$. Such operations may be understood as *refinement patterns*; more comprehensive pattern catalogues for the refinement of hierarchical state machines may be found, e.g., in [15, 24]. The utility of our refinement operations and the HTS setting is then demonstrated by means of a small example that illustrates the incremental, hierarchical design of an embedded controller.

3.1   Refinement Operations

The following operations describe some typical refinement practices employed by engineers (Ops. (A)–(C)) and the utility of closing states by declaring them as non-refinable and non-extensible (Ops. (D) and (E), resp.). We refrain from explicitly assigning names to operations, but we always refer to the original HTS as n and the refined HTS as m, so that $m \sqsubseteq_{HTS} n$.

A. Refining a simple, refinable state by a compound state. Let $n = (ext, true)$ be a simple HTS and $m = (\{m_1, \ldots, m_k\}, \longmapsto, m_0, ext', ref')$ be a compound HTS such that $ext'(e) \Longrightarrow ext(e)$ for all $e \in E$. Then, $m \sqsubseteq_{HTS} n$, because $MTS(n)$ has an e-may-loop for each $e \in E$ and no must-transitions. Due to this and Theorem 7, one may refine any simple, refinable state inside an HTS by a compound state.

B. Adding an e-transition to an e-extensible state. Let $n = (\{n_1, \ldots, n_k\}, \longmapsto, n_0, ext, true)$, $e \in E$ and $1 \leq i, j \leq k$ such that $ext(n_i, e)$, and define $m =_{df} (\{n_1, \ldots, n_k\}, \longmapsto \cup \{(n_i, e, n_j)\}, n_0, ext, true)$. Then, $m \sqsubseteq_{HTS} n$; by Theorem 7, this also holds for compound states inside a more complex HTS. The validity of $m \sqsubseteq_{HTS} n$ follows from the fact that there is an e-may-transition to tt for all states of the form $n.n_{i.\_}$ in $MTS(n)$. Thus, the (new) must-transitions (and underlying may-transitions) of $MTS(m)$ are permitted by $MTS(n)$.

C. Adding a simple state to a refinable compound state. Let $n = (\{n_1, \ldots, n_k\}, \longmapsto, n_0, ext, true)$ and $n_{k+1} = (ext', ref')$ be a compound and a simple HTS, resp. Then, $m =_{df} (\{n_1, \ldots, n_k, n_{k+1}\}, \longmapsto, n_0, ext, true)$ is a compound HTS, which trivially satisfies $m \sqsubseteq_{HTS} n$ as there are no transitions connected to n_{k+1}.

D. Closing a refinable state. This operation recursively closes all inner states by marking each state non-refinable and its inner states non-extensible for all events. If $n = (ext, true)$ is a simple HTS, let $m =_{df} (ext, false)$. Then, $m \sqsubseteq_{HTS} n$ as the e-may-loops are removed from the states in $MTS(n)$, for all $e \in E$.

If $n = (\{n_1, \ldots, n_k\}, \longmapsto, n_0, ext, true)$ is a compound HTS, we define $m =_{df} (\{n_1, \ldots, n_k\}, \longmapsto, n_0, ext, false)$. Moreover, all children n_i and all of their descendants get their refinability flag and extensibility flags set to *false*. Then, $m \sqsubseteq_{HTS} n$ because the e-may-loops and, provided $ext(e) = false$, also the e-may-transitions to tt are removed from all states of the form $n.\_$ in $MTS(n)$, for all $e \in E$. Note that syntactic consistency is preserved.

E. Restricting an e-extensible state for event e. Let $n = (ext, ref)$ be a simple HTS with $ext(e) = true$, and define $m =_{df} (ext', ref)$ where $ext'(e') = false$ if $e' = e$, and $ext'(e') = ext(e')$, otherwise. Then, $m \sqsubseteq_{HTS} n$; only the e-may-transition to tt is removed from $MTS(n)$, and $MTS(n)$ has no must-transitions.

Let $n = (\{n_1, \ldots, n_k\}, \longmapsto, n_0, ext, ref)$ be a compound HTS with $ext(e) = true$, define $m =_{df} (\{n_1, \ldots, n_k\}, \longmapsto, n_0, ext', ref)$ with ext' as above, and set the e-extensibility flag of all descendants of n to *false*. Then, $m \sqsubseteq_{HTS} n$; again, only the e-may-transitions to tt are removed from all states of the form $n.n_{i.\_}$ in $MTS(n)$, for all $1 \leq i \leq k$. Syntactic consistency is unaffected.

3.2 Example Application

We illustrate the above refinement operations on HTS by means of a simple example, the incremental development of a controller for a washing machine, which is illustrated in Figs. 1 and 2. In the HTS shown on the left in these figures, initial states are marked with a dangling incoming arrow, a refinable (non-refinable) state n has an unfilled (filled) circle to the left of its name. If n is e-extensible for all $e \in E' \subseteq E$, then we draw an unfilled circle labelled E' besides n's top-right corner; we also write $\bar{e}$ for the event set $E \setminus \{e\}$. If n is not extensible for any event, then the circle is filled and not labelled. Moreover, a may-transition labelled E' stands for a bunch of may-transitions, one for each $e \in E'$. Finally, illustrating the complete MTS with all its may-transitions would be visually overwhelming. Thus, we do not draw may-transitions that underlie must-transitions. Additionally, all E-may-loops in the MTS on the right in Figs. 1 and 2 are omitted, and only those may-transitions with target tt that emanate from the closest, still extensible outer context state are drawn.

The design of the controller starts with an empty canvas at Step (0), i.e., a single, simple, refinable and extensible state WM. Refinement Step (1) applies Op. A to place a state machine with states ON and OFF inside WM, between which one can switch via events off and on. The non-off-extensibility of OFF specifies that the machine cannot be switched off if it is already off, and analogously for ON. Step (2) refines ON further, by declaring that an active washing

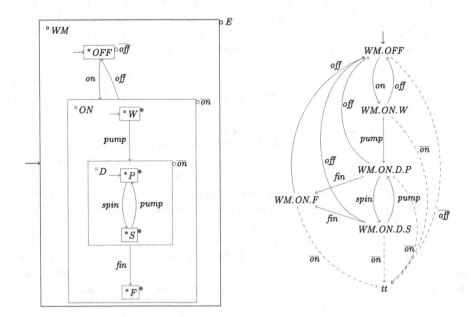

Fig. 1. Example illustrating incremental vertical refinement (Steps (0)–(3)), where the HTS WM and MTS $MTS(WM)$ are displayed on the left and right, resp. *Colour coding:* black (Step (0)), blue (Step (1)), green (Step (2)), red (Step (3)). (Colour figure online)

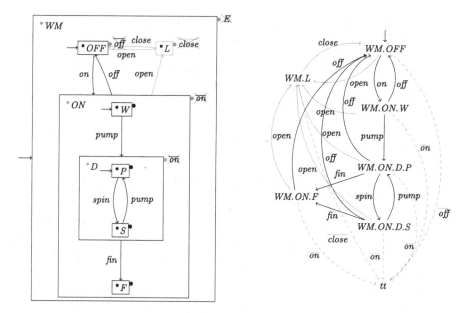

Fig. 2. Example illustrating incremental vertical refinement (Steps (4)–(6)). *Colour coding:* black (resulting HTS and MTS after Step (3), redrawn), pink (may-transitions removed in Step (4)), orange (Step (5)), gray (all may-transitions removed in Step (6)). (Colour figure online)

machine first washes (state W, for *Washing*), then drys (state D, for *Drying*) after initiating to pump out the water (event *pump*), and finally finishes (event *fin* leading to state F, for *Finishing*). Because this activity sequence is deemed complete except for state D, only D is refinable and $\overline{on}$-extensible. This state is refined in Step (3) by a state machine that toggles between the simple, non-refinable and non-extensible states P (*Pumping*) and S (*Spinning*).

Closing state ON in Step (4) via Ops. D and E means switching its refinability flag and all refinability and extensibility flags of its inner states to *false* (cf. Conds.(e) and (f) of Definition 1); thus, the refinability circle and extensibility circle of state D are also filled and the extensibility label $\overline{on}$ vanishes. Semantically, this leads to (i) the removal of the E-may-loops at states of the form $WM.ON._$ (not shown in Fig. 2, right) and (ii) the deletion of the $\overline{on}$-may-transition to tt at states of the form $WM.ON.D._$ (shown). The latter transitions are, however, re-inserted immediately (not shown), because ON itself is still $\overline{on}$-extensible. The analogue is true for the E-may-loops as state WM remains refinable. Note that these immediate reinsertions would not be automatic in case HTS would be extended by a mechanism for event scoping. Step (5) adds via Op. C state L (*Loading/Emptying*) as child state of WM, and successively inserts via Op. B *open*-transitions to and *close*-transitions from the *close*-extensible state L (opening and closing the washing machine's door). Finally, Step (6) declares WM as no longer refinable and extensible. The former implies by Condition (f) of

Definition 1 that states *OFF*, *ON* and *L* are also becoming non-extensible; hence, the now filled extensibility circles at those states and their crossed out labels.

This yields the final design of our washing machine controller, where all may-transitions that do not underly must-transitions are deleted. By the results of Sect. 3.1 and writing $WM^{(i)}$ for the HTS *WM* after refinement step i, we have $WM^{(6)} \sqsubseteq_{HTS} WM^{(0)}$ due to $WM^{(i)} \sqsubseteq_{HTS} WM^{(i-1)}$ for all $1 \leq i \leq 6$, as desired.

4   Conclusions

Hierarchical languages for specifying and designing reactive systems, such as UML state machines and Statecharts [6,16], offer the ability to refine designs by inserting states and transitions or by placing whole state machines inside simple states. This vertical refinement along state hierarchies adds behaviour and thus differs from the refinement concepts typically studied in concurrency theory, which focus on restricting non-determinism, i.e., on reducing behaviour.

This note sketched a proposal of how this apparent contradiction can be overcome. We demonstrated that the *Modal Transition Systems* (MTS) framework [18] can very well support vertical refinement, assuming that simple states are seen as empty canvases allowing arbitrary behaviour, and that inserting states and transitions into the canvas specifies required behaviour. For this to make practical sense, a state open for refinement or extension should be explicitly closed at some stage during the design process, thereby specifying that the state is in its final form and semantically cutting permitted but not required behaviour. As long as a state is open, required behaviour can be added and, hence, gradually more progress properties can be verified. When a state is closed, new safety properties can be verified. For example, the property "event *fin* cannot occur without event *pump* having occurred before" of our washing machine controller in the previous section can be proved once state *ON* becomes non-*fin*-extensible, and assuming that the scope of these two events is state *ON* only. Given that MTS has been well studied for component-based specification, e.g., in the context of interface theories [3–5,8] and assume-guarantee reasoning [22], it ideally lends itself to settings requiring both vertical and horizontal refinement and also demanding compositional reasoning.

Future work. Firstly, future work should evolve our semantics of HTS so that a general compositionality result is obtained, supporting direct substitution also at inner hierarchy levels. Secondly, because modal refinement is not fully abstract wrt. the notion of refinement on HTS described in Sect. 3.1, we plan to explore weaker refinement relations for hierarchical state machines. Thirdly, we wish to integrate our ideas in more fully featured languages for reactive systems design: HTS currently does *not* (i) permit any form of event scoping, which would imply changes to the semantic rules in Definition 4, (ii) specify priority along state hierarchy, (iii) consider concurrent behaviour, or (iv) address subtle questions such as *"What is in a step?"* [21,23], which becomes relevant when the execution of concurrent transitions may generate events. We also believe that the seminal compositional minimization technique co-invented by Graf [12], which is discussed by Garavel, Lang and Mounier in another contribution to this Festschrift volume [9], can be extended to support state hierarchy and the MTS framework.

Acknowledgements. Research support was provided by the German Research Foundation (DFG) under grant no. LU 1748/3-2. The author thanks Johannes Gareis for his helpful comments on drafts of this note and for carefully drawing the example figures.

References

1. de Alfaro, L., Henzinger, T.A.: Interface automata. In: ESEC/FSE, pp. 109–120. ACM (2001)
2. Basu, A., Bensalem, S., Bozga, M., Bourgos, P., Sifakis, J.: Rigorous system design: the BIP approach. In: Kotásek, Z., Bouda, J., Černá, I., Sekanina, L., Vojnar, T., Antoš, D. (eds.) MEMICS 2011. LNCS, vol. 7119, pp. 1–19. Springer, Heidelberg (2012). https://doi.org/10.1007/978-3-642-25929-6_1
3. Bauer, S.S., Mayer, P., Schroeder, A., Hennicker, R.: On weak modal compatibility, refinement, and the MIO workbench. In: Esparza, J., Majumdar, R. (eds.) TACAS 2010. LNCS, vol. 6015, pp. 175–189. Springer, Heidelberg (2010). https://doi.org/10.1007/978-3-642-12002-2_15
4. Benveniste, A., et al.: Contracts for system design. Found. Trends Electron. Des. Autom. **12**(2–3), 124–400 (2018)
5. Bujtor, F., Fendrich, S., Lüttgen, G., Vogler, W.: Nondeterministic modal interfaces. Theoret. Comput. Sci. **642**(C), 24–53 (2016)
6. Drusinsky, D.: Modeling and Verification Using UML Statecharts. Newnes (2006)
7. Eshuis, R.: Reconciling statechart semantics. Sci. Comput. Program. **74**(3), 65–99 (2009)
8. Fendrich, S., Lüttgen, G.: A generalised theory of interface automata, component compatibility and error. Acta Inf. (2018). https://doi.org/10.1007/s00236-018-0319-8
9. Garavel, H., Lang, F., Mounier, L.: Compositional verification in action. In: Howar, F., Barnat, J. (eds.) FMICS 2018. LNCS, vol. 11119, pp. 189–210. Springer, Cham (2018)
10. Glabbeek, R.J.: The linear time - branching time spectrum. In: Baeten, J.C.M., Klop, J.W. (eds.) CONCUR 1990. LNCS, vol. 458, pp. 278–297. Springer, Heidelberg (1990). https://doi.org/10.1007/BFb0039066
11. Graf, S., Quinton, S.: Contracts for BIP: hierarchical interaction models for compositional verification. In: Derrick, J., Vain, J. (eds.) FORTE 2007. LNCS, vol. 4574, pp. 1–18. Springer, Heidelberg (2007). https://doi.org/10.1007/978-3-540-73196-2_1
12. Graf, S., Steffen, B., Lüttgen, G.: Compositional minimisation of finite state systems using interface specifications. Formal Asp. Comput. **8**(5), 607–616 (1996)
13. Ben-Hafaiedh, I., Graf, S., Quinton, S.: Reasoning about safety and progress using contracts. In: Dong, J.S., Zhu, H. (eds.) ICFEM 2010. LNCS, vol. 6447, pp. 436–451. Springer, Heidelberg (2010). https://doi.org/10.1007/978-3-642-16901-4_29
14. Hamon, G., Rushby, J.M.: An operational semantics for Stateflow. STTT **9**(5–6), 447–456 (2007)
15. Harbird, L.: Patterns and Model Transformation Tools for Designing Contractual State Machines. Ph.D thesis, Univ. York, UK (2011)

16. Harel, D.: Statecharts: a visual formalism for complex systems. Sci. Comput. Program. **8**, 231–274 (1987)
17. Harel, D., Naamad, A.: The STATEMATE semantics of Statecharts. ACM Trans. Softw. Eng. Methodol. **5**(4), 293–333 (1996)
18. Larsen, K.G.: Modal specifications. In: Sifakis, J. (ed.) Computer Aided Verification. LNCS, vol. 407, pp. 232–246. Springer, Heidelberg (1990). https://doi.org/10.1007/3-540-52148-8_19
19. Lüttgen, G., von der Beeck, M., Cleaveland, R.: A compositional approach to Statecharts semantics. In: FSE, ACM Software Engineering Notes, vol. 25(6), pp. 120–129. ACM (2000)
20. Mikk, E., Lakhnechi, Y., Siegel, M.: Hierarchical automata as model for Statecharts. In: Shyamasundar, R.K., Ueda, K. (eds.) ASIAN 1997. LNCS, vol. 1345, pp. 181–196. Springer, Heidelberg (1997). https://doi.org/10.1007/3-540-63875-X_52
21. Pnueli, A., Shalev, M.: What is in a step: on the semantics of Statecharts. In: Ito, T., Meyer, A.R. (eds.) TACS 1991. LNCS, vol. 526, pp. 244–264. Springer, Heidelberg (1991). https://doi.org/10.1007/3-540-54415-1_49
22. Quinton, S., Graf, S.: Contract-based verification of hierarchical systems of components. In: SEFM, pp. 377–381. IEEE (2008)
23. de Roever, W.-P., Lüttgen, G., Mendler, M.: What Is in a step: new perspectives on a classical question. In: Manna, Z., Peled, D.A. (eds.) Time for Verification. LNCS, vol. 6200, pp. 370–399. Springer, Heidelberg (2010). https://doi.org/10.1007/978-3-642-13754-9_15
24. Schmidt, H.: On the Role of Nondeterminism and Refinement in Model-Driven Top-Down Development of Software Systems. Ph.D thesis, Univ. Kiel, Germany (2009)
25. Steffen, B., Murtovi, A.: M3C: modal meta model checking. In: Howar, F., Barnat, J. (eds.) FMICS 2018. LNCS, vol. 11119, pp. 223–241. Springer, Cham (2018)

$M3C$: Modal Meta Model Checking

Bernhard Steffen$^{(\boxtimes)}$ and Alnis Murtovi

Chair for Programming Systems, TU Dortmund University, Dortmund, Germany
{bernhard.steffen,alnis.murtovi}@tu-dortmund.de

Abstract. $M3C$ is a method and tool supporting meta-level product lining and evolution that comprises both context free system structure and modal refinement. The underlying Context-Free Modal Transition Systems can be regarded as loose specifications of meta models, and modal refinement as a way to increase the specificity of allowed DSLs by constraining the range of allowed syntax specifications. Model checking with $M3C$ allows one to verify properties specified in a branching-time logic for all DSLs of a given level of specificity in one go, which is illustrated by looking at variations of an elementary programming language. Technically, $M3C$ is based on second-order model checking which determines how procedure calls *affect* the validity of the properties of interest. The inherent compositionality of the second-order approach leads to a runtime complexity linear in the size of the procedural system representation, whose corresponding transition systems typically have infinitely many states. In fact, second-order model checking can be regarded as a means to tame state explosion via 'procedural abstraction', a technique which may well be beneficial also for regular (recursion-free) systems.

Keywords: Modal Transition Systems
Context-free/procedural transition systems · Modal refinement
Second-order model checking · Meta model
Domain-specific languages · Predicate/property transformers
Binary decision diagram · Compositionality

1 Introduction

In the last decades, model checking has developed as a very generic tool for automated analysis that can be applied in very different scenarios and in many variants. A particularly interesting development happened in the context of software product lining and evolution, where model checking has e.g., been applied to so-called modal transitions systems that, together with the inherent notion of refinement, allow one to capture not only individual system/programs but entire classes thereof. The point here is that the so-called *modal refinement* preserves all properties specified in the popular linear-time and branching-time temporal logics. Thus it is possible to verify properties of product lines or evolutionary steps by in one go as long as they are captured by a system specification in terms of a modal transitions system.

© Springer Nature Switzerland AG 2018
F. Howar and J. Barnat (Eds.): FMICS 2018, LNCS 11119, pp. 223–241, 2018.
https://doi.org/10.1007/978-3-030-00244-2_15

An alternative way to impose/control properties beyond single instances is the way of tailored domain specific languages (DSLs): all systems developed in such a language are typically guaranteed to satisfy the properties/constraints imposed by the DSLs' meta model (cf. [20]). Corresponding checks are typically done by parsers, but using context-free model checking [2–4], it is also possible to model check interesting properties of DSLs, whose impact on the individual systems typically increases with the specificity of the considered DSL. [19] proposes an approach that elaborates on the idea to control/guide software evolution and product lining by lifting the software evolution process (in part) to the meta level.

In this paper, we present $M3C$, a method and tool supporting meta-level product lining and evolution that comprises both context free system structure and modal refinement. The underlying Context-Free Modal Transition Systems (CFMTSs) can be regarded as loose specifications of meta models, and modal refinement as a way to increase the specificity of allowed DSLs by constraining the range of possible meta models (syntax specifications). Model checking with $M3C$ allows one to verify properties specified in a branching-time logic[1] for all DSLs of a given level of specificity in one go. Most of these properties can be directly interpreted as DSL-enforced program properties.[2]

The paper will illustrate the impact of the $M3C$ approach by interpreting model checking results both at the meta level and at the system level. We will show that the model checking results provide a good guidance in what one may call meta model engineering. More concretely, we will discuss the evolution step from a classical WHILE language to Wirth's PL/0, which comprise procedures [21]. We will start from a 'naive' modal specification of a family of languages that comprise, in particular the WHILE (sub) language and the entire PL/0, and discuss ways aiming at guaranteeing that called procedures are always declared (cf. Sect. 4.1).

Technically, $M3C$ is based on second-order model checking [2–4] which determines how procedure calls *affect* the validity of the properties of interest. The corresponding second-order analysis for determining the predicate transformers (the effects) for the individual procedures is characterized by its hierarchical fixpoint iteration: a higher-level iteration for exchanging approximate predicate transformers of the involved procedures, and a (local) lower level iteration for updating the individual predicates transformers on the basis of the current approximate transformers for the procedures. These iterations, which conceptually *separate the description of behavior of components from the way they interact* [11], may be arbitrarily intertwined because of monotonicity reasons.

The inherent compositionality of the second-order approach leads to a runtime complexity linear in the size of the procedural system representation, whose corresponding transition systems typically have infinitely many states. In fact, second-order model checking can be regarded as a means to tame state explosion via 'procedural abstraction', a technique which may well be beneficial also for

---

[1] We are focusing here on the alternation-free mu-calculus.

[2] Such properties are called rigid archimedean points in [20].

regular (recursion-free) systems: during higher-level iterations, entire subsystems are just considered as predicate transformers, i.e., as second-order versions of the predicate abstractions introduced in [12].

Abstraction, the art of focusing on the essential details, is also a guiding principle for modal refinement. In a sense, the may transitions of modal transition systems can be regarded as a form of don't care transition, providing future implementations with a freedom of choice, which may profitably be used for optimization or future system evolution. The fact that modal refinement supports a notion of property-preserving abstraction in the sense of [17] allows one to cover even infinite classes of implementations with one check or to minimize given implementations in a don't care fashion along the lines of [10,13,14].

After presenting the required background in Sect. 2, we present our model meta model checking algorithm in Sect. 3 and discuss its application in Sect. 4. The paper closes with our conclusions and direction to future work in Sect. 5.

2   Preliminaries

In this section we present *Context-Free Modal Transition Systems* (CFMTS) which extend *Modal Transition Systems* (MTSs) to mutually recursive systems of MTSs,[3] sketch PL/0, the programming language serving as an application scenario for our technology, and the considered property language, the (alternation-free) *modal μ-calculus*.

2.1   Context-Free Modal Transition Systems

Modal transitions systems and their extension with mutual recursion presented in this section come with a notion of refinement that establishes a powerful specification-implementation relation. They allow one to model check properties at the specification-level that are then guaranteed to hold for each implementation.

Definition 1 (Modal Transition Systems [15]). *Let S be a set of states and Act an alphabet of action symbols. $M = (S, s_0, Act, \dashrightarrow, \longrightarrow)$ is called a (rooted) Modal Transition System (MTS) with root s_0 if the following condition holds:*

$$\longrightarrow \subseteq \dashrightarrow \subseteq (S \times Act \times S)$$

Elements of $\dashrightarrow$ are called may transitions, those of $\longrightarrow$ must transitions. As usual, we will write $s \xrightarrow{a} s'$ iff $(s, a, s') \in \longrightarrow$ and $s \xrightarrow{a}$ to abbreviate $\exists s'. s \xrightarrow{a} s'$, $s \dashrightarrow{a} s'$ and $s \dashrightarrow{a}$ are defined analogously.

---

[3] Alternatively, one can regard CFMTS also as an extension of Context-Free Process Systems [2] to also allow *may transitions*.

MTSs denote sets of *Labelled Transition Systems* (LTS)s, which can simply be defined as MTS where all transitions are *must* transitions. Modal refinement, the corresponding specification-implementation relation, defines these sets as the minimal elements of the refinement ordering:

Definition 2 (MTS refinement [15]**).** *Let* $M_1 = (S_1, s_0^1, Act_1, {\dashrightarrow}_1, {\longrightarrow}_1)$, $M_2 = (S_2, s_0^2, Act_2, {\dashrightarrow}_2, {\longrightarrow}_2)$ *be two MTSs. A relation* $\leq_r \subseteq (S_1 \times S_2)$ *is called a refinement if the following holds for all* $(p, q) \in \leq_r$*:*

$$1. \ \forall(p, a, p') \in {\dashrightarrow}_1, \exists(q, a, q') \in {\dashrightarrow}_2 \colon (p', q') \in \leq_r$$
$$2. \ \forall(q, a, q') \in {\longrightarrow}_2, \exists(p, a, p') \in {\longrightarrow}_1 \colon (p', q') \in \leq_r$$

An MTS M_1 refines an MTS M_2, written $M_1 \leq_r M_2$, if there exists a refinement $\leq_r$ with $(s_0^1, s_0^2) \in \leq_r$. Intuitively, refinement is closed under node-splitting/duplication of states, allows may transitions to be either turned into must transitions or to be eliminated, while it requires all must transitions to be maintained. Like *bisimulation*, it preserves all temporal properties of finite state systems [16]. In fact, the restriction to finite state is not essential for the induction proof along the structure of the temporal formulas, which makes modal refinement an ideal tool for product line verification also for the here considered infinite state case.

The following notion of procedural modal transition system (PMTS) extends MTS to comprise *call transitions* that allows one to define mutually recursive sets of MTS, later formalized as Context-Free Modal Transition Systems (CFMTS).

Definition 3 (Procedural Modal Transition System). *A procedural modal transition system is defined as* $P = (\Sigma_P, Trans := Act \cup N, {\dashrightarrow}_P, {\longrightarrow}_P, \sigma_P^s, \sigma_P^e)$, *where:*

- Σ_P *is a set of state classes,*
- $Trans := Act \cup N$ *is a set of transformations (Act is a set of actions, N is a set of procedure names),*
- ${\longrightarrow}_P := {\longrightarrow}_P^{Act} \cup {\longrightarrow}_P^N$ *is the must transition relation*
- ${\dashrightarrow}_P := {\dashrightarrow}_P^{Act} \cup {\dashrightarrow}_P^N$ *is the may transition relation,*
  where ${\longrightarrow}_P^{Act} \subseteq {\dashrightarrow}_P^{Act} \subseteq \Sigma_P \times Act \times \Sigma_P$ *and* ${\longrightarrow}_P^N \subseteq {\dashrightarrow}_P^N \subseteq \Sigma_P \times N \times \Sigma_P$
- $\sigma_P^s \in \Sigma_P$ *is a class of start states and* $\sigma_P^e \in \Sigma_P$ *is a class of end states.*

A procedural MTS can be seen as an MTS that is extended by the possibility of having transitions whose effect is described by another MTS. For technical reasons, we require PMTSs P to satisfy the following two constraints:

1. The class of *end states* σ_P^e must be terminating in P, i.e. $\sigma_P^e \xrightarrow{\alpha}{\dashrightarrow}$ does not hold.
2. P must be guarded, i.e. all initial transitions of P must be labeled with atomic actions.

We call P *regular* if $\dashrightarrow_P^N = \emptyset$, i.e. P does not contain any process calls. In the following we denote the set of all regular PMTSs by G and define:

Definition 4 (Context-Free Modal Transition Systems (CFMTS)). *A context-free modal transition system is a quadruple $P = (N, Act, C, P_0)$, where:*

- *$N := \{N_0, \ldots, N_{n-1}\}$ is a set of names,*
- *Act is a set of actions,*
- *$C := \{N_i = PMTS_i \mid 0 \le i < n\}$ is a finite set of PMTS definitions where $PMTS_i$ is a finite PMTS with name $N_i \in N$ and*
- *P_0 is the main PMTS. Moreover we denote $\Sigma = \bigcup_{i=0}^{n-1} \Sigma_{P_i}$, $\longrightarrow = \bigcup_{i=0}^{n-1} \longrightarrow_{P_i}$ and $\dashrightarrow = \bigcup_{i=0}^{n-1} \dashrightarrow_{P_i}$.*

As detailed in [2,8,9],[4] CFMTSs serve as finite representations of the complete, typically infinite-state expansion of the corresponding main PMTS P_0 [2]. Figure 2 illustrates one step of such an expansion.

2.2 PL/0

The programming language PL/0 introduced by Wirth [21] is a general-purpose language which was intended to be used for educational purpose. Its Extended Backus-Naur form(EBNF) is given below.

```
Program    = Block "."
Block      = ["const" Ident "="Number {"," Ident "="Number} ";"]
             ["var" Ident {","Ident} ";"]
             {"procedure" Ident ";" Block ";"} Statement
Statement  = [Ident ":=" Expression | "call" Ident | "?" Ident
           |  "!" Expression
           |  "begin" Statement {";" Statement } "end"
           |  "if" Condition "then" Statement
           |  "while" Condition "do" Statement]
Condition  = "odd" Expression
           |  Expression ("=" | "#" | "<" | "<=" | ">" | ">=") Expression
Expression = ["+" | "-"] Term {("+" | "-") Term}
Term       = Factor {("*"|"/") Factor}
Factor     = Ident | Number | "("Expression")"
```

Applying our model checking technology to PL/0 requires to transform this EBNF into a corresponding CFMTS, which comprises one PMTS for each nonterminal.

Figure 1 shows the PMTSs for the non-terminals `Factor`, here enriched with the possibility of using curly braces alternatively to round braces for

---

[4] In [8,9] a conceptually similar structure to CFMTS is called *Systems of Procedural Automata* (SPAs) to better match the terminology used in the field of automata learning.

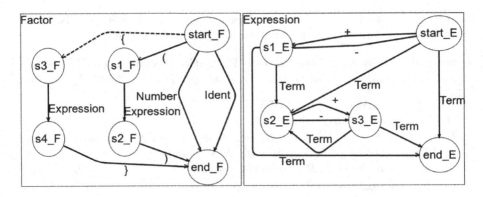

Fig. 1. Factor and Expression as PMTSs

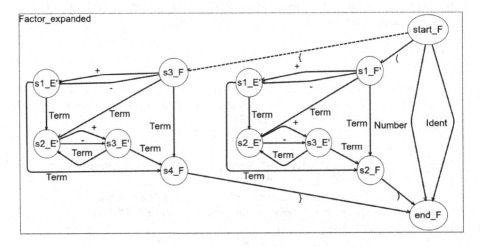

Fig. 2. Factor with Expression-calls expanded

an **Expression** as indicated by the outgoing may-transition from $start_F$, and **Expression**. The complete expansion process mentioned above is indicated in Fig. 2 by inlining the PMTS for **Expressions** into the **Factor** PMTS.[5]

2.3   The Alternation-Free Modal μ-Calculus

The *modal μ-Calculus* is a branching-time logic that is used to specify properties of transition systems. Characteristic are its greatest fixed point operator ν and a least fixed point operator μ that provide an enormous expressive power, however at the price of increased intricacy [1].

---

[5] The figures generated by our tool.

Let Var be a (countable) set of variables, AP a set of atomic propositions and Act a set of Actions. Furthermore let $X \in Var$, $A \in AP$ and $a \in Act$. The syntax is then given by the following Backus-Naur form:

$$\phi ::= A \mid X \mid \phi \vee \phi \mid \phi \wedge \phi \mid \langle a \rangle \phi \mid [a]\phi \mid \nu X.\phi \mid \mu X.\phi.$$

The semantics are given with respect to an MTS $(S, Act, \dashrightarrow, \longrightarrow)$, a valuation V which maps atomic propositions to subset of states of S and an environment e, mapping variables to subsets of S. The semantic function $\llbracket \cdot \rrbracket_e$ maps a formula to the set of states which satisfy the formula [2].

$$\llbracket A \rrbracket_e = V(A)$$
$$\llbracket X \rrbracket_e = e(X)$$
$$\llbracket \phi_1 \vee \phi_2 \rrbracket_e = \llbracket \phi_1 \rrbracket_e \cup \llbracket \phi_2 \rrbracket_e$$
$$\llbracket \phi_1 \wedge \phi_2 \rrbracket_e = \llbracket \phi_1 \rrbracket_e \cap \llbracket \phi_2 \rrbracket_e$$
$$\llbracket \langle a \rangle \phi \rrbracket_e = \{s \mid \exists s'.s \xrightarrow{a} s' \wedge s' \in \llbracket \phi \rrbracket_e\}$$
$$\llbracket [a]\phi \rrbracket_e = \{s \mid \forall s'.s \overset{a}{\dashrightarrow} s' \wedge s' \in \llbracket \phi \rrbracket_e\}$$
$$\llbracket \nu X.\phi \rrbracket_e = \bigcup\{T \subseteq S \mid T \subseteq \llbracket \phi \rrbracket_{e[X:=T]}\}$$
$$\llbracket \mu X.\phi \rrbracket_e = \bigcap\{T \subseteq S \mid \llbracket \phi \rrbracket_{e[X:=T]} \subseteq T\}$$

Thus an atomic proposition A is true in a state s if $s \in V(A)$, s satisfies X if $s \in e(X)$, and conjunction and disjunction are defined as usual. Special are the 'diamond' operator $\langle a \rangle$ and 'box' operator $[a]$. The diamond-operator is true if there exists a $s' \in S$ with $s \xrightarrow{a} s'$ that satisfies ϕ, while the box-operator is true if all successors of s that are connected by an edge labeled by the action a satisfy ϕ.

The modal μ-Calculus is not very 'user friendly'. On the other hand, it is a very good basis for a tool as many more convenient temporal logics, like CTL, can easily be expressed in the μ-calculus [5,7].

3 Model Checking Context-Free Modal Transition Systems

We extend the second-order model checking algorithm described in [2] for capturing context-free modal transition systems. This only requires minor modifications in order to deal with the characteristics of may transitions. Our presentation follows the development given in [2]. Like there, our algorithmic description also requires the representation of the μ calculus formulas that serve as input in terms of hierarchical equational systems.

3.1 Hierarchical Equational Systems

Hierarchical equational systems are composed of equational blocks which, due to the underlying hierarchy, can be evaluated in a hierarchical fashion.

Definition 5 (Equational Block [2]). *An equational block has one of two forms, min$\{E\}$ or max$\{E\}$, where E is a list of (mutually recursive) equations*

$$X_1 = \phi_1, \ldots, X_n = \phi_n$$

where $\phi_1, \ldots, \phi_n$ are basic formulas, i.e., can be written using the following grammar:

$$\phi^{basic} ::= A \mid X \vee X \mid X \wedge X \mid \langle a \rangle X \mid [a]X$$

The set of all variables X_i appearing in a block B are denoted by V_B, or simply by V in case B is clear from the context.

Min-blocks are used for capturing the least fixed point operator and Max-blocks for capturing the greatest fixed point operator, respectively. An *equational system* is a list of equational blocks $B = (B_1, \ldots, B_m)$ where the variables appearing on the left-hand side of some block are all distinct.

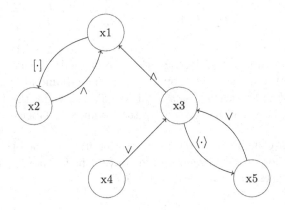

Fig. 3. Dependency graph of the equational system of ϕ

Example 1. Let $\phi = \nu X.[\cdot]X \wedge (\mu Y.A \vee \langle \cdot \rangle Y)$
The formula ϕ specifies that "it is always possible that A will hold". The dot '·' specifies that the box-/diamond-operator holds regardless of the transition label. In CTL we could express this as AG EF A [1]. The equational system consists of two blocks. We need one block for greatest fixed point νX and one for the least fixed point μY. The equational system corresponding to ϕ then looks as follows:

$$max\{ \; X_1 = X_2 \wedge X_3 \qquad\qquad min\{ \; X_3 = X_4 \vee X_5$$
$$X_2 = [\cdot]X_1\} \qquad\qquad\qquad X_4 = A$$
$$X_5 = \langle \cdot \rangle X_3\}$$

'Hierarchical' in the term hierarchical equational systems means that there are no cyclic dependencies between blocks in the sense defined below:

Definition 6 (Hierarchical Equational System [2]**).** *An Equational System* $B = (B_1, \ldots, B_n)$ *is hierarchical if the existence of a left-hand side variable of a block B_j, $1 \le j \le n$, appearing in a right-hand side formula of a block B_i implies $i \le j$.*

The constraint to exclude cyclic dependencies between blocks limits the expressive power of hierarchical equational systems to the alternation-free fragment of the μ calculus [6].

The model checking algorithm presented in the next section propagates information between the variables of equational blocks in an ordering reverse to the dependency relation: Fig. 3 shows the dependency graph of the formula $\phi = \nu X.[\cdot]X \wedge (\mu Y.A \vee \langle \cdot \rangle Y)$ presented in the previous example. Please note that in this graph every loop has an edge labeled with some box or diamond modality, a property of equational systems which we can enforce without loosing expressive power, and which is sufficient to guarantee a hierarchical evaluation/updating strategy for each state. In the following we will therefore assume that the dependency graphs of all equational blocks have this property.

3.2   The Second-Order Model Checking Algorithm

The fact that we only consider basic formulas on the right hand side of equations guarantees that keeping track of the truth values of variables is sufficient to propagate all the required information during the fixpoint computation of (first order) model checking. (Classical) first-order model checking for a block B computes a mapping that associates each state s of the considered MTS with the subset of V that contains all formulas that are valid at s. This means that model checking computes a fixpoint in the power set lattice 2^V.

Second-order model checking lifts the fixpoint computation to the lattice of corresponding (monotonic) predicate transformers $D = 2^V \longrightarrow 2^V$. This allows one to formulate model checking as a fixpoint computation that computes a predicate transformer $PT_\sigma \in D$ for each state class σ of a PMTS P in the considered CFMTS that aggregates the effect of the fragment of P that starts in σ and terminates with P's end state σ_P^e in the following sense: For any $V' \in 2^V$, $PT_\sigma(V')$ is the set of all variables of V that hold at σ in case that all formulas of V' hold at the end state of P. After this fixpoint computation the original model checking problem can be answered for the considered CFMTS simply by checking whether the input formula X_1 lies in $PT_{\sigma_P^s}(V_{deadlock})$, where $V_{deadlock}$ denotes the set of variables that hold for the deadlocked state. E.g., for the block whose dependency graph is shown in Fig. 3 this would only be X_4 in case A happens to hold at the considered deadlocked state, otherwise $V_{deadlock}$ would just be the empty set.

In the following we sketch how $PT_{\sigma_P^s}$ can be computed for all CFMTSs P and equational systems E while focusing on the peculiarities of the second-order approach and, in particular, of the implications of allowing also may transitions.

The global structure for hierarchically dealing with hierarchical equational systems in a 'depth first' fashion is identical to the first-order case. Thus we only need to consider the treatment of blocks in more detail, and we can focus on min blocks only, as the treatment of max blocks is completely dual.

Algorithm 1 shows the classical workset pattern for the corresponding fixpoint computation, which consists of an initialization phase, an iterative update of the property transformers, and the update of the workset.

Initialize the property transformers PT_σ of all state classes σ.
workset $= \Sigma$
while $workset \neq \emptyset$ **do**
> LET $\sigma \in$ workset;
> workset $=$ workset$\setminus\{\sigma\}$;
> $PT_\sigma.old = PT_\sigma$;
> $\alpha_1, \ldots \alpha_n =$ outgoing edge labels of σ;
> $PT_\sigma = \diamond^\sigma_{j=1,\ldots,n} PT_{[a_j]} \circ PT_{\sigma_j}$;
> **if** $PT_\sigma \neq PT_\sigma.old$ **then**
>> **if** $\sigma = \sigma^s_{P_i}$ *for some* $i \in N$ **then**
>>> workset $=$ workset $\cup \{\sigma' \mid \sigma' \xrightarrow{P_i} \}$;
>>
>> **end**
>> workset $=$ workset $\cup \{\sigma' \mid \sigma' \xrightarrow{\alpha} \sigma\}$;
>
> **end**

end

Algorithm 1. Algorithm: Model checking of context-free modal transition systems [2]

The property transformers associated with end states are generally initialized with the identity function, and this setting is maintained during the fixpoint computation. As we are considering min blocks, all other property transformers are initialized to the constant function *false*.

Also the update of the workset is simple. As in the classical case of a backward analysis, all predecessors of a state whose property transformer has changed are added to the workset. Special is only the situation for start states. Changes there affect all states that 'call' the corresponding PMTS. Thus they must also be added to the workset.

The most intricate part is the iterative update of the property transformers for a state class σ which proceeds in two steps: the determination of the property transformers for the individual choices of σ's outgoing transitions, and the aggregation of the common effect of all these individual property transformers on σ's property transformer.

The property transformer for an outgoing transition $\sigma \xrightarrow{\alpha} \sigma'$ is defined as

$$PT_{[\alpha]} \circ PT_{[\sigma']}$$

where $PT_{[\alpha]}$, the effect of taking step α, is defined as follows:

In case $\alpha = P_i$, we have $PT_{[\alpha]} = PT_{[P_i]} = PT_{\sigma_{P_i}^s}$, i.e., $PT_{[\alpha]}$ is the current approximation of the effect of P_i. Otherwise, i.e., in case $\alpha = a \in Act$, $PT_{[\alpha]}$ is characterized by

$$X_i \in PT_{[\alpha]}(M) \text{ iff } \left\{ \begin{array}{l} \phi_i = \langle a \rangle X_j \text{ and } X_j \in M \text{ and } \xrightarrow{\alpha} \in \longrightarrow \\ \phi_i = [a]X_j \text{ and } X_j \in M \\ \phi_i = [b]X_j \text{ and } b \neq a \end{array} \right\}$$

for $M \subseteq V$ and an equation $X_i = \phi_i$ of block B.

Please note that may transitions do not contribute when considering diamond-subformulas, as they cannot be guaranteed to exist in an actual implementation. In contrast, box subformulas are insensitive to the nature of may and must transitions.

Finally, the aggregation of the common effect of all the individual property transformers for outgoing transitions on σ's property transformer is defined by the function $(\diamond_{i=1,\ldots,k}^{\sigma} PT_i(M)) = M'$ which is characterized by

$$X_j \in M' \text{ iff } \left\{ \begin{array}{ll} \phi_j = A & \text{and } \sigma \in V(A) \\ \phi_j = X_{j_1} \wedge X_{j_2} & \text{and } (X_{j_1} \in M' \text{ and } X_{j_2} \in M') \\ \phi_j = X_{j_1} \vee X_{j_2} & \text{and } (X_{j_1} \in M' \text{ or } X_{j_2} \in M') \\ \phi_j = \langle a \rangle \psi & \text{and } \exists.1 \leq i \leq k \text{ with } X_j \in \boldsymbol{PT_i}(M) \\ \phi_j = [a]\psi & \text{and } \forall.1 \leq i \leq k \text{ with } X_j \in PT_i(M) \end{array} \right\}$$

for $M \subseteq V$, equations $X_j = \phi_j$ of B, and the convention that property transformers belonging to outgoing must transitions are emphasized in bold face (see line four). Like before, also here only the diamond subformulas are sensitive to the distinction between may and must transitions.

The following section will discuss our modal meta model checking approach along variations of Wirth's PL/0.

4   *M3C* at Work

This section starts by considering variations of Wirth's PL/0 in order to illustrate how modal meta model checking can provide vital feedback when engineering (specification/programming) languages. Subsequently, we present our *M3C* tool by discussing one concrete iteration step of a second-order fixpoint computation.

4.1   Playing with Variations of PL/0

In order to illustrate the impact of may transitions, we will consider the eleven variations of PL/0 listed in Table 1 which already also summarizes the model

Table 1. Truth table for 1)–11) and A)–D)

Nr.	Variant	Decl	Call	A)	B)	C)	D)
1)	WHILE(W)	-	-	1	0	0	1
2)	WD	Must	-	1	0	1	0
3)	WC	-	Must	0	1	0	1
4)	DC	Must	Must	0	1	1	1
5)	DC^t	Must	Must	1	1	1	1
6)	dc	May	May	?	?	?	?
7)	dc^t	May	May	1	?	?	?
8)	dC	May	Must	0	1	?	1
9)	dC^t	May	Must	1	?	?	1
10)	Dc	Must	May	?	?	1	?
11)	Dc^t	Must	May	1	?	1	?

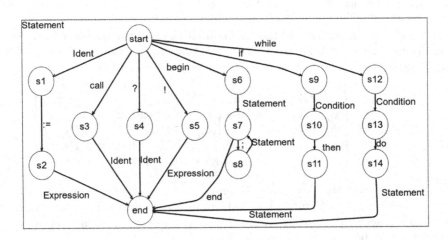

Fig. 4. The Statement PMTS

checking results for the four formulas we are going to discuss. The theme of this discussion is set by the popular property that *no call is possible unless the called procedure is declared.*

Figures 4, 5 and 6 illustrate essential differences between the considered variants. In Fig. 4 we see the PMTS for Statement which contains a 'call' transition. Whenever we say that 'call' is a may-transition we mean the transition from *start* to s_3. We denote the standard PL/0 by DC, PL/0 with a may 'call'-transition by Dc, PL/0 with a may 'decl'-transition by dC, and PL/0 where both, 'call' and 'decl' are may transitions, by dc.

The language WHILE(W) is the subset of PL/0 which contains neither decl- nor call-transitions. Consequently, e.g., state s_3 does not exist in the Statement

PMTS of this language. The variants WD and WC are defined likewise, i.e. WD is the WHILE language extended by procedure declarations and WC is the WHILE language extended procedure calls.

For the ease of presentation we will assume for the rest of the section that there is just one procedure which is declared by 'Decl' and called by 'Call'. Then property A) in Fig. 7 is a μ-calculus formulation of this (intuitive) property, i.e. *no call is possible unless the called procedure is declared.*

The second and third column of Table 1 specify the variants by indicating in which way the considered language supports declarations and calls. E.g., **WHILE(W)** does not support these features at all, while PL/0 supports both of them in a must fashion. Not all of these languages make sense. E.g., every program of WC that is not already in WHILE(W) is deemed to violate property A, and any program in WD that is not in WHILE(W) has redundant declarations. The situation is not as bad for dC and Dc, as they allow for language implementations that permit programs with correct calls.

These are exactly the kind of properties we want to check automatically with our *M3C* tool in order to, e.g., reveal transformations as the one indicated in Figs. 5 and 6: As indicated in the fifth column of Table 1 the node split that results in Fig. 6 is sufficient to guarantee property A for all corresponding specification variants (here are marked by an exponential 't').[6]

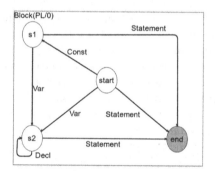

Fig. 5. The Block PMTS of PL/0 (Nr.4 *DC*)

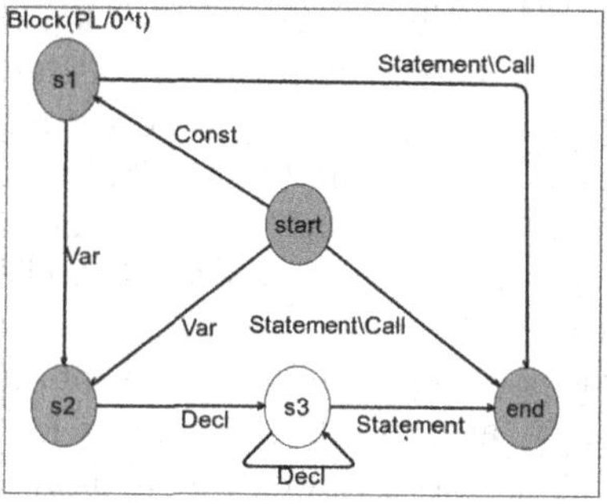

Fig. 6. The Block PMTS of $PL/0^t$ (Nr.5 DC^t)

In order to simplify the presentation of the four properties we are going to discuss we use the following conventional notation

$$[\neg\alpha]\,\phi = \bigwedge_{\beta\in Act,\alpha\neq\beta}[\beta]\,\phi$$

where Act is the action alphabet and ϕ is an arbitrary formula of the modal μ-calculus:

---

[6] For readability, in comparison to the specification in Sect. 2, we factored the constant-, variable- and procedure-declarations out here as own PMTSs.

We have already briefly discussed that property A) does not hold for 'standard' PL/0 and how to overcome this problem by an easy transformation. Let us nevertheless discuss Table 1 in more detail.

As mentioned above, already the interpretation of the first 5 rows is interesting. They concern five individual languages of increasing power and specificity. However, languages WD and WD are odd: as indicated by columns B and C, all programs of WC with call statements are deemed to violate the property that procedures need to be declared, whereas declarations of language WD will never be used. Language DC, PL/0, requires, as traditional, users to keep track of the declaration requirements, whereas language DC^t guarantees the property through its syntax definition. That language 1 (as well as 2) also satisfy property A is a consequence of the fact that universal quantification over the empty set is true.

The specifications of rows 6–11 are all the modal refinements of 6 which result from turning may to must transitions: Whereas the mere switch from may to must is sufficient to arrive at the specifications of rows 8 and 10, rows 7, 9, and 11 require some additional unrolling of the specification of row 6 along the lines indicated in Figs. 5 and 6.[7]

The question marks in Table 1 indicate that the corresponding property can neither be verified nor falsified. This means that the specification allows both languages that satisfy the property and languages that do not. In particular, the specification for row 6 allows the first five languages as implementations. In fact it is the largest of the eleven specifications according to the refinement ordering. The corresponding Hasse diagram, enriched to illustrate the fact that the refinement ordering preserves all temporal properties, is shown in Fig. 8.

$M3C$ allows one to check all temporal properties for each of the eleven languages. In particular, one can check the effectiveness of the transformation to the transformed versions for establishing property A by a single check of dc^t.

In [20] we called properties that can be enforced directly by an appropriate meta model rigid archimedean points. As grammar-based syntax specifications certainly are considered part of a meta model, the four properties discussed here can all be made rigid without imposing unwanted additional constraints.

$$
\begin{aligned}
A) &: \quad \nu X.([call]\mathit{ff} \wedge [\neg decl]X) \\
B) &: \quad \mu X.(\langle call\rangle tt \vee \langle \cdot \rangle X) \qquad\qquad (\text{In CTL}{:} EF\langle call\rangle tt) \\
C) &: \quad \mu X.(\langle decl\rangle tt \vee \langle \cdot \rangle) \qquad\qquad\ \ (\text{In CTL}{:} EF\langle decl\rangle tt) \\
D) &: \quad \nu X.[decl](\mu Y.\langle call\rangle tt \vee \langle \cdot \rangle Y) \wedge [\cdot]X
\end{aligned}
$$

Fig. 7. The properties to be checked

---

[7] The reader is invited to consider other refinement options. Please note, due to unrolling there are infinitely many options!

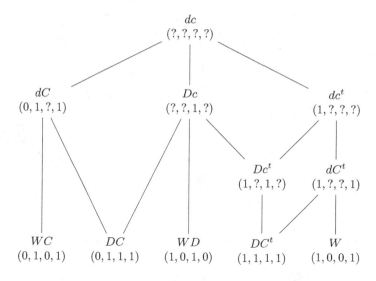

Fig. 8. Hasse-Diagram: Refinement ordering of variations

4.2 Second-Order Update with *M3C*

In this section, we consider a concrete update during the model checking process for property A in the representation shown in Fig. 9 concerning:

- the red state class ($s3$) of the Block PMTS for $PL/0^t (= DC^t)$ shown in Fig. 10, and
- the approximate predicate transformers for the relevant state classes whose representations as multi-source BDDs is shown in Fig. 11 (the correct association of these transformation to 'their' states is indicated by their color).

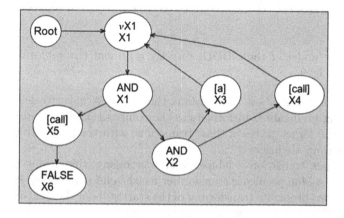

Fig. 9. The syntax tree of the input formula showing variable naming

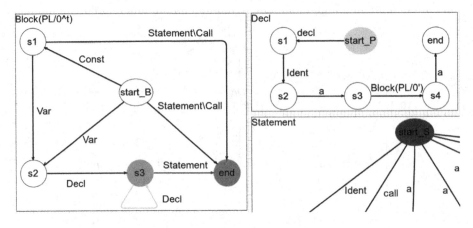

Fig. 10. The relevant states for the update (Color figure online)

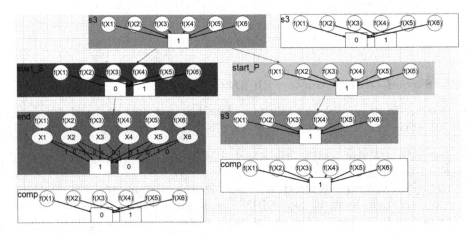

Fig. 11. The property transformers of the states which are relevant for the update (Color figure online)

The source nodes of these BDDs directly represent the subformulas (nodes) shown in Fig. 9.

s_3 has two outgoing edges. This means that we first have to determine their corresponding predicate transformers as the composition of the predicate transformers for the target states of these transitions with the predicate transformers of the transitions themselves.

As the green transition is labeled with **Statement**, this means that we have to compose the blue predicate transformer for the end state of the **Block** PMTS with the (green) predicate transformer of the start state of the **Statement** PMTS. This results in the leftmost white predicate transformer.

Similarly, as the yellow (cyclic) transition is labeled with `Procedure`, this means that we have to compose the red predicate transformer for state $s3$ of the `Block` PMTS with the (yellow) predicate transformer of the start state of the `Procedure` PMTS. This results in the other bottom-level white predicate transformer.

The update step is now completed by applying the $\diamond^\sigma$-operator to the two white predicates transformers at the bottom of Fig. 11. Intuitively, the resulting (white at the top) predicate transformer very much resembles a conjunction of the two composite argument transformers, because Proposition A does not contain a diamond modality.

All pictures displayed in this section are taken from our *M3C* tool whose visual support is ideal to support users in establishing a good intuition about our second-order approach. In fact, we use *M3C* in lectures as educational support.

5 Conclusion

We have presented *M3C*, a method and tool supporting meta-level product lining and evolution that comprises both context free system structure and modal refinement. The underlying CFMTSs can be regarded as loose specifications of meta models, and modal refinement as a way to increase the specificity of allowed DSLs by constraining the range of allowed syntax specifications. The inherent compositionality of the second-order approach leads to a runtime complexity linear in the size of the procedural system representation, whose corresponding transition systems typically have infinitely many states. It has been shown how model checking with *M3C* can be used to verify properties specified in a branching-time logic for all DSLs of a given level of specificity in one go. This has been illustrated by looking at variations of Wirth's PL/0.

We are planning to experiment with *M3C* as a tool for validating the specificity of defined DSLs, in particular to better understand which properties of a programming language can elegantly be realized as rigid archimedean points [20], i.e., be expressed in terms of adequate syntactic definitions. The treatment of Property A in Sect. 4.1 can be regarded as a first step in this direction. In the long term it is our goal to integrate *M3C* in our CINCO Meta Tooling Suite [18] as a guiding tool for what we call meta model engineering.

References

1. Blackburn, P., van Benthem, J.F.A.K., Wolter, F.: Handbook of Modal Logic. Studies in Logic and Practical Reasoning, vol. 3. Elsevier Science Inc., New York (2006)
2. Burkart, O., Steffen, B.: Model checking for context-free processes. In: Cleaveland, W.R. (ed.) CONCUR 1992. LNCS, vol. 630, pp. 123–137. Springer, Heidelberg (1992). https://doi.org/10.1007/BFb0084787
3. Burkart, O., Steffen, B.: Pushdown processes: parallel composition and model checking. In: Jonsson, B., Parrow, J. (eds.) CONCUR 1994. LNCS, vol. 836, pp. 98–113. Springer, Heidelberg (1994). https://doi.org/10.1007/978-3-540-48654-1_9

4. Burkart, O., Steffen, B.: Model checking the full modal mu-calculus for infinite sequential processes. Theor. Comput. Sci. **221**(1–2), 251–270 (1999). https://doi.org/10.1016/S0304-3975(99)00034-1

5. Clarke Jr., E.M., Grumberg, O., Peled, D.A.: Model Checking. MIT Press, Cambridge (1999)

6. Cleaveland, R., Steffen, B.: A linear-time model-checking algorithm for the alternation-free modal mu-calculus. Form. Methods Syst. Des. **2**(2), 121–147 (1993). https://doi.org/10.1007/BF01383878

7. Emerson, E.A.: Model checking and the mu-calculus. In: DIMACS Series in Discrete Mathematics, pp. 185–214. American Mathematical Society (1997)

8. Frohme, M., Steffen, B.: Active mining of document type definitions. In: Howar, F., Barnat, J. (eds.) FMICS 2018. LNCS, vol. 11119, pp. 147–161. Springer, Cham (2018)

9. Frohme, M., Steffen, B.: Compositional learning of mutually recursive procedural systems (2018, under submission)

10. Garavel, H., Lang, F., Mounier, L.: Compositional verification in action. In: Howar, F., Barnat, J. (eds.) FMICS 2018. LNCS, vol. 11119, pp. 189–210. Springer, Cham (2018)

11. Gössler, G., Graf, S., Majster-Cederbaum, M., Martens, M., Sifakis, J.: An approach to modelling and verification of component based systems. In: van Leeuwen, J., Italiano, G.F., van der Hoek, W., Meinel, C., Sack, H., Plášil, F. (eds.) SOFSEM 2007. LNCS, vol. 4362, pp. 295–308. Springer, Heidelberg (2007). https://doi.org/10.1007/978-3-540-69507-3_24

12. Graf, S., Saidi, H.: Construction of abstract state graphs with PVS. In: Grumberg, O. (ed.) CAV 1997. LNCS, vol. 1254, pp. 72–83. Springer, Heidelberg (1997). https://doi.org/10.1007/3-540-63166-6_10

13. Graf, S., Steffen, B.: Compositional minimization of finite state systems. In: Computer-Aided Verification, Proceedings of a DIMACS Workshop 1990, New Brunswick, New Jersey, USA, 18–21 June 1990, pp. 57–74 (1990)

14. Graf, S., Steffen, B., Lüttgen, G.: Compositional minimisation of finite state systems using interface specifications. Form. Asp. Comput. **8**(5), 607–616 (1996). https://doi.org/10.1007/BF01211911

15. Larsen, K.G., Thomsen, B.: A modal process logic. In: Proceedings of the Third Annual Symposium on Logic in Computer Science, pp. 203–210 (1988). https://doi.org/10.1109/LICS.1988.5119

16. Larsen, K.G.: Modal specifications. In: Sifakis, J. (ed.) CAV 1989. LNCS, vol. 407, pp. 232–246. Springer, Heidelberg (1990). https://doi.org/10.1007/3-540-52148-8_19

17. Loiseaux, C., Graf, S., Sifakis, J., Bouajjani, A., Bensalem, S.: Property preserving abstractions for the verification of concurrent systems. Form. Methods Syst. Des. **6**(1), 11–44 (1995). https://doi.org/10.1007/BF01384313

18. Naujokat, S., Lybecait, M., Kopetzki, D., Steffen, B.: CINCO: a simplicity-driven approach to full generation of domain-specific graphical modeling tools. STTT **20**(3), 327–354 (2018). https://doi.org/10.1007/s10009-017-0453-6

19. Steffen, B., Gossen, F., Naujokat, S., Margaria, T.: Language-driven engineering: from general-purpose to purpose-specific languages. In: Steffen, B., Woeginger, G. (eds.) Computing and Software Science. LNCS, vol. 10000, pp. 311–344. Springer, Cham (2018)

20. Steffen, B., Naujokat, S.: Archimedean points: the essence for mastering change. Trans. Found. Mastering Chang. **1**, 22–46 (2016). https://doi.org/10.1007/978-3-319-46508-1_3
21. Wirth, N.: Compilerbau - Eine Einführung. Teubner (1977)

Wholly!: A Build System
For The Modern Software Stack

Loic Gelle[1], Hassen Saidi[2(✉)], and Ashish Gehani[2]

[1] Ecole Polytechnique, Palaiseau, France
[2] SRI International, Menlo Park, USA
`hassen.saidi@sri.com`

Abstract. *Wholly!* is an automated build system for the modern software stack. It is designed for reproducible and verifiable builds of optimized and debloated software that runs uniformly on traditional desktops, the cloud, and IoT devices. *Wholly!* uses Linux containers to ensure the integrity and reproducibility of the build environment. It uses the `clang` compiler to generate LLVM bitcode for all produced libraries and binaries to allow for whole program analysis, specialization, and optimization. The `clang` compiler and install tools are all built with *Wholly!* as well. *Wholly!* has been applied to build Alpine Linux, Docker containers, microservices, and IoT software. We show that software packages built in *Wholly!* are faster, smaller, and more amenable to whole program analysis.

1 Introduction

The modern software stack has evolved from desktops to monolithic servers, and finally to the cloud and IoT devices. Driven by the need for rapid scalability, developers can either deploy an application on a thin operating system layer such as OSv [14], an operating system designed for the cloud, or in a container such as Docker [3] running on a traditional operating system. Applications can also be broken up into a number of microservices. Microservices can run in individual distinct containers, in virtual machines (VMs), as unikernels [8,10,16] running on a hypervisor or on bare metal, or even as a single function as a service. The diversity of these computing platforms creates new challenges for formal verification. We are particularly interested in applying source code analysis such as *abstract interpretation* [2] and *predicate abstraction* [6]. When analyzing source code, it is necessary to understand the build process for different platforms, and to account for all used libraries so that whole program analysis is possible. This requires dealing with the following challenges:

Bloated software: Running a simple application in a container often involves building a container image that includes a number of libraries that are not necessary to run the application. For microservices, the bloatware is worse. Running a

---

L. Gelle—While visiting SRI.

© Springer Nature Switzerland AG 2018
F. Howar and J. Barnat (Eds.): FMICS 2018, LNCS 11119, pp. 242–257, 2018.
https://doi.org/10.1007/978-3-030-00244-2_16

single Javascript function on Amazon Lambda or a service like Standard Library [18] requires running the entire Node.js interpreter on top of an Ubuntu image that contains libraries that are not needed for running Node.js. On a typical desktop running a Linux distribution, hundreds of packages and thousands of possibly extraneous libraries are installed.

Complex build processes and dependencies: gcc is the most popular compiler on Linux platforms. Even when using clang, gcc libraries are used during compilation. One has to carefully trace the build process to know precisely which supporting libraries, which build scripts, which linker, and which install tools have been used during any build process.

Lack of reproducibility: Given the complexity of build processes, and the reliance on dynamic linking and bloated deployment environments, it is often impossible to guarantee that software built in two different builds is going to behave exactly the same. This is particularly important in domains such as scientific computing [15], where reproducing the same results may be paramount to the integrity of the scientific method.

We present *Wholly!* [20], a tool for building and packaging software that explicitly defines dependencies, produces build processes that are repeatable and verifiable, and allows for whole program analysis. The result is leaner, faster, and debloated software packages that can be deployed on a variety of platforms. *Wholly!* is a tool for building and releasing software packages with C/C++ code. gcc is the de-facto standard compiler on Linux systems today. However, *Wholly!* uses the clang compiler to generate LLVM bitcode. *Wholly!* uses musl-libc, an efficient implementation of libc to produce leaner packages. clang has been used to build entire operating systems, such as FreeBSD and macOS. musl-libc is used to build Alpine Linux [1] with gcc. *Wholly!* is the first project to combine both clang and musl-libc to build Alpine and Docker containers.

We use a clang compiler that was built in *Wholly!* producing a faster and leaner compiler. The produced LLVM bitcode is used to further optimize the code using partial evaluation [17] and software winnowing [11], and for applying formal verification techniques [7]. In this paper, we describe the design, philosophy, evaluation, and applications of *Wholly!*, explaining how it enables whole program analysis of large and complex software.

2   System Overview

Each package is described in *Wholly!* by a simple recipe that contains all the information needed to build the package. Builds are performed in Docker containers to control the environment and provide isolation. For each package, build products are organized in fine-grained packages such as libraries, binaries, headers, and runtime support. *Wholly!* eventually releases the fine-grained sub-packages in the form of Docker images [3] that are easily reusable as dependencies to build more complex packages, or as production software. *Wholly!* uses static linking to produce small packages. Sub-packages can either be used as containers, or can be used on any Linux platform, making them highly portable across the different flavors of the Linux operating system.

2.1   Package Description

Two files are needed to describe a *Wholly!* package: a *recipe* file that is used for building the package, and a *contents* file that is used for releasing it. The *recipe* file describes what happens at build time. It is a small YAML-formatted file that contains the:

- link to download the source code for the package,
- name of the other *Wholly!* sub-packages that are build dependencies,
- invocations that need to be run in order to build the package, and
- for some packages, the path to additional resource files – patches for example – that will be used during the build stage.

Figure 1 shows a *Wholly!* package recipe for the `sqlite` database, version 3.18.

```
1   release_date: 2017-07-18
2   variables:
3     - pkg_name: sqlite
4     - pkg_ver: '3.18.0'
5
6   # Dependencies
7   dependencies:
8     musl-libc:
9       - headers
10      - libs
11    readline-7.0:
12      - headers
13
14  # Source
15  source:
16    http://www.sqlite.org/2017/{pkg_name}-autoconf-3180000.tar.gz
17
18  # Build stage
19  build:
20    - CC=gclang
21      CFLAGS="-static"
22      ./configure --prefix={__INSTALL_DIR__} --enable-shared=no
23    - make
24    - make install
```

Fig. 1. Recipe file for the package `sqlite-3.18`.

Figure 2 shows the *contents* file for the package. The contents file also uses the YAML format. It splits the package into different sub-packages, each of which is described by the:

- list of files that compose the sub-package, and
- checksum that is used to check the integrity of the build and to refine dependency management.

```
1    bc:
2        checksum: sha256:4f9170f7c2cb4f701dac9826509ed14de8a0aeb1597d36bbeb499dd8bdbee00c
3        files:
4        - /usr/bc
5    bin:
6        checksum: sha256:557f6deeeafc8dc3bff27f8ed97ef65ed15b5060f6e6f1f646e190db96573eb0
7        files:
8        - /usr/bin/sqlite3
9    headers:
10       checksum: sha256:0663e892fbb7fbcfb1f9402de9ff8efdaddb09c6730cfba88218273967880c38
11       files:
12       - /usr/include/sqlite3.h
13       - /usr/include/sqlite3ext.h
14   libs:
15       checksum: sha256:e99ccebd1c087ee4137fffe6cf5efb04cbb78b14a9460da60fdd2c7ce8038328
16       files:
17       - /usr/lib/libsqlite3.a
```

Fig. 2. Contents file for the package `sqlite-3.18`.

2.2 Building

Each package is built separately in a Docker container. This guarantees isolation and control over the:

- system files that are present during the build,
- environment variables being set,
- compiler and tools being used, and
- dependencies that are brought in.

Docker is an open platform to build, ship, and run distributed applications on desktops, data center VMs, or the cloud. Docker uses the resource isolation features of the Linux kernel, such as `cgroups` and kernel `namespaces`, and a union-capable file system, such as `OverlayFS`, to allow independent *containers* to run within a single Linux instance, avoiding the overhead of starting and maintaining virtual machines. Docker can build images automatically by reading the instructions from a *Dockerfile*. A Dockerfile is a text document that contains all the commands a user would issue at a shell command line to assemble an image. The execution of each command defines a layer in the file system that is cached by Docker. Each layer is referred to by a random identifier that can be used to "pull" only that specific layer of the file system.

In order to build the desired package, *Wholly!* turns the recipe file into a Dockerfile that will be read and executed by the Docker Engine. Each build follows this pattern:

1. A Docker container is launched and populated with a base image that contains the elements common to all the builds – compiler, linker, and environment.
2. Files from the dependency sub-packages are copied into the container.
3. Source code for the package to build is downloaded.
4. Build commands in the recipe file are executed (Fig. 3).

At the end of this process, the Docker image contains, among other artifacts, the files from the desired package that have been built and installed. Using

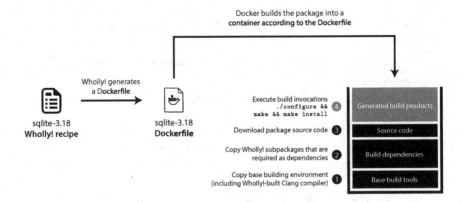

Fig. 3. Schematic view of the build stage for the *Wholly!* sqlite-3.18 package.

Docker's layered file system, we can determine the exact list of files that have been created during the build process. From these files, *Wholly!* creates a contents file that lists the files contained in each produced sub-package.

2.3 Sub-packaging

The image that is obtained from the previous step contains a lot of extraneous files, since it reflects the final state of the entire build environment. Starting from that, interesting files from the package are copied into different sub-packages, based on the specification in the contents file. The sub-package sqlite-3.18-bin, for example, only contains the file /usr/bin/sqlite3 that has been built.

After all the sub-packages have been released in the form of new Docker images, *Wholly!* verifies that the checksums of these images are consistent with the ones provided in the contents file. This ensures the integrity of the build, while at the same time serving as a proof of reproducibility. Initially, the checksum is written to the contents file when the subpackage is first created. Fine-grained sub-packaging also enables fine-grained dependency management. The package sqlite-3.18, for example, only requires the headers from musl-libc and readline-7.0 and the libraries from musl-libc instead of the whole contents of these packages (Fig. 4).

3 Design

In this section, we provide an in-depth description of the components and the design motivations of our build mechanism. In particular, we describe how *Wholly!* ensures traceability and reproducibility of builds.

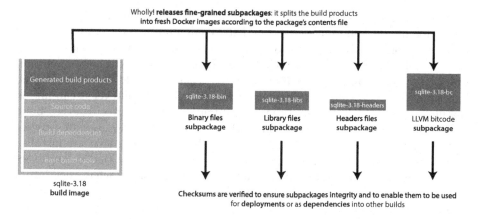

Fig. 4. Schematic view of the release stage for the *Wholly!* `sqlite-3.18` package.

3.1 Traceability of Builds

Wholly! uses recipes that are as simple and small as possible. They are designed to be understood easily, yet they contain every element that is necessary to the build. In particular, the dependencies are clearly stated, and since we want to keep the build environment as minimal as possible, only the required subpackages are imported at compile time. *Wholly!* then transforms this recipe into a Dockerfile that will be used to launch the build container. Since Dockerfiles are becoming increasingly complex as new features are implemented in Docker, we chose a simple YAML format, completely independent from Docker, for our recipes.

```
1   FROM wholly-readline-7.0-headers as wholly-readline-7.0-headers-files
2   FROM wholly-musl-libc-headers as wholly-musl-libc-headers-files
3   FROM wholly-musl-libc-libs as wholly-musl-libc-libs-files
4   FROM wholly-base-image
5
6   # Bringing dependencies in
7   COPY --from=wholly-readline-7.0-headers-files / /
8   COPY --from=wholly-musl-libc-headers-files / /
9   COPY --from=wholly-musl-libc-libs-files / /
10
11  # Getting source
12  WORKDIR /build
13  RUN curl \
14      "http://www.sqlite.org/2017/sqlite-autoconf-3180000.tar.gz" \
15      -o src.tar.gz
16  RUN mkdir sqlite-3.18 && tar xf src.tar.gz -C sqlite-3.18 \
17      --strip-components 1
18
19  # Building
20  WORKDIR /build/sqlite-3.18
21  RUN WLLVM_CONFIGURE_ONLY=1 CC=gclang CFLAGS="-static" \
22      ./configure --prefix=/usr --enable-shared=no
23  RUN make
24  RUN make install
```

Fig. 5. Dockerfile generated by *Wholly!* to build `sqlite-3.18`.

Figure 5 describes the Dockerfile generated automatically by *Wholly!* from the recipe file described in Fig. 1. The FROM command in the Dockerfile is used to import a previously built Docker image to build a more complex one. It allows users to control what goes into their Docker image. This is extremely important when controlling how packages are built. On a desktop, a build script would often look for dependencies in multiple locations, and will use whatever it can find in the file system. Tracing a build therefore often involves monitoring every build step for file accesses, for instance. Similarly, at runtime the execution of software will depend on the version of the dynamically linked libraries that are installed on the particular system. This makes it impossible to ensure that the software will execute uniformly across platforms. We control exactly what goes into a Docker image when we build a package. This allows us to trace the provenance of every single build product.

The contents file also greatly improves the clarity and the traceability of the builds. It can be used to account for every single file that is present in a released sub-package, and then in a container that runs in production.

3.2 Systematic Production of LLVM Bitcode

Wholly! uses clang as its C/C++ compiler. clang is capable of generating LLVM bitcode, an intermediate representation that is platform-independent and can be used for program transformation and optimization.

In order to benefit from this feature, *Wholly!* uses *gllvm* [5], a fast and concurrent wrapper for clang that generates both native objects and LLVM bitcode files. During a build, the bitcode for the whole package can easily be produced by calling the wrapper gclang instead of clang. Using this, *Wholly!* produces LLVM bitcode systematically for each of its packages, making it easier to analyze, transform, or optimize the packages at the LLVM bitcode level.

Wholly! uses musl-llvm [13], a fork of musl-libc [12]. musl's efficiency is unparalleled in Linux libc implementations. Designed from the ground up for static linking, musl carefully avoids importing large amounts of code or data that the application will not use. The advantage of musl-llvm over musl-libc is that there is LLVM bitcode generated for all of musl-llvm except for a handful of functions that require assembly for part of their implementation.

3.3 Clarity of Build Environment

The build environment is kept as minimal as possible. It runs atop an Alpine Linux Docker image that contains only the tools necessary for the builds – in particular, a compiler and a linker – and can be reproduced using the Dockerfile below.

The minimalism of Alpine Linux as a build environment is consistent with the idea of lean builds: only the necessary runtime is present to ensure working builds, and there are no extra files that are not needed. Additionally, the build container is completely transparent and can be replicated by anyone using Docker.

An important aspect of the workflow is that the build environment is used as a disposable container: it is launched, populated with the base build environment and the build dependencies; when building and release of the package have completed successfully, the container is just killed and never reused. This way, every build is performed in a fresh and isolated environment.

3.4   Reproducibility of Builds

The build environment is a mere container, populated by following simple Dockerfiles. It is thus easily replicable, ensuring that builds are always performed in exactly the same way.

To imbue the builds with determinism and reproducibility, *Wholly!* also relies on sub-package checksum verification. After every build, sub-package checksums are consistently checked against the reference checksums in the contents file. A match attests to the correctness of the package's contents. To ensure that identical recipes produce the same sub-packages, *Wholly!* sets the last modification and access time of every file that is copied into a sub-package image since this metadata feeds into the checksum calculation.

3.5   Static Building

Although *Wholly!* can be used to build any suitable recipe, we chose to use only static linking of binaries and libraries instead of dynamic linking (Fig. 6).

The reason is that we consider dynamic linking as being inconsistent with deployments on the modern software stack. With the popularity of cloud computing and emerging microservices, we need deployments that are smaller, faster and more specialized. While dynamic linking is suitable for general-purpose desktops, it leads to bloated and heavy deployments when applied to the container ecosystem, the cloud in general, and IoT devices. Indeed, using shared libraries instead of static binaries delays to runtime things that could have been determined at compile time:

- External symbols are resolved at runtime by a dynamic linker, adding a non negligible overhead to execution time.
- Unused functions from shared libraries are included in the deployment, whereas they could have been eliminated by link-time optimization.
- Dynamically-linked applications are dependent on a specific runtime that needs to be replicated in the target platform – including correct libraries and dynamic linker path and versions.

The *Wholly!* recipes that we created enforce the use of static linking so as to get specialized and smaller deployments easily. It allows us to release packages that make the most of link-time optimization to eliminate unused code while ensuring that these packages can run on a wide range of Linux-based systems, without assumptions being made about the runtime environment. Indeed, as a positive side effect of this, our static deployments are smaller than the ones

```
1   FROM alpine
2
3   # Building dependencies
4   RUN apk update
5   RUN apk add make binutils file git curl
6
7   # Copy build tools
8   RUN mkdir -p /tools/bin
9   COPY musl-clang/bin/* /tools/bin/
10  COPY clang-4.0/bin/* /tools/bin/
11  RUN ln -s /tools/bin/clang-4.0 /tools/bin/clang
12  RUN ln -s /tools/bin/clang-4.0 /tools/bin/clang++
13  RUN ln -s /tools/bin/clang-4.0 /tools/bin/clang-cpp
14
15  # Install gllvm
16  RUN apk add go musl-dev
17  ENV GOPATH="/usr/local/bin"
18  RUN go get github.com/SRI-CSL/gllvm/cmd/gclang
19  RUN go get github.com/SRI-CSL/gllvm/cmd/gclang++
20  RUN go get github.com/SRI-CSL/gllvm/cmd/get-bc
21  RUN mv ./usr/local/bin/bin/gclang /tools/bin
22  RUN mv ./usr/local/bin/bin/gclang++ /tools/bin
23  RUN mv ./usr/local/bin/bin/get-bc /tools/bin
24
25  RUN apk del go musl-dev
26
27  # Install tools
28  RUN chmod +x /tools/bin/*
29
30  # Folders
31  RUN mkdir -p /usr/bc
32  RUN mkdir -p /build
33  RUN mkdir -p /install
34
35  # Static environment variables
36  ENV PATH="/tools/bin:/root/go/bin:${PATH}"
37  ENV LLVM_CC_NAME musl-clang
38  ENV LLVM_CXX_NAME musl-clang++
39  ENV WLLVM_BC_STORE /usr/bc
```

Fig. 6. Dockerfile for *Wholly!* base build environment.

found in the Docker ecosystem, since our resulting binaries ship with less runtime and library code. They are also faster, since they require no runtime symbol resolution and thus less time is spent in kernel code and context switches.

4   Evaluation

Wholly! recipes and Docker containers can be used to build arbitrary software packages for multiple target platforms. We applied *Wholly!* to Linux packages, targeting the x86-64 platform, and focused on efficient and debloated packaging. In this section, we evaluate the packages built by *Wholly!* against those provided by the lightweight and minimal Alpine Linux distribution. We directly compare selected packages from the two systems, using size and performance as metrics. We also evaluate how *Wholly!* contributes to performing GNU-independent builds of packages.

4.1   Size of Packages

Wholly! particularly targets minimal Docker deployments of applications. Given this, we compare the size of ready-to-deploy Docker images built on top of

Wholly! packages on the one hand, and on Alpine Linux packages on the other hand. In the interest of ensuring a fair comparison, the packages that we compare have the same version, ship the same files, and are confirmed to run.

For the example of `nginx-1.12`, a small and popular HTTP server, Figs. 7 and 8 show the two Dockerfiles that we use to construct images that will be compared. The Alpine Linux version is the smallest possible deployment that we can make using Alpine and its `apk` package manager. Some *Wholly!* packages need additional configuration and runtime details; in the case of `nginx-1.12`, we need to import a `busybox` shell, set up directories, and create users. Since our packages are independent of the platform and runtime, this configuration step is not performed at build time.

```
1    FROM alpine:latest
2    RUN apk update
3    RUN apk add nginx
```

Fig. 7. Dockerfile for Alpine's `nginx-1.12` deployment. Only packages from distribution repositories are imported.

```
1     FROM wholly-nginx-1.12-bin as bin
2     FROM wholly-nginx-1.12-rt as rt
3     FROM wholly-nginx-1.12-conf as conf
4     FROM busybox
5
6     COPY --from=bin / /
7     COPY --from=rt / /
8     COPY --from=conf / /
9
10    RUN mkdir /var/cache && mkdir /var/cache/nginx && mkdir /var/run \
11       && touch /var/run/nginx.pid && addgroup -S nginx \
12       && adduser -D -S -h /var/cache/nginx -s /sbin/nologin -G nginx nginx \
13       && ln -sf /dev/stdout /var/log/nginx/access.log && ln -sf /dev/stderr /var/log/nginx/error.log
14
15    # Patch default configuration file to use port 80
16    COPY nginx.conf.patched /usr/conf/nginx.conf
17
18    EXPOSE 80
19
20    STOPSIGNAL SIGTERM
21
22    CMD ["nginx", "-g", "daemon off;"]
```

Fig. 8. Dockerfile that we use to build a runnable *Wholly!* `nginx-1.12` server.

Table 1 compares the size of the Docker images built for a representative set of packages.

For most of the packages, the *Wholly!* version is smaller, which is not surprising since the binaries are built statically and benefit from link-time optimization. The only exception among the tested packages is Node.js; this is because the vanilla Alpine package is built differently than the *Wholly!* version, and contains less functionality. The size of *Wholly!* packages makes them more consistent with small and specialized deployments in the cloud or in constrained environments, such as embedded systems.

Table 1. Size comparison for Docker images between *Wholly!* and Alpine. *Wholly!* packages are usually significantly smaller than their Alpine equivalent.

	Alpine-based image (in MB)	*Wholly!*-based image (in MB)
nginx-1.12	6.44	4.32
bzip2-1.0	5.31	0.425
sqlite-3.18	8.73	1.24
python-2.7	43.6	35.4
nodejs-6.11	36.8	54.4
clang-4.0	225	165

4.2 Performance of Deployments

In what follows, we try to see how *Wholly!* packages compete with commonly used applications and deployments in terms of performance. For this purpose, we analyzed the performance of different `nginx` servers and `clang` compilers.

We use the Dockerfile shown in Fig. 8 to build our *Wholly!* nginx server. Note that we include configuration commands so as to be able to connect to the server on port 80. The other servers that we use for this comparison are the official Docker images – available at Docker Hub – `nginx:mainline-alpine` and `nginx:official`, the latter being the default image available for `nginx`. We chose the other servers because they are amongst the most pulled and deployed Docker images, according to Docker Hub [4]. We then apply the following process to all three images:

1. Run the `nginx` image in a Docker container on the host machine.
2. Check that `http://localhost:80/index.html` is reachable and returns the default `nginx` web page.
3. Run and benchmark 10,000 successive requests to this webpage using Apache's `ab` tool.

The results of the benchmark are available in Fig. 9. The *Wholly!* deployment is slightly faster, and most importantly much smaller than the other ones.

We also compare *Wholly!*'s `clang` compiler to the one provided by Alpine Linux. To achieve this, we generate a number of random C files using `Csmith` [21], and measure the time needed to compile all these files sequentially with each compiler. We ensure that both compilers produce the exact same object files using hash comparisons. The results of the benchmark are provided in Fig. 10 and show that *Wholly!*'s version of `clang` is significantly faster than the Alpine Linux version. Since we use our *Wholly!*-generated compiler in *Wholly!*, we get very good build performance for our packages. More detailed benchmarks using `perf` show that *Wholly!*'s statically built version of `clang` triggers fewer time-consuming operations, such as context switches.

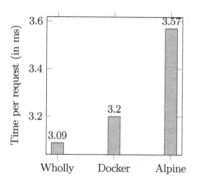
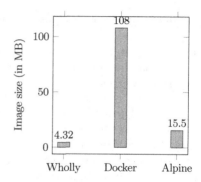

Fig. 9. Benchmarks for the **nginx** server show that the *Wholly!*-based version is slightly faster and much smaller than equivalents pulled from the Docker Hub.

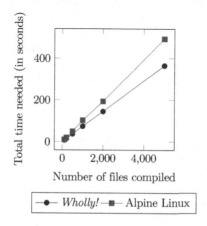

Fig. 10. Performance benchmark for **clang**: the *Wholly!*-built binary outperforms the one from the Alpine Linux repository by close to 40%.

4.3 Contribution to Environment-Independent Builds

One of the objectives of *Wholly!* is to make builds easily reproducible. We achieve this by providing a Docker-based build environment that is minimal and easy to replicate. We also note that most of Linux's user space software is implicitly dependent on the GNU build environment and provide a workaround to avoid this.

Like Alpine Linux, we chose to build all of our C packages against musl-libc, a lightweight C standard library that is an alternative to GNU's glibc. Unlike Alpine, *Wholly!* uses clang instead of gcc as its C compiler. Indeed, this non-GNU toolchain makes it harder to build packages that would compile without modification using gcc and glibc. In particular, some functional differences between musl-libc and glibc require patching, and we make use of wrapper scripts for the compiler and linker to automatically build with our non-standard libraries. Still, some packages like busybox just don't support clang and require gcc to build. The Tuscan Catalog [19] illustrates how this issue plagues many Linux packages.

However, most of the packages can be built using *Wholly!*, provided we create appropriate patches for them. In what follows, we give examples of packages that require such processing:

– `nodejs-6.11` provides the `fully-static` flag to statically build the binary, but still passes the `--rdynamic` flag to the compiler, which prevents the creation of a statically-linked executable. This shows that `nodejs-6.11`'s build scripts were not even tested to build a real statically-linked executable. We created a patch to fix the build in *Wholly!*.

– Statically building a full-featured `python-2.7` executable is anticipated in the build scripts, but is not officially documented. Designing a recipe to build it is quite complicated and requires manually editing setup files.

– Surprisingly, `clang-4.0` package required the most patching. Despite its aim at being a replacement for `gcc` and related tools, it is incompatible out-of-the-box with `musl-libc`'s macros, for which we needed 4 patch files. One extra patch was required to remove the `-Wl,-rpath-link` flag that was consistently passed at compile time. Figure 11 shows a sample patch.

```
 1   diff -uNr cmake.old/modules/AddLLVM.cmake cmake/modules/AddLLVM.cmake
 2   --- cmake.old/modules/AddLLVM.cmake 2017-01-17 13:47:58.000000000 -0800
 3   +++ cmake/modules/AddLLVM.cmake 2017-06-05 08:40:55.000000000 -0700
 4   @@ -671,7 +671,7 @@
 5         list(APPEND ALL_FILES "${LLVM_MAIN_SRC_DIR}/cmake/dummy.cpp")
 6       endif()
 7       if( EXCLUDE_FROM_ALL )
 8         add_executable(${name} EXCLUDE_FROM_ALL ${ALL_FILES})
 9       else()
10   @@ -1314,7 +1314,7 @@
11       if(NOT ARG_OUTPUT_DIR)
12   @@ -1426,10 +1426,6 @@
13         if(${CMAKE_SYSTEM_NAME} MATCHES "(FreeBSD|DragonFly)")
14           set_property(TARGET ${name} APPEND_STRING PROPERTY
15                       LINK_FLAGS " -Wl,-z,origin ")
16   -     elseif(${CMAKE_SYSTEM_NAME} STREQUAL "Linux"
17   -             AND NOT LLVM_LINKER_IS_GOLD)
18   -       set_property(TARGET ${name} APPEND_STRING PROPERTY
19   -               LINK_FLAGS " -Wl,-rpath-link,
20   -                     ${LLVM_LIBRARY_OUTPUT_INTDIR} ")
21         endif()
22       else()
23         return()
```

Fig. 11. The patch `cmake_fix_no_dynlinker_build.patch` is required for `clang-4.0` to handle static building correctly.

Our effort shows that it is possible to build the Linux user space in an environment that is not tied to the GNU toolchain. Indeed, *Wholly!* uses `clang` as its C compiler and `musl-libc/libc++` as its C/C++ standard libraries to build Alpine Linux's user space.

5   Applications

Wholly! has been used to construct efficient and portable builds of software packages for a number of platforms. We have built an entire Linux distribution, an entire Linux container ecosystem, and specialized virtual machines with microservices using *Wholly!*.

Alpine Linux: This is an independent, non-commercial, general-purpose Linux distribution. It is built around `musl-libc` and `busybox`. It is therefore smaller and more resource efficient than traditional GNU/Linux distributions. Alpine Linux uses its own package manager, called `apk`, and was designed with security in mind. Alpine Linux has a dedicated build infrastructure that consists of a number of scripts used to build packages. We chose it as a target platform because it is a Linux distribution that is built exclusively using `musl-libc`. However, it uses `gcc`, and not `clang`. We aim to build an entire Linux distribution with *Wholly!*, producing fine-grained packages, precise definitions of package dependencies, and for each library and executable, produce the corresponding LLVM bitcode to enable whole program analysis, transformations, and optimizations.

We have automatically translated Alpine build scripts to *Wholly!* recipe files. Our recipes are often simpler, more intuitive, and readable than Alpine build scripts. Another reason we chose Alpine Linux is the growing popularity of Docker containers. Docker has started using Alpine Linux for its base container images.

Docker Containers: Docker is the world's leading software container management platform. Containers are rapidly gaining traction as the preferred platform for deploying cloud applications and microservices. Docker containers are built using Dockerfiles and *Wholly!* uses Dockerfiles to build arbitrary software packages. As a result, it is possible to directly export packages and sub-packages as Docker images. Because we use static linking and link-time optimization, Docker images produced by *Wholly!* are both smaller in size and faster. When utilizing microservices, it is desirable to support a fast deployment cycle. Being able to build images efficiently also enhances developer productivity by speeding up the debug and test cycle.

Minimal VMs: In 2017, Docker unveiled LinuxKit [9], a toolkit for building secure, lean, and portable Linux subsystems. It allows to bundle a number of Docker images, along with kernel support, to be built into a stand-alone VM. Because our Docker images are leaner and faster than those provided by Docker, we are able to produce more efficient VMs that can be booted on IoT devices, as well as on typical cloud infrastructure.

6   Whole Program Analysis

It is well known that when applying formal verification to source code, what is verified is not what is executed. Because an application can be compiled with different compilers and may be deployed with different versions of libraries, it is not possible to guarantee that source code verification translates into correct execution.

The systematic production of LLVM bitcode for any application built with *Wholly!*, allows us to apply formal verification to all of the application code and the libraries it is dependent on. We use SeaHorn [7], a fully automated analysis framework for LLVM-based languages, to perform a number of program analyses, such as abstract interpretation, invariant generation, memory safety, and bounded model-checking. Because of the reproducibility of builds, guaranteed by *Wholly!*, a formally analyzed applications is proved to exhibit the same behavior on different platforms.

The verification at the LLVM bitcode level can be done after code specialization using partial evaluation and code winnowing techniques, such as the ones implemented in OCCAM [11]. These techniques can be taken one step further so that I/O operations are specialized and all read and writes to files are replaced with in-memory loads and stores. This often improves performances by avoiding the execution of expensive system calls. Of note is that it also ensures that what is being verified is close to what is being executed.

7   Conclusion

We have presented *Wholly!*, a tool for building efficient, fine-grained, and LLVM-based packages for Alpine Linux, Docker containers, and LinuxKit VMs. *Wholly!* can be used in the future for cross-compiling these and arbitrary packages to support multiple architectures and operating systems. *Wholly!*'s uniform and reproducible build process will avoid many of the portability issues reported in recent studies [19], and can provide reproducible builds for a range of areas, including scientific computing. Combined with LLVM-based software specialization and optimization frameworks, such as OCCAM [11], and formal verification tools, such as SeaHorn [7], *Wholly!*supports the production of debloated, efficient, and verified code that can be deployed in practice.

Acknowledgement. This material is based upon work supported by the US National Science Foundation (NSF) under Grant ACI-1440800, Department of Homeland Security (DHS) Science and Technology Directorate, and the Office of Naval Research (ONR) under Contract No. N68335-17-C-0558. Any opinions, findings, and conclusions or recommendations expressed in this material are those of the authors and do not necessarily reflect the views of NSF, DHS, or ONR.

References

1. Alpine Linux. https://alpinelinux.org/
2. Cousot, P., Cousot, R.: Abstract interpretation: a unified lattice model for static analysis of programs by construction or approximation of fixpoints. In: 4th ACM Symposium on Principles of Programming Languages (POPL) (1977)
3. Docker. https://www.docker.com/
4. Docker Hub. https://hub.docker.com/

 5. gllvm. https://github.com/SRI-CSL/gllvm
 6. Graf, S., Saidi, H.: Construction of abstract state graphs with PVS. In: Grumberg, O. (ed.) CAV 1997. LNCS, vol. 1254, pp. 72–83. Springer, Heidelberg (1997). https://doi.org/10.1007/3-540-63166-6_10
 7. Gurfinkel, A., Kahsai, T., Komuravelli, A., Navas, J.A.: The SeaHorn verification framework. In: Kroening, D., Păsăreanu, C.S. (eds.) CAV 2015. LNCS, vol. 9206, pp. 343–361. Springer, Cham (2015). https://doi.org/10.1007/978-3-319-21690-4_20
 8. Haskell Lightweight Virtual Machine. https://galois.com/project/halvm/
 9. LinuxKit. https://github.com/linuxkit/linuxkit
10. Madhavapeddy, A. et al.: Unikernels: library operating systems for the cloud. In: 18th ACM International Conference on Architectural Support for Programming Languages and Operating Systems (ASPLOS) (2013)
11. Malecha, G., Gehani, A., Shankar, N.: Automated software winnowing. In: 30th ACM Symposium on Applied Computing (SAC) (2015)
12. musl libc. https://www.musl-libc.org/
13. LLVM musl libc. https://github.com/SRI-CSL/musllvm
14. OSv. http://osv.io/
15. Piccolo, S., Frampton, M.: Tools and techniques for computational reproducibility. GigaScience 5(1), 30 (2016)
16. Rumprun unikernel. https://github.com/rumpkernel/
17. Smowton, C.: I/O Optimisation and elimination via partial evaluation, Ph.D. thesis, Cambridge University (2014)
18. Standard Library. https://stdlib.com/
19. Tuscan Catalog. https://karkhaz.github.io/tuscan/
20. Wholly! https://github.com/SRI-CSL/Wholly/
21. Yang, X., Chen, Y., Eide, E., Regehr, J.: Finding and understanding bugs in C compilers. In: 32nd ACM Conference on Programming Language Design and Implementation (PLDI) (2011)

A Modeling Language for Security Threats of IoT Systems

Delphine Beaulaton[1], Ioana Cristescu[2](✉), Axel Legay[2], and Jean Quilbeuf[2]

[1] Univ. South Brittany, Irisa, Vannes, France
[2] Inria Rennes, Rennes, France
ioana-domnina.cristescu@inria.fr

Abstract. We propose a security-based modeling language for IoT systems with two important features: (i) vulnerabilities are explicitly represented and (ii) interactions are allowed or denied based on the information stored on the IoT devices. An IoT system is transformed in BIP, a component-based modeling language, in which can execute the system and perform security analysis. As proof-of-concept for our approach we model an attack on the Amazon Smart-Key system.

Keywords: IoT systems · Component-based specifications · Security

1 Introduction

IoT systems are part of our daily lives, as we are surrounded by computing devices that communicate through the Internet. The IoT devices often have access to personal, confidential information that needs to be shared with other devices in order to provide *smart* services. Security attacks on IoT systems exploit the vulnerabilities of the different devices, and their interactions, to steal the sensitive data [2,13].

We propose a modeling language for IoT systems in which vulnerabilities are explicitly represented. A malicious *entity*, that we usually call an Attacker, tries to break a security property of the system by using different attack scenarios. The other entities in the system can accidentally help the Attacker by *leaking* sensitive data. If one attack scenario violates the security property, our analysis concludes that the system is vulnerable to security threats.

Another feature of our language is that the interactions are permitted only between entities that share some *knowledge*. It is often the case that IoT devices require a password or share security keys to ensure their identity and to communicate with the rest of the system. In our approach, *protocols* supervise the interactions and verify that the two communicating entities have some common knowledge. The Attacker assumes the identity of the other entities by obtaining their knowledge.

© Springer Nature Switzerland AG 2018
F. Howar and J. Barnat (Eds.): FMICS 2018, LNCS 11119, pp. 258–268, 2018.
https://doi.org/10.1007/978-3-030-00244-2_17

Running Example. In the Amazon Smart-Key [1] system, shown in Fig. 1, Amazon provides Home Owners with a Smart Lock and a Camera. The Camera can communicate with the Amazon Server to send all its recordings. A Home Owner asks for a delivery at a time when she is not home (step 1). The Delivery Guy sends the package number to the Amazon server (step 2) from which it receives a temporary code (step 3) that, if communicated to the Smart Lock, can open the door (step 4). The Smart Lock is also in charge for turning on the Camera as soon as the door is unlocked (step 5). The Delivery Guy leaves the package inside and asks the Smart Lock to close the door (step 6) and to turn off the Camera (step 7). The Camera sends the video of the delivery to the Amazon Server (step 8) which forwards it to the Home Owner (step 9).

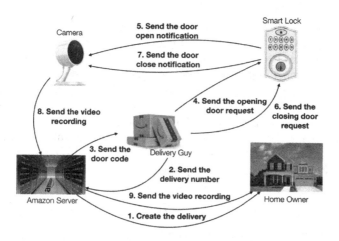

Fig. 1. Amazon Smart-Key

In our example, the security property is that the camera is recording as long as the door is open, to prevent thefts. Let us suppose that an Attacker intercepts the communication between the Delivery Guy and the Smart Lock. The Delivery Guy leaks the code for closing the door, which never reaches the Smart Lock. The communication between the Smart Lock and the Camera also has to be intercepted. The Attacker assumes the identity of the Smart Lock and sends a message to the Camera to turn off the recording. If this two-steps scenario succeeds the home is vulnerable to thefts as the door is open and the camera is turned off.

Outline. In Sect. 2 we introduce our language and show how we can model the Amazon Smart-Key system. An IoT model is translated in BIP in Sect. 3, which is equipped with an execution framework. We use the system's executions in Sect. 4 to verify whether a system is vulnerable to security attacks. As this is preliminary work for integrating probabilities and performing more complex analysis on IoT systems, we sketch the future works and conclude in Sect. 5.

2   A Modeling Language for IoT Systems

We model interconnected devices in an IoT systems as *entities*, that have each an identifier, ranged over by $e_1, \cdots, e_n$. Entities communicate using protocols and exchange values. Formally we write E for the set of identifiers, C for the set of protocols and *Val* for the set of values.

Protocols supervise the interactions, by verifying that some knowledge is shared between the communicating entities. We model the *knowledge* of an entity as a function $k : E \times C \rightarrow PowerSet(Val)$ which associates to an entity e and a protocol c a set of values. For simplicity we write k_i^c for the application of k to the entity e_i and the protocol c. Then an interaction between entities e_1 and e_2 is permitted by the protocol c if there exists one common value between k_1^c and k_2^c.

Each entity has a CCS-like process [11] defined by the grammar in Fig. 2. A process $a.P$ executes an action a and continues as P. The process $a.P + b.Q$ chooses between two execution branches, either $a.P$ or $b.Q$. We use A to denote (recursive) definitions, and 0 to denote the inactive process.

Two entities communicate through a pair of actions (Send, Receive), that represent "safe" interactions or (Leak, Collect) which signal an inadvertent interaction with a malicious entity. Actions have to specify the identifiers of the sender and the receiver and a value v which is exchange during the interaction. Moreover safe interactions also specify a *protocol* c. Entities can also compute *internally*, without involving any interaction, represented by the action τ.

$$Process \quad P, Q \ ::= \ a.P \mid a.P + b.Q \mid A \mid 0$$

$$Action \quad a, b \ ::= \ e_1 \xrightarrow[v]{c} e_2 \ (Send) \mid e_1 \xleftarrow{c} e_2 \ (Receive)$$

$$\mid \ e_1 \underset{v}{\rightarrowtail} e_2 \ (Leak) \mid e_1 \leftarrowtail e_2 \ (Collect) \mid \tau \ (Internal)$$

$$Definition \quad A \ \overset{def}{=} \ P$$

Fig. 2. The Syntax of the IoT calculus

IoT Transition Systems. An entity's state $\langle P, k \rangle$ consists of a running process and a current knowledge. A global state (of an IoT system) s is defined by the following grammar:

$$s ::= \emptyset \ \Big| \ \langle P, k \rangle \ \Big| \ s \mid s.$$

that is it can be either empty, a local state or the composition of the local states of each of its constituents. An IoT transition system consists of the tuple (S, T, i) where S is a set of global states, $i \in S$ is an initial state and $T \subseteq S \times S$ is a set of transitions that are derived by the rules in Fig. 3. We write $s \rightarrow s'$ for a transition and $s_0 \rightarrow s_1 \cdots s_{n-1} \rightarrow s_n$ for an *execution* of the system.

$$\text{SENDRECEIVE } \frac{k_1^c \cap k_2^c \neq \emptyset \qquad c' = \mathsf{protocol}(v)}{\langle e_1 \xrightarrow{c}_v e_2.P_1, k_1 \rangle | \langle e_2 \xleftarrow{c} e_1.P_2, k_2 \rangle \rightarrow \langle P_1, k_1 \rangle | \langle P_2, k_2^{c'} \uplus \{v\} \rangle}$$

$$\text{LEAKCOLLECT } \frac{c' = \mathsf{protocol}(v)}{\langle e_1 \rightsquigarrow_v e_2.P_1, k_1 \rangle | \langle e_2 \leftharpoondown e_1.P_2, k_2 \rangle \rightarrow \langle P_1, k_1 \rangle | \langle P_2, k_2^{c'} \uplus \{v\} \rangle}$$

$$\text{INTERNAL } \langle \tau.P, k \rangle \rightarrow \langle P, k \rangle \qquad \text{CONGRUENCE } \frac{s \equiv_s t \rightarrow s' \equiv_s t'}{s \rightarrow s'}$$

$$\text{SUM } \frac{\langle P_i, k_i \rangle | \langle P_j, k_j \rangle \rightarrow \langle P_i', k_i' \rangle | \langle P_j', k_j' \rangle}{\langle P_i + Q_i, k_i \rangle | \langle P_j + Q_j, k_j \rangle \rightarrow \langle P_i', k_i' \rangle | \langle P_j', k_j' \rangle} \qquad \text{PAR } \frac{s \rightarrow s'}{s \mid t \rightarrow s' \mid t}$$

Fig. 3. The Operational Semantics of the IoT calculus

The rules SENDRECEIVE and LEAKCOLLECT describe the communication between two entities e_1 and e_2 with the knowledge functions k_1 and k_2, respectively. The two entities exchange a value v which is added to the knowledge of e_2 under protocol c'. The SENDRECEIVE interaction also verifies that the two entities share a common value in their knowledge for a protocol c. An internal computation is derived by the rule INTERNAL. The rules PAR and SUM allow derivations inside the state's composition and the sum constructors. Lastly, the rule CONGRUENCE rewrites a state or a process into a syntactic form that is suitable for a derivation. It uses two *congruence* relations $\equiv_P$ and $\equiv_S$, defined as the smallest equivalence relations on processes and states, respectively, such that

- $\equiv_P$ includes the abelian monoid laws for $+$ and the unfolding law for definitions:

$$P + Q \equiv_P Q + P \quad (P + Q) + R \equiv_P P + (Q + R) \quad P + 0 \equiv_P P$$
$$A \equiv_P P \text{ if } A \overset{\text{def}}{=} P.$$

- $\equiv_S$ includes the abelian monoid laws for $|$ and generalizes $\equiv_P$ to states:

$$s|t \equiv_s t|s \quad (s|t)|q \equiv_s s|(t|q) \quad s|\emptyset \equiv_s s \quad \frac{P \equiv_P Q}{\langle P, k \rangle \equiv_S \langle Q, k \rangle}$$

The Amazon Smart-Key Example. In modeling our example, we have the following entities: the Home Owner H, the Amazon Server S, the Delivery Guy D, the Smart Lock L, the Camera C and the Attacker A. The initial process for each entity is given in Fig. 4. The protocols used in the example are delivery, doorControl, cameraCom and customerCom.

We define the initial knowledge of each entity such that all safe communications are possible. For instance, the Amazon Server and the Home Owner

$$AmazonServer = S \xleftarrow{customerCom} H.S \xleftarrow{delivery} D.S \underset{doorCode}{\xrightarrow{delivery}} D.S \xleftarrow{cameraCom} C.$$
$$S \underset{video}{\xrightarrow{customerCom}} H.AmazonServer$$

$$HomeOwner = H \underset{askDelivery}{\xrightarrow{customerCom}} S.H \xleftarrow{customerCom} S.HomeOwner$$

$$DeliveryGuy = D \underset{deliveryArrived}{\xrightarrow{delivery}} S.D \xleftarrow{delivery} S.D \underset{openDoor}{\xrightarrow{doorControl}} L.$$
$$(\tau.normal\_delivery + \tau.hijack\_delivery)$$
$$normal\_delivery = D \underset{closeDoor}{\xrightarrow{doorControl}} L.DeliveryGuy$$
$$hijack\_delivery = D \underset{lock1}{\rightarrowtail} A.DeliveryGuy$$

$$SmartLock = L \xleftarrow{doorControl} D.L \underset{startRecording}{\xrightarrow{cameraCom}} C.(\tau.normal\_lock + \tau.hijack\_lock)$$

$$normal\_lock = L \xleftarrow{doorControl} D.L \underset{stopRecording}{\xrightarrow{cameraCom}} C.SmartLock$$

$$hijack\_lock = L \xleftarrow{doorControl} A.L \underset{camera1}{\rightarrowtail} A.SmartLock$$

$$Camera = C \xleftarrow{cameraCom} L.(C \xleftarrow{cameraCom} L.C \underset{video}{\xrightarrow{cameraCom}} S.Camera+$$
$$C \xleftarrow{cameraCom} A.C \underset{video}{\xrightarrow{cameraCom}} S.Camera)$$

$$Attacker = A \leftarrowtail D.A \underset{getCameraId}{\xrightarrow{doorControl}} L.A \leftarrowtail L.A \underset{stopRecording}{\xrightarrow{cameraCom}} C.Attacker$$

Fig. 4. The Amazon Smart-Key system

can communicate because they both know the identity of the Home Owner: $k_S^{customerCom} = k_H^{customerCom} = homeOwner1$. However, initially the Attacker only knows the identity of the Delivery Guy and it is through the LeakCollect interactions that the Attacker acquires information that allows him to communicate with the Smart Lock and the Camera. To model this behaviour, the Delivery Guy and the Smart Lock have two execution branches, one called the *normal* behaviour, when the Attacker does not interfere and a second one, the *hijacked* one, where the system is vulnerable to the attack.

3 BIP: A Component-Based Modeling Language

BIP [3,10,12] is a component-based modeling language where a system is modeled as the *composition* of a set of interacting components. BIP stands for *Behaviour* (each component has an abstract behaviour), *Interaction* (components interact with each other) and *Priorities* (interactions have a priority order, and higher priority interactions occur first). We start by introducing the components, and then move on to the interactions and the priorities.

A component has an abstract behaviour, represented by a labeled transition system (LTS). Components communicate with each other through *ports*. Transitions are labeled by ports and the set of ports used by a components is called the *interface* of the component.

Definition 1. *A component K is an LTS, denoted as (P, Q, q^0, T), where P is a set of* ports *constituting the interface of K, Q is the set of states, $q^0 \in Q$ is the initial state, and $T \subseteq Q \times P \times Q$ is the set of transitions labeled by ports from the interface P.*

We write $q^1 \xrightarrow{a} q^2$ if the tuple (q^1, a, q^2) is in T. The previous transition is said to be enabled when the component is at state q^1. An execution is a sequence of transitions that starts from the initial state $q^0 \xrightarrow{a_1} q^1 \cdots q^{n-1} \xrightarrow{a_n} q^n$.

The definition above can be extended by including variables in components. In such an extended version, there are three additional mechanism:

- *guards:* each transition has a predicate, name guard, defined on the variables. For a transition to be enabled, the guard must evaluate to true.
- *variables exchange:* each port exports a set of variables. Any interaction through that port can read and write these variables.
- *update functions:* each transition is labeled with an update function that set new values to the variables according to the previous ones.

These mechanisms interact as follows. First the guards are evaluated to list the enabled transitions. Then, when an interaction takes place, the variables exported by the associated port are potentially modified. Finally, the update function is applied to modify the variables of the component. Sometimes there are no variables to verify or update, in which case the guard function is the constant true or the update function is the identity.

In our case, we use variables to encode the knowledge of the entities. As an example, consider the component Amazon Server from Fig. 5, representing the entity with the same name from our running example. The states $S_0, \cdots S_4$ represent the reachable processes from the *AmazonServer* of Fig. 4. The protocols used in *AmazonServer* become the ports **customerCom, develivery, cameraCom**. Initially the

Composition of BIP Components. BIP systems consists of several components that interact with each other. An *interaction* consists of the synchronization of some local transitions labeled by ports. In the following we define a BIP system of n components. We write (P_i, Q_i, q_i^0, T_i) for the transition system of the component K_i for $i \leq n$.

Definition 2. *Let $(K_i)_{i \leq n}$ be n components such that their interfaces are pairwise disjoint, that is $i \neq j \implies P_i \cap P_j = \emptyset$. We define the set of all ports by $Ports = \bigcup_{i \leq n} P_i$. An interaction (a, α) consists of an exported port $a \notin Ports$, a non-empty set of ports $\alpha \subseteq Ports$ such that there exists at most one port from each interface P_i in α.*

Interactions involve at least one component. In the case where only one component participate in the interaction, we say that it is *internal* transition and we denote it with τ.

As for transitions in the atomic components, interactions can be extended to handle data, using guards and update functions. For each interaction, the set of variables exported by the participating ports defines the set of variables that are visible to the interaction. The interaction can only take place if the guard evaluates to true. When the interaction takes place, the update function modifies the value of the variables exported by the port.

In Fig. 5 there is an interaction between the Amazon Server and the Home Owner defined on the ports **customerCom** of two components. These ports export the knowledge related to the corresponding protocol. The guard of interaction checks the existence of a common value between the the Amazon Server's knowledge and the Home Owner's knowledge. The update function simply propagates to the Amazon Server a message signaling a delivery request.

An *interaction model* γ is a set of interactions with distinct exported ports. An useful notation for the next definition is $I_a = \{i : \exists a \in P_i, a \in \alpha_i\}$ for the set of indexes of the components K_i that participate in the interaction. Note that, because in an interaction model the exported ports are distinct, we can distinguish an interaction (a, α) by the port a.

Definition 3. *Let γ be a set of interactions defined on the components $(K_i)_{i \leq n}$. We denote with $\langle \gamma \rangle (K_i)_{i \leq n}$ the component (P_γ, Q, q^0, T) where*

- $P_\gamma = a : (a, \alpha) \in \gamma$ *is the set of exported ports of γ;*
- $Q = \prod_{i \leq n} Q_i$ *with* $q^0 = (q_1^0, \cdots q_n^0)$ *and* $F = \prod_{i \leq n} F_i$;
- *T is the least set of transitions such that:*

$$\frac{(a, \alpha) \in \gamma \quad \forall i \in I_a, \exists a_i \in \alpha, q_i^1 \xrightarrow{a_i} q_i^2 \quad \forall i \notin I_a, q_i^2 = q_i^1}{(q_1^1, \cdots, q_n^1) \xrightarrow{a} (q_1^2, \cdots, q_n^2)}.$$

Priorities. A priority order on a set of ports is a partial order, where each element $a < b$ of the order is called a *priority*. Whenever the system has a choice between the two interactions on ports a or b, the interaction on b is chosen. Formally, we introduce priorities as in Definition 3, following the approach in [10].

Definition 4. *Let $<$ be a priority order on the ports P of a component $K = (P, X, Q, q^0, T)$. We define $\langle < \rangle (K)$ as the component (P, X, Q, q^0, T') where only T' is changed to be the least set of transitions such that*

$$\frac{q^1 \xrightarrow{a} q^2 \in T \quad \nexists b \in P, \exists q \in Q, (a < b \wedge q^1 \xrightarrow{b} q)}{q^1 \xrightarrow{a} q^2}.$$

We use a priority order, denoted $\ll$, which gives priority to the internal transitions over the binary interactions. We can also use the method in [10] to infer a priority order that avoids deadlocks (the system reaches states from which no transition is possible) as much as possible.

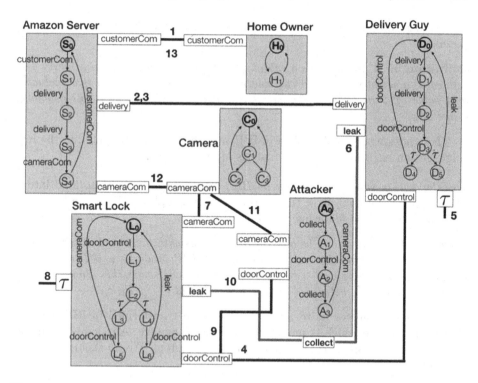

Fig. 5. The initial state of the Amazon Smart-Key transformed to BIP. Each IoT entity is transformed into the BIP component with the same name. The LTS of a BIP component represents the process of the corresponding IoT entity while the variables represent the knowledge. Each state in the LTS represents a reachable process. Actions connect the different states of the LTS. For simplicity, here the ports are the protocols, for the SendReceive interactions, τ denote the internal transitions and *leak*, *collect* the LeakCollect. Variables are sets of values, where each protocol has its own variable. Interactions are defined between ports that have the name, or are internal transitions, denoted τ.

Giving More Power to the Attacker. In our model, we explicitly model the knowledge of the Attacker by using a set of values to represent it. Furthermore, this knowledge focuses mainly on actual data rather than the state of a component. However, some attacks might require to send a message when a component is in a particular state, which makes it vulnerable to an attack. To that end we could use techniques similar to the ones used for the *distributed controller* in [8,9]. A distributed controller knows the behaviour of a system and can observe its executions to infer the global state of the system. An Attacker can analyze the behaviour of a system to detect in which state it is most vulnerable. For example, an Attacker that knows how Amazon Smart-Home works can detect when the Delivery Guy opens the door of a user's home and proceed with an attack at that moment. A more powerful Attacker can also observe the data exchanged during communications. An attack in our case could consists in reusing the code for opening and closing a door that was used during a "safe" execution of the system.

Definition 5. *A process π is a subset of states in a component. A property ϕ is defined as a set of value for a variable x and it holds in a state q if x evaluates to a value of ϕ in state q. We say that π knows ϕ if ϕ holds in all reachable states of π.*

These notions are well studied in BIP, and therefore if integrated in the IoT language can enrich the security analysis of an IoT system.

Transformation of an IoT System to BIP. An IoT system is translated into a BIP system. We do not show the transformation here, but is based on [4], along with the proof of the following theorem.

Theorem 1. *Let $e_1, \cdots e_n$ be a set of IoT entities with the initial states $\langle P_i, k_i \rangle$, $i \leq n$. The transformation in [4] from IoT to BIP produces a BIP component K_i for each e_i entity and a γ an interaction model such that there exists a bisimulation relation between $\langle \ll \rangle (\langle \gamma \rangle (K_i)_{i \leq n})$ and $\prod_{i \leq n} \langle P_i, k_i \rangle$.*

The theorem allows us to analyze the system transformed in BIP, instead of the original one which is modeled in the IoT language. Any analysis on the executions of the BIP system holds for the IoT system. We do this in the next section.

4   Verification

The BIP language is equipped with a simulator that we use to obtain executions of an IoT system. As future work we will use the simulations for more complicated security analysis, based on statistical model checking [6]. For the moment, we simply use the simulation framework to guide the executions of a system to discover execution paths leading to security failures.

By simulating the system we can extract two executions for the Amazon Smart-Key system. To clarify notations, in the following execution we write the global state as a list of the local states of the different BIP components.

Let us informally describe an execution where the Attacker succeeds. Each step of the attack also annotates the interactions in Fig. 5. The initial state is $(S_0, H_0, L_0, C_0, D_0, A_0)$.

1. the Home Owner contacts the Amazon Server using the protocol customer-Com, which verifies that $k_S^{\text{customerCom}} \cap k_H^{\text{customerCom}} = \{\text{homeOwner1}\}$, that is that both entities know the value *homeOwner1*. The Home Owner sends the message *askDelivery* to the Amazon Sever. The global state becomes $(\mathbf{S_1}, \mathbf{H_1}, L_0, C_0, D_0, A_0)$;

2. when the delivery arrives, the Delivery Guy sends the message *deliveryArrived* to the Amazon Server on protocol delivery, which verifies that both entities know the Delivery Guy identity, $k_D^{\text{delivery}} \cap k_S^{\text{delivery}} = \{\text{deliveryGuy1}\}$. The state changes to $(\mathbf{S_2}, H_1, L_0, C_0, \mathbf{D_1}, A_0)$;

3. the Amazon Server sends back the value *doorCode1* to the Delivery Guy, using the same protocol and the state is now $(\mathbf{S_3}, H_1, L_0, C_0, \mathbf{D_2}, A_0)$;

4. the Delivery Guy has the value *doorCode1* needed to communicate with the Smart Lock on protocol doorControl, $k_D^{\text{doorControl}} \cap k_L^{\text{doorControl}} = \{\text{doorCode1}\}$. The Delivery Guy sends the message *openDoor* and the state changes to $(S_3, H_1, \mathbf{L_1}, C_0, \mathbf{D_3}, A_0)$;

5. the Delivery Guy accidentally agrees to help the Attacker by choosing the internal transition leading to the global state $(S_3, H_1, L_1, C_0, \mathbf{D_5}, A_0)$;

6. the Delivery Guy leaks to the Attacker the value *doorCode1*. The state becomes $(S_3, H_1, L_1, C_0, \mathbf{D_0}, \mathbf{A_1})$;

7. the Smart Lock opens the door and sends the message *startRecording* to the Camera using the protocol cameraCom, for which the guard $k_L^{\text{cameraCom}} \cap k_C^{\text{cameraCom}} = \{\text{camera1}\}$ holds. The state is now $(S_3, H_1, \mathbf{L_2}, \mathbf{C_1}, D_0, A_1)$;

8. the Smart Lock is also recruited by the Attacker, when the Smart Lock chooses the internal transition leading to the global state $(S_3, H_1, \mathbf{L_4}, C_1, D_0, A_1)$;

9. the Attacker communicates with the Smart Lock using a safe communication, as now the Attacker knows the *doorCode1*. The condition of the protocol doorControl: $k_A^{\text{doorControl}} \cap k_L^{\text{doorControl}} = \{\text{doorCode1}\}$ holds. Then Attacker sends the message *getCameraId* and the state changes to $(S_3, H_1, \mathbf{L_6}, C_1, D_0, \mathbf{A_2})$;

10. the Smart Lock leaks the value *camera1* to the Attacker. The states is now $(S_3, H_1, \mathbf{L_0}, C_1, D_0, \mathbf{A_3})$;

11. the Attacker sends the message *stopRecording* to the Camera using the protocol cameraComwhich verifies that $k_A^{\text{cameraCom}} \cap k_C^{\text{cameraCom}} = \{\text{camera1}\}$. The global state is now $(S_3, H_1, L_0, \mathbf{C_3}, D_0, \mathbf{A_0})$;

12. unaware of the attack, the Camera sends an uncompromising *video* to the Amazon Server using the protocol cameraCom. The state is now $(\mathbf{S_4}, H_1, L_0, \mathbf{C_0}, D_0, A_0)$;

13. lastly, the Amazon Server forwards the *video* to the Home Owner using the protocol customerCom. The system is back in its initial state $(\mathbf{S_0}, \mathbf{H_0}, L_0, C_0, D_0, A_0)$.

The Smart Lock never received a message for closing the door, while the Camera did received a message to stop the recording. Therefore the door is open, the Camera switched off, and the home is vulnerable to thefts.

The Attacker proceeds in two steps: it first compromises the Delivery Guy and then compromises the Smart Lock. If either one of these two steps fails, the attack fails. An example of a safe execution is one in which everything is as above, except for the step 5, where the Delivery Guy does an internal transition to the local state D_4 (instead of state D_5). The Attacker cannot then collect the value *doorCode1* and cannot communicate with the Smart Lock. Another possibility is for the Delivery Guy to leak the value *doorCode1* (and thus proceed as in step 5 and 6 described above), but the Smart Lock does not collaborate with the Attacker in step 8.

5   Conclusion

We introduced a modeling language for IoT systems, where the malicious entities are explicitly part of the system. The malicious entities interfere with the rest of the system to steal confidential data and leave the system vulnerable. A system modeled in our language is transformed into a BIP system which is then executed. Execution traces leading to successful attacks are proofs of the vulnerabilities of a system.

As future work we plan to add probabilities to the IoT language, similarly to the probabilistic CCS [7] and use *statistical* BIP [5] to simulate these systems. In the plasma tool [6] we can then apply statistical model checking techniques to provide more complex security analysis.

References

1. Amazon key. https://www.amazon.com/key. Accessed 22 June 2018
2. Antonakakis, M., et al.: Understanding the Mirai botnet. In: 26th USENIX Security Symposium (2017)
3. Basu, A., Bozga, M., Sifakis, J.: Modeling heterogeneous real-time components in BIP. In: 4th SEFM Conference (2006)
4. Beaulaton, D., et al.: A language for analyzing security of IoT systems. In: 13th SOSE Conference (2018)
5. Bensalem, S., Bozga, M., Delahaye, B., Jegourel, C., Legay, A., Nouri, A.: Statistical model checking QoS properties of systems with SBIP. In: Margaria, T., Steffen, B. (eds.) ISoLA 2012. LNCS, vol. 7609, pp. 327–341. Springer, Heidelberg (2012). https://doi.org/10.1007/978-3-642-34026-0_25
6. Boyer, B., Corre, K., Legay, A., Sedwards, S.: PLASMA-lab: a flexible, distributable statistical model checking library. In: Joshi, K., Siegle, M., Stoelinga, M., D'Argenio, P.R. (eds.) QEST 2013. LNCS, vol. 8054, pp. 160–164. Springer, Heidelberg (2013). https://doi.org/10.1007/978-3-642-40196-1_12
7. Van Glabbeek, R., Smolka, S., Steffen, B.: Reactive, generative, and stratified models of probabilistic processes. Inf. Comput. **121**(1), 59–80 (1995)
8. Graf, S.: Distributed implementation of constrained systems based on knowledge. In: 13th ISPDC Conference (2014)
9. Graf, S., Quinton, S.: Knowledge for the distributed implementation of constrained systems. Softw. Syst. Model. **15**, 1163–1180 (2013)
10. Ben Hafaiedh, I., Graf, S., Quinton, S.: Building distributed controllers for systems with priorities. J. Log. Algebr. Program. **80**(3), 194–218 (2011)
11. Milner, R. (ed.): A Calculus of Communicating Systems. LNCS, vol. 92. Springer, Heidelberg (1980). https://doi.org/10.1007/3-540-10235-3
12. Sifakis, J.: A framework for component-based construction extended abstract. In: 3rd SEFM Conference (2005)
13. TrapX Security Inc., TrapX LAbs: Anatomy of an attack, medjack (medical device attack). Technical report, May 2015

Revisiting Bounded Reachability Analysis of Timed Automata Based on MILP

Iulian Ober[✉]

University of Toulouse - IRIT,
118 Route de Narbonne, 31062 Toulouse, France
`iulian.ober@irit.fr`

Abstract. We study the reduction of bounded reachability analysis of timed automata (TA) to a Mixed Integer Linear Programming (MILP) problem. While bounded model checking of timed automata has been explored in the literature based on the satisfiability of Boolean constraint formulas over linear arithmetic constraints verified using SAT Modulo Theory (SMT) solvers, the approach presented in this paper opens up the alternative of using MILP solvers. We present some preliminary results comparing the two approaches and provide ideas on how linear optimization can be useful for analyzing the behavior of TA. The results are supported by a prototype implementation which relies either on a MILP solver (Gurobi) or an SMT solver (MathSAT). Certain techniques for reducing the search space and improving the performance are also discussed.

1 Introduction

Timed automata [1] allow the specification of time-dependent behavior and they have been used as underlying semantic model for real-world, industry-grade languages used in the design and analysis of real-time systems, such as SDL [7,14] and extensions of UML [11,15,17]. As S. Graf remarked in [14], "at the semantic level, it is interesting to have a minimal number of basic primitives allowing expression of all concepts" [related to time], and timed automata primitives fill this need both for functional design elements and for non-functional aspects.

Since the applications for these models are often safety-critical (e.g., real-time systems, communication protocols), their formal verification has received wide attention in the research literature. There are several mature tools for verifying or simulating various flavors of timed automata-based models, including [3,8,26,27]. Although timed automata give raise to infinite state spaces due to the dense domain of time, both reachability and model checking of various logics are decidable based on finite representations of the state space. The tools and analysis methods cited above rely on symbolic representations of state sets, such as the Difference Bound Matrices (DBMs, introduced in [12]), or more efficient ones such as CDDs, RED [18,26].

Bounded model checking (BMC) [5] on the other hand is a successful method for analyzing models that yield very large state spaces. It relies on encoding the

© Springer Nature Switzerland AG 2018
F. Howar and J. Barnat (Eds.): FMICS 2018, LNCS 11119, pp. 269–283, 2018.
https://doi.org/10.1007/978-3-030-00244-2_18

next-state relationship as a logical formula and on instantiating this formula a bounded number of times to encode all possible runs of depth equal to the bound. Then, a valid run corresponds to an assignment of the variables that satisfies the formula. The verification of properties on runs is hence reduced to the Boolean satisfaction problem (SAT) for the logical formula encoding possible runs. BMC was initially introduced for discrete state-transition systems and formulas are expressed in plain propositional logic. BMC has also been studied for timed automata (see Sect. 5), generally based on formulations that use Boolean constraint formulas over linear arithmetic constraints, i.e., Boolean combinations of propositional variables and linear relations over real variables that can be fed to an SMT solver.

In this paper we study an alternative approach to bounded reachability analysis of timed automata, based on Mixed Integer Linear Programming (MILP). We propose several formulations that aim to increasingly improve performance through reducing the search space and we compare these formulations based on two benchmark examples. Since the formulation is also expressible as a Boolean constraint problem over linear arithmetic constraints, we are able to compare the performance of the MILP-based method with one based on SMT. In this first study we have limited the scope to the verification of simple reachability properties; the method can nevertheless be extended to bounded model-checking for more complex temporal properties.

The paper is structured as follows: Sect. 2 provides the definitions for the version of timed automata used in the paper and introduces MILP. Section 3 discusses different formulations of the bounded reachability as a MILP problem. Section 4 discusses and compares experimental results for the different variants and solvers. Sections 5 and 6 discuss the related work before concluding.

2   Preliminaries

2.1   Timed Automata

We rely on a standard definition of timed automata [1]. A timed automaton is a state-transition graph in which transitions may be guarded with conditions on *clock variables*, used to measure the progress of time. Clocks may be reset when a transition fires and they advance at the same rate.

Let X be a finite set of clock identifiers. A *valuation* is a function $\mathbf{v} : X \rightarrow \mathbb{R}$ assigning a real value to each clock. A *clock predicate* ζ over X is a logical conjunction of conditions of the form $x \bowtie \mathbf{c}$ where $x \in X$, $\mathbf{c} \in \mathbb{Z}$ (or $\mathbf{c} \in \mathbb{R}$ when the integrality hypothesis is not needed) and $\bowtie$ is one of $<, \leq, >, \geq$, or $=$. Our notation will not distinguish between the predicate and the set of valuations that satisfy it; thus, $\mathbf{v} \in \zeta$ denotes that the valuation $\mathbf{v}$ satisfies the predicate ζ. Let $Cond(X)$ be the set of clock predicates over X.

A *timed automaton* is a tuple $A = (L, l_{init}, X, Inv, Ch, T)$ where L is a finite set of identifiers (the *locations*), $l_{init} \in L$ is the initial location, X is a finite set of *clocks*, $Inv : L \rightarrow Cond(X)$ is a function associating an invariant to to each location, Ch is a set of identifiers (the synchronization channels), and T is a set of tuples of the form $t = (src, dst, syn, grd, rst)$ (the *transitions*) such that: $src, dst \in L$, $syn \in \{\epsilon\} \cup \{?, !\} \times Ch$, $grd \in Cond(X)$, $rst \subseteq X$. The components of t designate the source/destination location, synchronization action (ϵ for no synchronization), the guard condition and respectively a set of clocks that are reset to zero. When several automata are involved, we will use the superscripts to refer to the components of a particular automaton B, e.g., L^B, X^B; for the components of transition tuples, we will use projection functions having the same name as the respective component in the definition above (e.g., $src(t), dst(t)$).

The semantics of a timed automaton is given by its transition system, i.e. a graph in which vertices are configurations and edges represent transitions. A configuration is a pair $(l, \mathbf{v})$ where l is a location and $\mathbf{v}$ is a clock valuation such that $\mathbf{v} \in Inv(l)$. There are two kinds of transitions: elapsing of a duration $\delta \in \mathbb{R}$, denoted $(l, \mathbf{v}) \xrightarrow{\delta} (l, \mathbf{v} + \delta)$ (where $\mathbf{v} + \delta$ is the valuation such that $(\mathbf{v} + \delta)(x) = \mathbf{v}(x) + \delta$) and discrete transitions, denoted $(l, \mathbf{v}) \xrightarrow{t} (l', \mathbf{v}')$ where $t \in T$. Time elapsing is conditioned by $\mathbf{v} + \delta \in Inv(l)$. The discrete transition t is conditioned by $l = src(t)$, $l' = dst(t)$, $\mathbf{v} \in grd(t)$ and $\mathbf{v}'(x) = 0$ for all $x \in rst(t)$ and $\mathbf{v}'(x) = \mathbf{v}(x)$ for all $x \in X \setminus rst(t)$. A path in the transition system is called a *run*. A run is in *canonical form* if it starts and ends with a time elapsing transition (possibly of duration zero) and the sequence of transitions composing it strictly alternates time elapsing transitions and discrete transitions. It is easy to see that any run can be transformed into an equivalent cannonical run by summing up the delay of successive time transitions and by inserting zero-delay transitions where needed.

Given a set of timed automata $A_1, ..., A_n$ with pairwise disjoint sets of locations and clocks, the system of timed automata $\mathcal{A} = A_1 \parallel ... \parallel A_n$ is defined by its transition system as follows. The configurations are pairs of the form $((l_1, ..., l_n), \mathbf{v}_1 \sqcup ... \sqcup \mathbf{v}_n)$, where $(l_1, ..., l_n) \in L^{A_1} \times ... \times L^{A_n}$ and $\sqcup$ is the union operator for functions with disjoint domains. Time elapsing transitions $((l_1, ..., l_n), \mathbf{v}_1 \sqcup ... \sqcup \mathbf{v}_n) \xrightarrow{\delta} ((l_1, ..., l_n), \mathbf{v}'_1 \sqcup ... \sqcup \mathbf{v}'_n)$ are possible iff $\forall k, (l_k, \mathbf{v}_k) \xrightarrow{\delta} (l_k, \mathbf{v}'_k)$. Discrete transitions without synchronization $((l_1, ..., l_n), \mathbf{v}_1 \sqcup ... \sqcup \mathbf{v}_n) \xrightarrow{\epsilon} ((l'_1, ..., l'_n), \mathbf{v}'_1 \sqcup ... \sqcup \mathbf{v}'_n)$ are possible iff $\exists k, (l_k, \mathbf{v}_k) \xrightarrow{\epsilon} (l'_k, \mathbf{v}'_k)$ and $\forall j \neq k, l_j = l'_j$ and $\mathbf{v}_j = \mathbf{v}'_j$. Discrete transitions with synchronization are possible only in pairs of an output (!) and an input (?): $((l_1, ..., l_n), \mathbf{v}_1 \sqcup ... \sqcup \mathbf{v}_n) \xrightarrow{\mathbf{c}} ((l'_1, ..., l'_n), \mathbf{v}'_1 \sqcup ... \sqcup \mathbf{v}'_n)$ iff $\exists \mathbf{c} \in Ch^{A_1} \cup ... \cup Ch^{A_n}, k, l$ such that $(l_k, \mathbf{v}_k) \xrightarrow{!\mathbf{c}} (l'_k, \mathbf{v}'_k), (l_l, \mathbf{v}_l) \xrightarrow{?\mathbf{c}} (l'_l, \mathbf{v}'_l)$ and $\forall j \notin \{k, l\}, l_j = l'_j$ and $\mathbf{v}_j = \mathbf{v}'_j$. This version of non-associative n-ary composition is commonly used in practice, for example in the UPPAAL tool [3].

The reachability problem for timed automata is known to be decidable [1]. The decision procedure relies on the integrality of constants used in clock predicates. Our bounded reachability method, as well as others proposed in the literature, can relax this hypothesis and work with real constants (e.g., represented as floating point numbers). On the other hand, since MILP problems only admit non-strict linear constraints (see next paragraph), we forbid strict comparisons in clock predicates. One can replace strict comparisons used in the automata with non-strict ones by fixing a minimum gap.

2.2   MILP

A Linear Programming problem is a mathematical optimization problem in which constraints are linear inequalities and the objective function is also a linear. A Mixed-Integer Linear Programming (MILP) problem is an LP problem in which some of the variables are constrained to be integers [23]. Like SAT, MILP is NP-complete, but many solvers are capable of solving very large problems arising in practice and their performance has vastly improved during the past decades.

Binaries (i.e., integer variables with value 0/1) can be used to represent Booleans and MILP can encode arbitrary Boolean constraints through inequalities, sometimes more compactly than using the standard logical operators.

In addition to inequalities, some solvers may accept a number of additional constraint types, such as *indicator constraints* [16] which have the form $b \to C$ where b is a binary variable and C is a linear inequality that has to be satisfied by the solution only if b has the value 1. This is the only form of non-linear constraint that we will use in our formulation of the reachability problem.

3   Formulating Bounded Reachability in MILP

Let $\mathcal{A} = A_1 \parallel \ldots \parallel A_n$ be a system of timed automata. We discuss here the way in which reachable states and transitions of the system are encoded as variables and constraints of a MILP problem. Several options are available for the encoding, one of the goals of this section being to define the variants so that their performance can be compared in the experiments section.

Let us remind first that the formulation concerns the states of the system that can be reached through a sequence of transitions of bounded length. To simplify the definitions, we consider first that there is a total order between the states and between the transitions, although this constraint will be relaxed later on.

3.1   Encoding of State

The state of the automaton A_k at step i is characterized by the location in which it resides and the values of its clocks. To encode these, we use:

– a set of binary variables, one for each location of A_k:

$$VL_i^{A_k} = \{l_i | l \in L^{A_k}, 0 \le i \le \mathbf{B}\}$$

– a set of continuous variables, one for each clock of A_k, which will designate the last time (with respect to a time reference frame) when the clock was reset:

$$VX_i^{A_k} = \{reset_i^x | x \in X^{A_k}, 0 \le i \le \mathbf{B}\}$$

Since A_k can only be in one state at a time, the following constraint holds:

$$\sum_{l \in VL_i^{A_k}} l = 1 \tag{1}$$

To encode the initial state of each automaton, the following constraints have to hold:

$$\forall l \in L^{A_k} : \quad l_0 = 1 \quad \text{iff} \quad l = l_{init}^{A_k} \tag{2}$$

$$\forall x \in X^{A_k} : \quad reset_0^x = 0 \tag{3}$$

The global state of the system at step i also includes the time since the beginning of the run: now_i (with the constraint $now_0 = 0$). For the moment we consider the case where the transitions of the system are totally ordered in a sequence, hence we can use a global time reference frame. This will no longer be the case when the total order constraint is relaxed, later on.

The state of each automaton has to observe the invariant of its current location. Since each location invariant is a conjunction of atomic clock conditions, each of these can be treated as a separate MILP constraint. By notation abuse, we will write $c \in Inv(l)$ when c is an atomic clock condition part of the conjunction $Inv(l)$. At step i, an atomic condition $x \bowtie \alpha$ is equivalent to the linear expression $now_i - reset_i^x \bowtie \alpha$ and an atomic condition $x - y \bowtie \alpha$ is equivalent to the linear expression $reset_i^y - reset_i^x \bowtie \alpha$. Let LE_i^c denote the linear expression corresponding to condition c at step i. Then, the following constraints have to hold:

$$\forall l \in L^{A_k}, \quad \forall c \in Inv(l) : \quad l_i \to LE_i^c \tag{4}$$

The purpose of the model is to verify reachability of certain states. For the experiments, we specified the searched state as a conjunction of conditions on automata locations and clocks values at step **B**, for which the encoding is straightforward.

3.2   Encoding of Transitions

To allow for an efficient formulation of the possible runs of the system, our MILP model allows, by construction, only for canonical runs (in which discrete steps and time elapsing steps strictly alternate). Thus, a step i is in our case formed of a time elapsing step (possibly of delay equal to zero) followed by a discrete step. Thus, when we refer to a sequence of length **B**, this is actually a sequence of $2\mathbf{B} + 1$ steps: **B** pairs formed of a time step and a discrete step, plus a final time step in order to allow for time to go on after the last discrete step. Steps are numbered from 0 to **B**.

The time elapsing steps are not explicitly encoded, which further simplifies the model. Instead, we simply add the condition that time has to progress in the right direction:

$$\forall i : \quad now_i \leq now_{i+1} \tag{5}$$

With this in mind, now_i designates the current time before the pair (time delay, discrete transition) of rank i. Thus the discrete transition i takes place at time now_{i+1}.

A first consequence is that the constraint (4) given above models the satisfaction of location invariants *before* the time step i but not *after*. In order to ensure the satisfaction of the invariant *after* the step i (and hence, between the two, since invariants are convex), we need an additional constraint. Let LEA_i^c denote the linear expression corresponding to condition c *after* step i. It is easy to see that LEA_i^c can be built similarly to LE_i^c, based on now_{i+1} (time *after* the delay step i) and on the values of $reset_i^x$ (reset dates *before* the discrete step i).

$$\forall l \in L^{A_k}, \quad \forall c \in Inv(l) : \quad l_i \rightarrow LEA_i^c \tag{6}$$

For each discrete transition we will use an auxiliary binary variable that models the fact that the transition is triggered at step i. While this is not usually done in other formulations used for BMC, we find that this makes it easier to express the constraints and to reconstruct the sequence of transitions when the solver finds a feasible solution. Thus:

$$VT_i^{A_k} = \{t_i | t \in T^{A_k}, 0 \le i < \mathbf{B}\}$$

Except for synchronization which is discussed in the next section, the other necessary conditions for a discrete transition are given below. To simplify the formulas, the components of a transition t (i.e., $src(t), dst(t),...$) will also be denoted by $src(vt), dst(vt), ...$, for any $vt \in VT_i^{A_k}$ that corresponds to t.

$$\forall t \in VT_i^{A_k} : \quad t \rightarrow src(t_i) \wedge dst(t_{i+1}) \tag{7}$$

$$\forall t \in VT_i^{A_k}, \quad \forall c \in grd(t) : \quad t \rightarrow LEA_i^c \tag{8}$$

$$\forall t \in VT_i^{A_k}, \quad \forall x \in VX_i^{A_k} \text{ s.t. } x \in rst(t) : \quad t \rightarrow (reset_{i+1}^x = now_{i+1}) \tag{9}$$

$$\forall t \in VT_i^{A_k}, \quad \forall x \in VX_i^{A_k} \text{ s.t. } x \notin rst(t) : \quad t \rightarrow (reset_{i+1}^x = reset_i^x) \tag{10}$$

Instead of a discrete transition, an automaton A_k may perform a special "skip" transition at step any i, without changing either the state or the values of *reset* variables. In the following section we will discuss some additional conditions that ensure that *skip* steps of individual automata are only used under certain conditions, so that the global system runs continue to have the canonical form. To represent the *skip* transitions, a binary variable $skip_i^{A_k}$ is introduced for each i and A_k, along with these constraints:

$$\forall i, \forall x \in X^{A_k} : \quad skip_i^{A_k} \rightarrow (reset_{i+1}^x = reset_i) \tag{11}$$

$$\forall i, \forall l \in L^{A_k} : \quad skip_i^{A_k} \rightarrow (l_{i+1} = l_i) \tag{12}$$

Skip transitions are also useful for encoding the fact that a bounded sequence of length $\mathbf{B}$ may be followed by one final time step: we extend the length of the sequence by one and we require that the last discrete step (numbered $\mathbf{B}$) be a *skip*.

3.3   Relaxing the Order of Transitions and Handling Synchronization

From this point on, several variants of the model will be considered. They all share the variables and constraints described previously and differ essentially in the way in which transitions of individual automata are ordered within the global run and in how synchronization between automata is handled.

A first variant (denoted **SS** for *sequential steps*) is to consider that transitions are ordered sequentially. At each step, only one automaton may fire a discrete transition. In order to account for synchronization, the constraints ensure that an *input* on some channel can only be executed by an automaton immediately after an *output* on the same channel was executed by a different automaton (i.e., in the next step and so that now does not change between the two). To preserve the canonical form of runs, a constraint ensures that, once a *skip* transition appears, all subsequent transitions are *skips*. Let *inputs/outputs* designate the set of all transitions that specify an input (resp. output) synchronization and *conjugated(t)* be a function that gives the set of all transitions t' which specify an output synchronization with the same channel name as t. We do not formally define these, but it is relatively easy to see how they are syntactically derived from the definition of a system. The formulation is as follows:

$$\forall i : \sum_k (skip_i^{A_k} + \sum_{t \in VT_i^{A_k}} t) = 1 \tag{13}$$

$$\forall i, \forall t \in outputs : t_i \rightarrow \sum_{t' \in conjugated(t)} t'_{i+1} = 1 \tag{14}$$

$$\forall i > 0, \forall t \in inputs : t_i \rightarrow \sum_{t' \in conjugated(t)} t'_{i-1} = 1 \tag{15}$$

$$\forall i.0 < i < \mathbf{B}, \forall t \in inputs : t_i \rightarrow (now_i = now_{i+1}) \tag{16}$$

By experimenting with this formulation, one rapidly concludes it is inefficient, mainly for two reasons. Firstly, since only one automaton is allowed to step at a time, one has to choose a relatively large bound $\mathbf{B}$, which in itself penalizes performance. Secondly, if the model is used for establishing the unreachability of some configuration (as it is the case when one tries to verify a safety property), a positive result is achieved when the model is *infeasible* (the term used by MILP solvers, meaning *unsatisfiable*). However, the difficulty of proving infeasibility is generally correlated with the size of the Infeasible Irreducible System (IIS, equivalent of the UNSAT-core in SAT/SMT). Experiments show that with the **SS** formulation, the IIS is generally the entire model (i.e., no constraint can be removed without breaking infeasibility) – and therefore establishing infeasibility is hard.

This finding led us to seek more efficient formulations. A first variant (**MS1** for multi-step with unique time basis) is to allow for multiple automata to trigger discrete transitions within the same step. This also allows a simpler handling of input/output synchronization, which can now be performed within the same step. The formulation is as follows:

$$\forall i, \forall k : skip_i^{A_k} + \sum_{t \in VT_i^{A_k}} t = 1 \qquad (17)$$

$$\forall i, \forall t \in outputs : t_i \rightarrow \sum_{t' \in conjugated(t)} t'_i = 1 \qquad (18)$$

$$\forall i, \forall t \in inputs : t_i \rightarrow \sum_{t' \in conjugated(t)} t'_i = 1 \qquad (19)$$

This formulation is more efficient as it allows to use a lower value for the bound $\mathbf{B}$, since several automata can trigger during a step. However, the use of a unique time basis for all automata (the now_i variables) introduces dependencies between their behaviors. As a consequence, even when a safety property could in principle be proved locally on one or a small subset of the system's automata, the actual IIS is still usually the entire model, and therefore infeasibility remains hard to prove.

A solution to this problem can be to de-correlate time progress in the different automata forming a system. As long as an automaton progresses without synchronizing with others, it can use its own value of now which can be different from the others', in a way similar to what was proposed in [20]. Only when two automata synchronize, they must agree on their respective value of now. To encode this we replace each now_i variable by a set of variables $now_i^{A_k}$, and the constraints (4), (5), (6), (8) and (9) are rewritten to refer to the local now of the concerned automaton. Of course, this implies that an automaton can only read/reset its own clocks.

In this model, there are several ways to achieve input/output synchronization. A first variant (denoted $\mathbf{MSm}$ for multi-step with multiple time bases) will rely on the same constraints as $\mathbf{MS1}$, i.e., (17), (18) and (19), while adding two more:

$$\forall i, j, k, \forall t \in VT_i^{A_j}, \forall t' \in VT_i^{A_k} \text{ s.t. } t' \in conjugated(t) :$$
$$t \wedge t' \rightarrow (now_{i+1}^{A_j} = now_{i+1}^{A_k}) \qquad (20)$$

meaning that local $nows$ agree in case of synchronization, and

$$\forall j, k : now_{\mathbf{B}}^{A_j} = now_{\mathbf{B}}^{A_k}) \qquad (21)$$

meaning that local $nows$ agree at the end of the sequence.

To ensure that we obtain a canonical run with $\mathbf{MSm}$, we can add a constraint enforcing that, if all automata perform a $skip$ at step i, they will continue doing the same for all steps $j > i$. However, even with this constraint, an individual automaton may still perform a $skip$ at step i and some discrete transition at a later step. As this seems to be a source of combinatorial explosion, we have sought to remove it, by no longer relying on the fact that inputs/outputs have to take place in the same step (constraints (18) and (19)). This opens up interesting possibilities:

- The steps of the different automata forming the system are completely decorrelated. The run is no longer a unique sequence of (multi-)steps but a set of sequences, one for each automaton.
- The sequences can be of different length. One can imagine fixing the depth bound **B** differently for each automaton (e.g., depending on its own complexity).
- Each individual sequence can be constrained to be in canonical form, i.e., no more spurious *skip* transitions (except at the end of each run).

However, this also raises new challenges, as the global coherence of the model still has to be ensured. A solution is to use a matrix of auxiliary binary variables to represent the fact that step i of an automaton A_n synchronizes with step j of A_m. Constraints were added to ensure that synchronizations take place at the same time (similar to condition (20)), and that message overtaking does not occur. Details are omitted here, they can be found in the code of the prototype. Henceforth, this variant of the formulation will be denoted **ISs** (independent-steps with synchronization).

3.4   MILP Objective

The difference between an SMT-based bounded model checker/reachability analyzer and one based on MILP is that the latter may integrate an optimization objective. The objective has the form of a linear expression on model variables (depending on the solver, other forms of expressions, such as quadratic forms, may also be used). The objective proves to be useful for selecting a system run out of the set of feasible ones based on minimizing/maximizing various criteria. For example, for model debugging it is often convenient to obtain the shortest run that leads to the searched state, i.e. the run that contains the smallest number of (non-*skip*) discrete transitions. This can be obtained by minimizing the objective:

$$obj = \sum_{\substack{i,k \\ t \in VT_i^{A_k}}} t$$

Other examples of uses for the objective function include searching for runs that optimize the time of residence in certain locations. It is also easy to extend the model to handle weighted timed automata [6], which add costs on states/locations, so as to search for runs that optimize the total cost.

4   Experimental Results

The method described in the previous section was implemented in a prototype[1] written in Python and using Gurobi [16] as back-end MILP solver. In order to

---

[1] https://www.irit.fr/~Iulian.Ober/brat.

allow comparisons, the prototype can also encode the reachability problem as an SMT problem over linear arithmetic constraints, and use MathSAT [21] as backend (via the *pysmt* API). Both formulations use exactly the same constraints, therefore providing an interesting basis for comparison. The automata are specified programmatically directly in Python; however, the format is relatively close to the textual format of UPPAAL, to the point that we could adapt some benchmark generation scripts[2] to generate models for our experiments. Experiments were performed on a Linux machine with 8 Intel Core 2.4 GHz CPUs and 16 GB of memory. Note that the version based on Gurobi exploits the platform parallelism, whereas the one based on MathSAT only uses one of the processors.

4.1   Examples Used

Several examples have been built in order to exercise the prototype. We will concentrate in the following on two of them: the now-classical Train-Gate-Controller (TGC) example [1] and the CSMA/CD (Carrier Sense, Multiple-Access with Collision Detection) protocol, based on the model included in the UPPAAL benchmarks [22]. The CSMA/CD protocol allows to assign a broadcast network channel to one of several competing transmitters. A detailed description is given in [27]; let us note that the model is parametric in the number of transmitters.

4.2   Results for Feasible Models (Reachable States)

In the first experiment reported here, we search for a state for which we know that it may be reached at a certain depth. In the CSMA/CD example, for a model with N transmitters, an interesting candidate is the state *bus_collisionN* of the automaton corresponding to the bus, since we know that it may be reached at a minimum depth of $N + 1$. For each value of N two tests are performed, one with a depth bound $\mathbf{B} = N + 1$ and another one with a larger bound. For each combination of N and depth, the different variants of formulation presented in Sect. 3.3 have been tried, both using the MILP encoding (Gurobi) and the SMT encoding (MathSAT). The quantitative results are listed in the Fig. 1; the green background designates the solver which produced faster results for a particular configuration. In all experiments the time limit was set to 1000 s.

On this experiment the speed of the two solvers is generally comparable, with a slight advantage for the MILP solver for lower values of $\mathbf{B}$ and for the SMT solver for larger ones. It is worth noting however that the MILP encoding provides results that are qualitatively more interesting: we have set the objective of finding traces with a minimum number of (non-skip) discrete transitions. In the case where the bound is strictly larger than $N + 1$, the runs provided by the SMT solver contain many more transitions than necessary for reaching the goal state, while the runs provided by the MILP solver have exactly $N+1$ transitions. Thus, when reachability analysis is used for model understanding and debugging purposes, the MILP solution provides more interesting results.

---

[2] https://www.it.uu.se/research/group/darts/uppaal/benchmarks.

N / B	MS1		MSm		ISs	
	SMT	MILP	SMT	MILP	SMT	MILP
10 / 11	0.41	0.26	0.7	0.29	0.82	0.24
10 / 22	3.61	0.92	4.15	5.27	4.22	2.02
15 / 16	1.41	1.76	3.44	1.85	2.14	0.85
15 / 32	18.13	19.45	40.61	14.79	33.98	22.82
20 / 21	3.96	4.74	12.26	2.28	3.91	2.09
20 / 42	34.85	12.29	132.14	55.19	47.02	67.66
30 / 31	18.76	15.26	54.84	9.14	19.89	17.24
30 / 50	135.17	87.64	432.29	929.11	374.55	524.9
40 / 41	69.93	89.22	131.15	27.16	58.28	44.06
40 / 60	379.66	166.32	918.53	--	416.59	917.95

Fig. 1. Experiment 1 (CSMA/CD) – times in s.

As the numbers in Fig. 1 indicate, the CSMA/CD example does not benefit from the partially ordered runs afforded by the **MSm** and **ISs** variants. This is caused by the centralized nature of the example, as all the transitions of the transmitting stations synchronize with a transition of the bus, whose behavior is essentially sequential.

We proceed with a second experiment which exhibits an increased degree of parallelism. Based on the TGC example [1], we build a system composed of **N** Train-Gate-Controller triplets. In order to demonstrate the interest of having multiple time bases (the case of the **MSm** and **ISs** variants), the waiting delay before the Controller sends the signal to raise the Gate is set to a different value in each triplet. The reachable configuration that will be searched is one in which every Gate is in state *raising*, after a train has passed.

N	MS1		MSm		ISs	
	SMT	MILP	SMT	MILP	SMT	MILP
2	0.08	60.51	0.05	0.07	0.09	0.03
3	0.22	--	0.11	0.11	0.17	0.05
5	2.48	--	0.33	0.18	0.51	0.09
10	102.01	--	2.44	0.41	2.57	0.22
20	--	--	21.37	0.63	15.22	0.61
50	--	--	154.59	1.83	157.71	2.67
100	--	--	682.53	20.65	668.45	14.4

Fig. 2. Experiment 2 (TGC) – times in s.

The search times for different values of **N** are given in Fig. 2. Note that for the **MS1** variant, N+5 steps are necessary to reach the search state, whereas for the variants that use a separate time basis for each automaton (**MSm** and **ISs**) the same state can be reached in a constant number of steps (5). This explains the wide difference in performance between the three variants. It is also to be noted that the relative performance of the solvers is widely different depending on the variant: the SMT solver is orders of magnitude faster on **MS1** while the MILP solver is up to 50 times faster on **MSm** and **ISs**.

4.3   Results for Infeasible Models (Unreachable States)

When reachability analysis is used for verifying a safety property (i.e., that some "bad state" is never reached), the MILP model (respectively the SMT problem) will be infeasible (unsatisfiable) when the property is verified. Experiments show that the performance of the solvers is not uniform whether the purpose is finding scenarios in a feasible model or proving that the model is infeasible. This section is dedicated to experiments for the latter case.

For the TGC example, a safety property is that the Gate cannot be in a state other than *closed* when the Train passes the Gate. We try to prove this property holds up to a "reasonable" bound for depth. The choice of the bound is somewhat arbitrary, but is informed by the results of experiment 2, which show that a full cycle of gate lowering – train passing – gate raising can be achieved in **N+5** steps for **MS1** and in 5 steps for **MSm** and **ISs**. The bound is thus chosen to be 2*N for **MS1** and respectively 10 for **MSm** and **ISs**.

The computation times for deciding infeasibility are given in Fig. 3. Notice that the SMT solver performs significantly better on this task than the MILP solver. The **MSm** and **ISs** formulations also perform much better than **MS1** for large models, **ISs** being the only formulation for which the MILP solver can handle larger systems in a reasonable time.

N	MS1		MSm		ISs	
	SMT	MILP	SMT	MILP	SMT	MILP
2	0.01	1.55	0.04	31.3	0.25	0.36
3	0.03	13.74	0.06	80.16	0.34	0.56
5	0.07	--	0.09	993.15	0.56	1.17
10	0.41	--	0.21	--	1.13	2.44
20	3.27	--	0.45	--	2.4	7.41
50	68.92	--	1.54	--	6.46	26.03
99	--	--	5.81	--	16.09	70.66

Fig. 3. Experiment 3 (TGC with unreachable end state) – times in s.

5   Related Work

Applying bounded model checking [5] to timed automata has been the subject of many studies in the past, beginning with [2,24,25]. The problem is reduced to satisfiability of formulas in a decidable first order logic (e.g., propositional logic with linear arithmetic constraints or difference logic). Most recent works rely on SMT solvers, which have made significant progress in the past years and are able to handle large specifications. To our knowledge, Mixed Integer Linear

Programming has not yet been explored for formulating bounded model-checking problems, except in the realm of linear hybrid automata [13]. The authors of [13] concentrate on the integration of a DPLL-based SAT solver with a linear programming routine in order to benefit from the capacity of the LP routine to solve large conjunctive systems of linear inequalities over the reals. Although the method proposed by [13] could be adapted to fit our needs, we have chosen to rely on an off-the-shelf MILP solver and we concentrated on making the formulation as efficient as possible and on comparing the MILP solution with one based on SMT.

The idea of reducing the length of runs (and hence the size of the search space) by allowing several automata to make discrete transitions in the same (multi-)step has been explored in [20]. It follows up on work on partial order reductions for timed automata [4,19]. We take the multi-step idea two steps forward, first by allowing the clocks of different automata to be de-synchronized in the same multi-step, and then by allowing synchronizing transitions to take place in different steps, which allows to separate the representations of the runs of different TAs and use different bounds on the run length for each automaton. A similar approach was presented in [9] in the context of linear hybrid automata.

6   Conclusions

The results presented in this paper show that there is a place for MILP-based bounded reachability analysis in the spectrum of analysis methods used for timed systems. While the SMT-based method outperforms it when there are no satisfying runs, which makes SMT a better candidate for approaching model-checking problems, the MILP-based method proves to be relatively fast for finding satisfying runs when they exist. Moreover, the method allows to search for runs that optimize certain criteria. Since different criteria may be encoded in the optimization objective, such as run length or time of residence in certain states, our approach provides a convenient method for exploring behavior, model understanding and debugging.

The paper also discusses certain techniques for reducing the size of the search space based on allowing as much as possible independent progress of the different automata forming the system. Several different formulations of the reachability problem are presented and we provide experimental data allowing to compare their relative performance. One formulation (**ISs**) is particularly interesting, both from the point of view of raw performance, and because it separates the representations of the runs of different automata, which allows to set different bounds on their respective length. We think that this should allow to handle more efficiently large systems that mix components of varying complexity.

The prototype implemented for this study handles only a minimalist communicating timed automata model. Future work is needed for enriching the model, e.g., with local/shared data, data communication over synchronization, shared clocks, location and transition weights [6], etc. Although we do not aim for a full-fledged bounded model checker, it would be interesting to provide counterexample generation for more complex temporal logic properties.

This paper is dedicated to Susanne Graf on the occasion of her anniversary event, as a mark of my admiration and respect for her scientific achievements and for her human qualities. It is an honor and an inspiration to have her as colleague and friend.

References

1. Alur, R., Dill, D.L.: A theory of timed automata. Theor. Comput. Sci. **126**(2), 183–235 (1994)
2. Audemard, G., Cimatti, A., Kornilowicz, A., Sebastiani, R.: Bounded model checking for timed systems. In: Peled, D.A., Vardi, M.Y. (eds.) FORTE 2002. LNCS, vol. 2529, pp. 243–259. Springer, Heidelberg (2002). https://doi.org/10.1007/3-540-36135-9_16
3. Behrmann, G., David, A., Larsen, K.G., Pettersson, P., Yi, W.: Developing UPPAAL over 15 years. Softw. Pract. Exper. **41**(2), 133–142 (2011)
4. Bengtsson, J., Jonsson, B., Lilius, J., Yi, W.: Partial order reductions for timed systems. In: Sangiorgi, D., de Simone, R. (eds.) CONCUR 1998. LNCS, vol. 1466, pp. 485–500. Springer, Heidelberg (1998). https://doi.org/10.1007/BFb0055643
5. Biere, A., Cimatti, A., Clarke, E., Zhu, Y.: Symbolic model checking without BDDs. In: Cleaveland, W.R. (ed.) TACAS 1999. LNCS, vol. 1579, pp. 193–207. Springer, Heidelberg (1999). https://doi.org/10.1007/3-540-49059-0_14
6. Bouyer, P.: Weighted timed automata: model-checking and games. Electron. Notes Theor. Comput. Sci. **158**, 3–17 (2006). Proceedings of the 22nd Annual Conference on Mathematical Foundations of Programming Semantics (MFPS XXII)
7. Bozga, M., Graf, S., Mounier, L., Ober, I., Roux, J.-L., Vincent, D.: Timed extensions for SDL. In: Reed, R., Reed, J. (eds.) SDL 2001. LNCS, vol. 2078, pp. 223–240. Springer, Heidelberg (2001). https://doi.org/10.1007/3-540-48213-X_14
8. Bozga, M., Graf, S., Ober, I., Ober, I., Sifakis, J.: The IF toolset. In: Bernardo, M., Corradini, F. (eds.) SFM-RT 2004. LNCS, vol. 3185, pp. 237–267. Springer, Heidelberg (2004). https://doi.org/10.1007/978-3-540-30080-9_8
9. Bu, L., Cimatti, A., Li, X., Mover, S., Tonetta, S.: Model checking of hybrid systems using shallow synchronization. In: Hatcliff, J., Zucca, E. (eds.) FMOODS/FORTE-2010. LNCS, vol. 6117, pp. 155–169. Springer, Heidelberg (2010). https://doi.org/10.1007/978-3-642-13464-7_13
10. Damm, W., Olderog, E.-R. (eds.): FTRTFT 2002. LNCS, vol. 2469. Springer, Heidelberg (2002). https://doi.org/10.1007/3-540-45739-9
11. David, A., Möller, M.O., Yi, W.: Formal verification of UML statecharts with real-time extensions. In: Kutsche, R.-D., Weber, H. (eds.) FASE 2002. LNCS, vol. 2306, pp. 218–232. Springer, Heidelberg (2002). https://doi.org/10.1007/3-540-45923-5_15
12. Dill, D.L.: Timing assumptions and verification of finite-state concurrent systems. In: Sifakis, J. (ed.) CAV 1989. LNCS, vol. 407, pp. 197–212. Springer, Heidelberg (1990). https://doi.org/10.1007/3-540-52148-8_17
13. Fränzle, M., Herde, C.: Efficient proof engines for bounded model checking of hybrid systems. Electron. Notes Theor. Comput. Sci. **133**, 119–137 (2005)
14. Graf, S.: Expression of time and duration constraints in SDL. In: Sherratt, E. (ed.) SAM 2002. LNCS, vol. 2599, pp. 38–52. Springer, Heidelberg (2003). https://doi.org/10.1007/3-540-36573-7_3

15. Graf, S.: OMEGA: correct development of real time and embedded systems. Softw. Syst. Model. **7**(2), 127–130 (2008)
16. Gurobi Optimization Inc., Reference manual v. 7.5. https://www.gurobi.com/documentation/7.5/refman.pdf. Accessed on 8 June 2018
17. Knapp, A., Merz, S., Rauh, C.: Model checking - timed UML state machines and collaborations. In: Damm and Olderog [10], pp. 395–416
18. Larsen, K.G., Pearson, J., Weise, C., Yi, W.: Clock difference diagrams. Nord. J. Comput. **6**, 271–298 (1999)
19. Lugiez, D., Niebert, P., Zennou, S.: A partial order semantics approach to the clock explosion problem of timed automata. Theor. Comput. Sci. **345**(1), 27–59 (2005)
20. Malinowski, J., Niebert, P.: SAT based bounded model checking with partial order semantics for timed automata. In: Esparza, J., Majumdar, R. (eds.) TACAS 2010. LNCS, vol. 6015, pp. 405–419. Springer, Heidelberg (2010). https://doi.org/10.1007/978-3-642-12002-2_34
21. MathSAT 5. http://mathsat.fbk.eu. Accessed 8 June 2018
22. Möller, O.: CSMA/CD protocol specification (UPPAAL benchmark). https://www.it.uu.se/research/group/darts/uppaal/benchmarks/#CSMA. Accessed 8 June 2018
23. Nemhauser, G.L., Wolsey, L.A.: Integer and Combinatorial Optimization. Wiley-Interscience, New York (1988)
24. Niebert, P., Mahfoudh, M., Asarin, E., Bozga, M., Maler, O., Jain, N.: Verification of timed automata via satisfiability checking. In: Damm and Olderog [10], pp. 225–244
25. M. Sorea. Bounded model checking for timed automata. Electron. Notes Theor. Comput. Sci. **68**(5), 116–134 (2003). MTCS 2002, Models for Time-Critical Systems (CONCUR 2002 Satellite Workshop)
26. Wang, F.: Efficient verification of timed automata with BDD-like data structures. STTT **6**(1), 77–97 (2004)
27. Yovine, S.: KRONOS: A verification tool for real-time systems. STTT **1**(1–2), 123–133 (1997)

Evaluation and Comparison of Real-Time Systems Analysis Methods and Tools

Sophie Quinton[(⊠)]

Univ. Grenoble Alpes, INRIA, CNRS, Grenoble INP, LIG, Grenoble, France
`sophie.quinton@inria.fr`

Abstract. The verification of real-time systems has been an active area of research for several decades now. Some results have been successfully transferred to industry. Still, many obstacles remain that hinder a smooth integration of academic research and industrial application. In this extended abstract, we discuss some of these obstacles and ongoing research and community efforts to bridge this gap. In particular, we present several experimental and theoretical methods to evaluate and compare real-time systems analysis methods and tools.

Keywords: Real-time systems · Verification · Formal methods

1   Introduction

Critical embedded systems such as cars, satellites or planes are real-time in the sense that they must provide some type of timing guarantees, e.g., to ensure that a system will always react sufficiently quickly to some external event.

The verification of real-time systems has been an active area of research for several decades now since the seminal work of Liu and Layland [20] (see [8] for a survey). Some results have been successfully transferred to industry, as illustrated by the existence of numerous companies selling real-time systems analysis tools which are spin-offs from research institutions, e.g., AbsInt[1] (from Saarland University), Symtavision[2] (now part of Luxoft, from TU Braunschweig) and RTaW[3] (from INRIA). Four additional examples of successful technology transfer are described in [7].

Still, many obstacles remain that hinder a smooth integration of academic research and industrial application. To illustrate this on an example, the verification of timing properties in the automotive industry tends to be based on simulations rather than static analysis, complemented with monitoring to handle at runtime potential timing violations. The rapid evolution of real-time systems,

---

This work has been partially supported by the LabEx PERSYVAL-Lab (ANR-11-LABX-0025-01).

[1] https://www.absint.com/.
[2] https://auto.luxoft.com/uth/timing-analysis-tools/.
[3] http://www.realtimeatwork.com.

© Springer Nature Switzerland AG 2018
F. Howar and J. Barnat (Eds.): FMICS 2018, LNCS 11119, pp. 284–290, 2018.
https://doi.org/10.1007/978-3-030-00244-2_19

with the advent of multicore architectures and the shift toward heterogeneous, high-performance platforms, is increasing the gap between the analysis tools and methods proposed by the research community and the needs of industry [25].

At the same time, this trend represents a unique opportunity, because systems are becoming so complex that simulation is not a viable verification method anymore. There is currently a need for simple mechanisms to make these new, complex platforms more predictable, and for associated verification techniques. For example, several automotive OEMs and suppliers are now using the Logical Execution Time (LET) [18] paradigm to achieve predictable communication [14,17]. This choice has led to renewed interactions between academia and industry in order to identify where more research is needed on the topic [9].

In this context, we argue that one major obstacle to the application of academic results in industry is the difficulty, both for academics and practitioners, to evaluate how existing analysis techniques and their associated tools can perform on real systems. In the following, we discuss some criteria for such an evaluation that deserve more attention from the research community. We then present current efforts toward experimental and theoretical methods to evaluate and compare real-time systems analysis methods and tools.

2   Evaluation Criteria

In this section, we would like to draw attention to several criteria that are key to evaluating the usability of a method or a tool, and which we feel are currently underestimated.

2.1   Expressivity of the Underlying Model

One major difficulty that practitioners face whenever trying to use a tool from academia, e.g. pyCPA[4], MAST[5] or Cheddar[6], is the mismatch between the models they work with and the expressivity of the tool they would like to use [16]. Many papers still assume a simple model where independent software tasks execute on a uniprocessor. In practice, systems are now much more complex, with multiple cores, communication buses, shared caches, etc. Even uniprocessor systems require more complex models than the one introduced in [20].

One example is illustrated in [15]: Due to minor uncertainties in clock implementations, the exact value of a task period (describing the frequency with which the task is activated) may not be known. This means that the activations of two tasks that are specified with the same period may shift if mapped onto different processors, which must be taken into account by the analysis. This requires support for parameters in the system model.

Another example related to the description of task activations concerns tasks implementing engine control. Such tasks, which are commonly referred to as

---

[4] https://pycpa.readthedocs.io.

[5] https://mast.unican.es/mast.html.

[6] http://beru.univ-brest.fr/~singhoff/cheddar/.

adaptive variable-rate (AVR) tasks, are activated whenever the crankshaft of the engine reaches a specific angle. Recent theoretical works [3, 22] provide solutions for precisely analyzing such tasks, but most tools do not implement them.

These are just two examples to illustrate the complexity of modeling industrial systems. Reality is even more complex, with tasks often implemented with some degree of intra-task parallelism [23], and the additional complexity due to multicore architectures. Many existing tools and analysis techniques do take into account some level of complexity in their model, including those cited above, but they apply to different, incomparable models with no systematic way of comparing them. Despite existing efforts [21], we still lack a clear understanding of how different abstractions can be compared semantically.

2.2   Expressivity of the Provided Guarantees

A second, related issue is the fact that academic research has largely focused on guaranteeing schedulability, that is, on ensuring that no task in a given task set can ever miss its deadline. Schedulability is usually established by computing an upper bound on the worst-case response time of tasks, i.e., the maximal delay between the activation of a task resulting in the creation of a job to be executed, and the completion of that job. This is often not the most critical issue.

First, one is generally not interested in the response time of a single task, but rather in the end-to-end latency of a so-called cause-effect chain of tasks which are independently activated but communicate via shared variables [10]. Although this problem was formalized ten years ago, it has only recently become an active research topic [1].

Besides, the notion of schedulability itself (even if the notion of deadline is applied to cause-effect chains rather than single tasks) is restrictive [2]: In particular, it has been shown that many real-time systems are weakly-hard rather than hard, meaning that they can tolerate a bounded number of deadline misses without this leading to system failure [11, 19].

These two examples illustrate the fact that researchers and tool providers must pay closer attention to which timing guarantees are used in practice. A better understanding about how the real-time aspects interface with other viewpoints such as function or energy consumption is needed for that [13].

2.3   Precision of the Computed Results

Another problem that hinders the use of academic solutions for the verification of real-time systems is the lack of support to estimate the precision of the computed results. Indeed, for scalability reasons, existing solutions compute upper bounds on worst-case behaviors, which introduces some pessimism in the analysis. The problem is that there is no method to quantify that pessimism, other than comparing the computed upper bounds with results obtained by simulation. In general, there is a large gap between the values thus obtained (through analysis and simulation) and the user does not know whether it is due to the imprecision of the simulation, or whether it results from the pessimism of the analysis. Exhibiting a possible scenario leading to a deadline miss would be valuable to practitioners because it would help them to redesign the system to make it schedulable. The need to investigate this issue further and some initial results are provided in [12].

3   Methods for Evaluation and Comparison

Let us now present several initiatives aiming to help researchers and practitioners compare their methods and tools.

3.1   Empirical Approaches

The objective of the WATERS industrial challenge[7] is to address the need for closer interaction between academia and industry that is underlined by the observations made in the previous sections. The principle of the challenge is to provide researchers with a concrete industrial problem related to real-time systems design and analysis, which they try to solve with their preferred method and tool. So far, Thales, Bosch and Dassault have contributed (Bosch has proposed multiple challenges). The WATERS industrial challenge has proven over the years to be an extremely attractive and valuable exercice to share and compare solutions and results.

While we need more case studies such as the WATERS industrial challenge, we also need synthetic test cases, or tools to generate them, on which there is a consensus. Unfortunately, there is no such tool at the moment – authors use custom made generators for their publications. Some rules to generate meaningful test cases are provided in [6], but the targeted models are too simple to tackle realistic sytems and need to be extended.

RTSpec [24] represents a significant effort towards a unified format for describing such test cases. It is a formalism for real-time systems specification with flexible syntax and rigorous semantics based on UPPAAL models. Based on this library, the timing model of various analyzers can be formalized, and mappings between their respective input formats can be rigorously defined. The overall target is a framework which comprises the RTSpec formalism, a tool chain for automatically translating RTSpec into the input of various analysis tools, and a set of benchmarks which are synthetic or derived from industrial case studies. Such a framework would provide a systematic, automated and rigorous methodology for evaluating analyzers.

3.2   Theoretical Approaches

Few research papers have focused on the issue of comparing real-time systems analysis techniques. A recent publication [5] (building upon [6]) is tackling the problem while identifying pitfalls in the use of metrics such as resource augmentation factors and utilization bounds to compare methods or tools.

---

[7] https://www.ecrts.org/industrialchallenge.

One theoretical tool which seems promising to provide a solid formal background for comparing models and analysis techniques is the Prosa[8] library, a repository of definitions and proofs for real-time schedulability analysis [4] using the Coq proof assistant[9]. One of the objectives of the ongoing CASERM project[10] is to build the RTSpec framework on top of Prosa instead of UPPAAL, thus allowing for formal proofs on model transformations, as needed for comparison purposes.

4   Conclusion

In this short paper, we have illustrated the need for a better theoretical and practical support to evaluate and compare methods and tools for real-time systems analysis. We have underlined the importance of being able to formally relate models used by different approaches, as well as the need to look beyond schedulability analysis and to develop methods to quantify the pessimism of existing analyses. In addition, we have presented recent and ongoing initiatives targeting these goals, which we hope will help reducing the gap between academic research and industrial practice.

References

1. Becker, M., Dasari, D., Mubeen, S., Behnam, M., Nolte, T.: End-to-end timing analysis of cause-effect chains in automotive embedded systems. J. Syst. Archit. Embed. Syst. Des. **80**, 104–113 (2017). https://doi.org/10.1016/j.sysarc.2017.09.004
2. Beyond the deadline: new interfaces between control and scheduling for the design and analysis of critical embedded systems. Tutorial at ESWeek 2017 (2017). https://team.inria.fr/spades/beyond-the-deadline/
3. Biondi, A., Natale, M.D., Buttazzo, G.C.: Response-time analysis of engine control applications under fixed-priority scheduling. IEEE Trans. Comput. **67**(5), 687–703 (2018). https://doi.org/10.1109/TC.2017.2777826
4. Cerqueira, F., Stutz, F., Brandenburg, B.B.: PROSA: a case for readable mechanized schedulability analysis. In: 28th Euromicro Conference on Real-Time Systems, ECRTS 2016, pp. 273–284 (2016). https://doi.org/10.1109/ECRTS.2016.28
5. Chen, J.J., von der Brüggen, G., Huang, W.H., Davis, R.I.: On the pitfalls of resource augmentation factors and utilization bounds in real-time scheduling. In: 29th Euromicro Conference on Real-Time Systems, ECRTS 2017, vol. 76, pp. 9:1–9:25 (2017). https://doi.org/10.4230/LIPIcs.ECRTS.2017.9
6. Davis, R.I.: On the evaluation of schedulability tests for real-time scheduling algorithms. In: 7th International Workshop on Analysis Tools and Methodologies for Embedded and Real-time Systems, WATERS 2017 (2017)
7. Davis, R.I., et al.: Transferring real-time systems research into industrial practice: four impact case studies. In: 30th Euromicro Conference on Real-Time Systems, ECRTS 2018, pp. 7:1–7:24 (2018). https://doi.org/10.4230/LIPIcs.ECRTS.2018.7

---

[8] http://prosa.mpi-sws.org.
[9] https://coq.inria.fr/.
[10] https://project.inria.fr/caserm.

8. Davis, R.I., Burns, A.: A survey of hard real-time scheduling for multiprocessor systems. ACM Comput. Surv. (CSUR) **43**(4), 35 (2011)

9. Ernst, R., Kuntz, S., Quinton, S., Simons, M.: The logical execution time paradigm: new perspectives for multicore systems (dagstuhl seminar 18092). Dagstuhl Rep. **8**(2), 122–149 (2018). https://doi.org/10.4230/DagRep.8.2.122

10. Feiertag, N., Richter, K., Nordlander, J., Jonsson, J.: A compositional framework for end-to-end path delay calculation of automotive systems under different path semantics. In: 1st Workshop on Compositional Theory and Technology for Real-Time Embedded Systems, CRTS 2008 (2008)

11. Frehse, G., Hamann, A., Quinton, S., Woehrle, M.: Formal analysis of timing effects on closed-loop properties of control software. In: Proceedings of the IEEE 35th IEEE Real-Time Systems Symposium, RTSS 2014, pp. 53–62 (2014). http://dx.doi.org/10.1109/RTSS.2014.28

12. Girault, A., Henia, R., Prévot, C., Quinton, S., Sordon, N.: Improving and estimating the precision of bounds on the worst-case latency of task chains. In: ACM SIGBED International Conference on Embedded Software, EMSOFT 2018 (2018, to appear)

13. Graf, S., Quinton, S., Girault, A., Gössler, G.: Building correct cyber-physical systems: why we need a multiview contract theory. In: 23rd International Conference on Formal Methods for Industrial Critical Systems, FMICS 2018 (2018, to appear)

14. Hamann, A., Dasari, D., Kramer, S., Pressler, M., Wurst, F.: Communication centric design in complex automotive embedded systems. In: 29th Euromicro Conference on Real-Time Systems, ECRTS 2017, pp. 10:1–10:20 (2017). https://doi.org/10.4230/LIPIcs.ECRTS.2017.10

15. Henia, R., Rioux, L.: WATERS industrial challenge by Thales. https://www.ecrts.org/industrialchallenge-thales

16. Henia, R., Rioux, L., Sordon, N., Garcia, G., Panunzio, M.: Integrating model-based formal timing analysis in the industrial development process of satellite on-board software. In: 2nd International Conference on Model-Driven Engineering and Software Development, MODELSWARD 2014, pp. 619–625 (2014). https://doi.org/10.5220/0004874306190625

17. Hennig, J., von Hasseln, H., Mohammad, H., Resmerita, S., Lukesch, S., Naderlinger, A.: Towards parallelizing legacy embedded control software using the LET programming paradigm. In: WiP Session at the 2016 IEEE Real-Time and Embedded Technology and Applications Symposium, RTAS 2016, p. 51 (2016). http://dx.doi.org/10.1109/RTAS.2016.7461355

18. Kirsch, C.M., Sokolova, A.: The logical execution time paradigm. In: Advances in Real-Time Systems, pp. 103–120 (2012). http://dx.doi.org/10.1007/978-3-642-24349-3_5

19. Linsenmayer, S., Allgöwer, F.: Stabilization of networked control systems with weakly hard real-time dropout description. In: 56th IEEE Annual Conference on Decision and Control, CDC 2017, pp. 4765–4770 (2017). https://doi.org/10.1109/CDC.2017.8264364

20. Liu, C.L., Layland, J.W.: Scheduling algorithms for multiprogramming in a hard-real-time environment. J. ACM **20**(1), 46–61 (1973). http://doi.acm.org/10.1145/321738.321743

21. Long, A.B., Ouhammou, Y., Grolleau, E., Fejoz, L., Rioux, L.: Bridging the gap between practical cases and temporal performance analysis: a models repository-based approach. In: Proceedings of the 25th International Conference on Real-Time Networks and Systems, RTNS 2017, pp. 178–187 (2017). http://doi.acm.org/10.1145/3139258.3139286

22. Mohaqeqi, M., Abdullah, J., Ekberg, P., Yi, W.: Refinement of workload models for engine controllers by state space partitioning. In: 29th Euromicro Conference on Real-Time Systems, ECRTS 2017, vol. 76, pp. 11:1–11:22 (2017). https://doi.org/10.4230/LIPIcs.ECRTS.2017.11
23. Serrano, M.A., Melani, A., Kehr, S., Bertogna, M., Quiñones, E.: An analysis of lazy and eager limited preemption approaches under DAG-based global fixed priority scheduling. In: 20th IEEE International Symposium on Real-Time Distributed Computing, ISORC 2017, pp. 193–202 (2017). https://doi.org/10.1109/ISORC.2017.9
24. Shan, L., Graf, S., Quinton, S., Fejoz, L.: A framework for evaluating schedulability analysis tools. In: Models, Algorithms, Logics and Tools - Essays Dedicated to Kim Guldstrand Larsen on the Occasion of His 60th Birthday, pp. 539–559 (2017). https://doi.org/10.1007/978-3-319-63121-9_27
25. Kramer, S., Ziegenbein, D., Hamann, A.: Real world automotive benchmark for free. In: 5th International Workshop on Analysis Tools and Methodologies for Embedded and Real-time Systems, WATERS 2015 (2015)

Author Index

Printed in the United States
By Bookmasters